Mackerel pike...

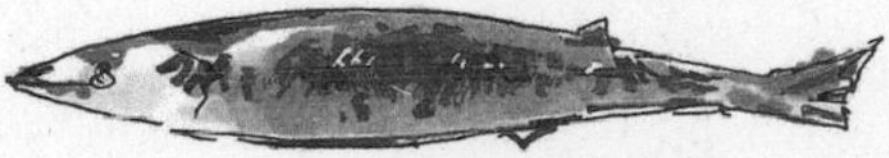

...is tasty.

Thank you for picking up *Haikyu!!* volume 28! Ever since I started this job, I've come to realize I'm not good at directing people. Now I know just how great my bosses were back when I worked in an office. They were always there to point out what I needed to do and keep me on track. Maybe you shouldn't go against the grain!

HARUICHI FURUDATE began his manga career when he was 25 years old with the one-shot *Ousama Kid* [King Kid], which won an honorable mention for the 14th Jump Treasure Newcomer Manga Prize. His first series, *Kiben Gakuha, Yotsuya Sensei no Kaidan* [Philosophy School, Yotsuya Sensei's Ghost Stories], was serialized in *Weekly Shonen Jump* in 2010. In 2012, he began serializing *Haikyu!!* in *Weekly Shonen Jump*, where it became his most popular work to date.

HAIKYU!!
VOLUME 28
SHONEN JUMP Manga Edition

Story and Art by
HARUICHI FURUDATE

Translation  **ADRIENNE BECK**
Touch-Up Art & Lettering ▣ **ERIKA TERRIQUEZ**
Design ▣ **JULIAN [JR] ROBINSON**
Editor ▣ **MARLENE FIRST**

HAIKYU!! © 2012 by Haruichi Furudate
All rights reserved.
First published in Japan in 2012 by SHUEISHA Inc., Tokyo.
English translation rights arranged by SHUEISHA Inc.

The stories, characters and incidents mentioned
in this publication are entirely fictional.

Printed in the U.S.A.

Published by VIZ Media, LLC
P.O. Box 77010
San Francisco, CA 94107

10 9 8 7 6 5 4 3 2 1
First printing, October 2018

SHONEN JUMP MANGA

HAIKYU!!

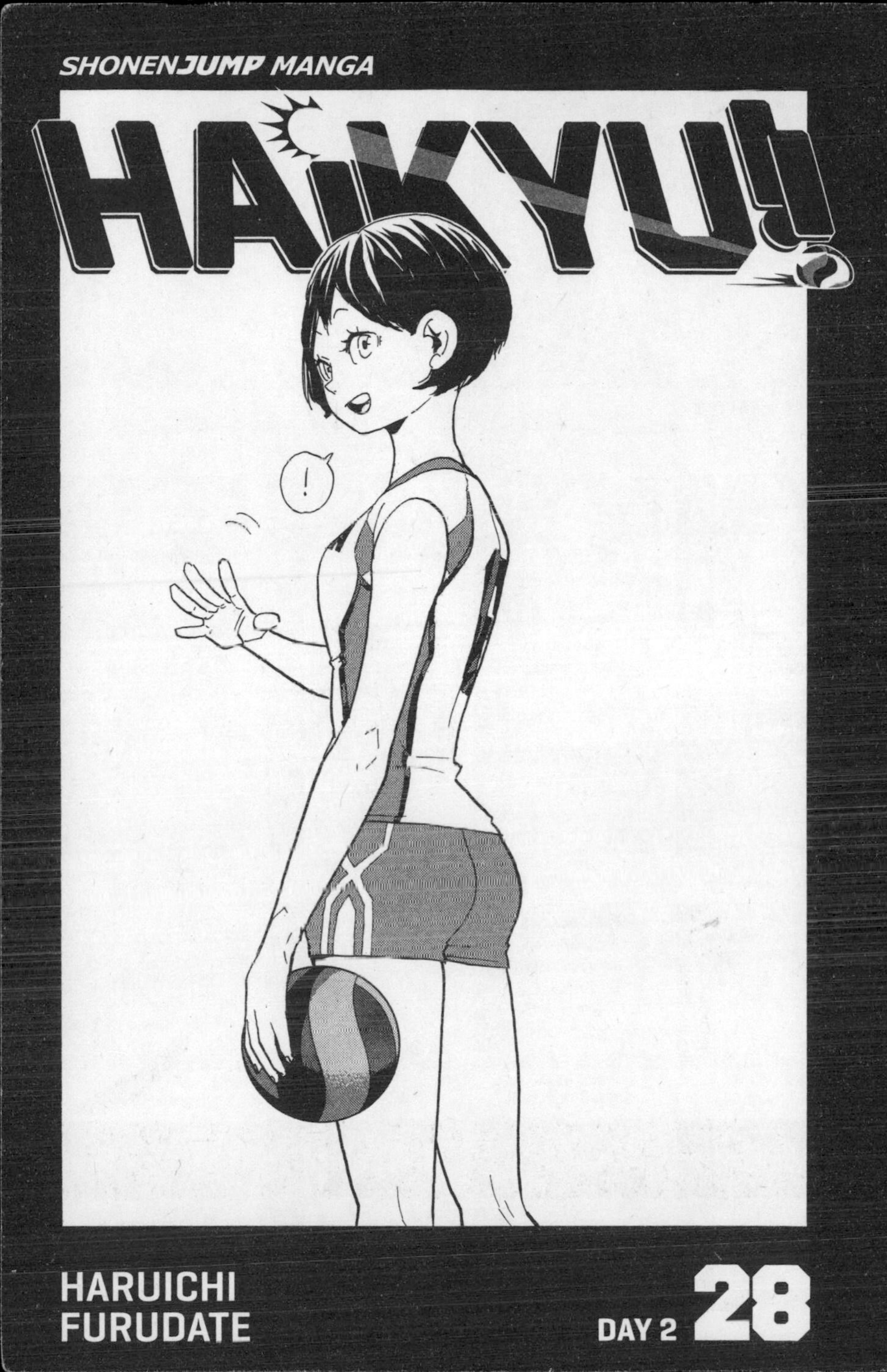
!

HARUICHI
FURUDATE

DAY 2

28

Karasuno High School Volleyball Club

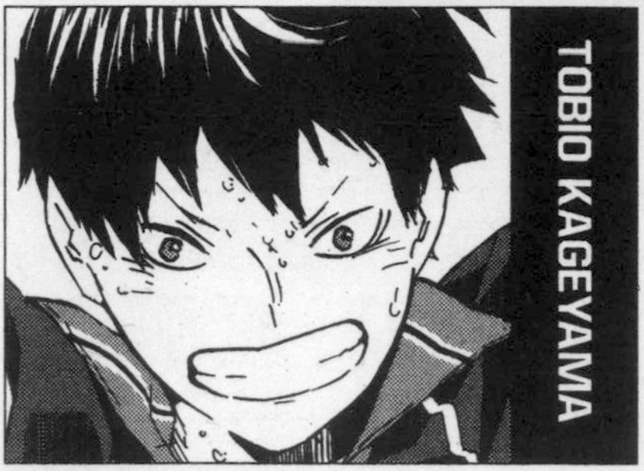
TOBIO KAGEYAMA

1ST YEAR / SETTER
His instincts and athletic talent are so good that he's like a "king" who rules the court. Demanding and egocentric.

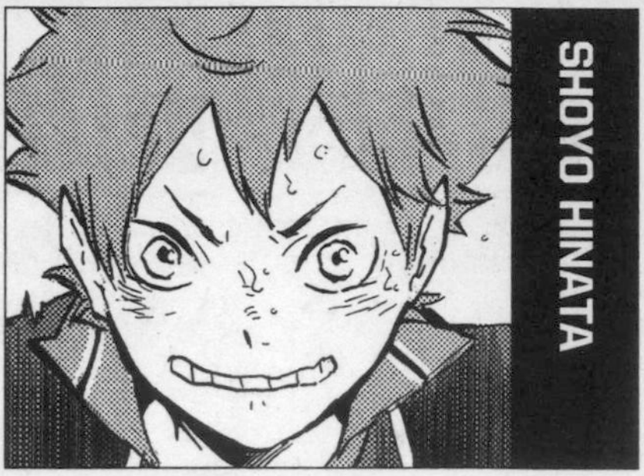
SHOYO HINATA

1ST YEAR / MIDDLE BLOCKER
Even though he doesn't have the best body type for volleyball, he is super athletic. Gets nervous easily.

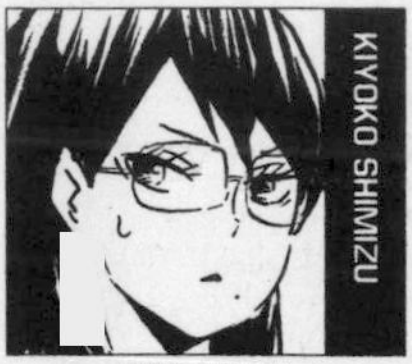
KIYOKO SHIMIZU

3RD YEAR
MANAGER

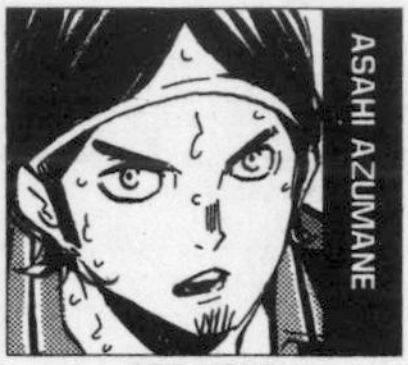
ASAHI AZUMANE

3RD YEAR
WING SPIKER

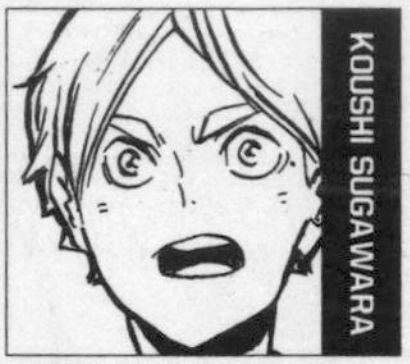
KOUSHI SUGAWARA

3RD YEAR (VICE CAPTAIN)
SETTER

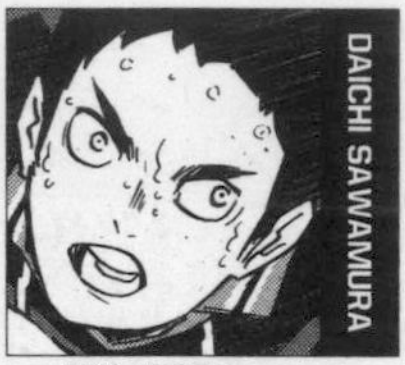
DAICHI SAWAMURA

3RD YEAR (CAPTAIN)
WING SPIKER

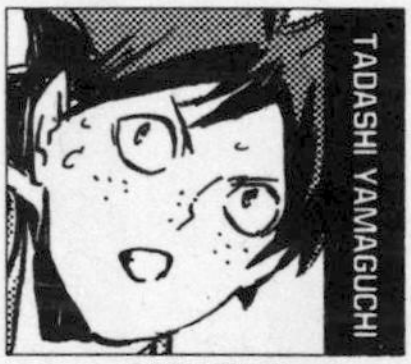
TADASHI YAMAGUCHI

1ST YEAR
MIDDLE BLOCKER

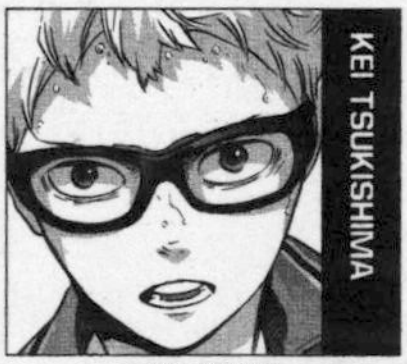
KEI TSUKISHIMA

1ST YEAR
MIDDLE BLOCKER

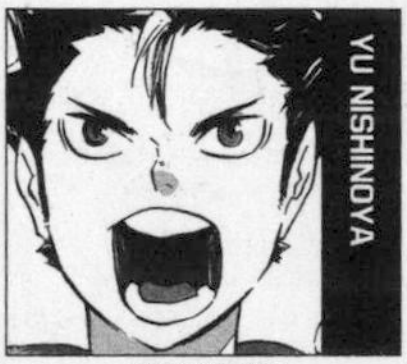
YU NISHINOYA

2ND YEAR
LIBERO

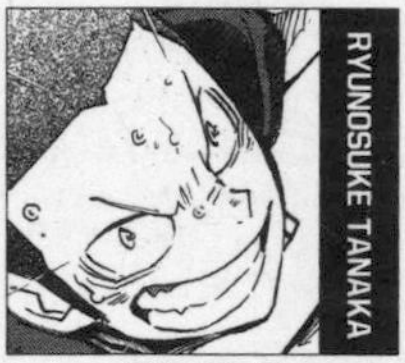
RYUNOSUKE TANAKA

2ND YEAR
WING SPIKER

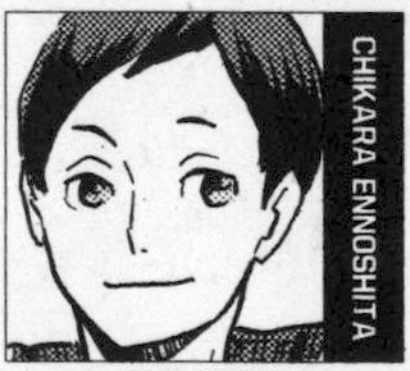
CHIKARA ENNOSHITA

2ND YEAR
WING SPIKER

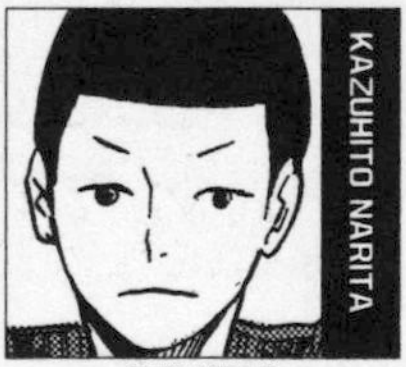
KAZUHITO NARITA

2ND YEAR
MIDDLE BLOCKER

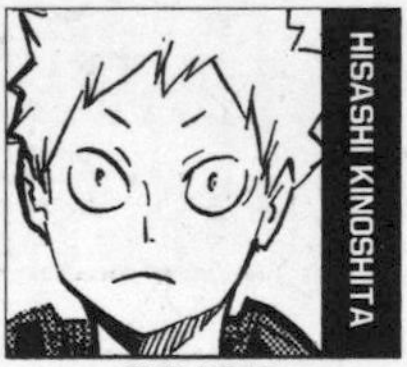
HISASHI KINOSHITA

2ND YEAR
WING SPIKER

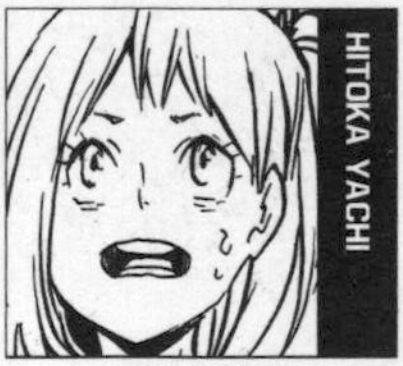
HITOKA YACHI

1ST YEAR
MANAGER

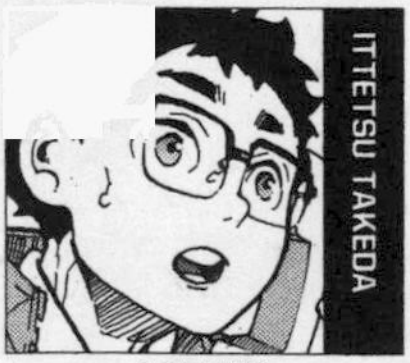
ITTETSU TAKEDA

ADVISER

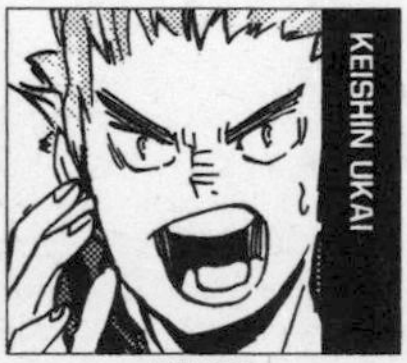
KEISHIN UKAI

COACH

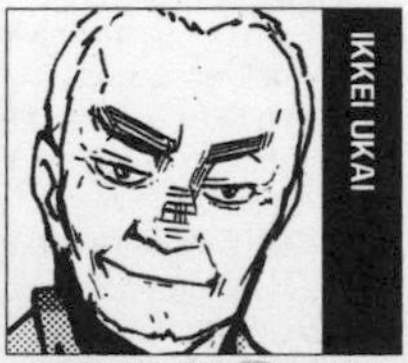
IKKEI UKAI

FORMER HEAD COACH

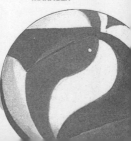

CHARACTERS

NATIONAL SPRING TOURNAMENT

Fukurodani Academy

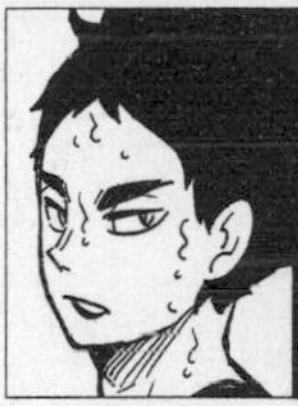

KEIJI AKAASHI

2ND YEAR
SETTER

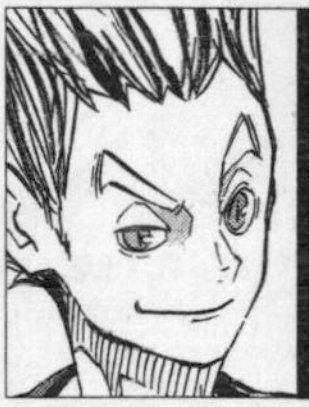

KOTARO BOKUTO

3RD YEAR (CAPTAIN)
WING SPIKER

Nekoma High School

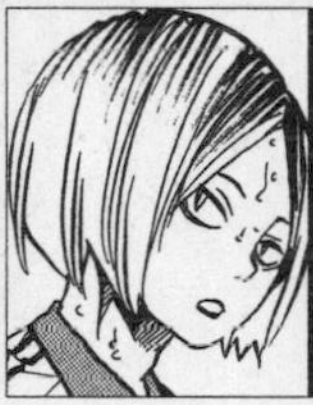

KENMA KOZUME

2ND YEAR
SETTER

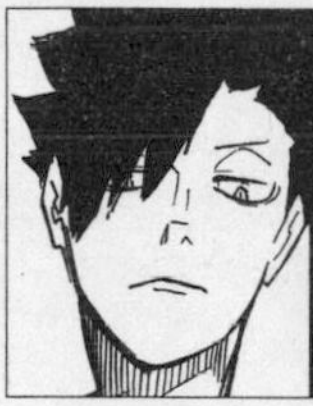

TETSURO KUROO

3RD YEAR (CAPTAIN)
MIDDLE BLOCKER

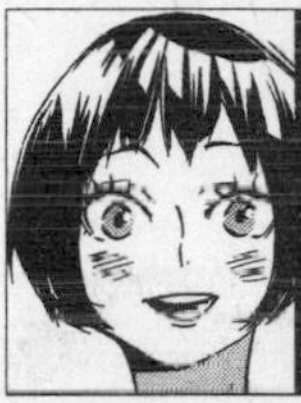

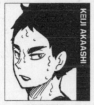

KANOKA AMANAI

NIIYAMA GIRLS' HIGH SCHOOL 2ND YEAR
WING SPIKER

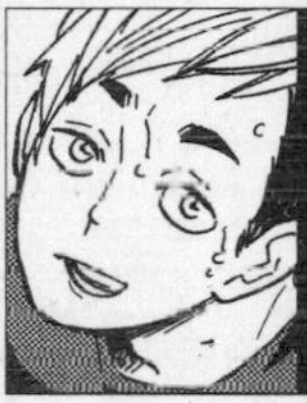

ATSUMU MIYA

2ND YEAR
SETTER

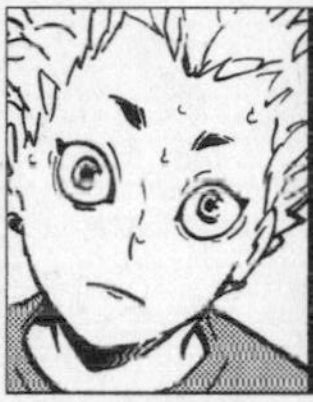

KORAI HOSHIUMI

2ND YEAR
WING SPIKER

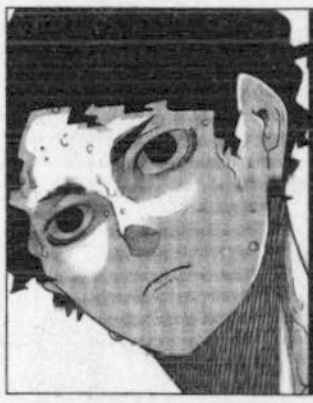

KIYOOMI SAKUSA

ITACHIYAMA 2ND YEAR
WING SPIKER

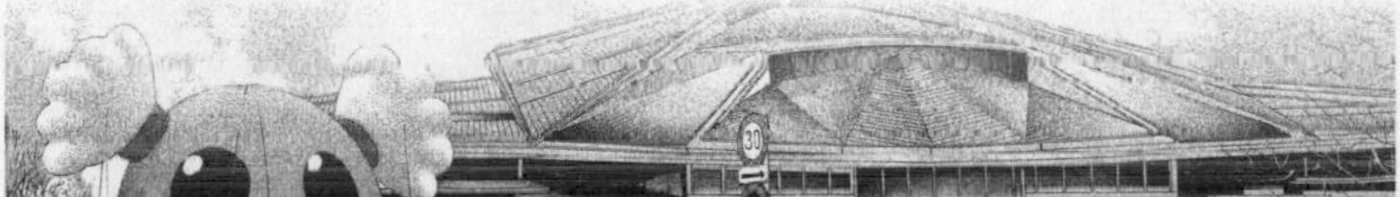
30

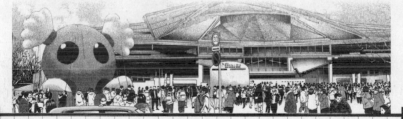

Ever since he saw the legendary player known as "the Little Giant" compete at the national volleyball finals, Shoyo Hinata has been aiming to be the best volleyball player ever! He decides to join the volleyball club at his middle school and gets to play in an official tournament during his third year. His team is crushed by a team led by volleyball prodigy Tobio Kageyama, also known as "the King of the Court." Swearing revenge on Kageyama, Hinata graduates middle school and enters Karasuno High School, the school where the Little Giant played. However, upon joining the club, he finds out that Kageyama is there too! The two of them bicker constantly, but they bring out the best in each other's talents and become a powerful combo. Then the Spring Tournament begins! Karasuno's first opponent is Tsubakihara Academy. Kageyama quickly acclimates to the huge auditorium, and with all its players showing off their new skills, Karasuno takes the lead! Looking to recover, Tsubakihara sends out rookie pinch server Himekawa. Despite messing up once, Himekawa tries again, and his ceiling serve gives Tsubakihara the momentum it needs. However, Sugawara's quick thinking leads Karasuno to victory!

HAIKYU!!

28 DAY 2

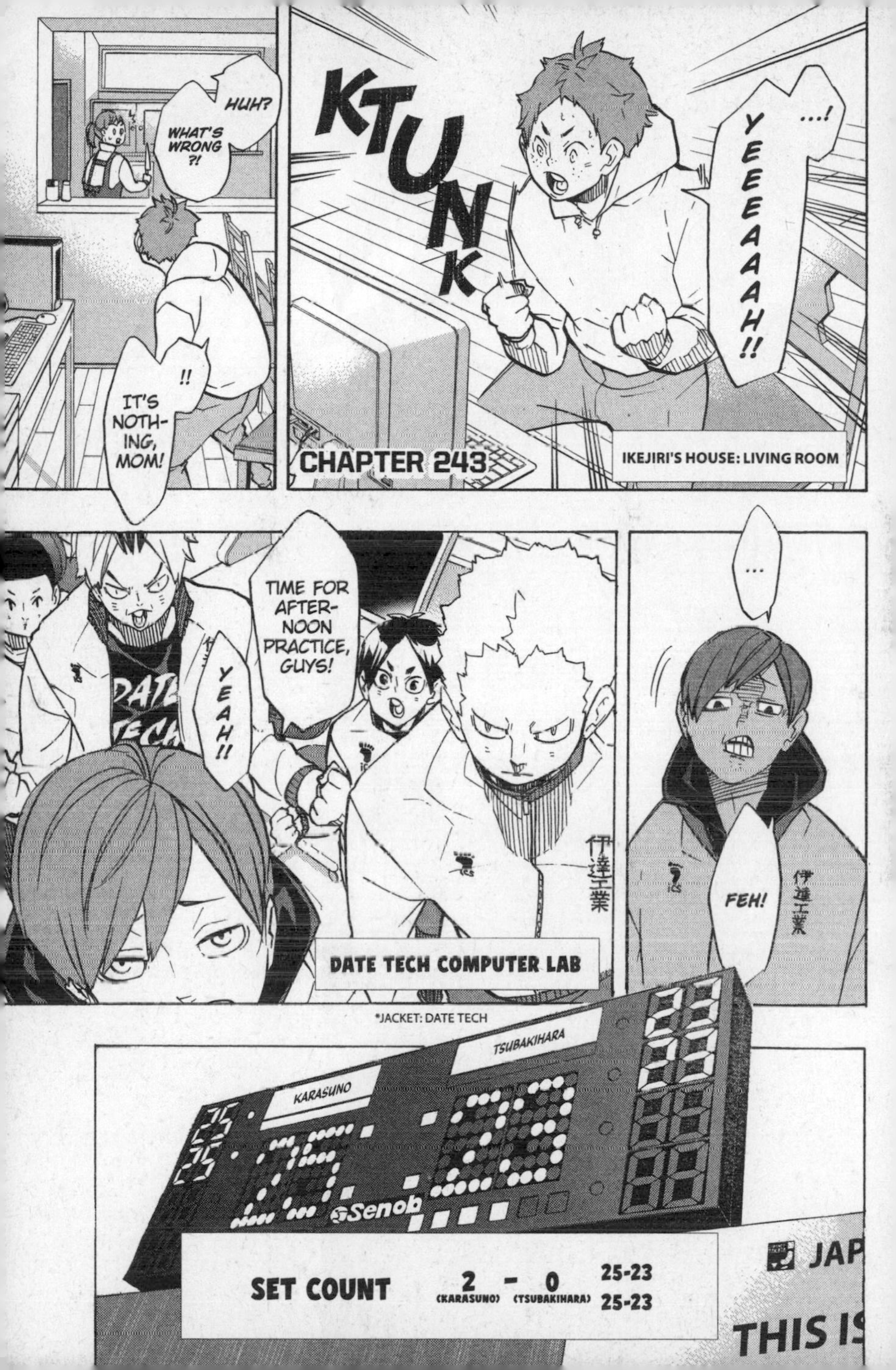
...!
YEEEAAAAH!!
KTUNK
CHAPTER 243
IKEJIRI'S HOUSE: LIVING ROOM
HUH? WHAT'S WRONG ?!
!!
IT'S NOTHING, MOM!
...
FEH!
伊達工業
TIME FOR AFTERNOON PRACTICE, GUYS!
YEAH!!
伊達工業
DATE TECH COMPUTER LAB
*JACKET: DATE TECH
TSUBAKIHARA
KARASUNO
Senob
SET COUNT 2 - 0 (KARASUNO) (TSUBAKIHARA) 25-23 25-23
JAP
THIS IS

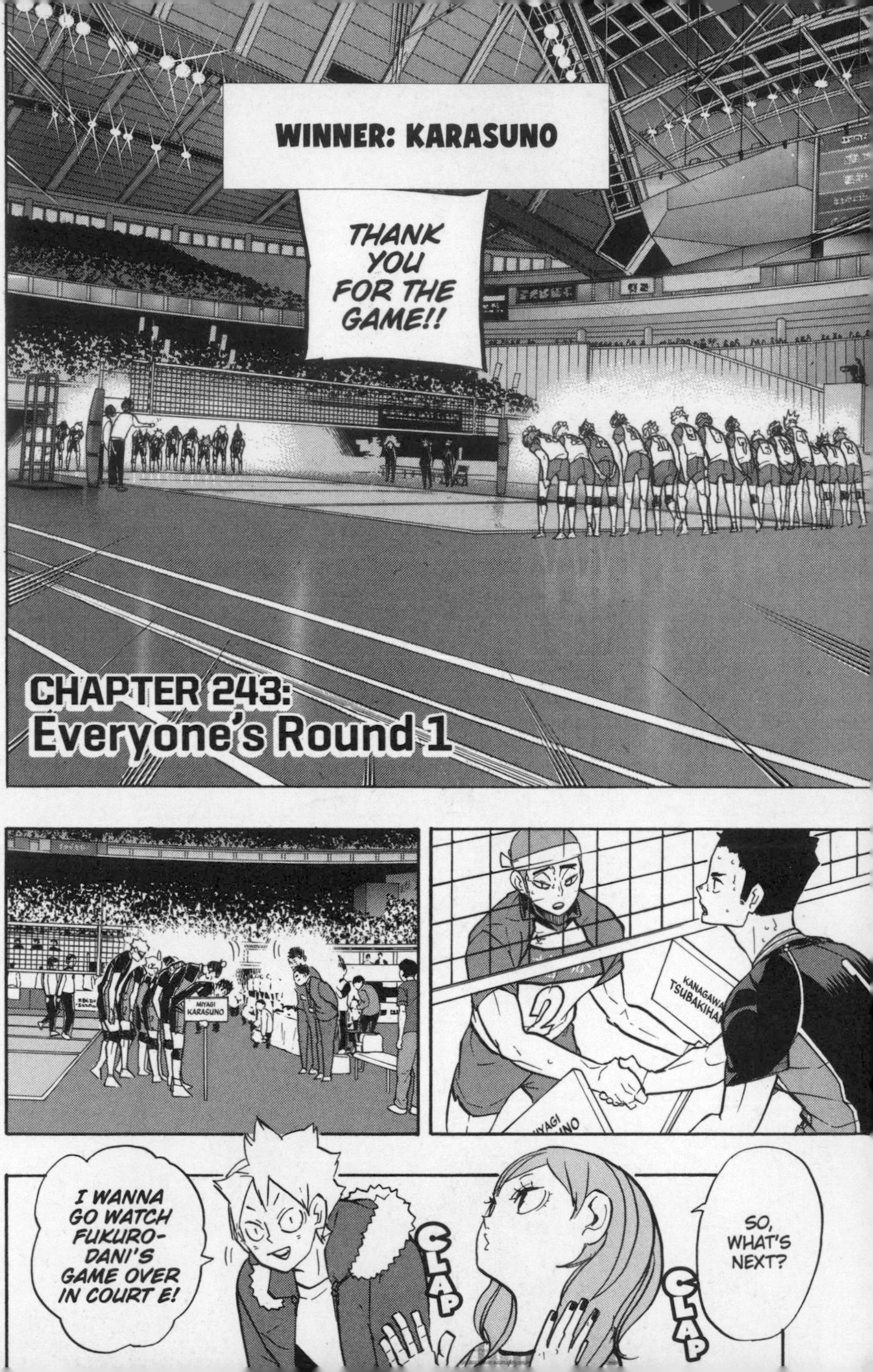

WINNER: KARASUNO
THANK YOU FOR THE GAME!!
CHAPTER 243:
Everyone's Round 1
MIYAGI KARASUNO
SO, WHAT'S NEXT?
CLAP
CLAP
I WANNA GO WATCH FUKURO-DANI'S GAME OVER IN COURT E!

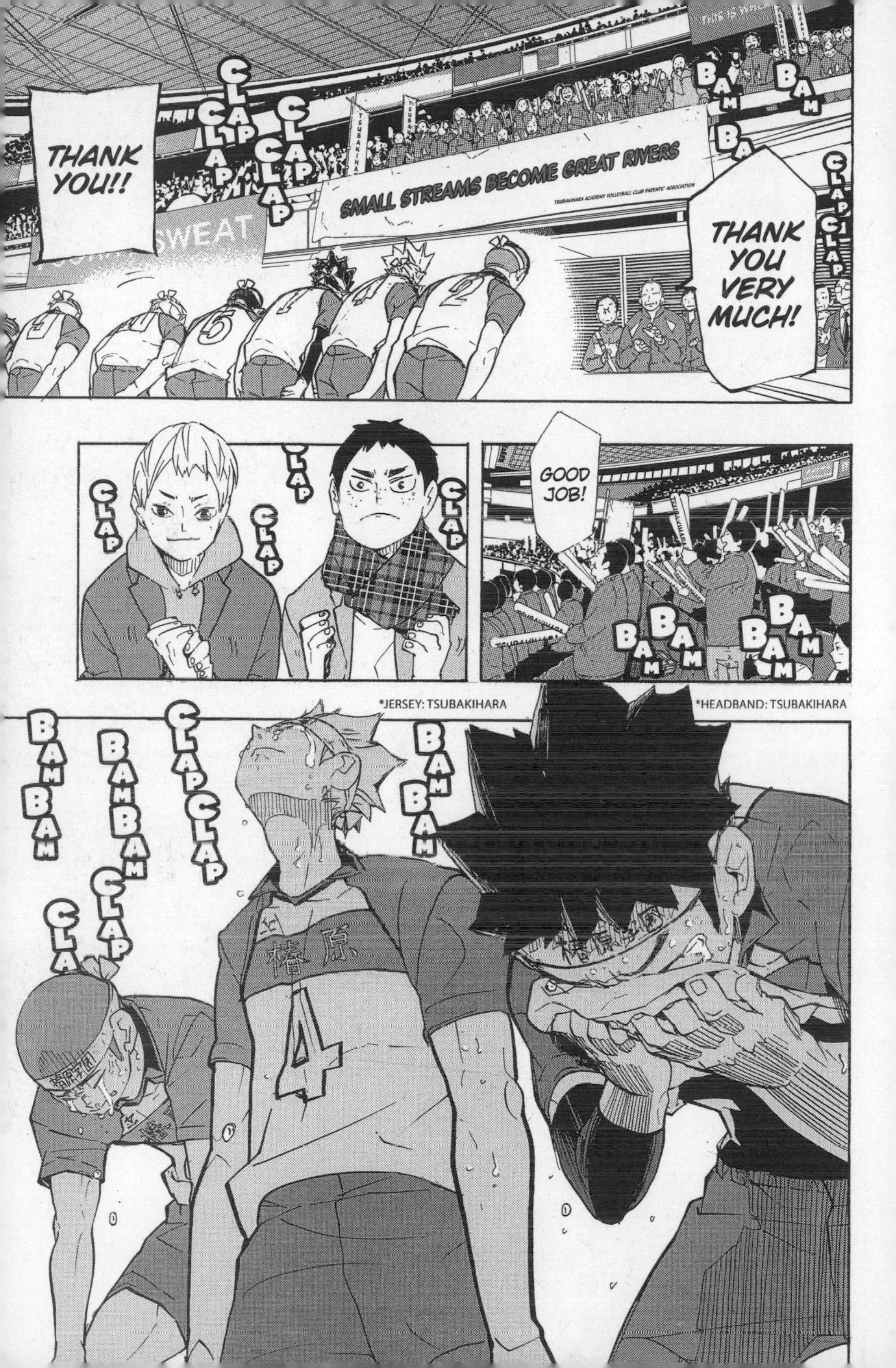
BAM BAM
BAM
CLAP CLAP
THANK YOU VERY MUCH!
SMALL STREAMS BECOME GREAT RIVERS
TSUBAKIHARA ACADEMY VOLLEYBALL CLUB PARENTS' ASSOCIATION
CLAP CLAP
CLAP CLAP
THANK YOU!!
SWEAT
GOOD JOB!
BAM BAM
BAM BAM
CLAP
CLAP
CLAP
CLAP
*HEADBAND: TSUBAKIHARA
*JERSEY: TSUBAKIHARA
BAM BAM
CLAP CLAP
BAM BAM
CLAP
BAM BAM
CLA

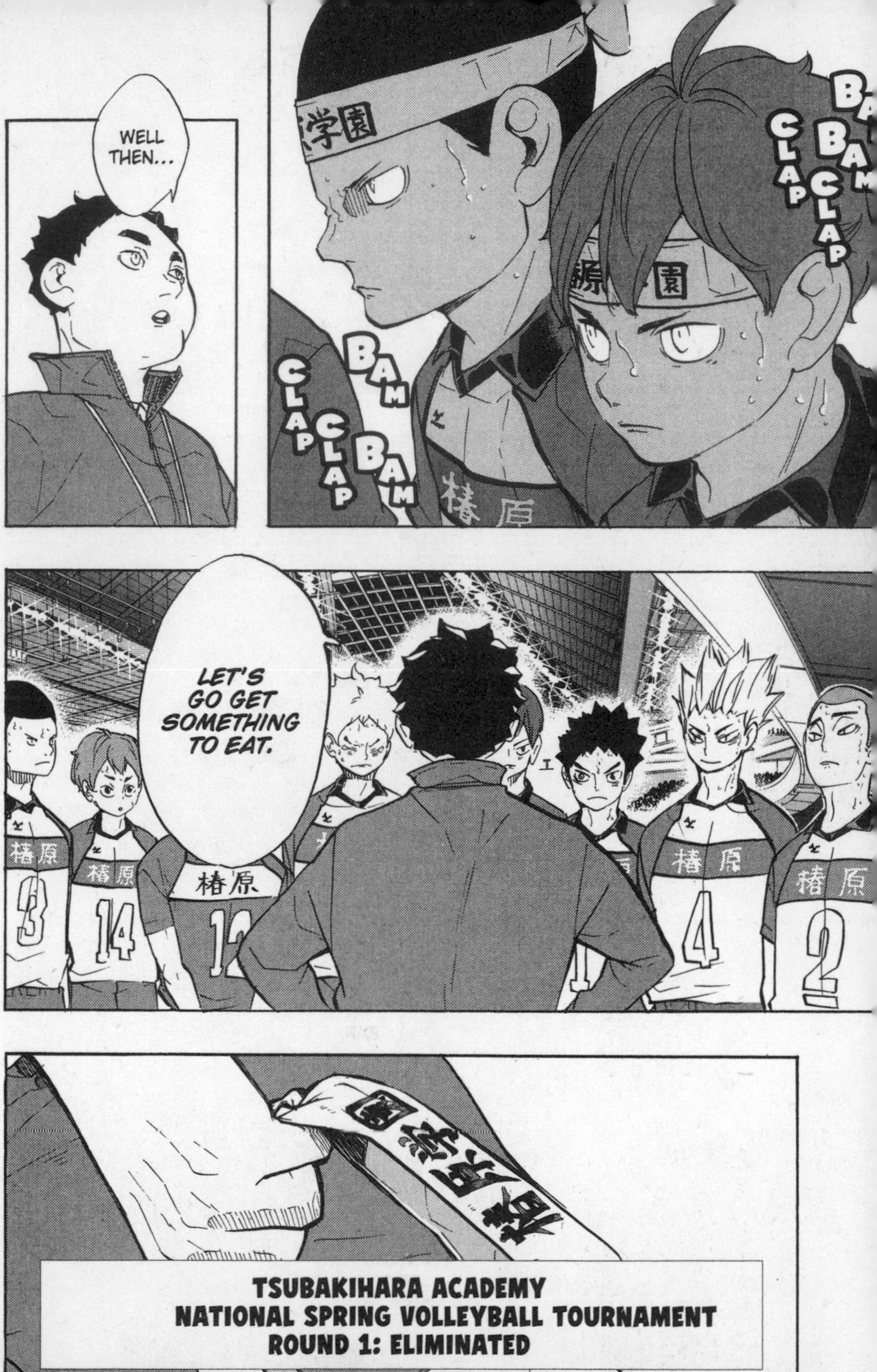
BAM
CLAP
BAM
CLAP
BAM
CLAP
CLAP
BAM
WELL THEN...
LET'S GO GET SOMETHING TO EAT.
TSUBAKIHARA ACADEMY
NATIONAL SPRING VOLLEYBALL TOURNAMENT
ROUND 1: ELIMINATED

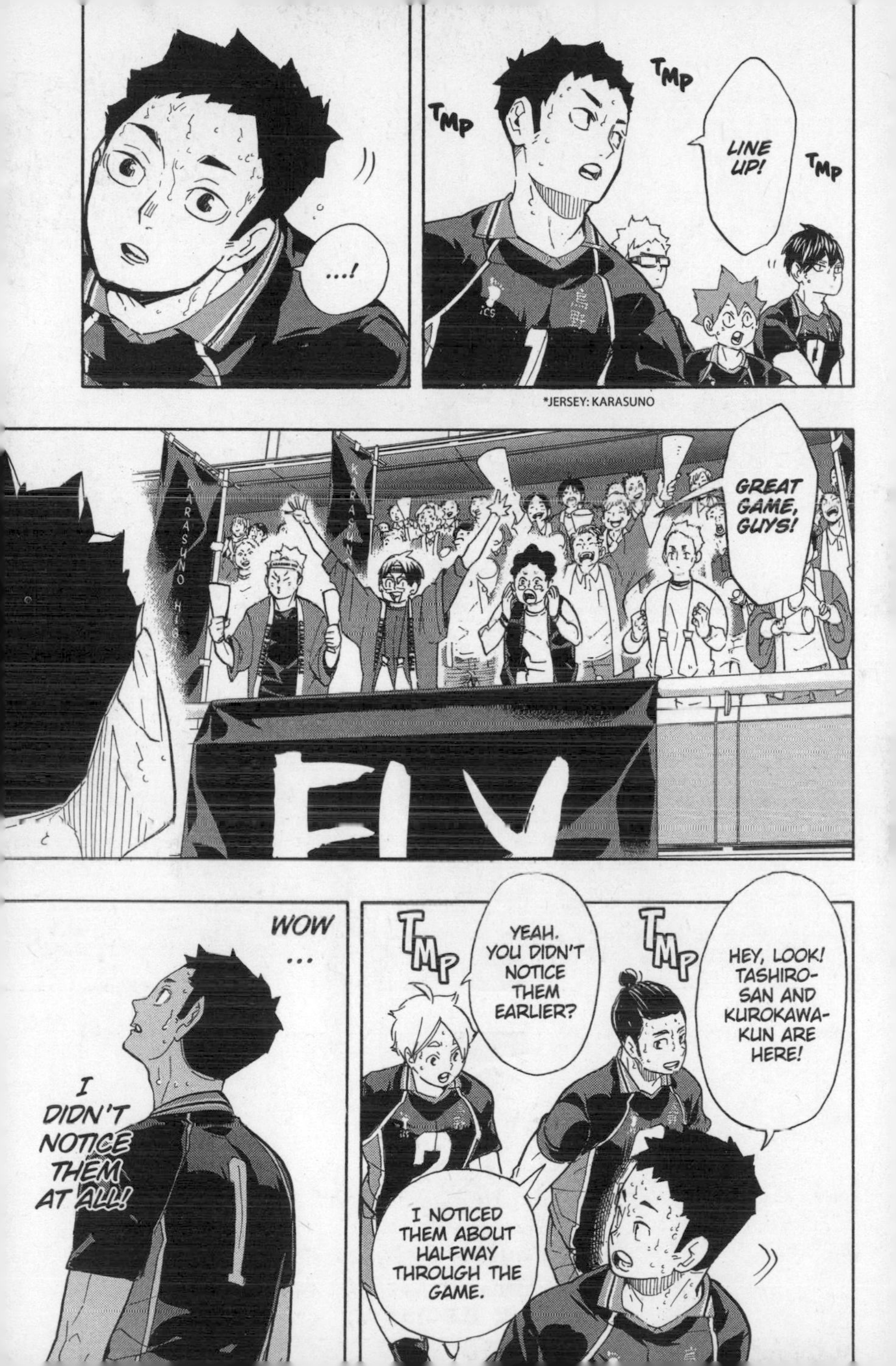
TMP
TMP
LINE UP!
TMP
...!
*JERSEY: KARASUNO
GREAT GAME, GUYS!
TMP
HEY, LOOK! TASHIRO-SAN AND KUROKAWA-KUN ARE HERE!
TMP
YEAH. YOU DIDN'T NOTICE THEM EARLIER?
I NOTICED THEM ABOUT HALFWAY THROUGH THE GAME.
WOW ...
I DIDN'T NOTICE THEM AT ALL!

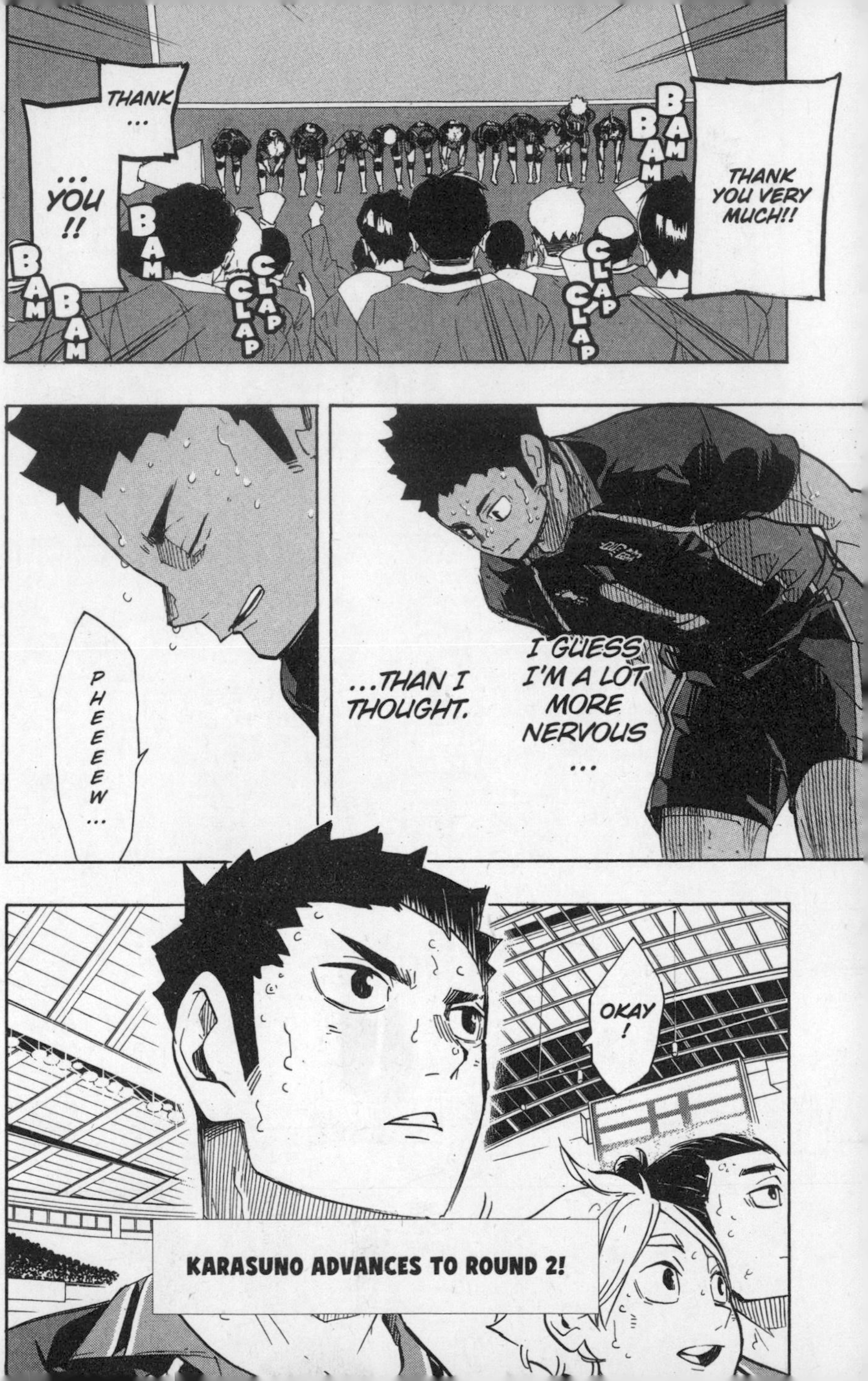
BAM BAM
THANK YOU VERY MUCH!!
CLAP CLAP
CLAP CLAP
THANK...
...YOU!!
BAM BAM
BAM BAM
BAM BAM
I GUESS I'M A LOT MORE NERVOUS...
...THAN I THOUGHT.
PHEEEEEW...
OKAY!
KARASUNO ADVANCES TO ROUND 2!

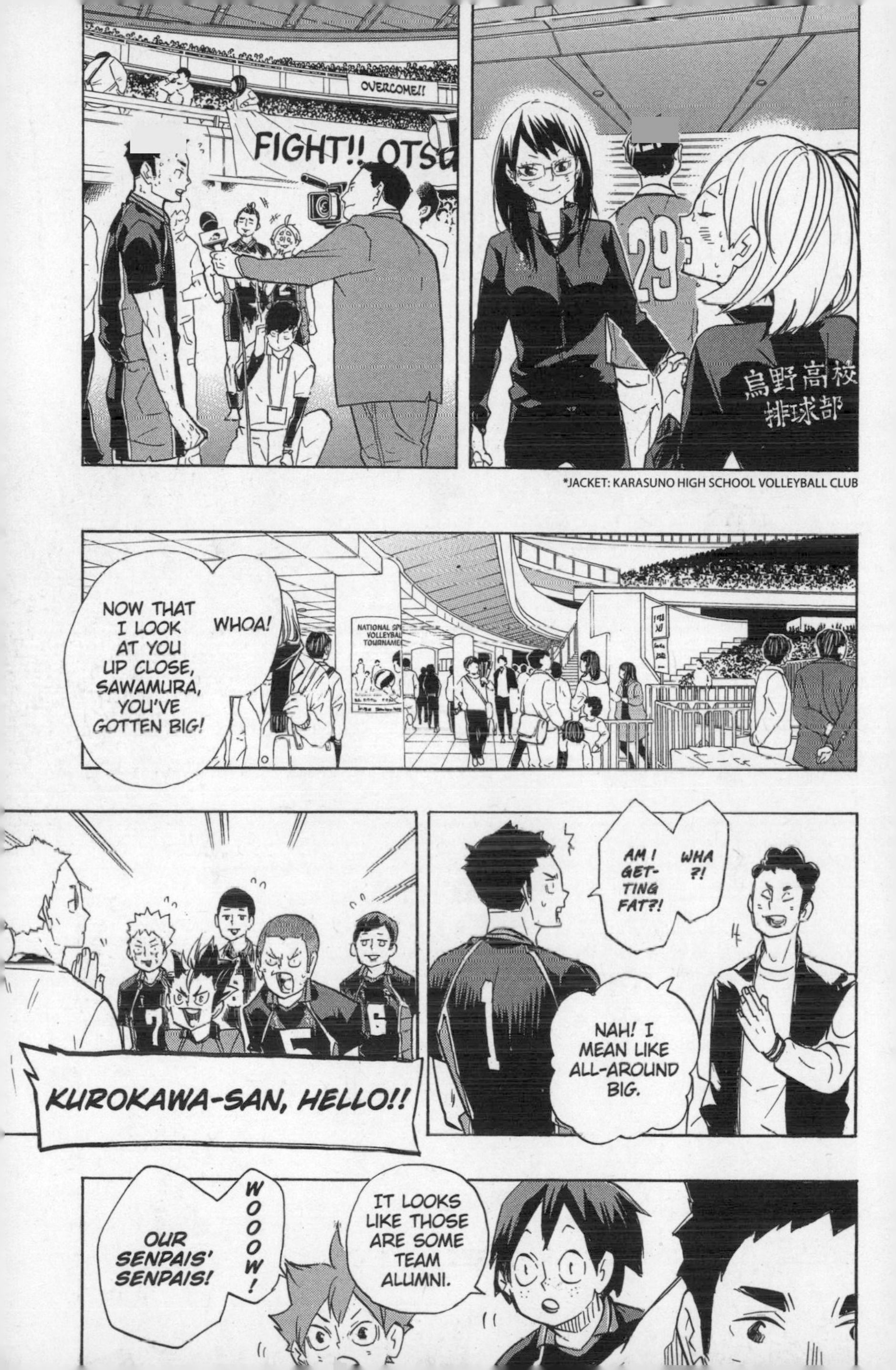

烏野高校 排球部
*JACKET: KARASUNO HIGH SCHOOL VOLLEYBALL CLUB
OVERCOME!!
FIGHT!! OTSU
WHOA!
NOW THAT I LOOK AT YOU UP CLOSE, SAWAMURA, YOU'VE GOTTEN BIG!
WHA ?!
AM I GETTING FAT?!
NAH! I MEAN LIKE ALL-AROUND BIG.
KUROKAWA-SAN, HELLO!!
IT LOOKS LIKE THOSE ARE SOME TEAM ALUMNI.
WOOOOW!
OUR SENPAIS' SENPAIS!

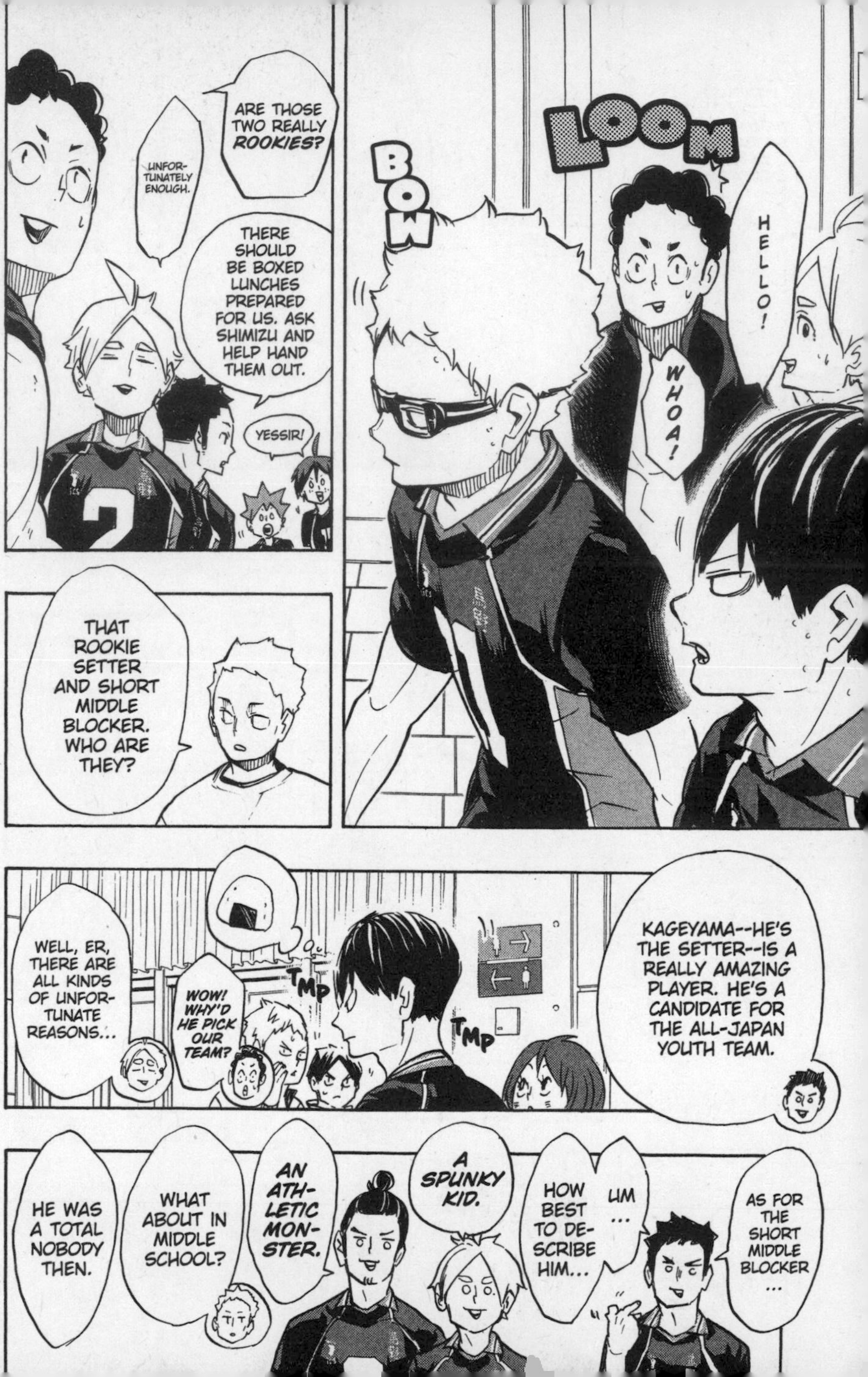
HELLO!
LOOM
BOW
WHOA!
ARE THOSE TWO REALLY ROOKIES?
UNFORTUNATELY ENOUGH.
THERE SHOULD BE BOXED LUNCHES PREPARED FOR US. ASK SHIMIZU AND HELP HAND THEM OUT.
YESSIR!
THAT ROOKIE SETTER AND SHORT MIDDLE BLOCKER. WHO ARE THEY?
KAGEYAMA--HE'S THE SETTER--IS A REALLY AMAZING PLAYER. HE'S A CANDIDATE FOR THE ALL-JAPAN YOUTH TEAM.
TMP
TMP
WOW! WHY'D HE PICK OUR TEAM?
WELL, ER, THERE ARE ALL KINDS OF UNFORTUNATE REASONS...
AS FOR THE SHORT MIDDLE BLOCKER...
UM...
HOW BEST TO DESCRIBE HIM...
A SPUNKY KID.
AN ATHLETIC MONSTER.
WHAT ABOUT IN MIDDLE SCHOOL?
HE WAS A TOTAL NOBODY THEN.

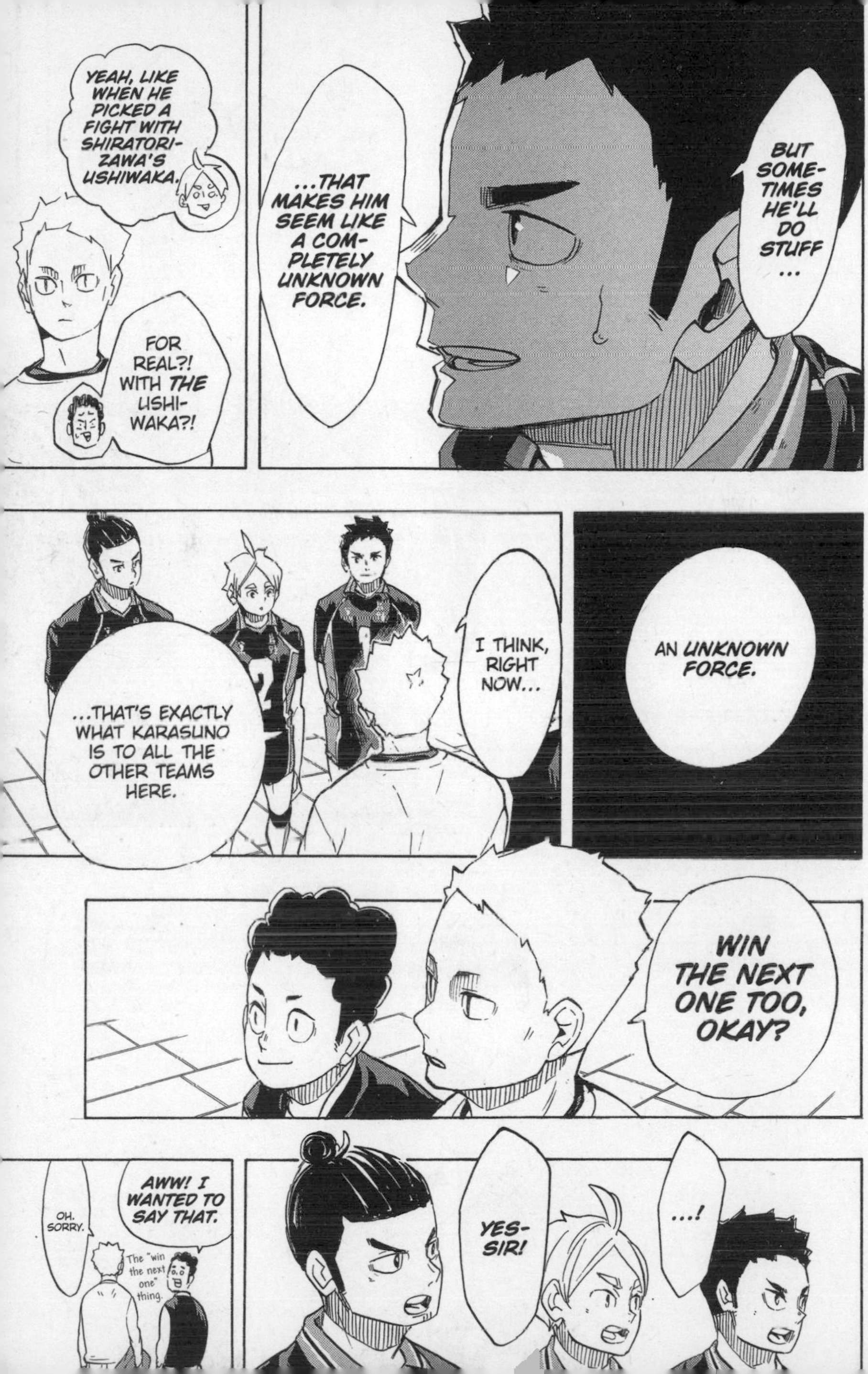

BUT SOMETIMES HE'LL DO STUFF...
...THAT MAKES HIM SEEM LIKE A COMPLETELY UNKNOWN FORCE.
YEAH, LIKE WHEN HE PICKED A FIGHT WITH SHIRATORIZAWA'S USHIWAKA.
FOR REAL?! WITH THE USHIWAKA?!
AN UNKNOWN FORCE.
I THINK, RIGHT NOW...
...THAT'S EXACTLY WHAT KARASUNO IS TO ALL THE OTHER TEAMS HERE.
WIN THE NEXT ONE TOO, OKAY?
...!
YES-SIR!
AWW! I WANTED TO SAY THAT.
OH. SORRY.
The "win the next one" thing.

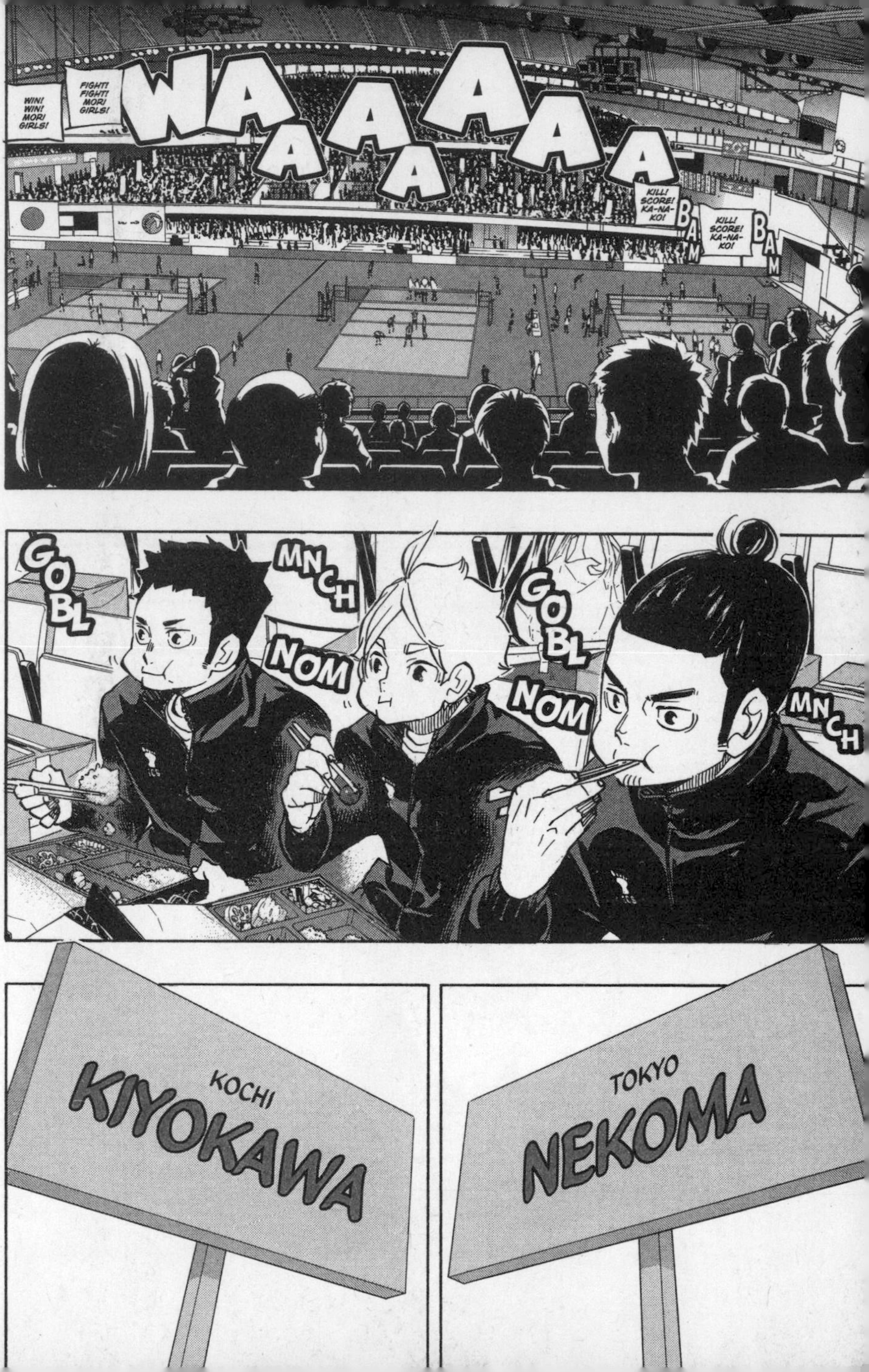

KILL! SCORE! KA-NA-KO!
BAM
KILL! SCORE! KA-NA-KO!
BAM
WAAAAAAA
FIGHT! FIGHT! MORI GIRLS!
WIN! WIN! MORI GIRLS!
MNCH
NOM
GOBL
MNCH
NOM
GOBL
TOKYO
NEKOMA
KOCHI
KIYOKAWA

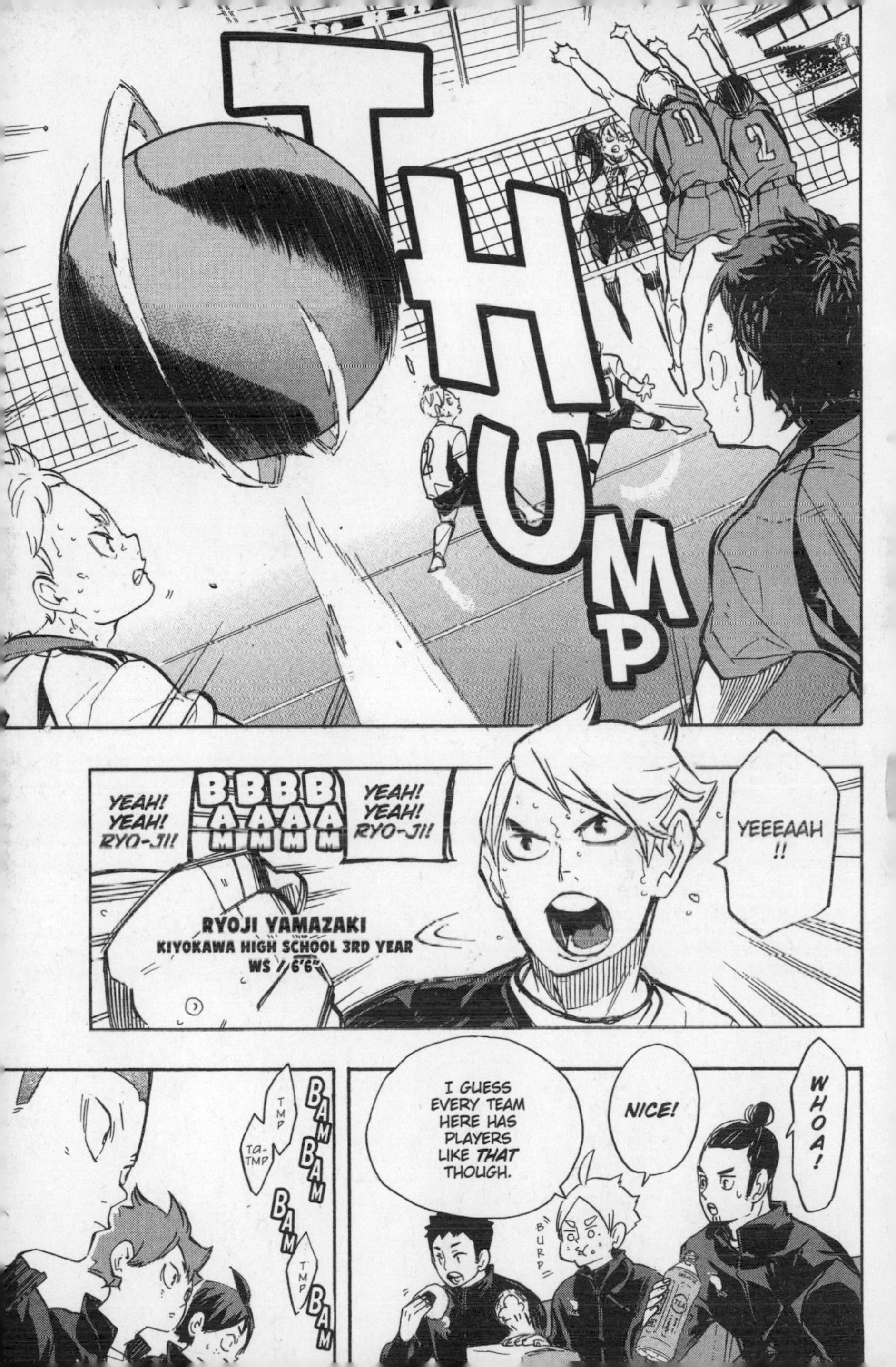
THUMP
YEEEAAH!!
RYOJI YAMAZAKI
KIYOKAWA HIGH SCHOOL 3RD YEAR
WS / 6'6"
YEAH! YEAH! RYO-JI!
BAM BAM BAM BAM
YEAH! YEAH! RYO-JI!
WHOA!
NICE!
I GUESS EVERY TEAM HERE HAS PLAYERS LIKE *THAT* THOUGH.
BURP
BAM BAM BAM BAM
TMP
TA-TMP
TMP

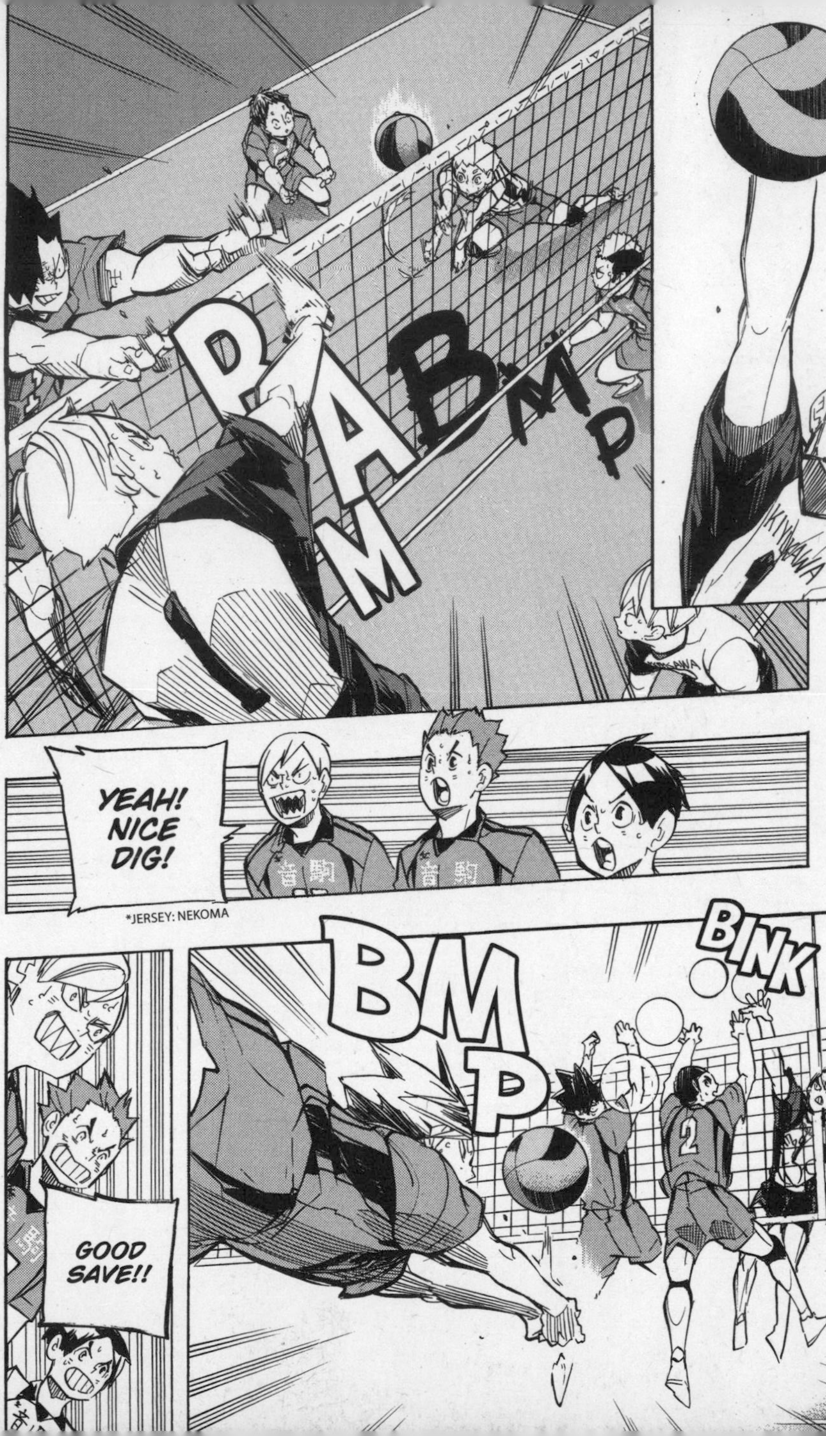
BAM
BMP
YEAH! NICE DIG!
*JERSEY: NEKOMA
BINK
BMP
GOOD SAVE!!

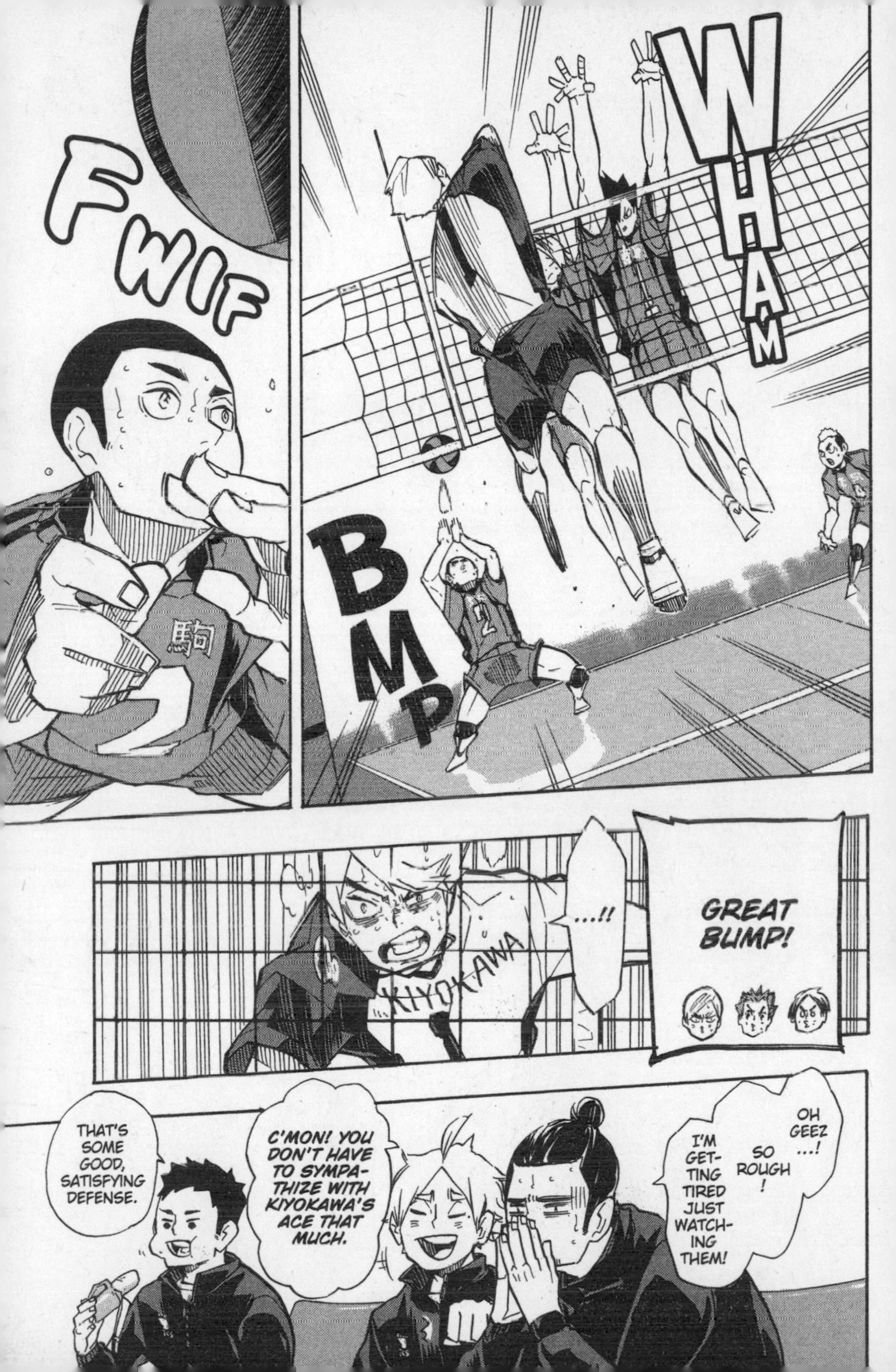
WHAM
BMP
FWIF
GREAT BUMP!
...!!
KIYOKAWA
OH GEEZ ...!
SO ROUGH!
I'M GETTING TIRED JUST WATCHING THEM!
C'MON! YOU DON'T HAVE TO SYMPATHIZE WITH KIYOKAWA'S ACE THAT MUCH.
THAT'S SOME GOOD, SATISFYING DEFENSE.

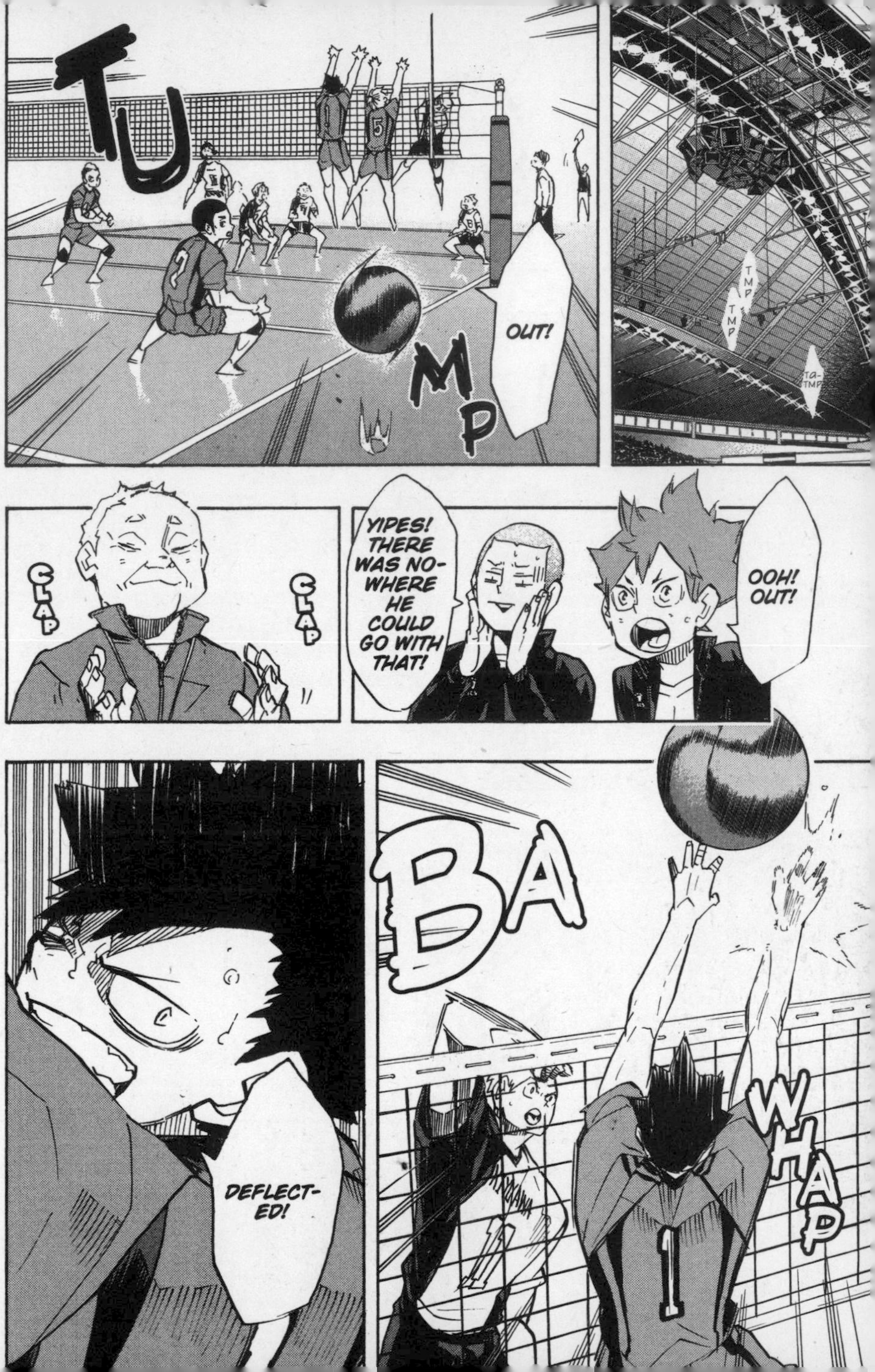
TMP
TMP
TA-TMP
TU
MP
OUT!
OOH! OUT!
YIPES! THERE WAS NO-WHERE HE COULD GO WITH THAT!
CLAP
CLAP
BA
WHAP
DEFLECT-ED!

FUKU-NAGA!

FWIF

TUMP

GAME OVER

YEAH! GREAT SHOT!

FWUP

IN!

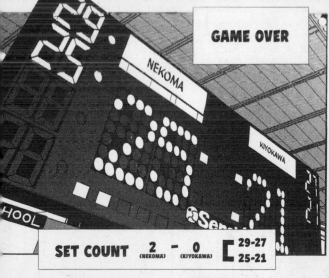

NEKOMA

KIYOKAWA

HOOL

SET COUNT **2** (NEKOMA) **-** **0** (KIYOKAWA) [29-27
25-21

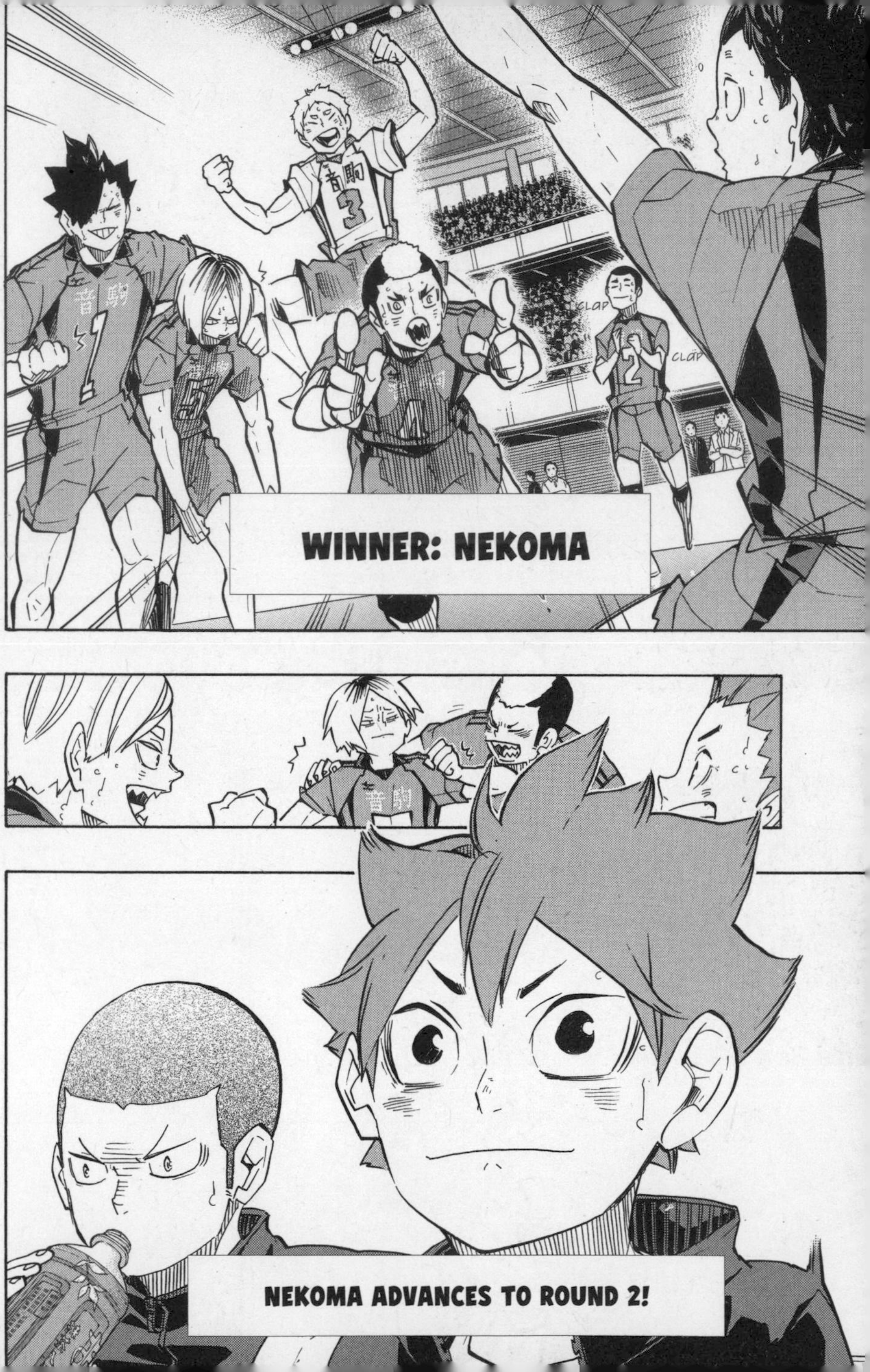
CLAP
CLAP
WINNER: NEKOMA
NEKOMA ADVANCES TO ROUND 2!

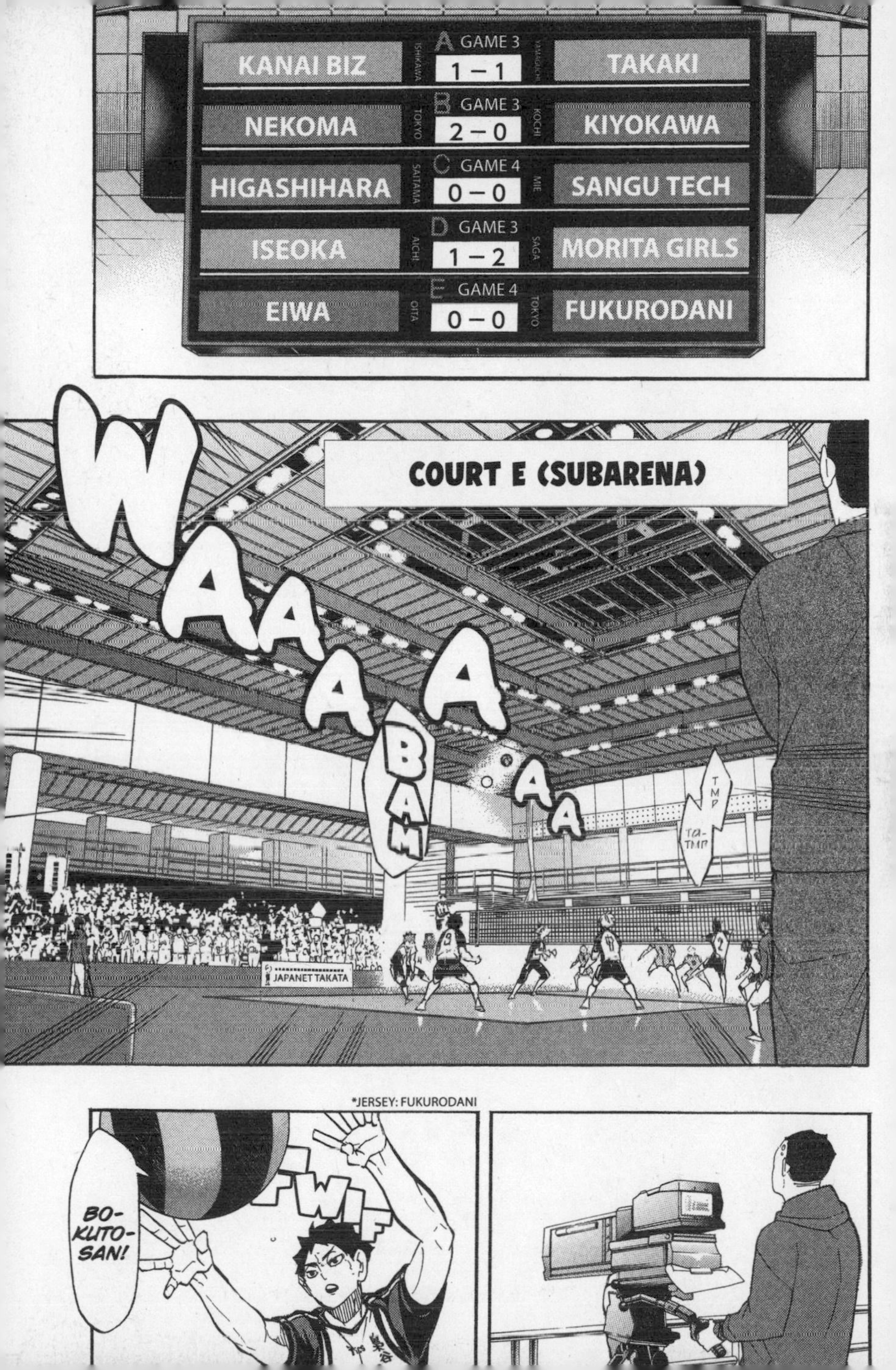
A GAME 3
KANAI BIZ
ISHIKAWA
1 – 1
YAMAGUCHI
TAKAKI
B GAME 3
NEKOMA
TOKYO
2 – 0
KOCHI
KIYOKAWA
C GAME 4
HIGASHIHARA
SAITAMA
0 – 0
MIE
SANGU TECH
D GAME 3
ISEOKA
AICHI
1 – 2
SAGA
MORITA GIRLS
E GAME 4
EIWA
OITA
0 – 0
TOKYO
FUKURODANI
COURT E (SUBARENA)
WAAAAAAA
BAM
TMP
TA-TMP
JAPANET TAKATA
*JERSEY: FUKURODANI
FWIF
BO-KUTO-SAN!

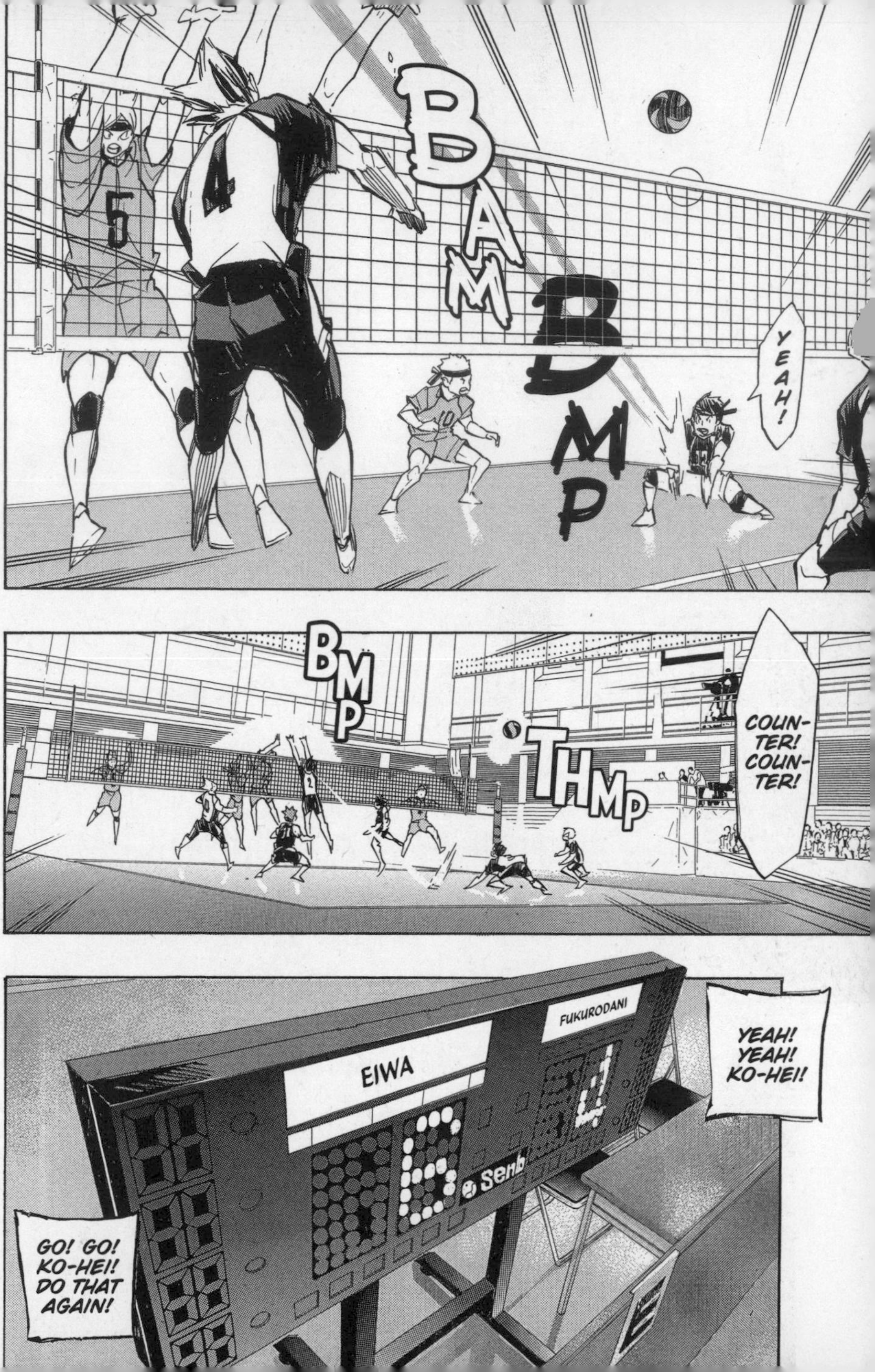
YEAH!
BAM
BAMP
BMP
THMP
COUNTER! COUNTER!
YEAH! YEAH! KO-HEI!
FUKURODANI
EIWA
Senb
GO! GO! KO-HEI! DO THAT AGAIN!

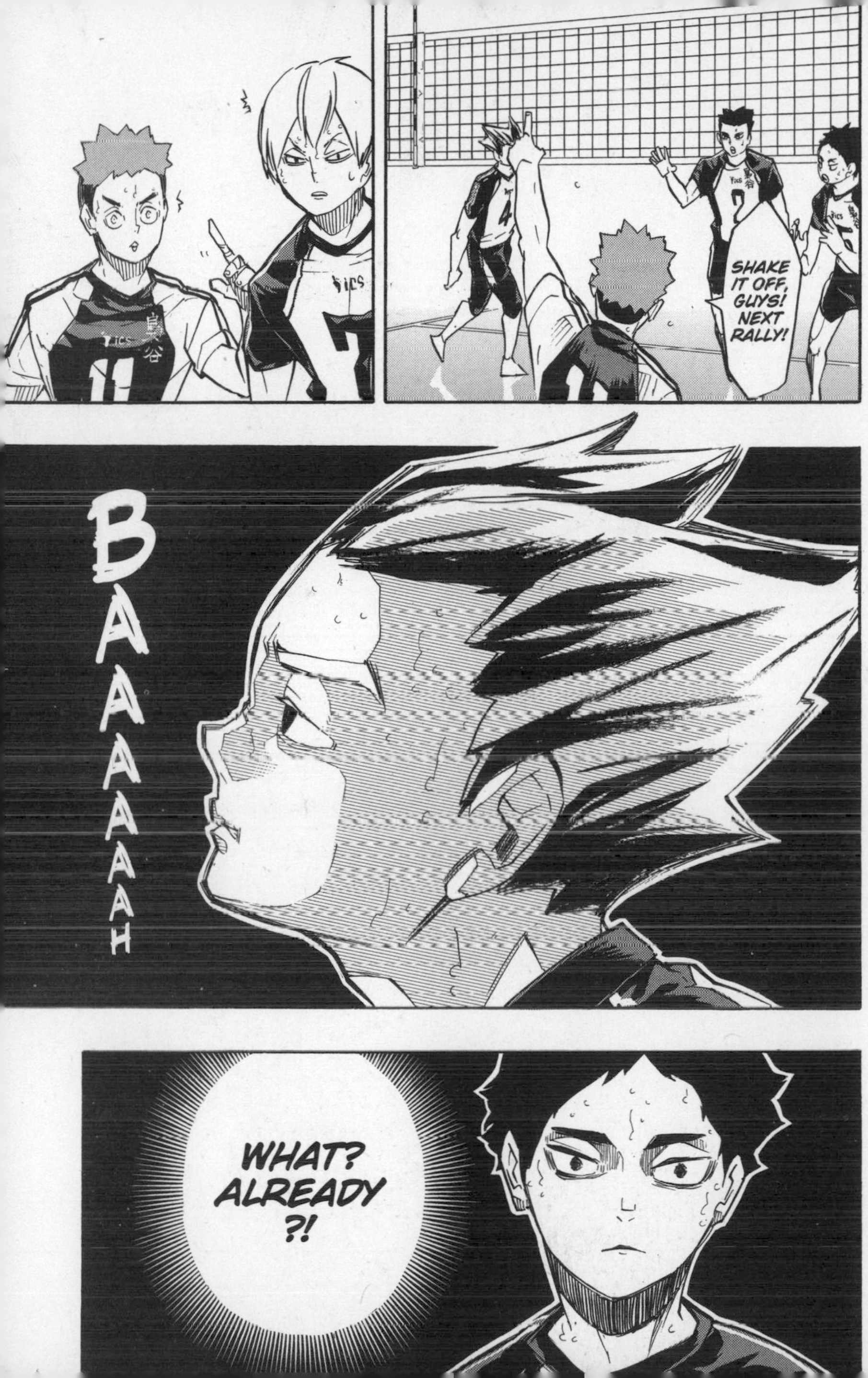
SHAKE IT OFF, GUYS! NEXT RALLY!
BAAAAAAAH
WHAT? ALREADY ?!

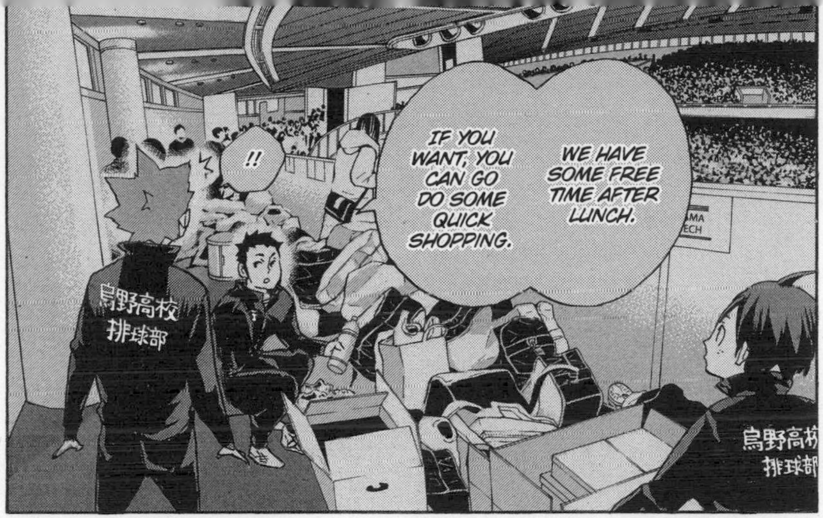
WE HAVE SOME FREE TIME AFTER LUNCH.
IF YOU WANT, YOU CAN GO DO SOME QUICK SHOPPING.
!!
烏野高校 排球部
烏野高校 排球部

CHAPTER 244

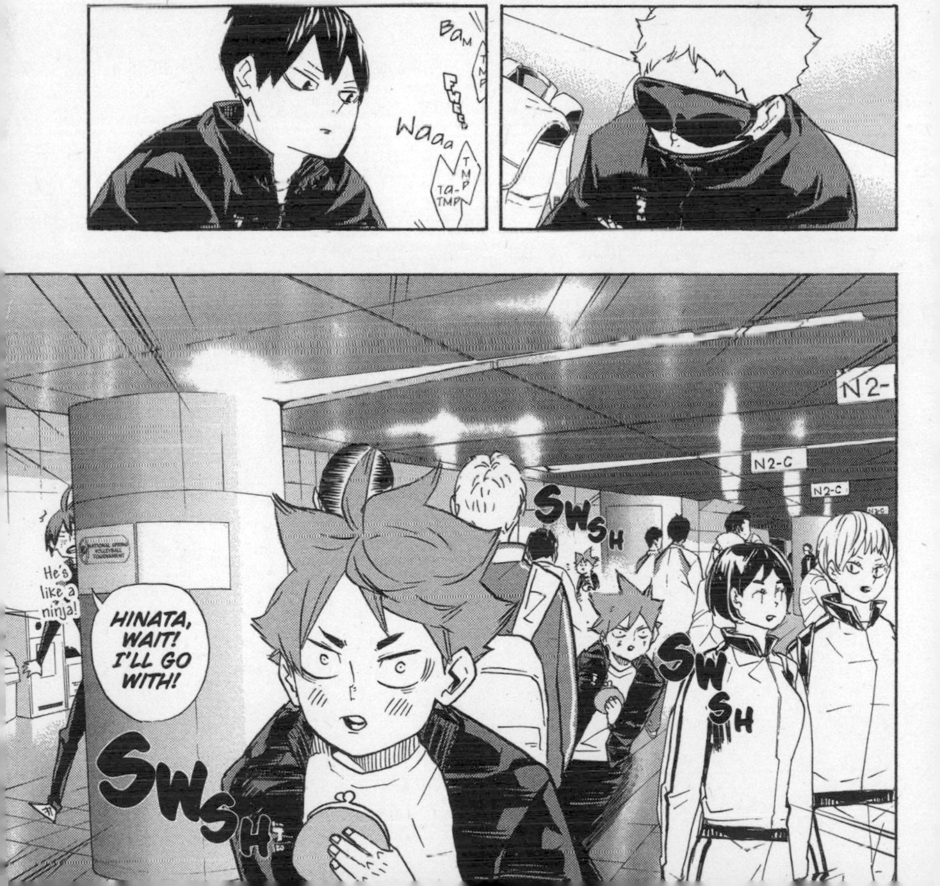
BAM
TMP
WAAA
TMP TA-TMP
SWSH
SWSH
HINATA, WAIT! I'LL GO WITH!
He's like a ninja!
SWSH

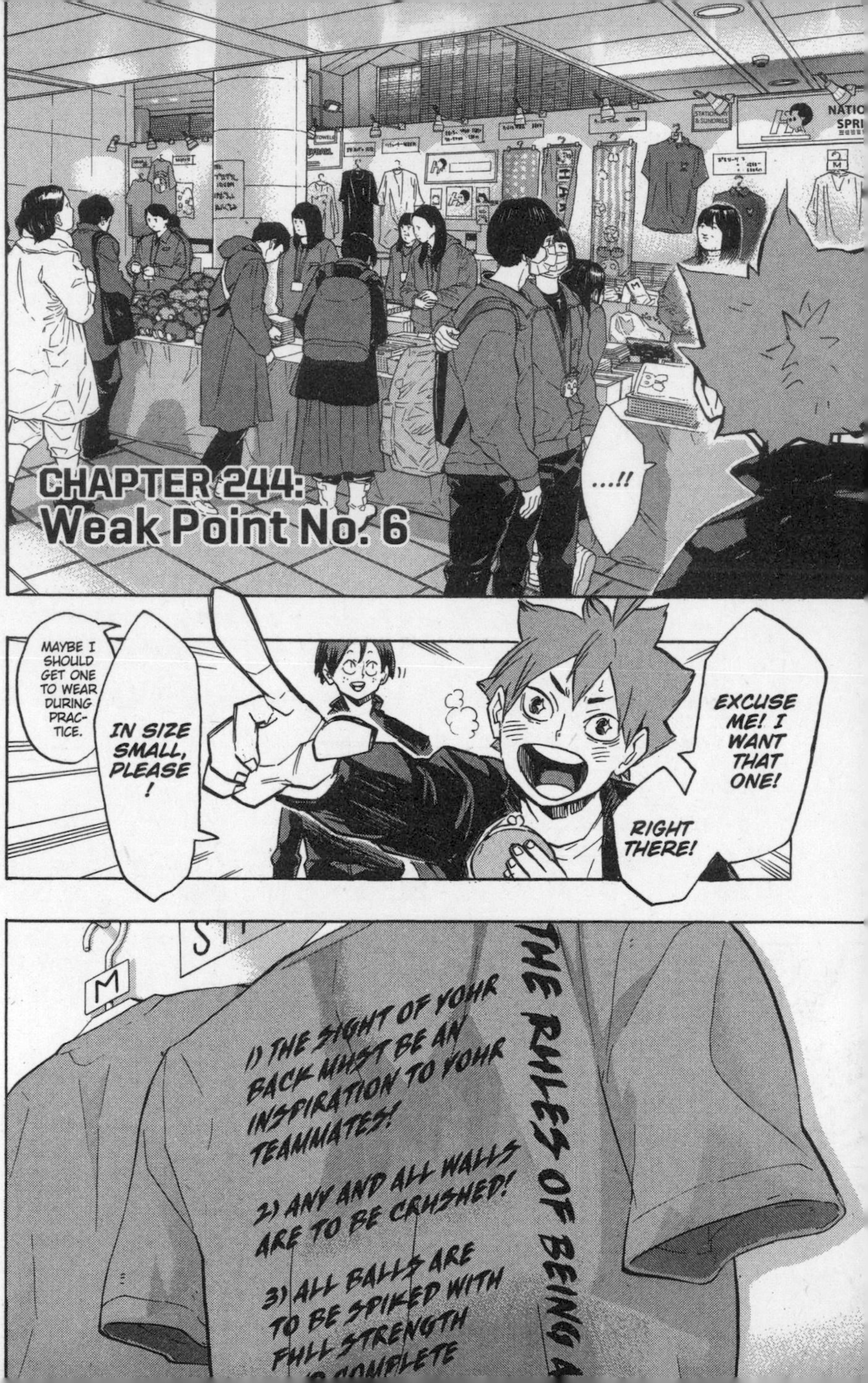
CHAPTER 244:
Weak Point No. 6
...!!
EXCUSE ME! I WANT THAT ONE!
RIGHT THERE!
IN SIZE SMALL, PLEASE!
MAYBE I SHOULD GET ONE TO WEAR DURING PRAC-TICE.
M
THE RULES OF BEING A
1) THE SIGHT OF YOUR BACK MUST BE AN INSPIRATION TO YOUR TEAMMATES!
2) ANY AND ALL WALLS ARE TO BE CRUSHED!
3) ALL BALLS ARE TO BE SPIKED WITH FULL STRENGTH
COMPLETE

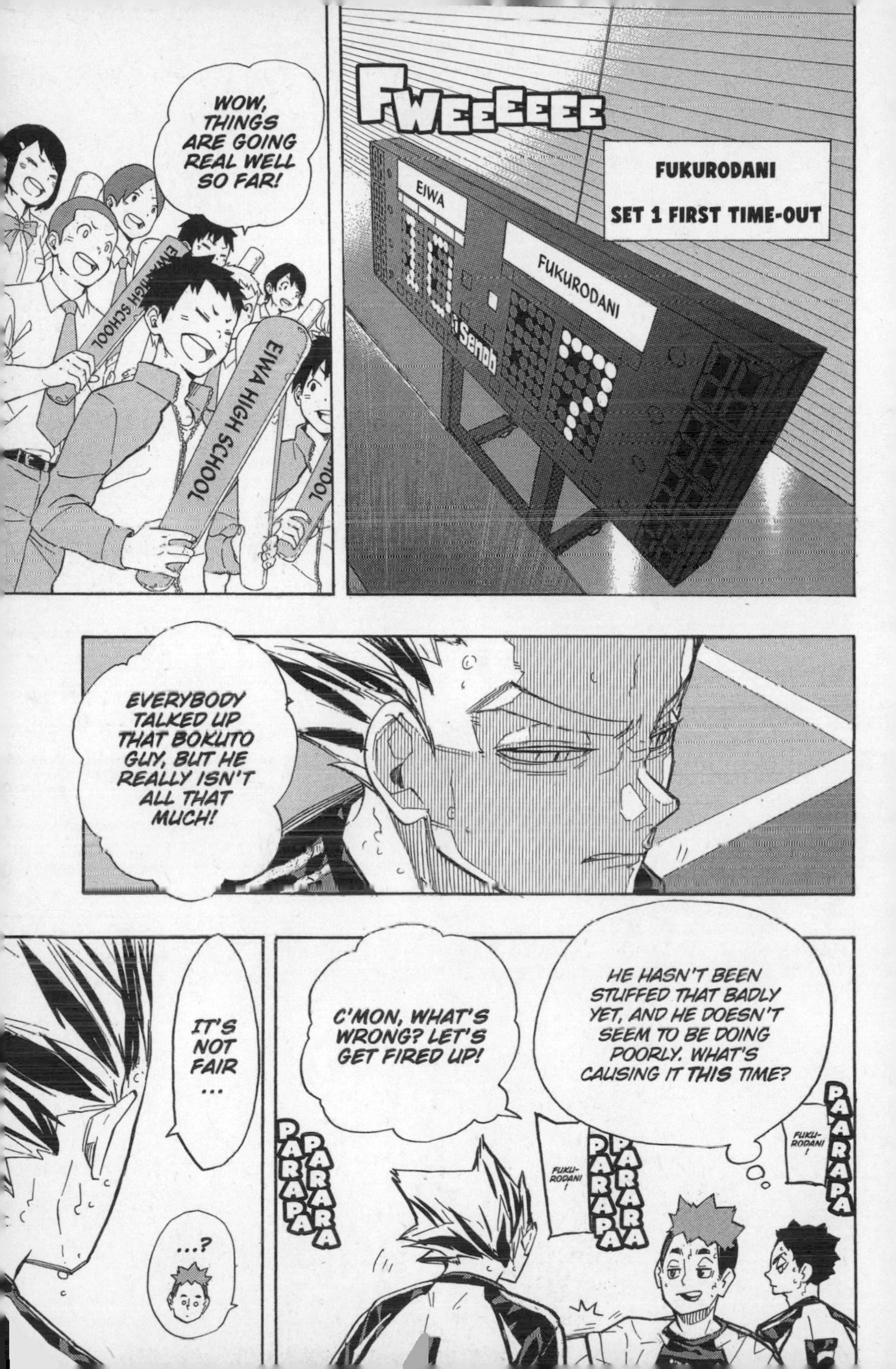
FWEEEEEE
FUKURODANI
SET 1 FIRST TIME-OUT
EIWA
10
FUKURODANI
7
WOW, THINGS ARE GOING REAL WELL SO FAR!
EIWA HIGH SCHOOL
EIWA HIGH SCHOOL
EVERYBODY TALKED UP THAT BOKUTO GUY, BUT HE REALLY ISN'T ALL THAT MUCH!
PAARAPA
FUKU-RODANI!
HE HASN'T BEEN STUFFED THAT BADLY YET, AND HE DOESN'T SEEM TO BE DOING POORLY. WHAT'S CAUSING IT THIS TIME?
PARAPA PARARA
FUKU-RODANI!
C'MON, WHAT'S WRONG? LET'S GET FIRED UP!
PARAPA PARARA
IT'S NOT FAIR...
...?

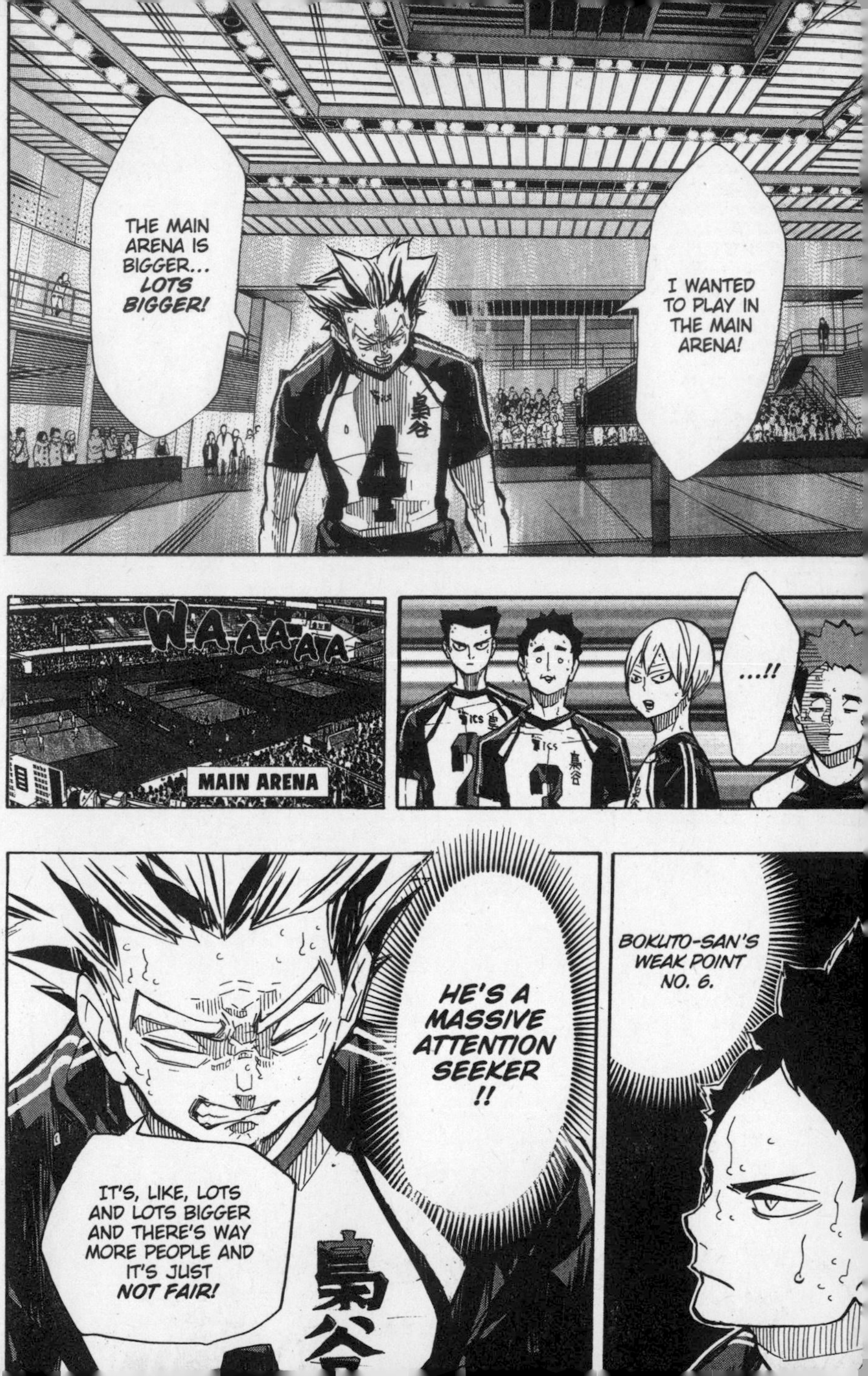
I WANTED TO PLAY IN THE MAIN ARENA!
THE MAIN ARENA IS BIGGER... LOTS BIGGER!
...!!
WAAAAA
MAIN ARENA
BOKUTO-SAN'S WEAK POINT NO. 6.
HE'S A MASSIVE ATTENTION SEEKER !!
IT'S, LIKE, LOTS AND LOTS BIGGER AND THERE'S WAY MORE PEOPLE AND IT'S JUST NOT FAIR!

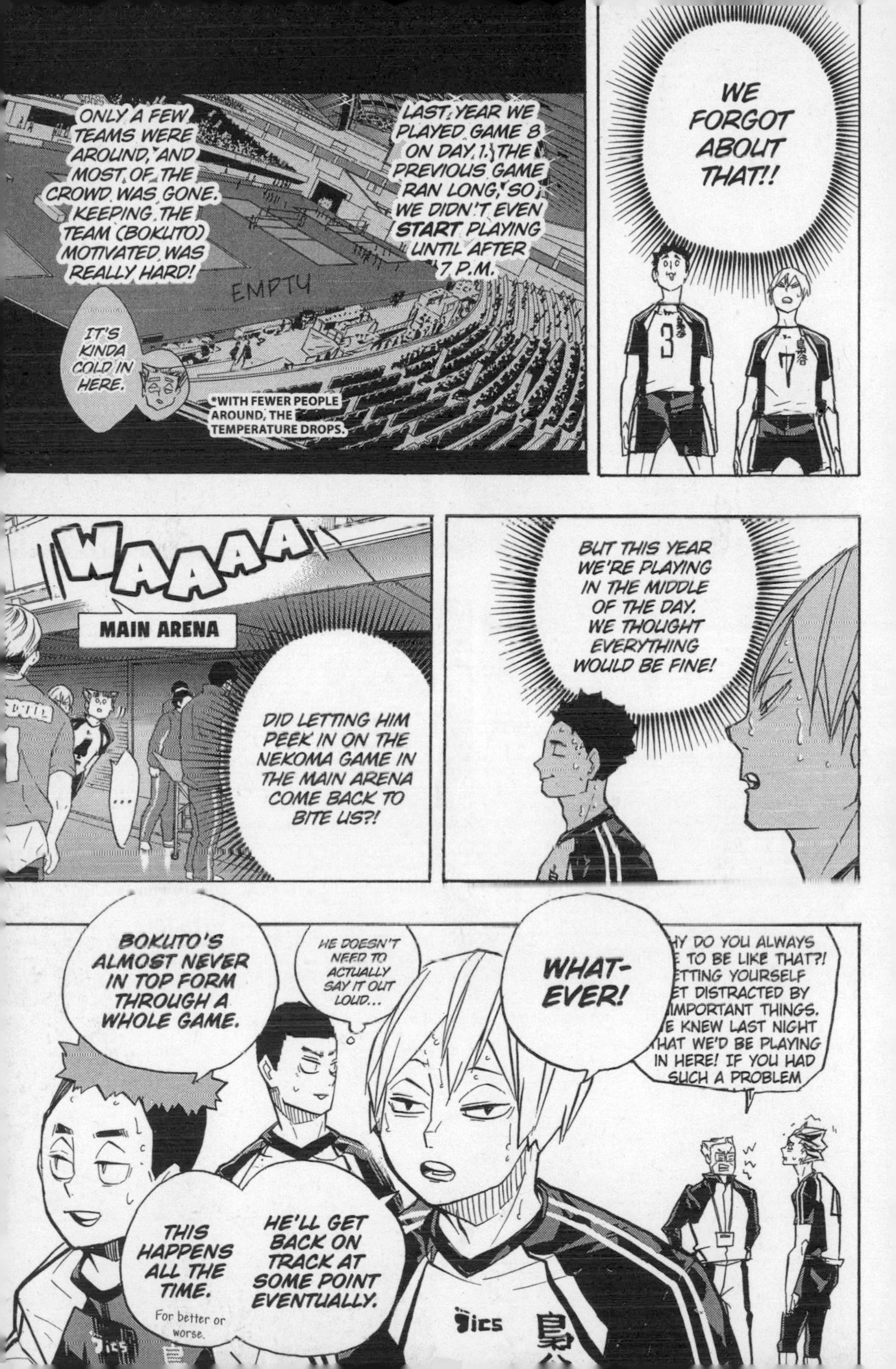
WE FORGOT ABOUT THAT!!
LAST YEAR WE PLAYED GAME 8 ON DAY 1. THE PREVIOUS GAME RAN LONG, SO WE DIDN'T EVEN START PLAYING UNTIL AFTER 7 P.M.
ONLY A FEW TEAMS WERE AROUND, AND MOST OF THE CROWD WAS GONE. KEEPING THE TEAM (BOKUTO) MOTIVATED WAS REALLY HARD!
EMPTY
IT'S KINDA COLD IN HERE.
*WITH FEWER PEOPLE AROUND, THE TEMPERATURE DROPS.
BUT THIS YEAR WE'RE PLAYING IN THE MIDDLE OF THE DAY. WE THOUGHT EVERYTHING WOULD BE FINE!
WAAAAA
MAIN ARENA
DID LETTING HIM PEEK IN ON THE NEKOMA GAME IN THE MAIN ARENA COME BACK TO BITE US?!
...
HY DO YOU ALWAYS E TO BE LIKE THAT?! ETTING YOURSELF ET DISTRACTED BY IMPORTANT THINGS. E KNEW LAST NIGHT THAT WE'D BE PLAYING IN HERE! IF YOU HAD SUCH A PROBLEM
WHAT-EVER!
HE DOESN'T NEED TO ACTUALLY SAY IT OUT LOUD...
BOKUTO'S ALMOST NEVER IN TOP FORM THROUGH A WHOLE GAME.
HE'LL GET BACK ON TRACK AT SOME POINT EVENTUALLY.
THIS HAPPENS ALL THE TIME.
For better or worse.

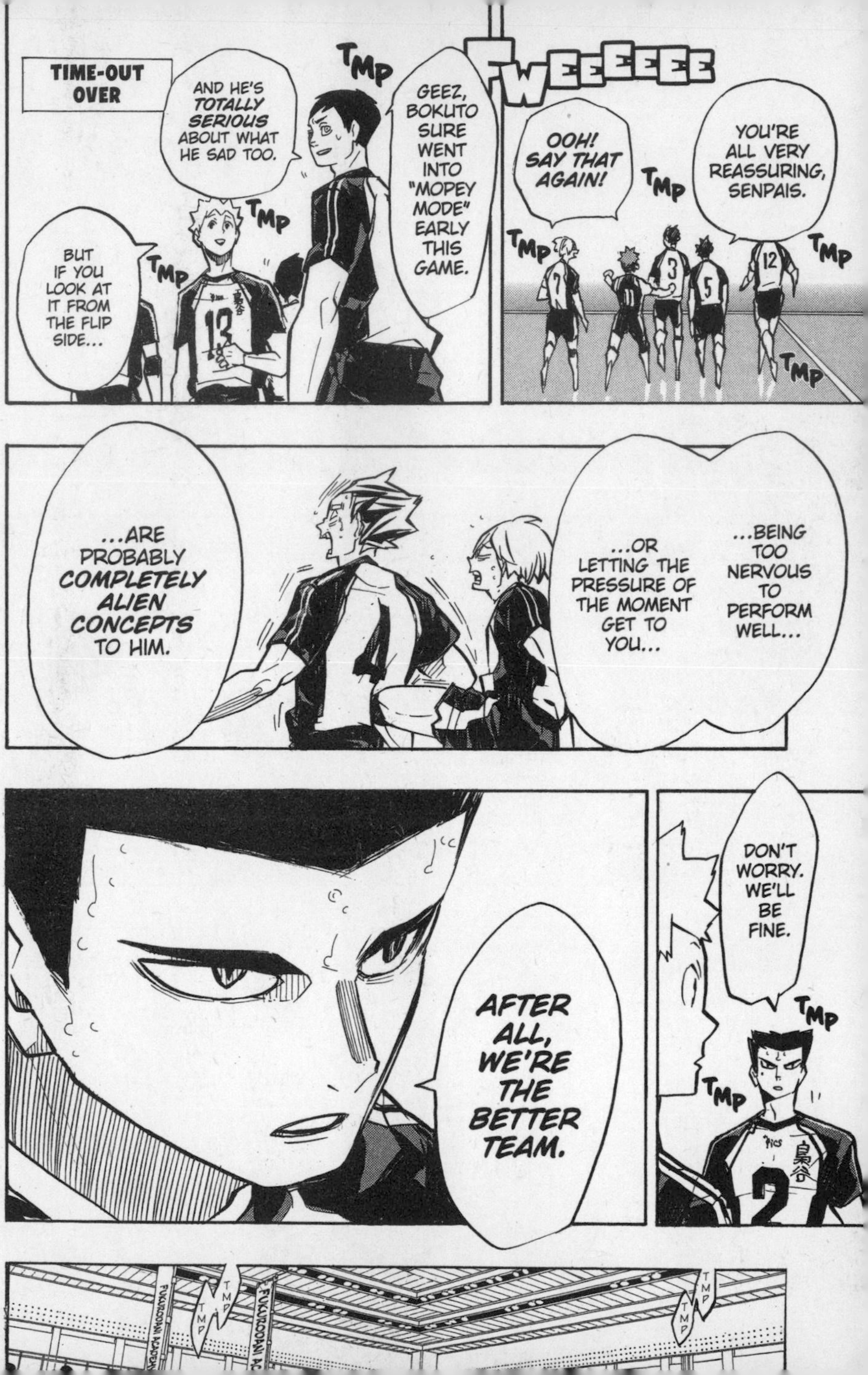
FWEEEEEE
YOU'RE ALL VERY REASSURING, SENPAIS.
TMP
OOH! SAY THAT AGAIN!
TMP
TMP
TMP
TMP
GEEZ, BOKUTO SURE WENT INTO "MOPEY MODE" EARLY THIS GAME.
AND HE'S TOTALLY SERIOUS ABOUT WHAT HE SAD TOO.
TIME-OUT OVER
TMP
TMP
BUT IF YOU LOOK AT IT FROM THE FLIP SIDE...
...BEING TOO NERVOUS TO PERFORM WELL...
...OR LETTING THE PRESSURE OF THE MOMENT GET TO YOU...
...ARE PROBABLY COMPLETELY ALIEN CONCEPTS TO HIM.
DON'T WORRY. WE'LL BE FINE.
TMP
TMP
AFTER ALL, WE'RE THE BETTER TEAM.
TMP
TMP
TMP
TMP
FUKURODANI

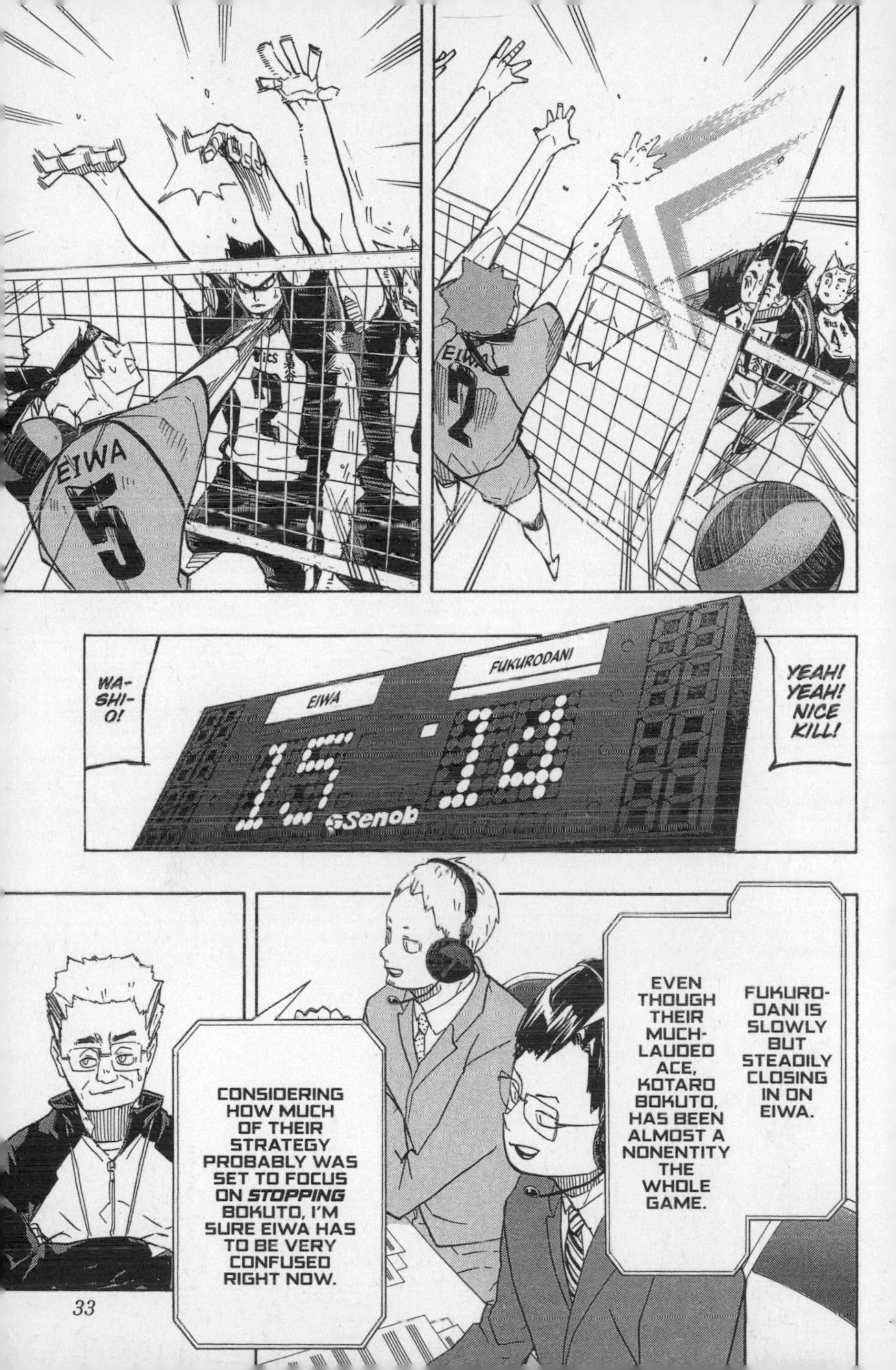
YEAH! YEAH! NICE KILL!
FUKURODANI
EIWA
WA-SHIO!
Senob
FUKURO-DANI IS SLOWLY BUT STEADILY CLOSING IN ON EIWA.
EVEN THOUGH THEIR MUCH-LAUDED ACE, KOTARO BOKUTO, HAS BEEN ALMOST A NONENTITY THE WHOLE GAME.
CONSIDERING HOW MUCH OF THEIR STRATEGY PROBABLY WAS SET TO FOCUS ON *STOPPING* BOKUTO, I'M SURE EIWA HAS TO BE VERY CONFUSED RIGHT NOW.

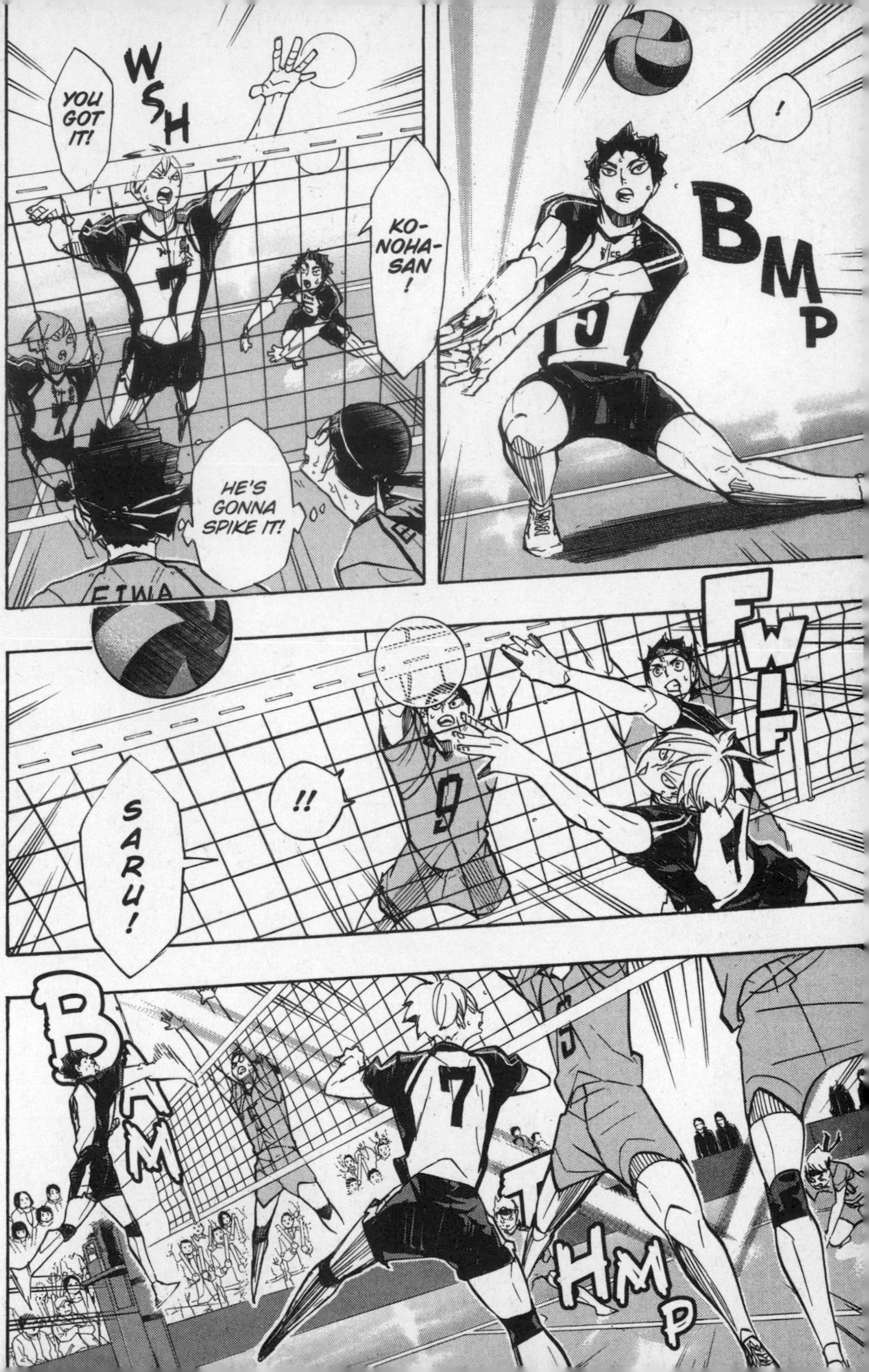

!
BMP
KO-NOHA-SAN!
YOU GOT IT!
WSH
HE'S GONNA SPIKE IT!
FWIF
!!
SARU!
THMP
BM

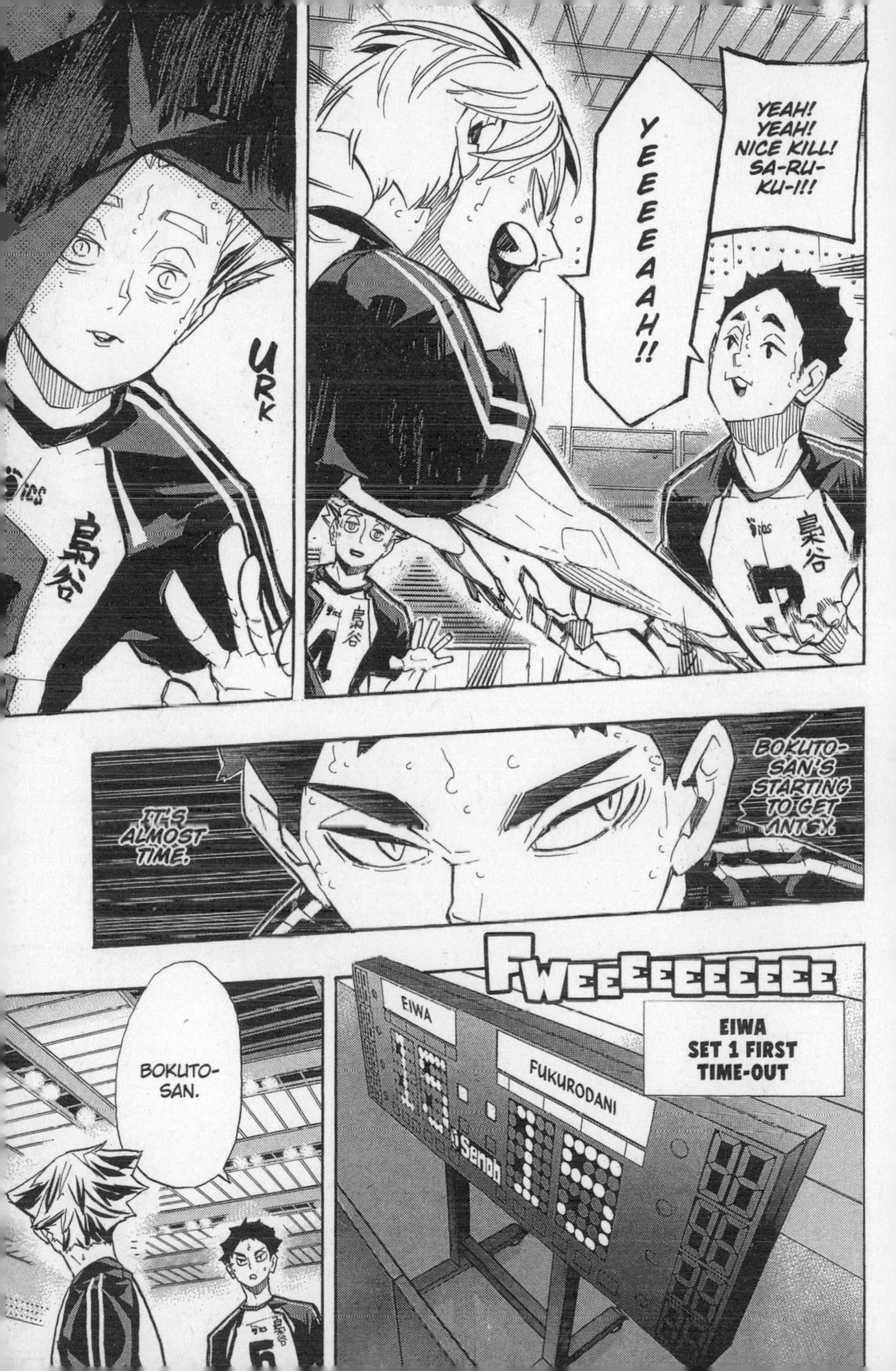

YEAH! YEAH! NICE KILL! SA-RU-KU-!!!
YEEEEAAH!!
URK
BOKUTO-SAN'S STARTING TO GET ANTSY.
IT'S ALMOST TIME.
FWEEEEEEEEEE
EIWA SET 1 FIRST TIME-OUT
EIWA
FUKURODANI
BOKUTO-SAN.

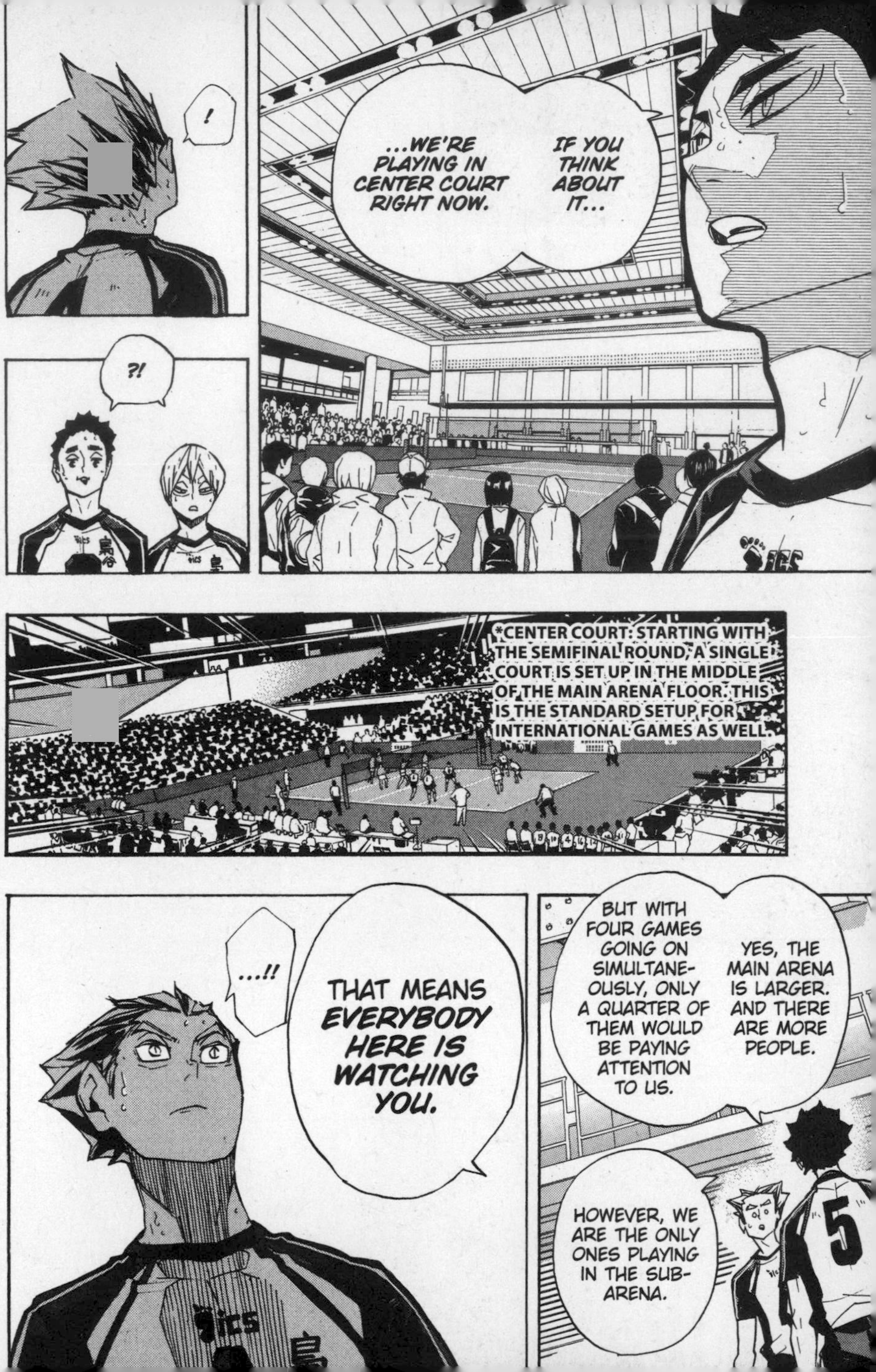
IF YOU THINK ABOUT IT...
...WE'RE PLAYING IN CENTER COURT RIGHT NOW.
!
?!
*CENTER COURT: STARTING WITH THE SEMIFINAL ROUND, A SINGLE COURT IS SET UP IN THE MIDDLE OF THE MAIN ARENA FLOOR. THIS IS THE STANDARD SETUP FOR INTERNATIONAL GAMES AS WELL.
YES, THE MAIN ARENA IS LARGER. AND THERE ARE MORE PEOPLE.
BUT WITH FOUR GAMES GOING ON SIMULTANE-OUSLY, ONLY A QUARTER OF THEM WOULD BE PAYING ATTENTION TO US.
HOWEVER, WE ARE THE ONLY ONES PLAYING IN THE SUB-ARENA.
THAT MEANS EVERYBODY HERE IS WATCHING YOU.
...!!

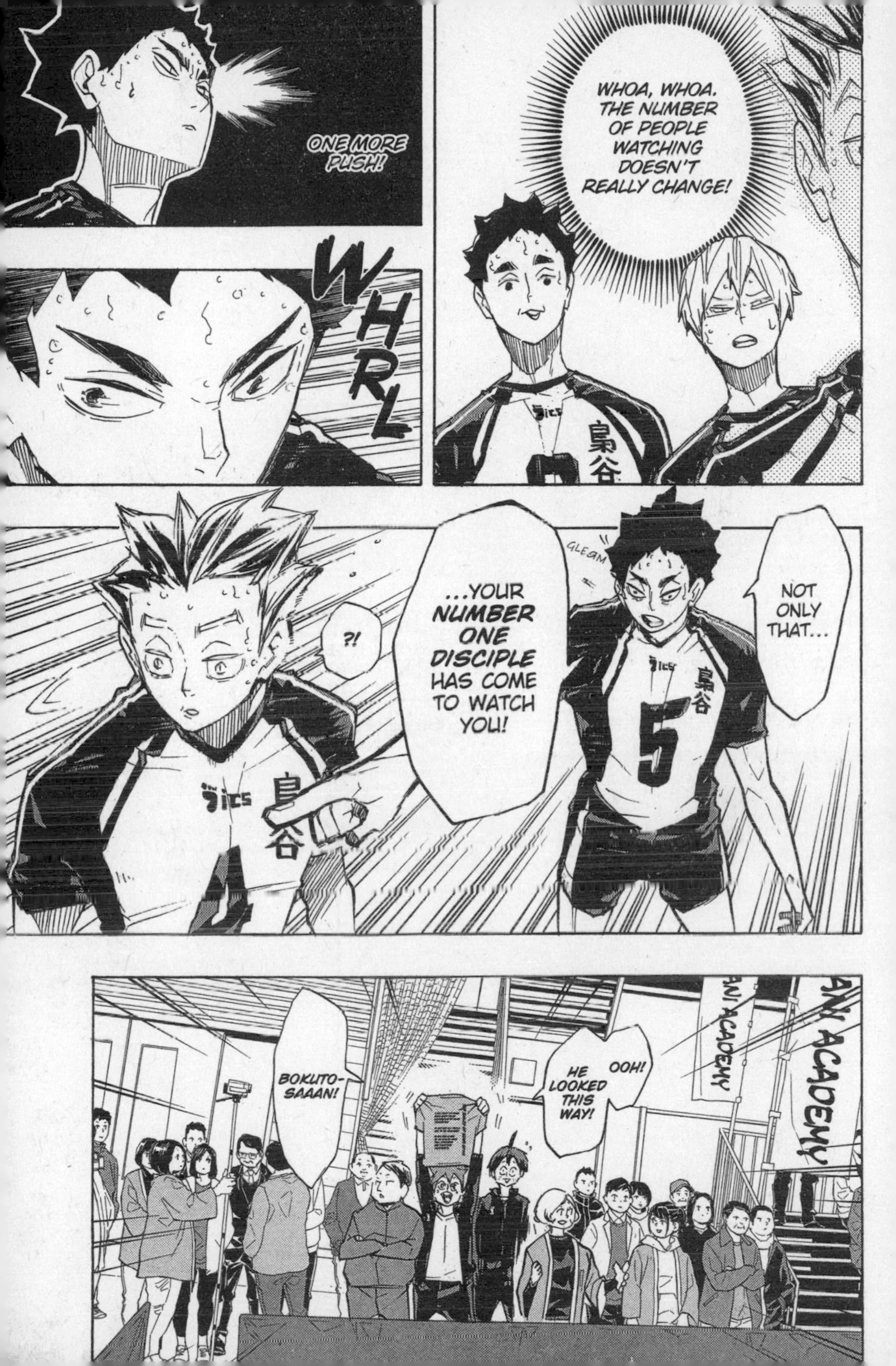
WHOA, WHOA. THE NUMBER OF PEOPLE WATCHING DOESN'T REALLY CHANGE!
ONE MORE PUSH!
WHRL
NOT ONLY THAT...
GLEAM
...YOUR NUMBER ONE DISCIPLE HAS COME TO WATCH YOU!
?!
ANI ACADEMY
ACADEMY
ANI ACADEMY
OOH!
HE LOOKED THIS WAY!
BOKUTO-SAAAN!

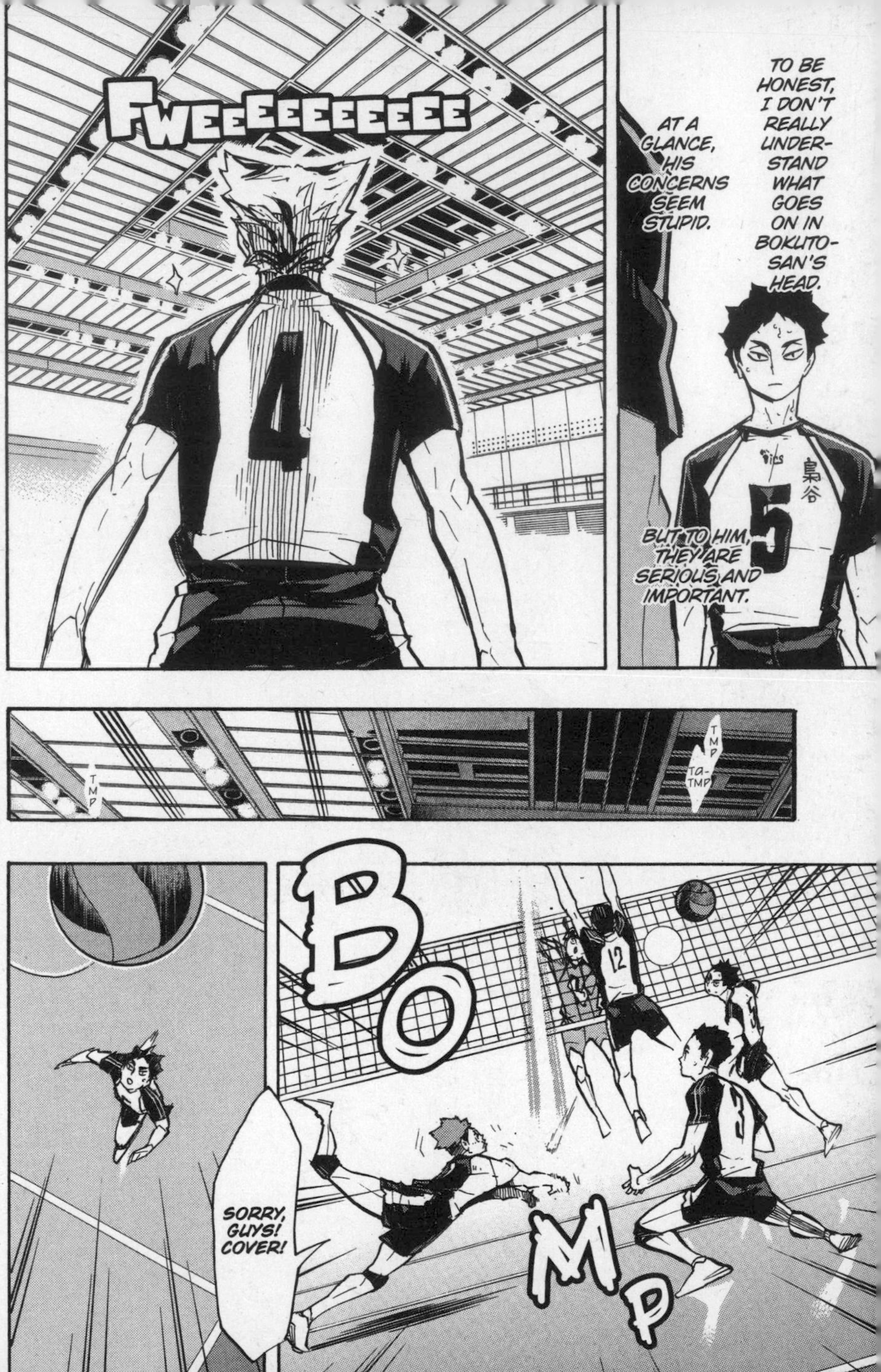
TO BE HONEST, I DON'T REALLY UNDERSTAND WHAT GOES ON IN BOKUTO-SAN'S HEAD.
AT A GLANCE, HIS CONCERNS SEEM STUPID.
BUT TO HIM, THEY ARE SERIOUS AND IMPORTANT.
FWEEEEEEEEEE
TMP
TA-TMP
TMP
BOOMP
SORRY, GUYS! COVER!

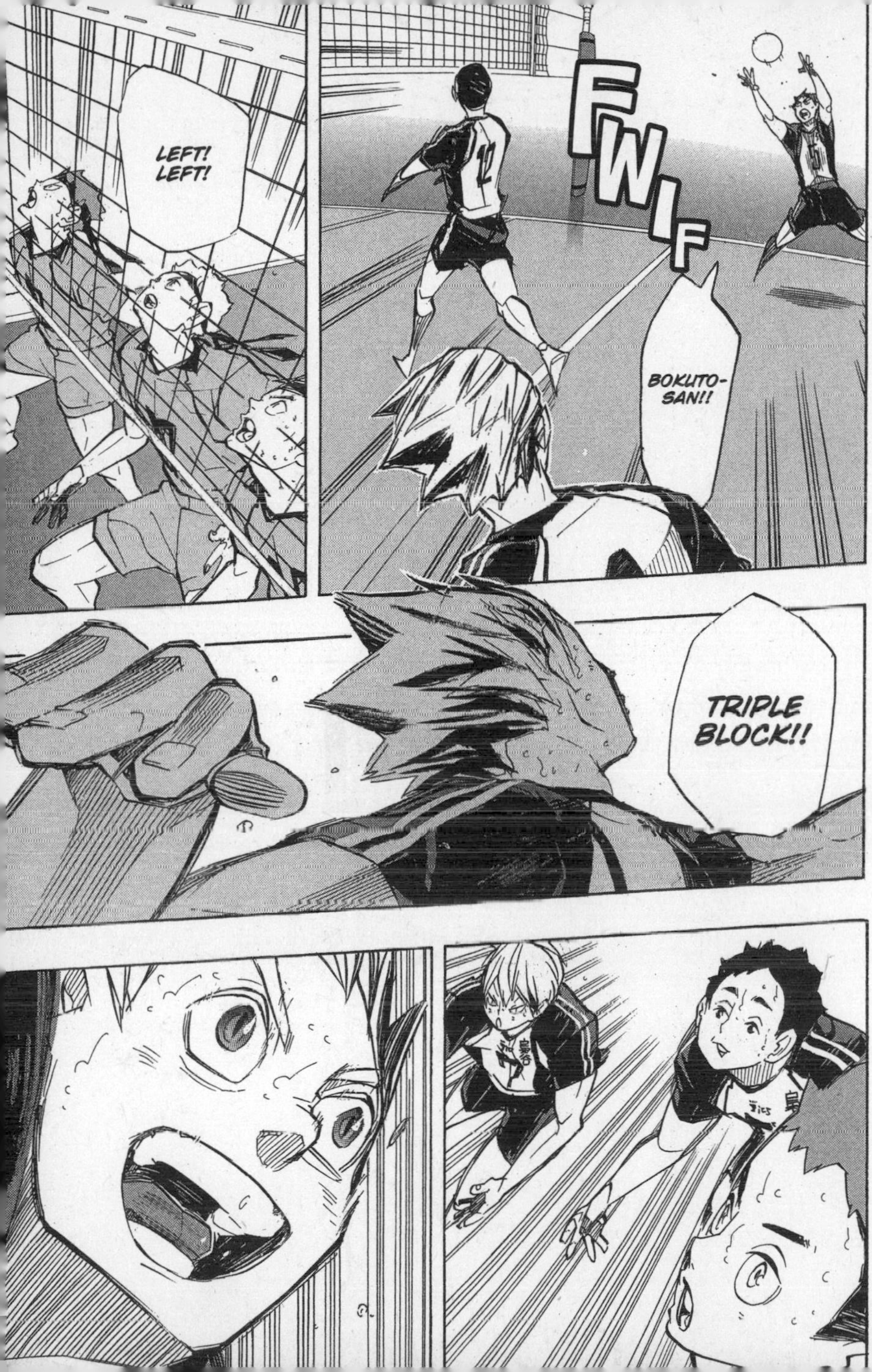
FWIF
BOKUTO-SAN!!
LEFT! LEFT!
TRIPLE BLOCK!!

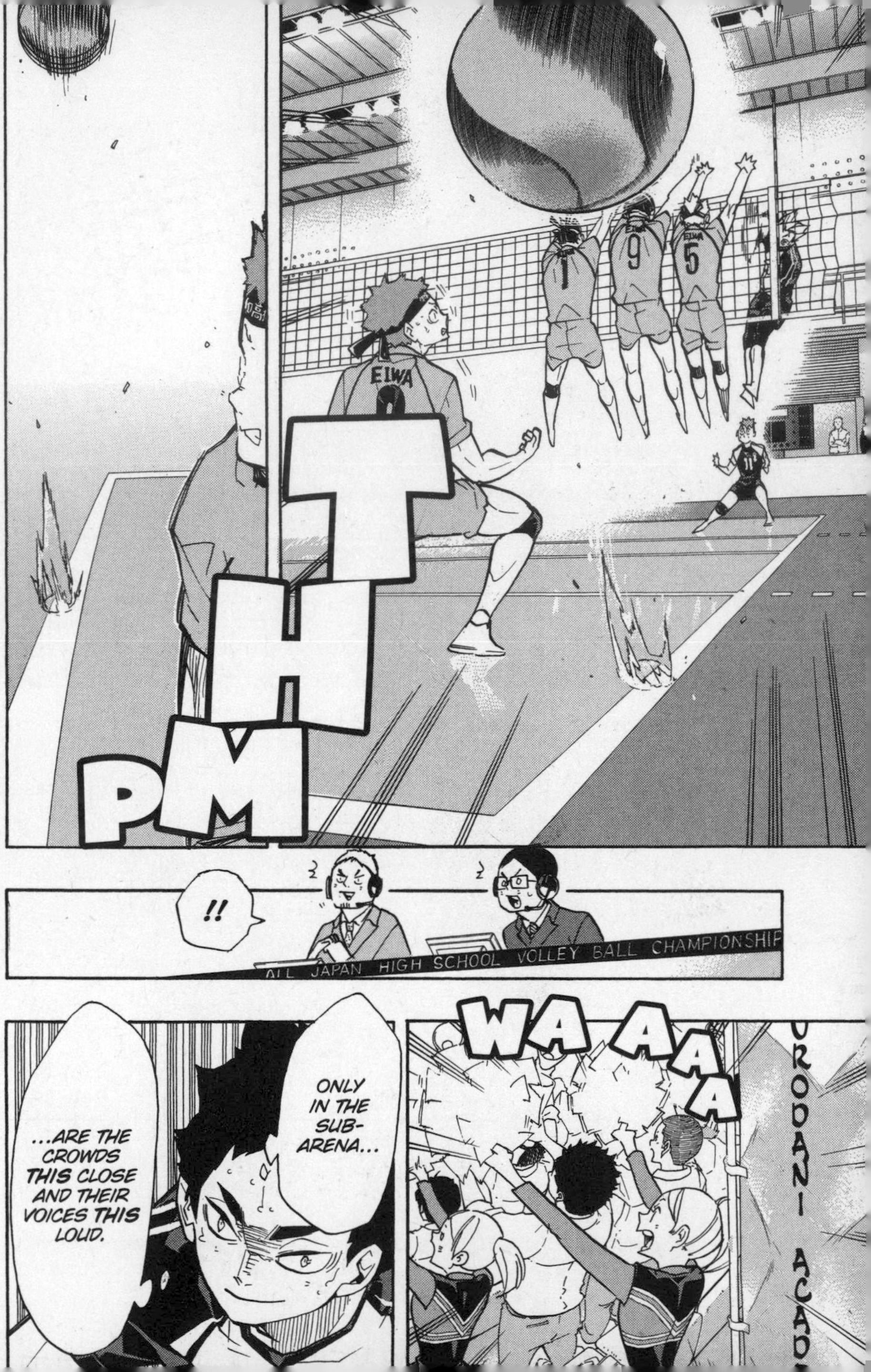
THMP
!!
ALL JAPAN HIGH SCHOOL VOLLEY BALL CHAMPIONSHIP
WA AAAA
ONLY IN THE SUB-ARENA...
...ARE THE CROWDS THIS CLOSE AND THEIR VOICES THIS LOUD.

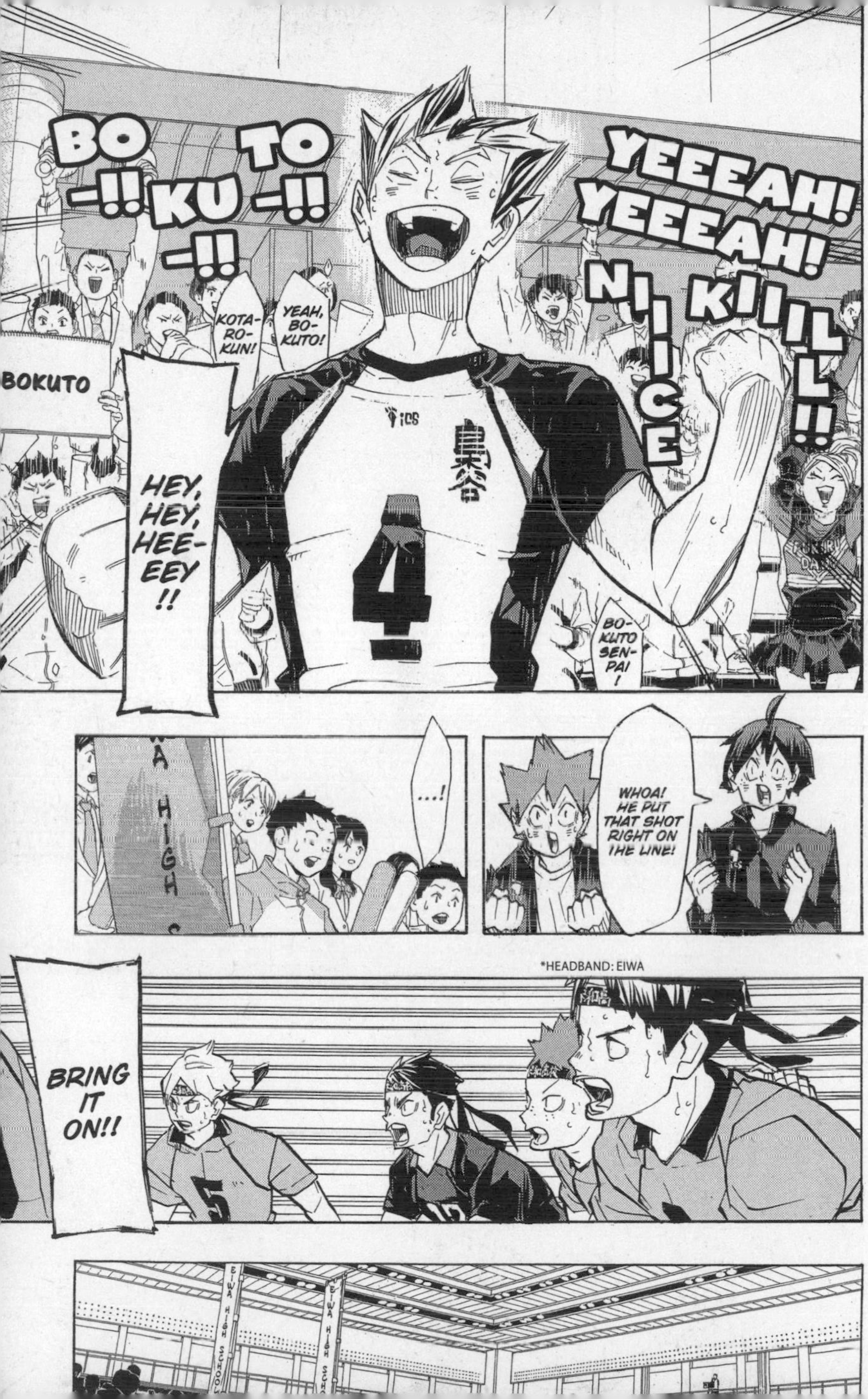
YEEEAH! YEEEAH!
NIIICE KIIILL!!
BOKUTO SENPAI!
HEY, HEY, HEEEEY!!
YEAH, BOKUTO!
KOTAROKUN!
BO-!! KU-!! TO-!!
BOKUTO
WHOA! HE PUT THAT SHOT RIGHT ON THE LINE!
...!
*HEADBAND: EIWA
BRING IT ON!!
EIWA HIGH SCHOOL
EIWA HIGH SCHOOL

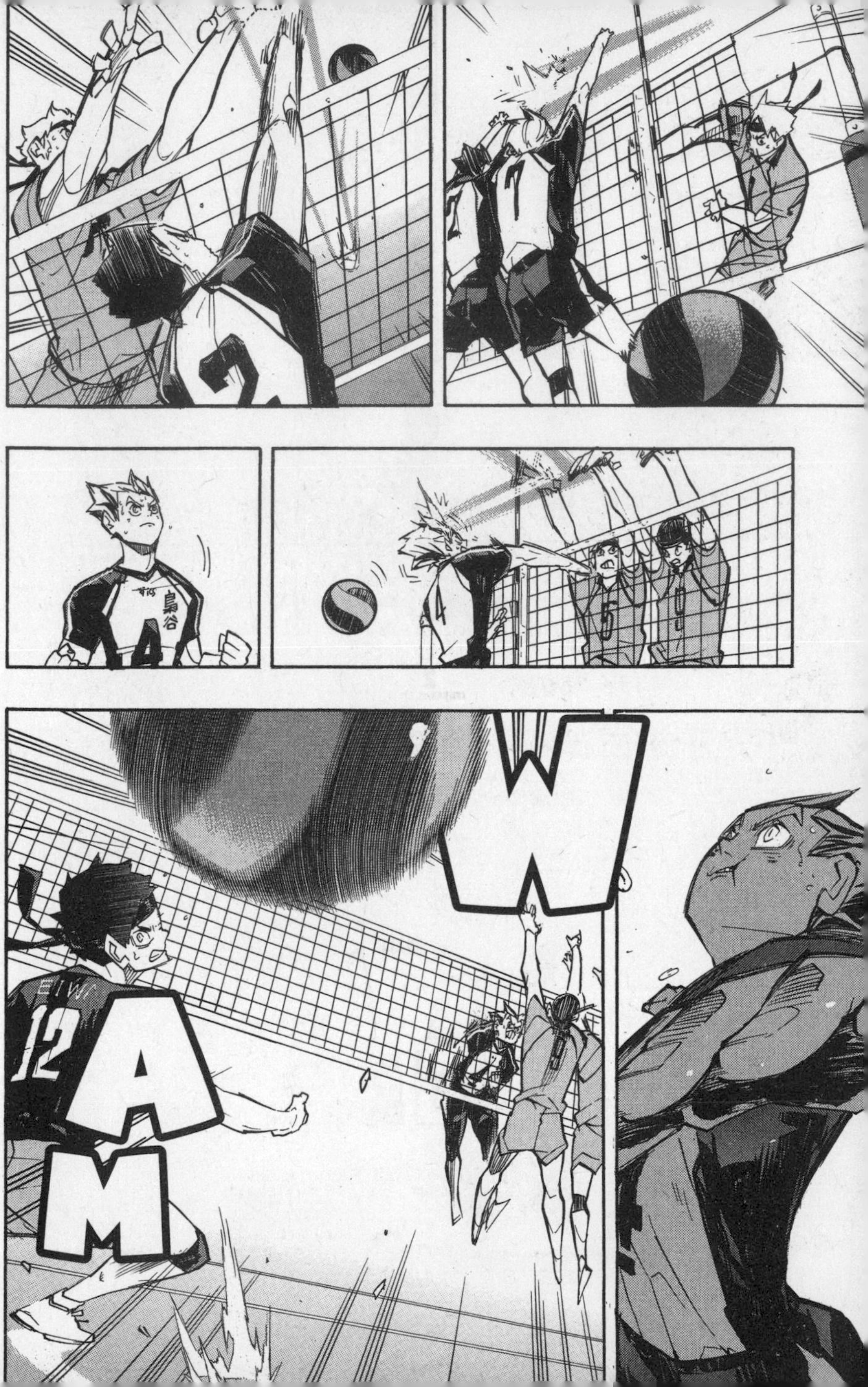

WAM

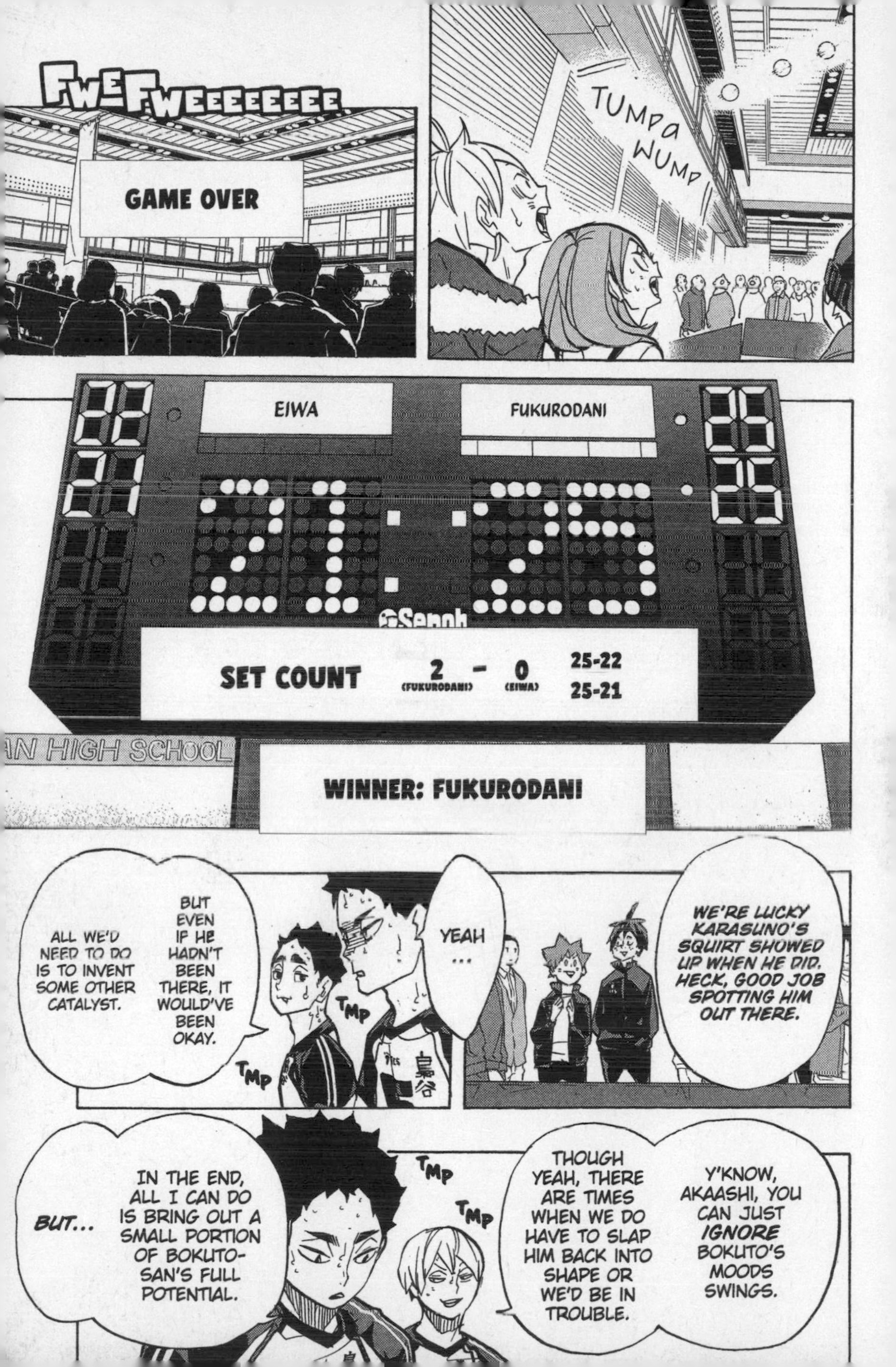
TUMPA WUMP
FWEFWEEEEEEEE
GAME OVER
EIWA
FUKURODANI
SET COUNT 2 - 0 (FUKURODANI) (EIWA) 25-22 25-21
AN HIGH SCHOOL
WINNER: FUKURODANI
WE'RE LUCKY KARASUNO'S SQUIRT SHOWED UP WHEN HE DID. HECK, GOOD JOB SPOTTING HIM OUT THERE.
YEAH...
BUT EVEN IF HE HADN'T BEEN THERE, IT WOULD'VE BEEN OKAY.
ALL WE'D NEED TO DO IS TO INVENT SOME OTHER CATALYST.
TMP
TMP
Y'KNOW, AKAASHI, YOU CAN JUST IGNORE BOKUTO'S MOODS SWINGS.
THOUGH YEAH, THERE ARE TIMES WHEN WE DO HAVE TO SLAP HIM BACK INTO SHAPE OR WE'D BE IN TROUBLE.
TMP
TMP
IN THE END, ALL I CAN DO IS BRING OUT A SMALL PORTION OF BOKUTO-SAN'S FULL POTENTIAL.
BUT...

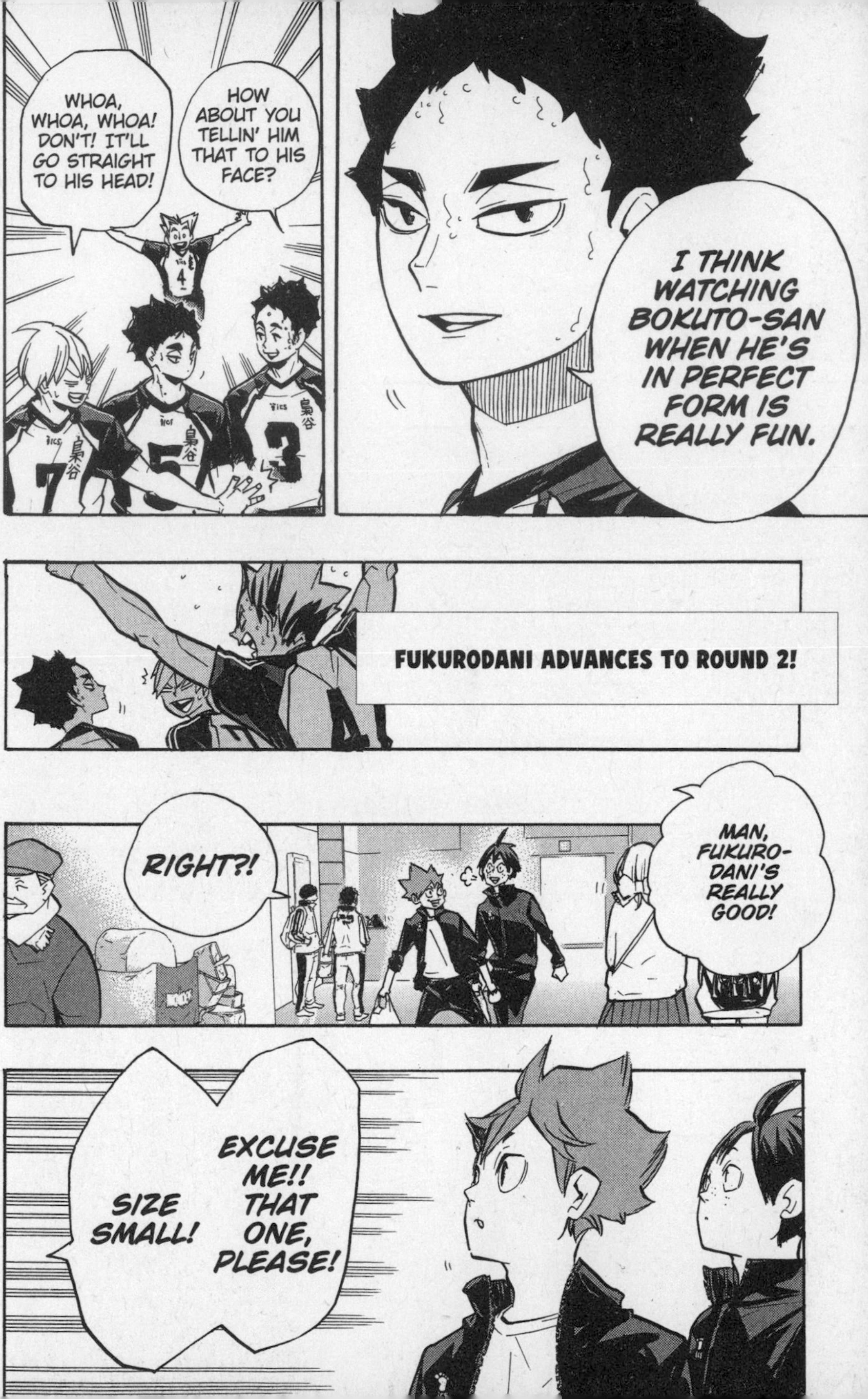
I THINK WATCHING BOKUTO-SAN WHEN HE'S IN PERFECT FORM IS REALLY FUN.
HOW ABOUT YOU TELLIN' HIM THAT TO HIS FACE?
WHOA, WHOA, WHOA! DON'T! IT'LL GO STRAIGHT TO HIS HEAD!
FUKURODANI ADVANCES TO ROUND 2!
MAN, FUKURO-DANI'S REALLY GOOD!
RIGHT?!
EXCUSE ME!! THAT ONE, PLEASE!
SIZE SMALL!

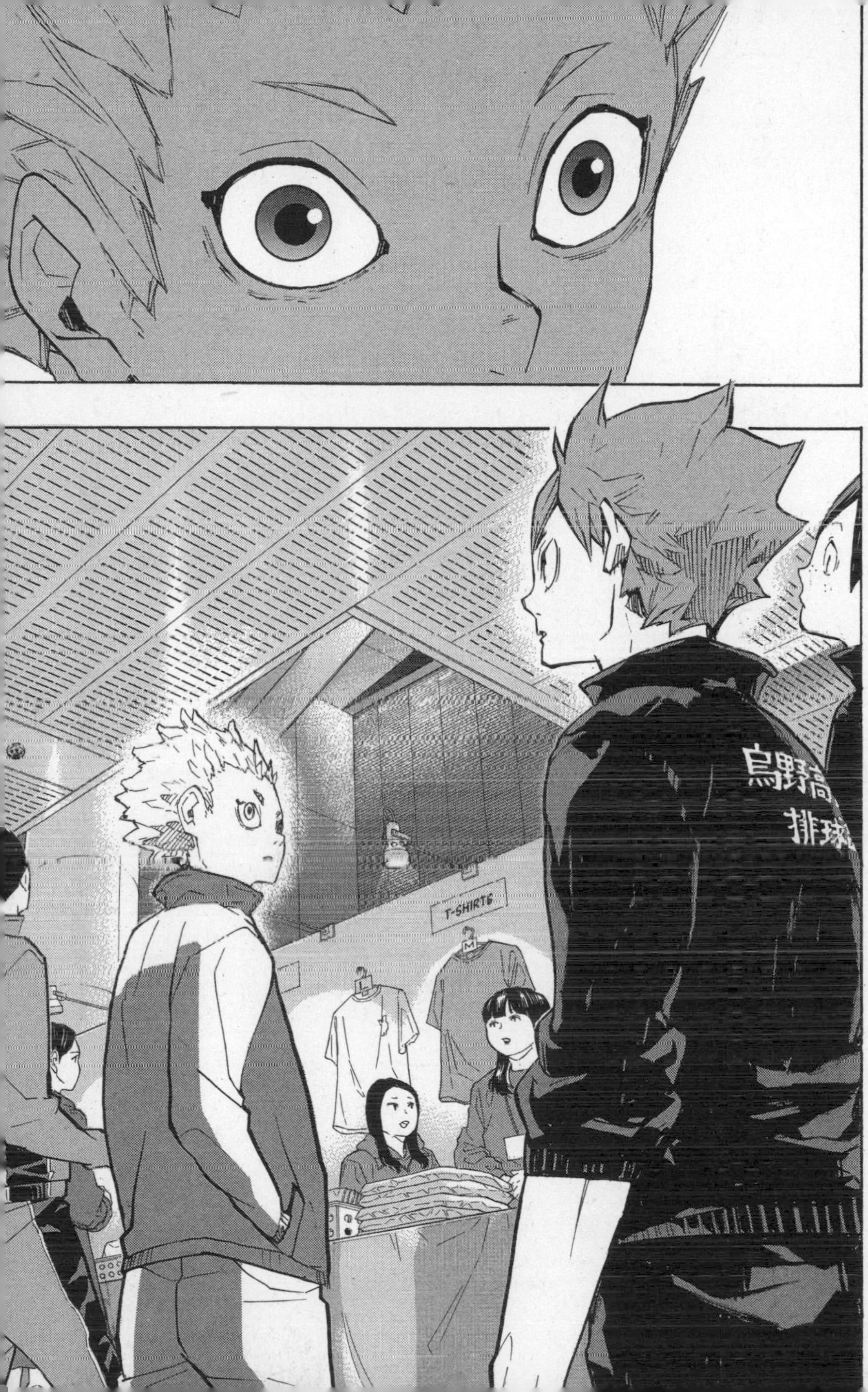

T-SHIRTS
烏野高
排球

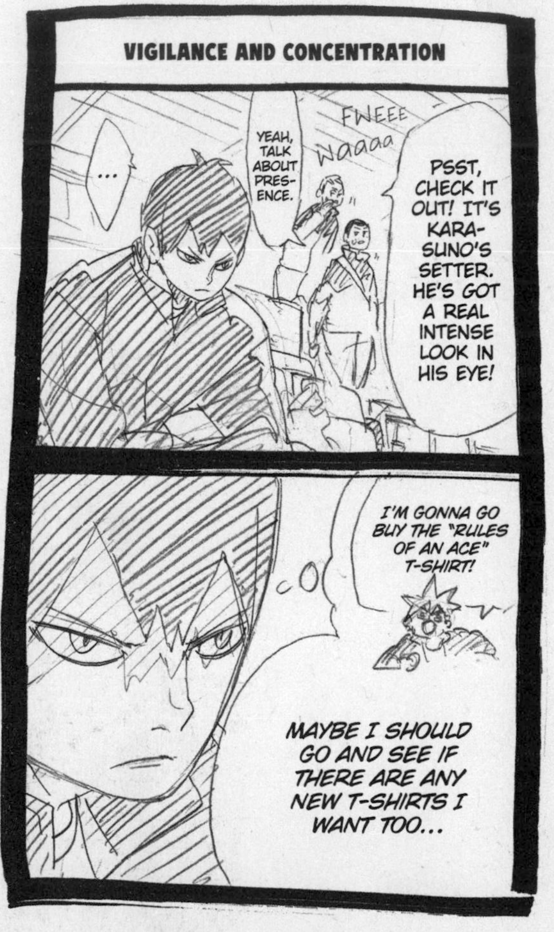
VIGILANCE AND CONCENTRATION
FWEEE
Waaaa
PSST, CHECK IT OUT! IT'S KARA-SUNO'S SETTER. HE'S GOT A REAL INTENSE LOOK IN HIS EYE!
YEAH, TALK ABOUT PRES-ENCE.
...
I'M GONNA GO BUY THE "RULES OF AN ACE" T-SHIRT!
MAYBE I SHOULD GO AND SEE IF THERE ARE ANY NEW T-SHIRTS I WANT TOO...

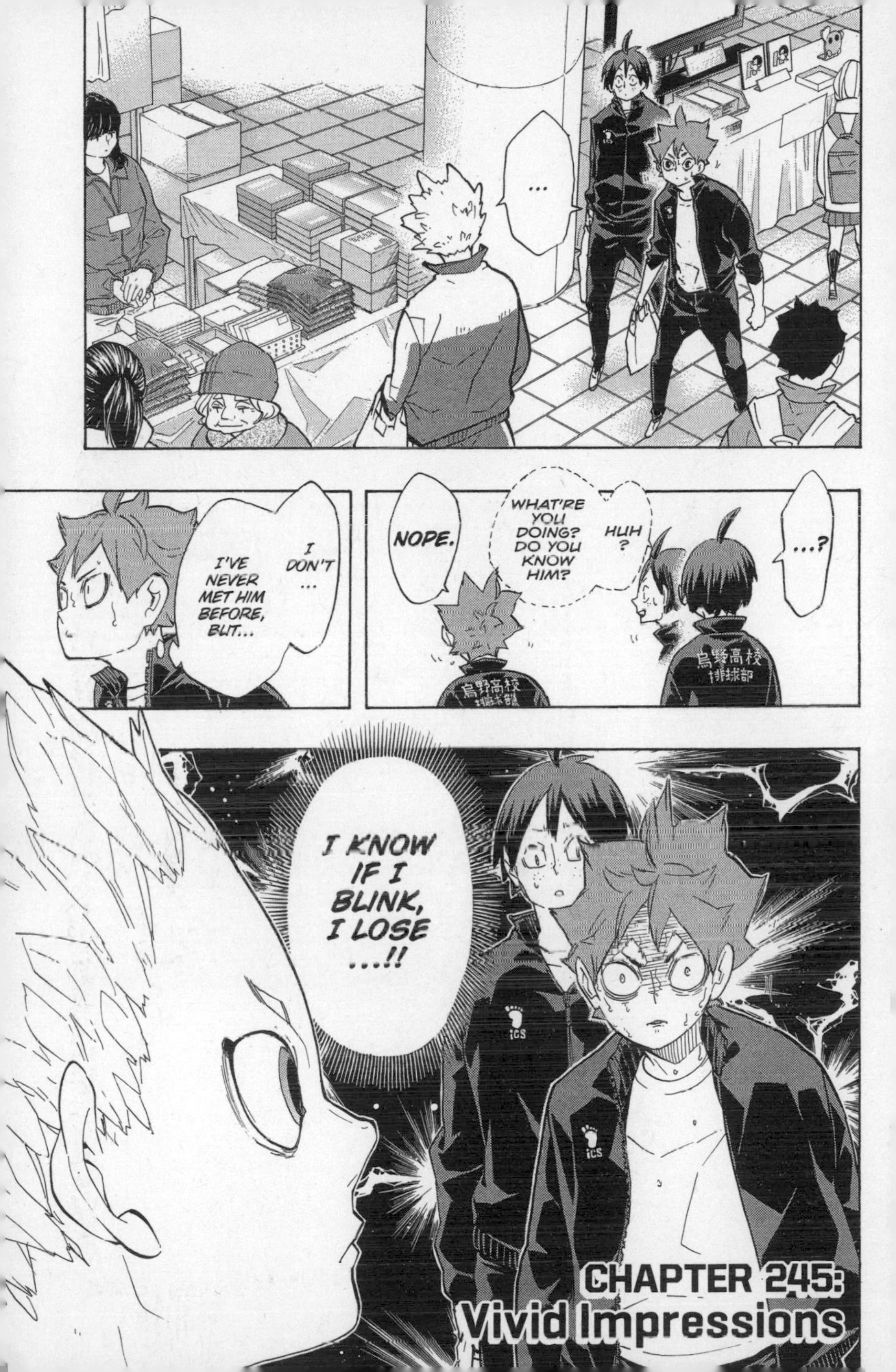
...
...?
HUH?
WHAT'RE YOU DOING? DO YOU KNOW HIM?
NOPE.
I DON'T...
I'VE NEVER MET HIM BEFORE, BUT...
I KNOW IF I BLINK, I LOSE...!!
CHAPTER 245:
Vivid Impressions

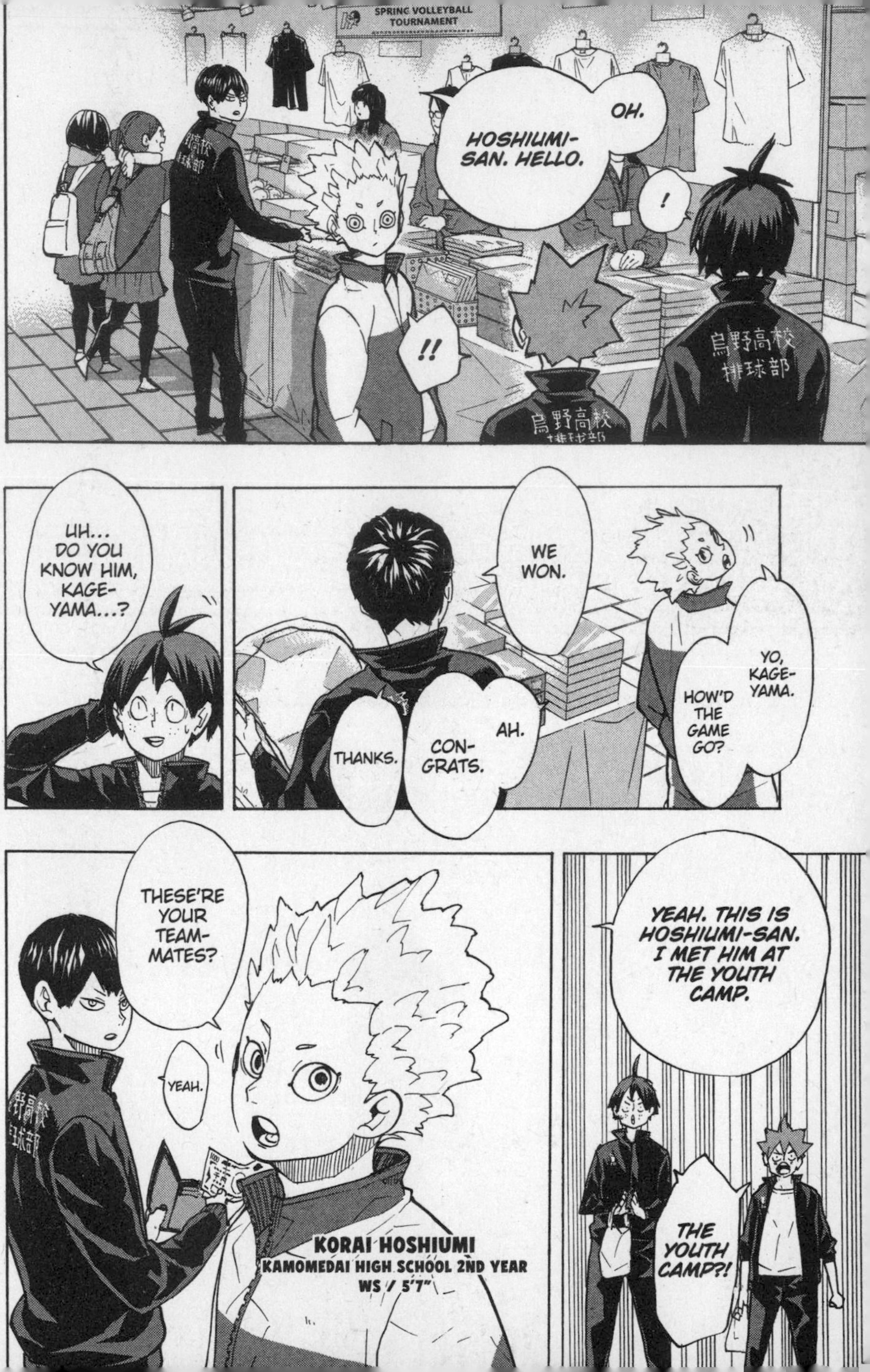
SPRING VOLLEYBALL TOURNAMENT
OH.
HOSHIUMI-SAN. HELLO.
!
!!
烏野高校 排球部
YO, KAGE-YAMA.
HOW'D THE GAME GO?
WE WON.
AH.
CON-GRATS.
THANKS.
UH... DO YOU KNOW HIM, KAGE-YAMA...?
YEAH. THIS IS HOSHIUMI-SAN. I MET HIM AT THE YOUTH CAMP.
THE YOUTH CAMP?!
THESE'RE YOUR TEAM-MATES?
YEAH.
KORAI HOSHIUMI
KAMOMEDAI HIGH SCHOOL 2ND YEAR
WS / 5'7"

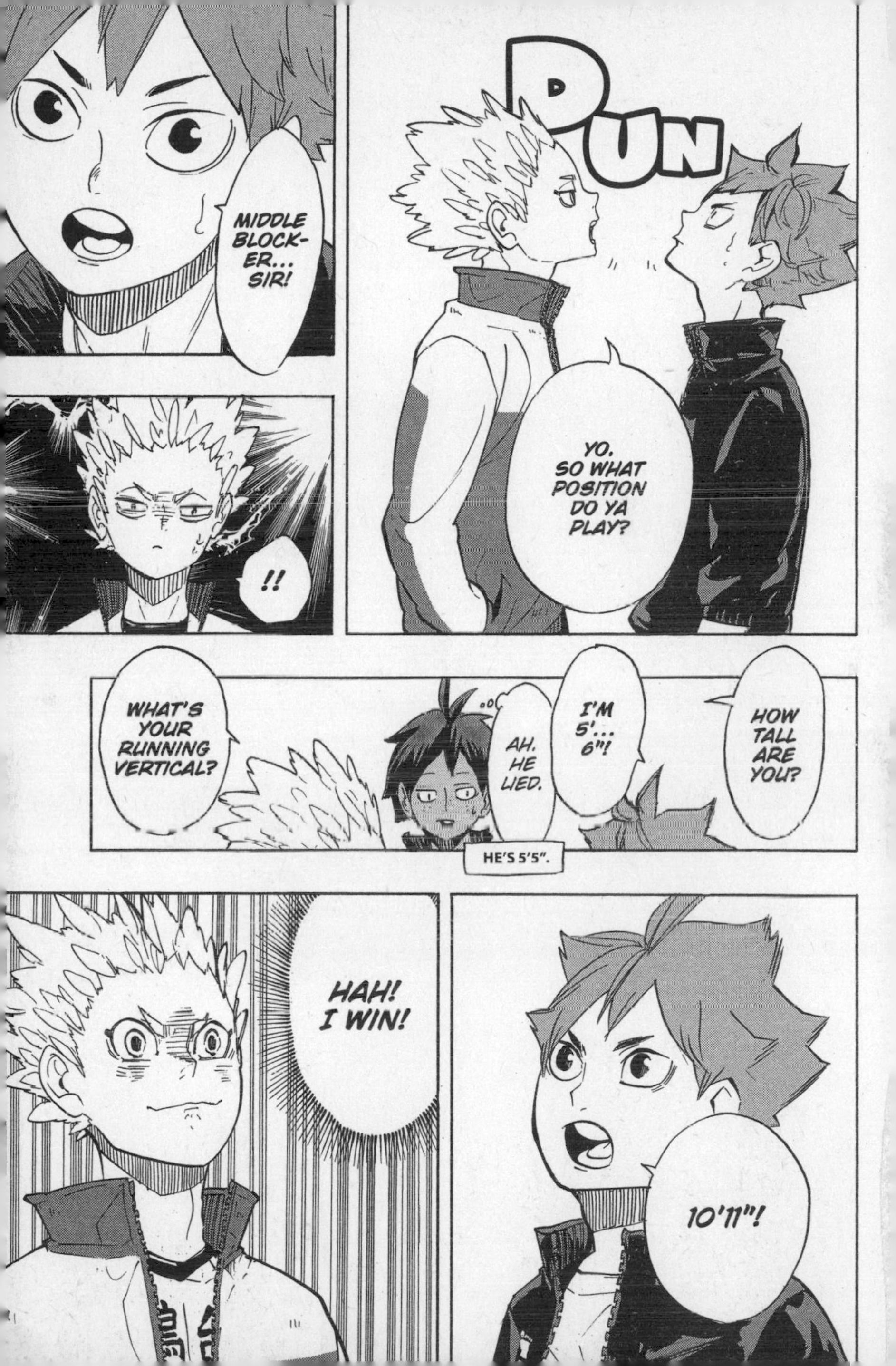
DUN
YO. SO WHAT POSITION DO YA PLAY?
MIDDLE BLOCKER... SIR!
!!
HOW TALL ARE YOU?
I'M 5'... 6"!
AH. HE LIED.
HE'S 5'5".
WHAT'S YOUR RUNNING VERTICAL?
10'11"!
HAH! I WIN!

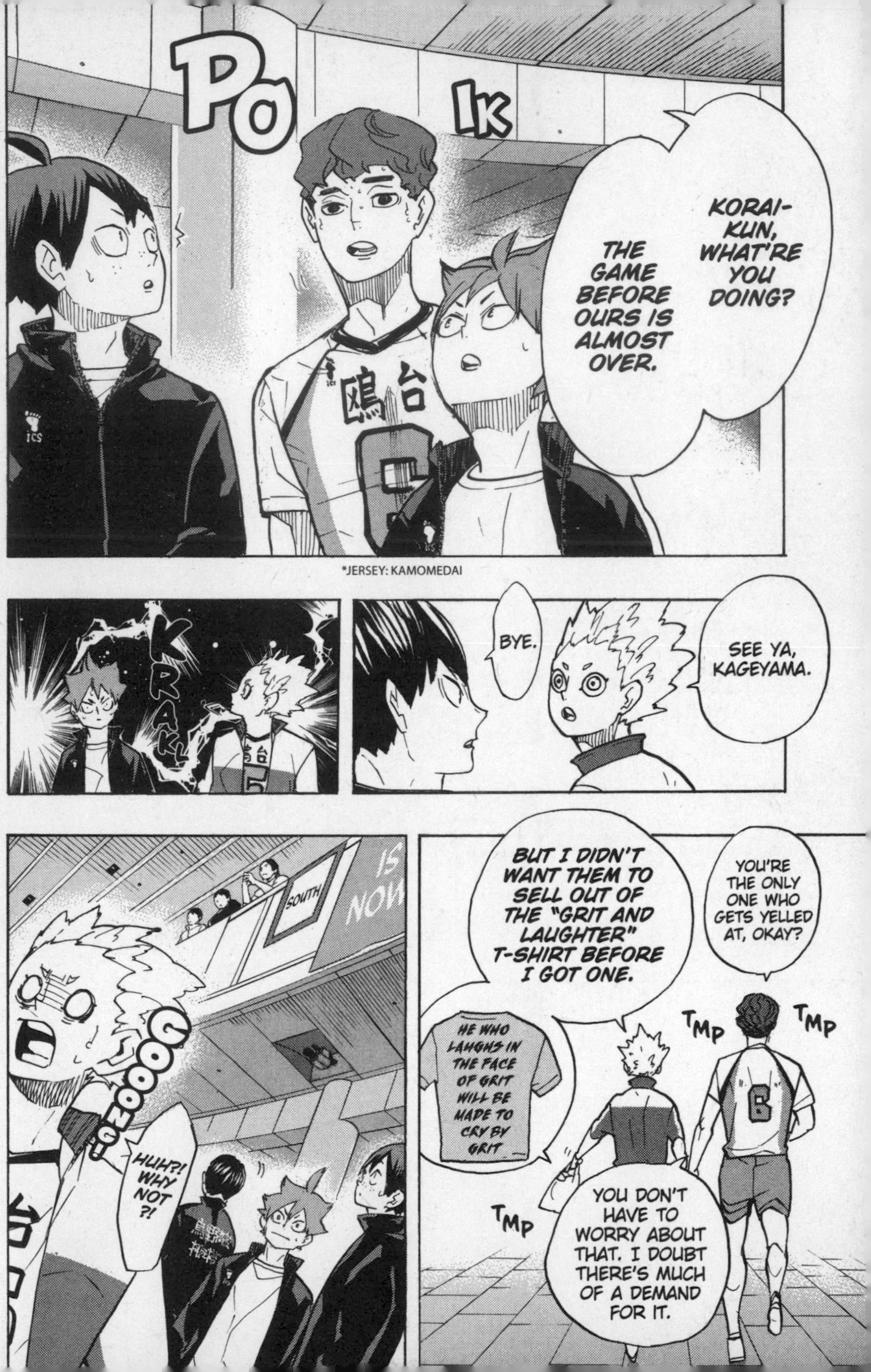
POIK
KORAI-KUN, WHAT'RE YOU DOING?
THE GAME BEFORE OURS IS ALMOST OVER.
*JERSEY: KAMOMEDAI
SEE YA, KAGEYAMA.
BYE.
KRAK
YOU'RE THE ONLY ONE WHO GETS YELLED AT, OKAY?
BUT I DIDN'T WANT THEM TO SELL OUT OF THE "GRIT AND LAUGHTER" T-SHIRT BEFORE I GOT ONE.
HE WHO LAUGHS IN THE FACE OF GRIT WILL BE MADE TO CRY BY GRIT
TMP TMP
TMP
YOU DON'T HAVE TO WORRY ABOUT THAT. I DOUBT THERE'S MUCH OF A DEMAND FOR IT.
SOUTH
GOOOONG!
HUH?! WHY NOT ?!

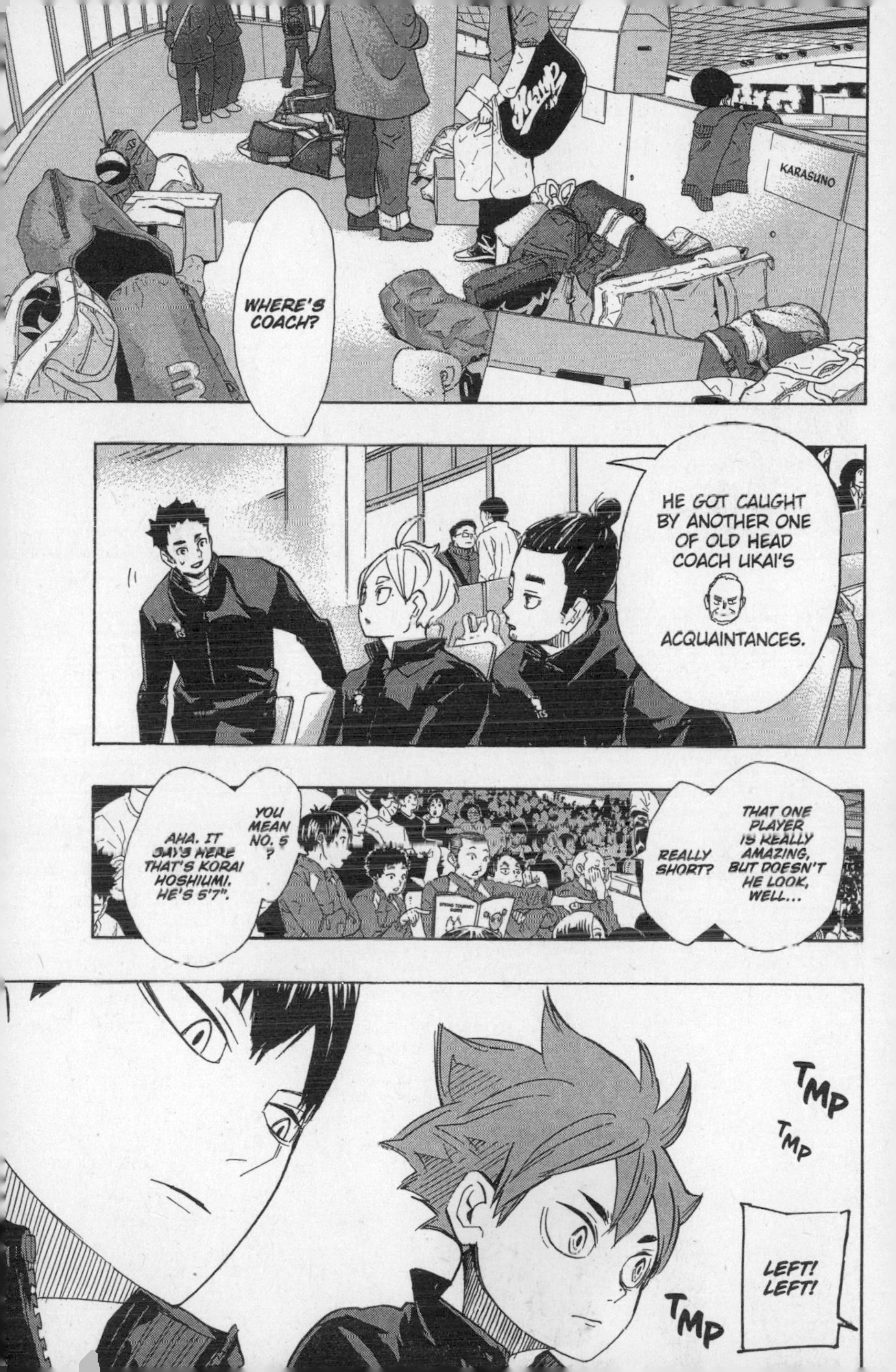
KARASUNO
WHERE'S COACH?
HE GOT CAUGHT BY ANOTHER ONE OF OLD HEAD COACH UKAI'S
ACQUAINTANCES.
THAT ONE PLAYER IS REALLY AMAZING, BUT DOESN'T HE LOOK, WELL...
REALLY SHORT?
YOU MEAN NO. 5?
AHA. IT SAYS HERE THAT'S KORAI HOSHIUMI. HE'S 5'7".
TMP
TMP
LEFT! LEFT!
TMP

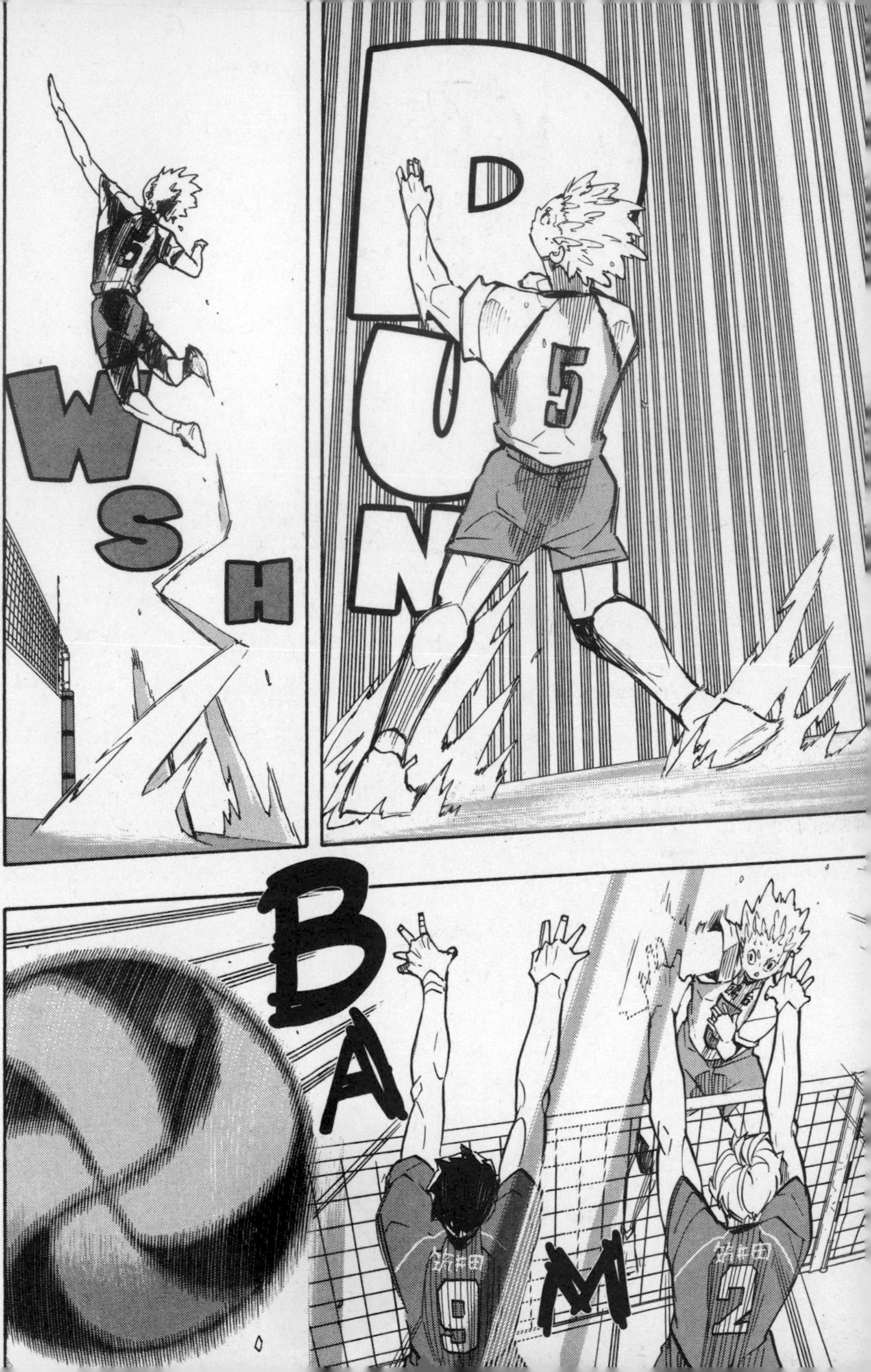
DUN
WSH
BAM

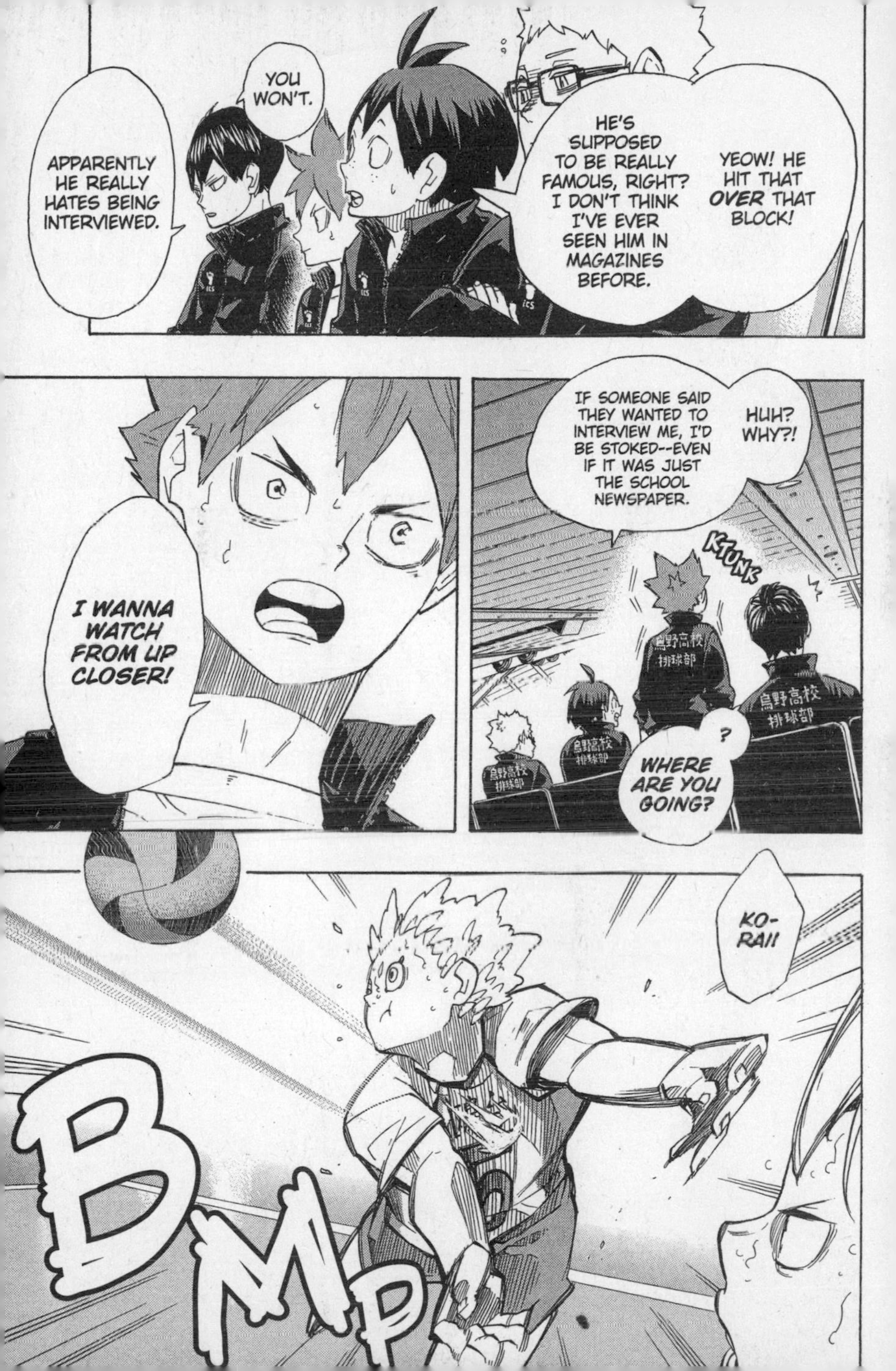
YEOW! HE HIT THAT *OVER* THAT BLOCK!
HE'S SUPPOSED TO BE REALLY FAMOUS, RIGHT? I DON'T THINK I'VE EVER SEEN HIM IN MAGAZINES BEFORE.
YOU WON'T.
APPARENTLY HE REALLY HATES BEING INTERVIEWED.
HUH? WHY?!
IF SOMEONE SAID THEY WANTED TO INTERVIEW ME, I'D BE STOKED--EVEN IF IT WAS JUST THE SCHOOL NEWSPAPER.
KTUNK
?
WHERE ARE YOU GOING?
I WANNA WATCH FROM UP CLOSER!
KO-RAII
BMP

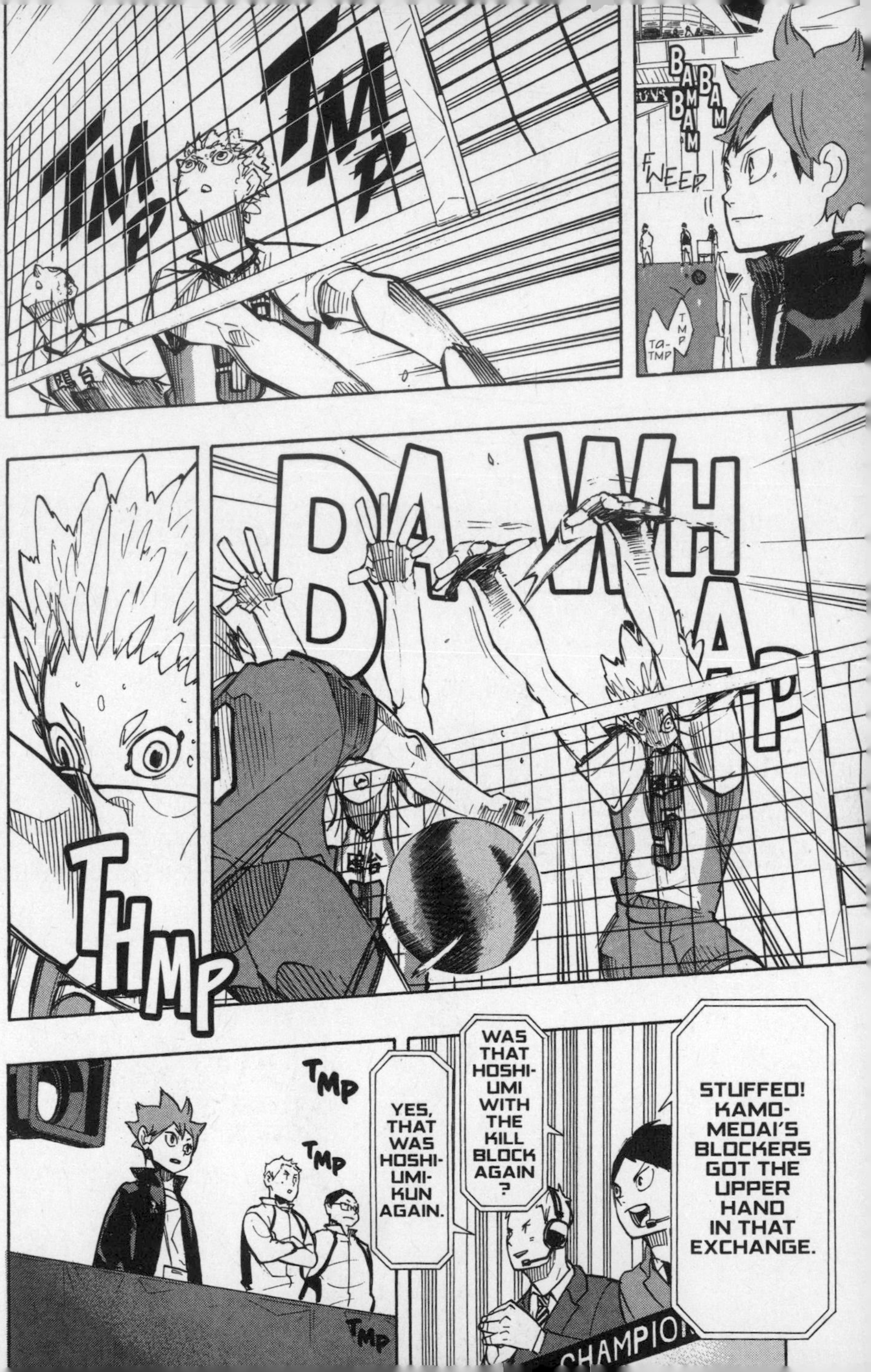
BAM
BAM
BAM
BAM
FWEEP
TMP
Ta-TMP
TMP
TMP
BADWHAP
THMP
STUFFED! KAMOMEDAI'S BLOCKERS GOT THE UPPER HAND IN THAT EXCHANGE.
WAS THAT HOSHIUMI WITH THE KILL BLOCK AGAIN?
YES, THAT WAS HOSHIUMI-KUN AGAIN.
TMP
TMP
TMP
CHAMPIO

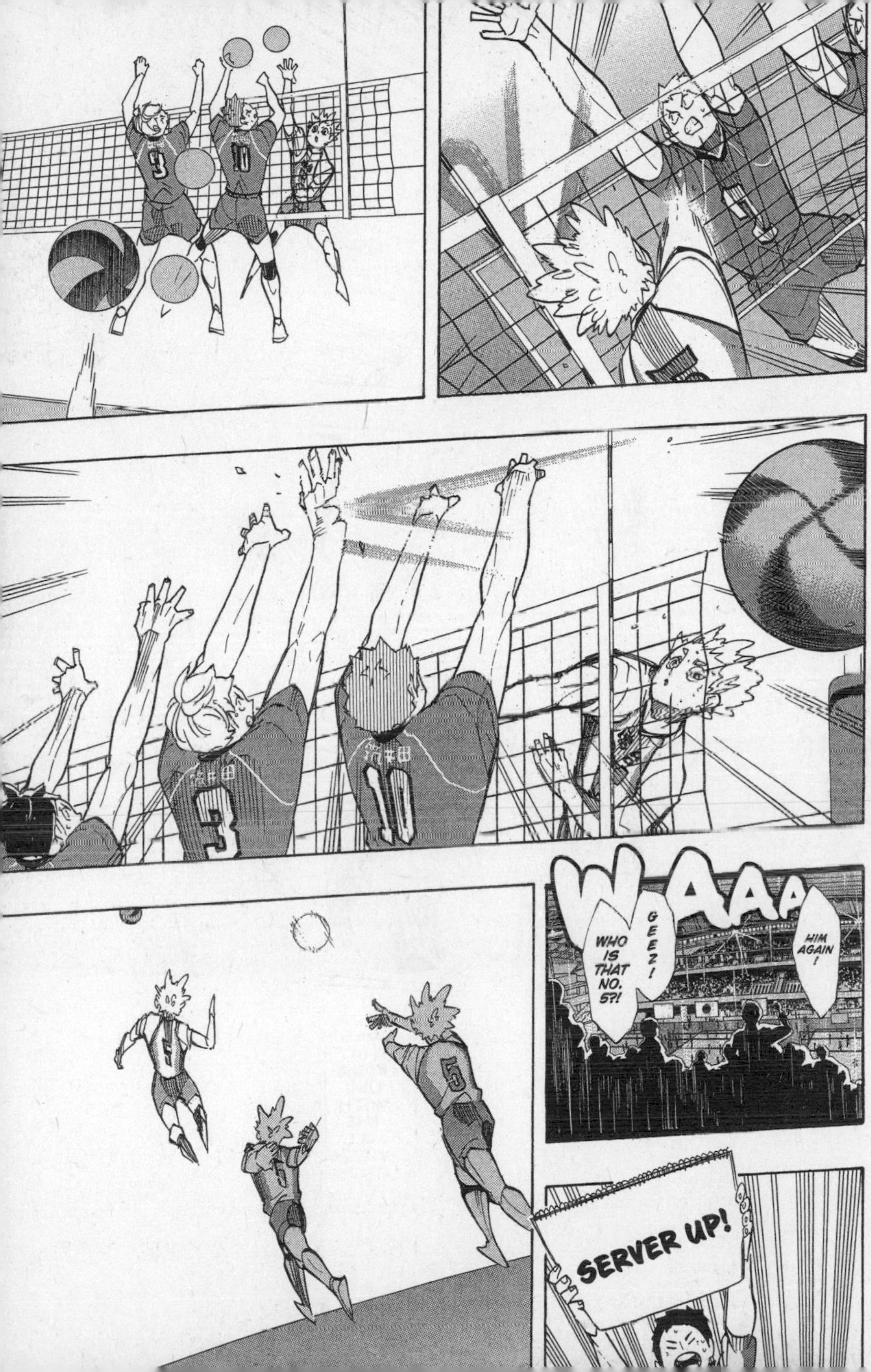
WAAA
HIM AGAIN!
GEEZ!
WHO IS THAT NO. 5?!
SERVER UP!

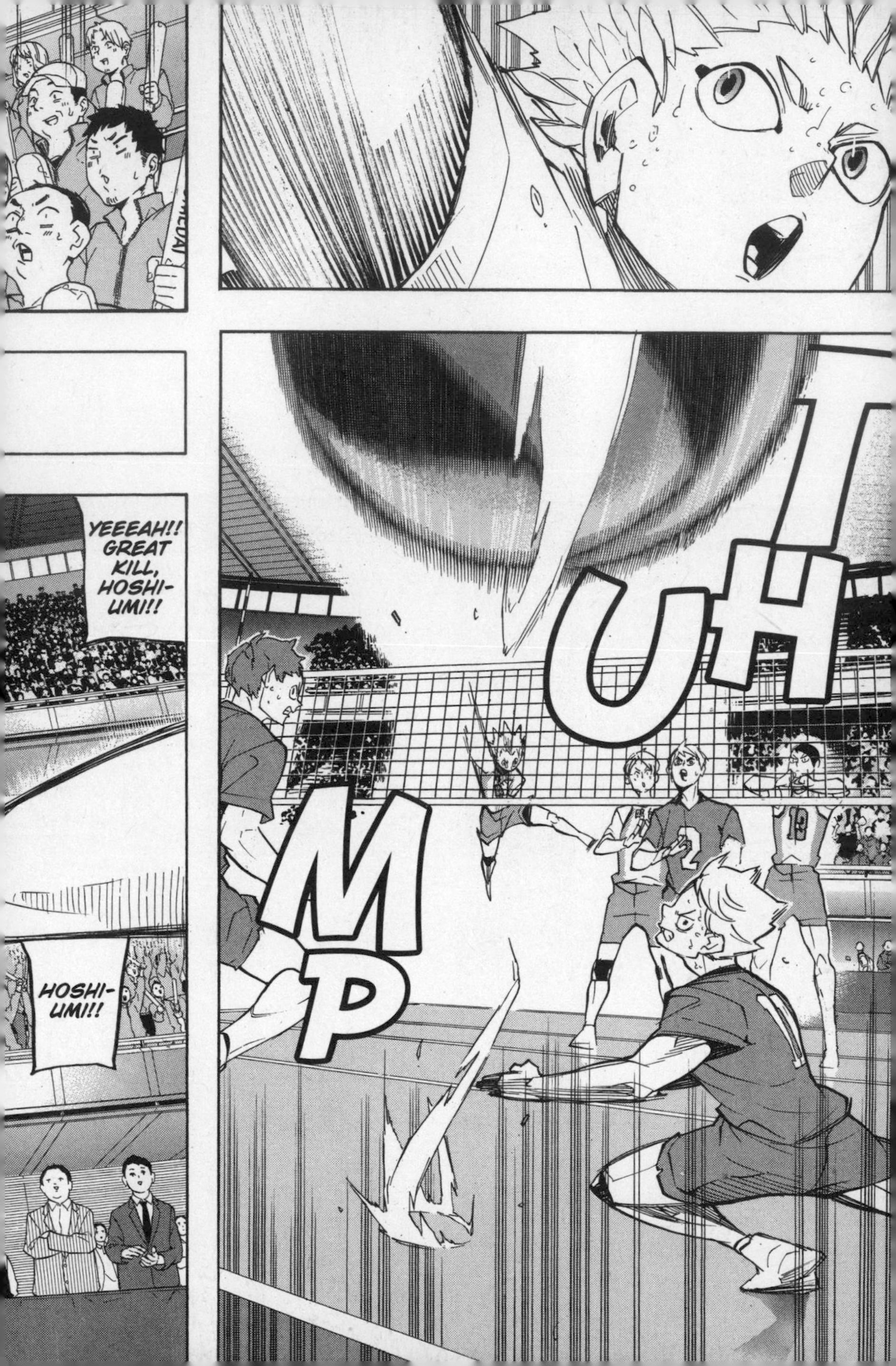
THUMP
YEEEAH!! GREAT KILL, HOSHI-UMI!!
HOSHI-UMI!!

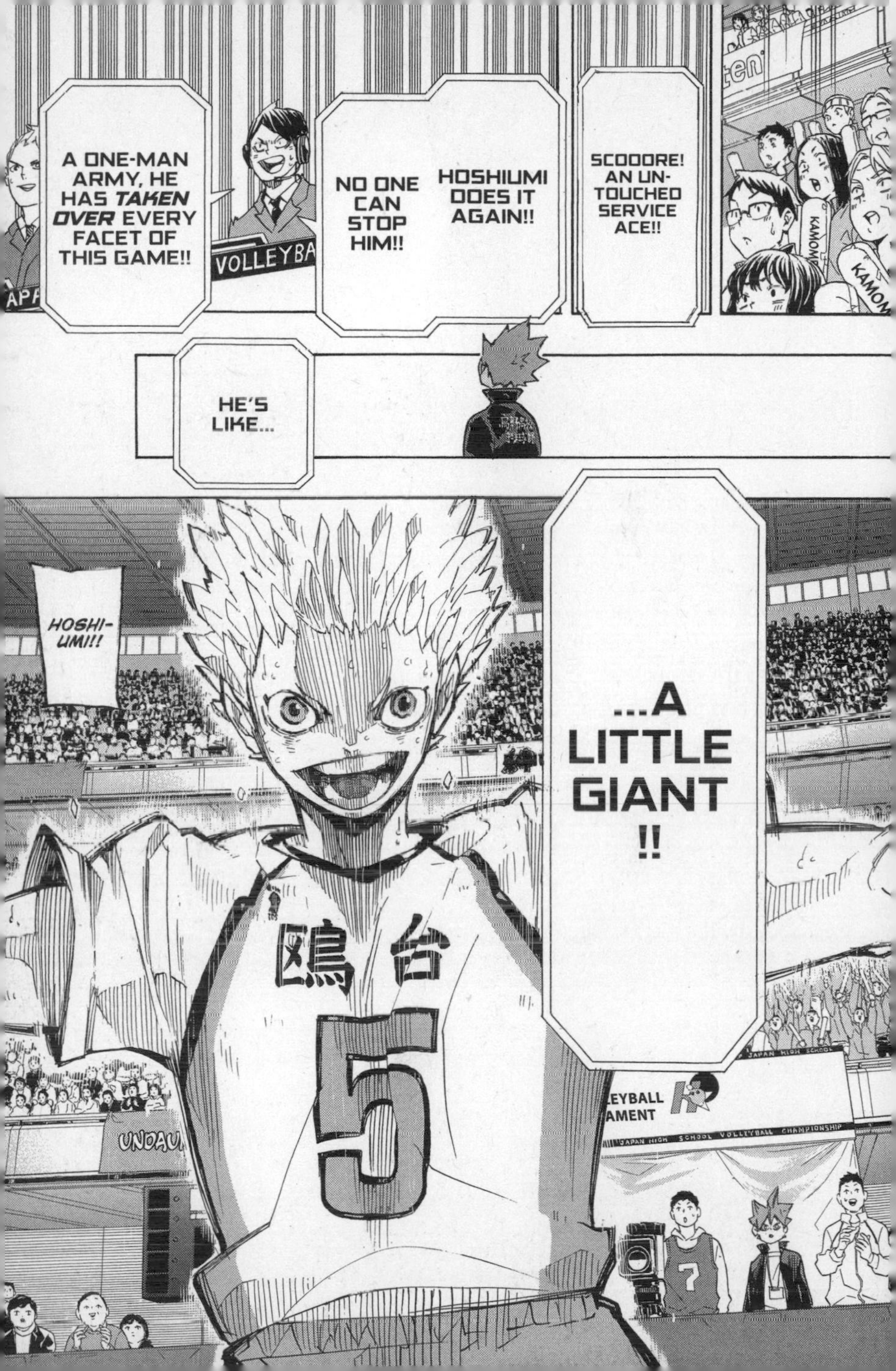

SCOOORE! AN UN-TOUCHED SERVICE ACE!!
HOSHIUMI DOES IT AGAIN!!
NO ONE CAN STOP HIM!!
A ONE-MAN ARMY, HE HAS ***TAKEN OVER*** EVERY FACET OF THIS GAME!!
HE'S LIKE...
...A LITTLE GIANT!!
HOSHI-UMI!!
JAPAN HIGH SCHOOL VOLLEYBALL CHAMPIONSHIP

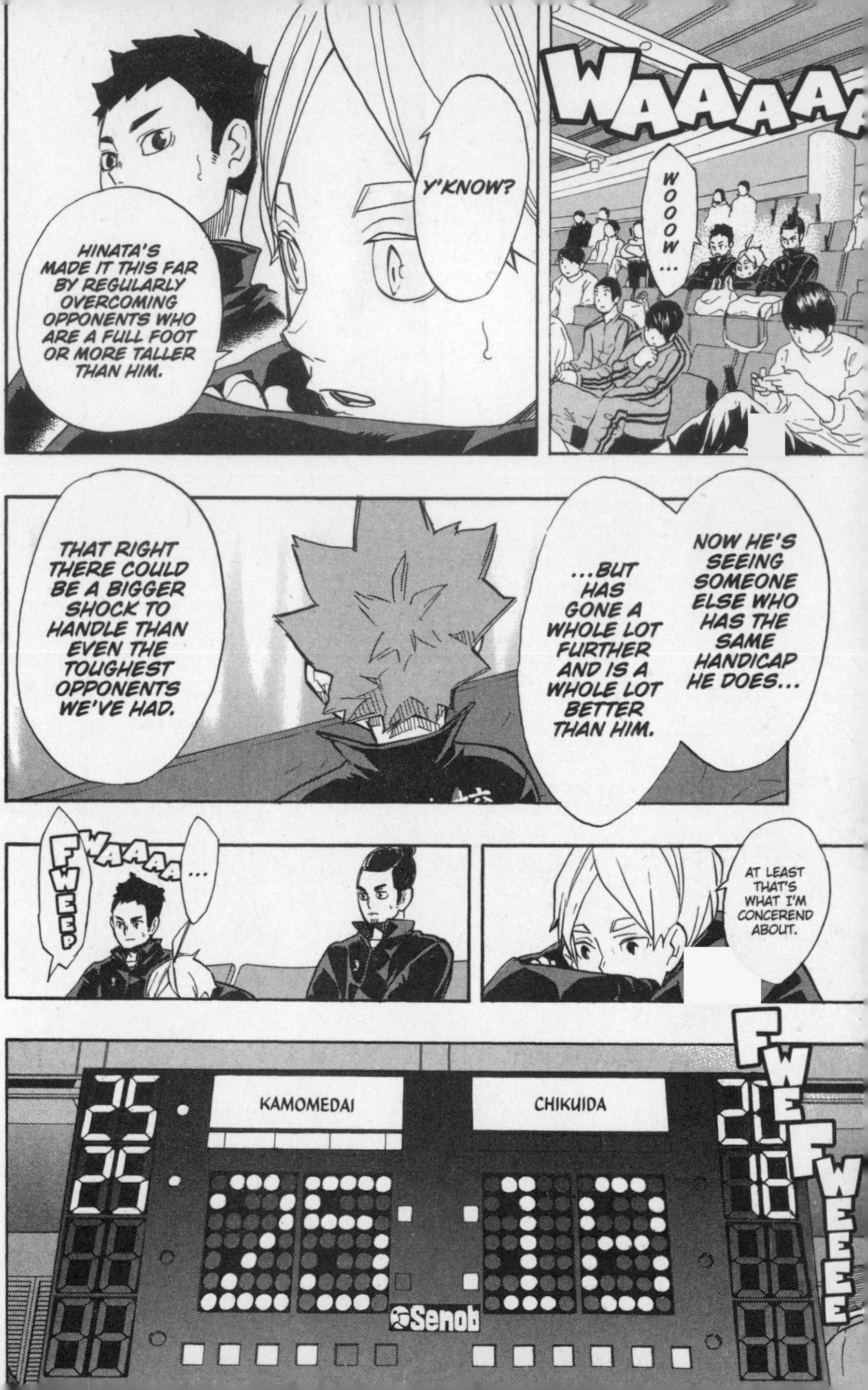
WAAAAA
WOOOW...
Y'KNOW?
HINATA'S MADE IT THIS FAR BY REGULARLY OVERCOMING OPPONENTS WHO ARE A FULL FOOT OR MORE TALLER THAN HIM.
NOW HE'S SEEING SOMEONE ELSE WHO HAS THE SAME HANDICAP HE DOES...
...BUT HAS GONE A WHOLE LOT FURTHER AND IS A WHOLE LOT BETTER THAN HIM.
THAT RIGHT THERE COULD BE A BIGGER SHOCK TO HANDLE THAN EVEN THE TOUGHEST OPPONENTS WE'VE HAD.
AT LEAST THAT'S WHAT I'M CONCEREND ABOUT.
...
FWAAAAA
FWEEEP
FWEE
FWEEEE
KAMOMEDAI
CHIKUIDA
Senob

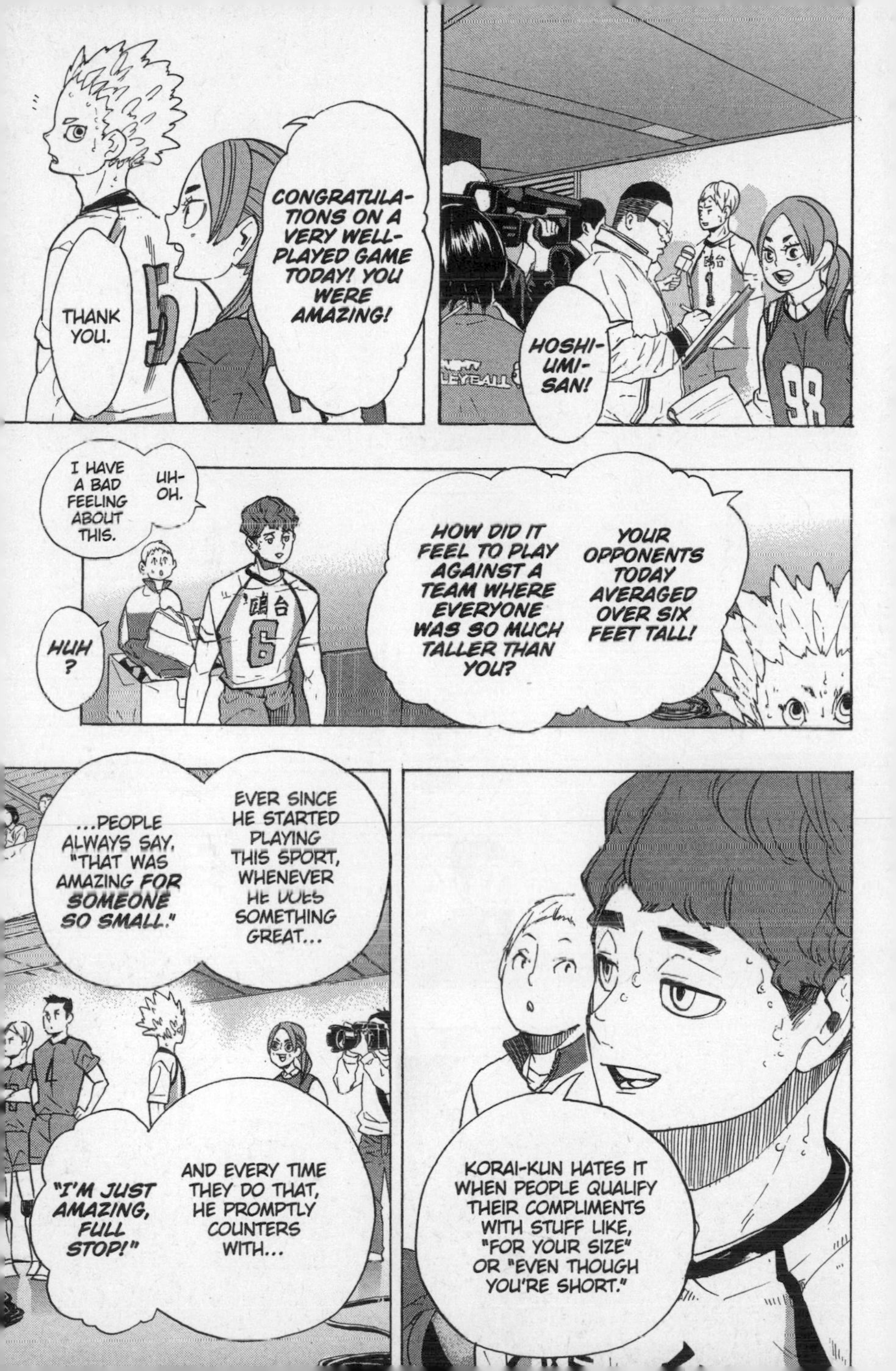
HOSHI-UMI-SAN!
CONGRATULATIONS ON A VERY WELL-PLAYED GAME TODAY! YOU WERE AMAZING!
THANK YOU.
YOUR OPPONENTS TODAY AVERAGED OVER SIX FEET TALL!
HOW DID IT FEEL TO PLAY AGAINST A TEAM WHERE EVERYONE WAS SO MUCH TALLER THAN YOU?
UH-OH.
I HAVE A BAD FEELING ABOUT THIS.
HUH?
KORAI-KUN HATES IT WHEN PEOPLE QUALIFY THEIR COMPLIMENTS WITH STUFF LIKE, "FOR YOUR SIZE" OR "EVEN THOUGH YOU'RE SHORT."
EVER SINCE HE STARTED PLAYING THIS SPORT, WHENEVER HE DOES SOMETHING GREAT...
...PEOPLE ALWAYS SAY, "THAT WAS AMAZING FOR SOMEONE SO SMALL."
AND EVERY TIME THEY DO THAT, HE PROMPTLY COUNTERS WITH...
"I'M JUST AMAZING, FULL STOP!"

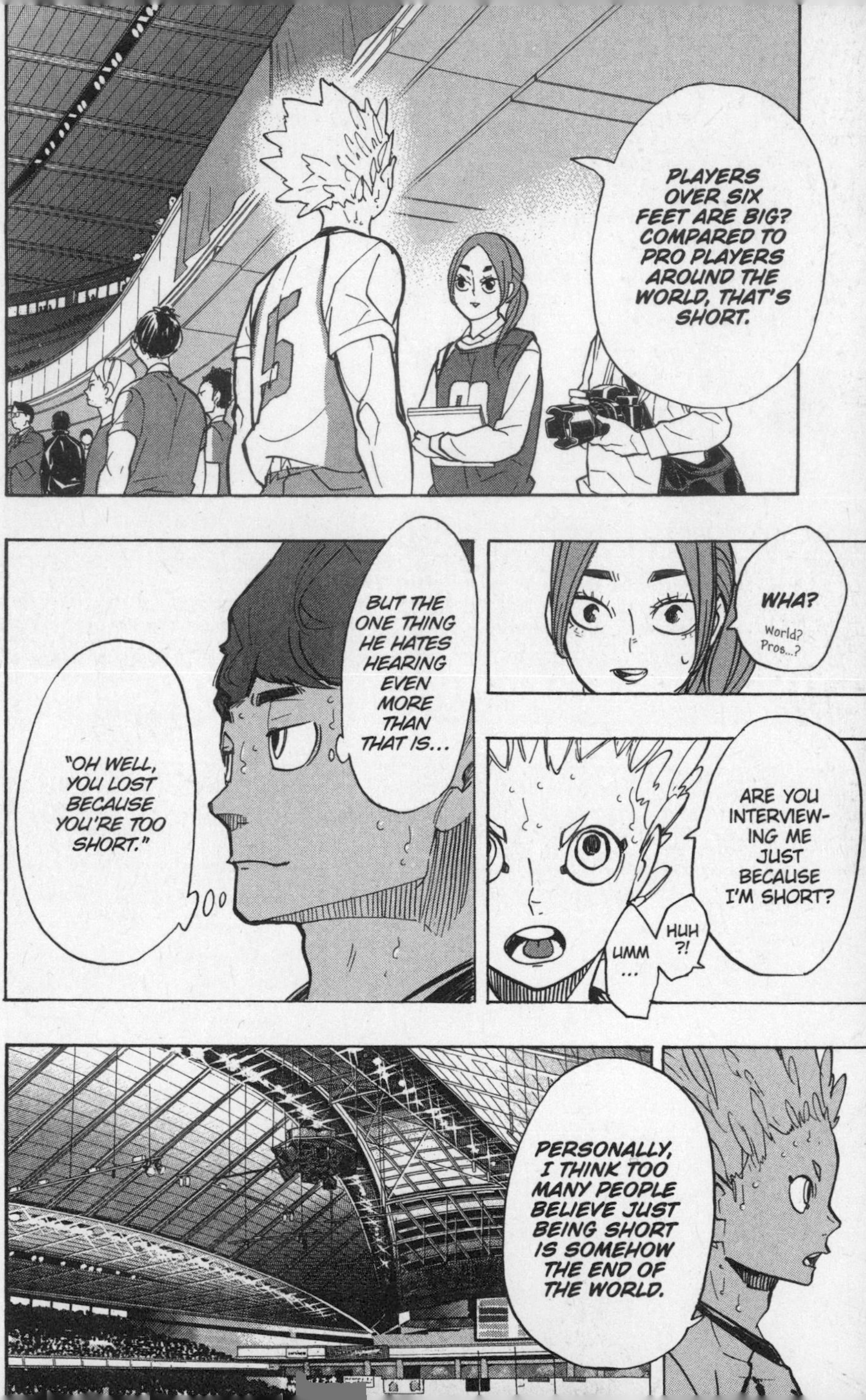
PLAYERS OVER SIX FEET ARE BIG? COMPARED TO PRO PLAYERS AROUND THE WORLD, THAT'S SHORT.
WHA?
World? Pros...?
ARE YOU INTERVIEW-ING ME JUST BECAUSE I'M SHORT?
HUH ?!
UMM ...
BUT THE ONE THING HE HATES HEARING EVEN MORE THAN THAT IS...
"OH WELL, YOU LOST BECAUSE YOU'RE TOO SHORT."
PERSONALLY, I THINK TOO MANY PEOPLE BELIEVE JUST BEING SHORT IS SOMEHOW THE END OF THE WORLD.

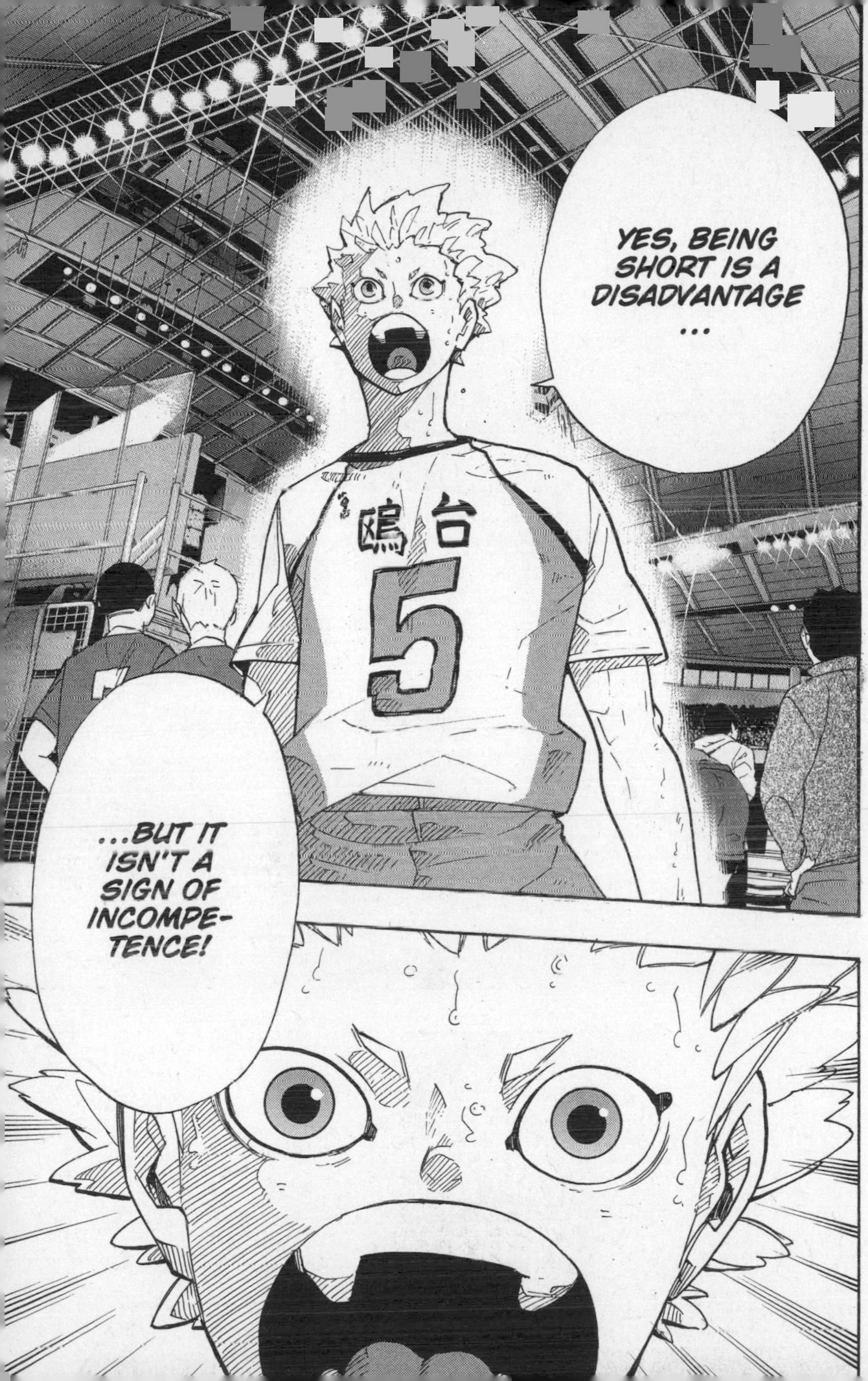
YES, BEING SHORT IS A DISADVANTAGE ...
鴎台
5
...BUT IT ISN'T A SIGN OF INCOMPE-TENCE!

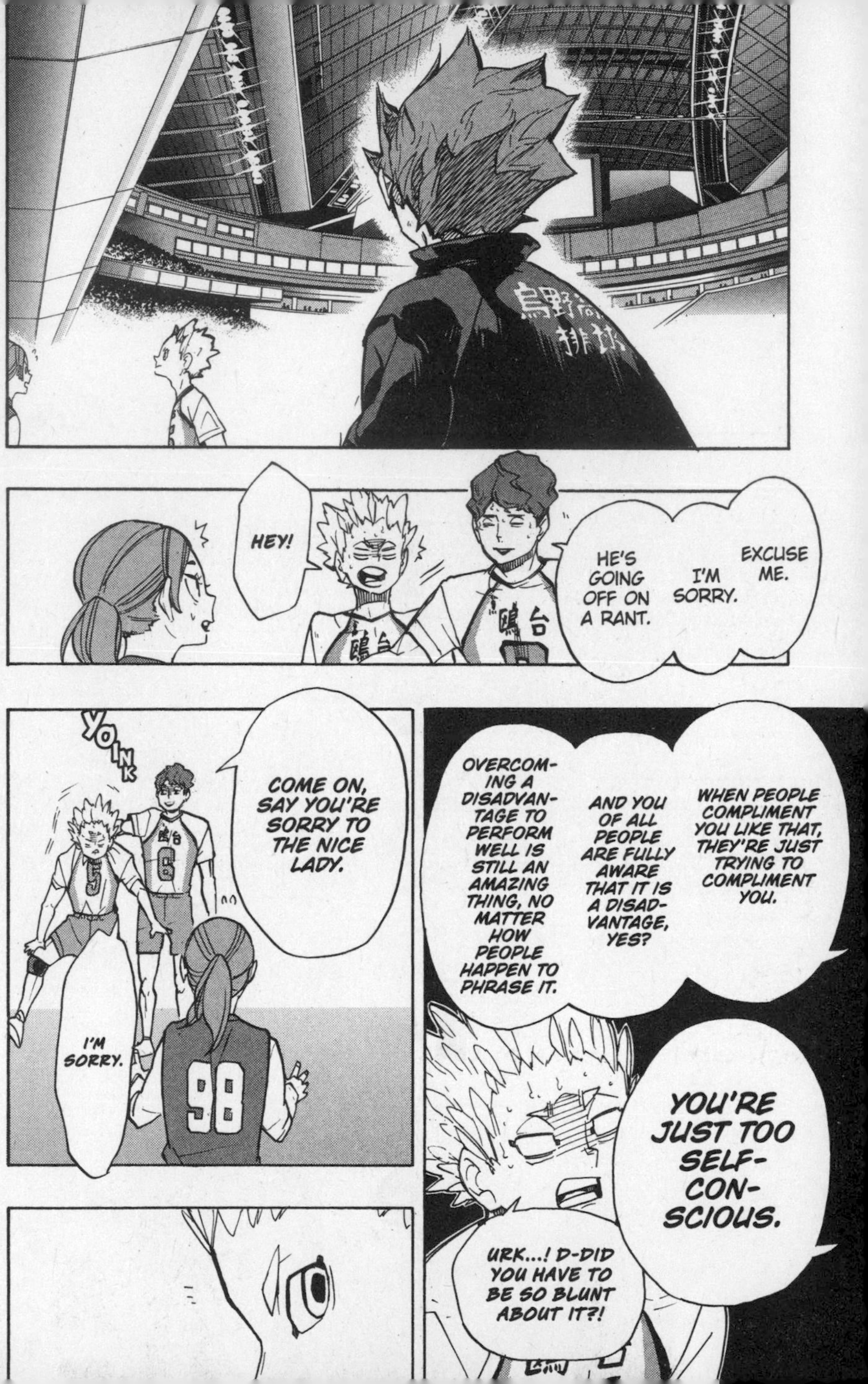
EXCUSE ME.
I'M SORRY.
HE'S GOING OFF ON A RANT.
HEY!
WHEN PEOPLE COMPLIMENT YOU LIKE THAT, THEY'RE JUST TRYING TO COMPLIMENT YOU.
AND YOU OF ALL PEOPLE ARE FULLY AWARE THAT IT IS A DISADVANTAGE, YES?
OVERCOMING A DISADVANTAGE TO PERFORM WELL IS STILL AN AMAZING THING, NO MATTER HOW PEOPLE HAPPEN TO PHRASE IT.
YOU'RE JUST TOO SELF-CONSCIOUS.
URK...! D-DID YOU HAVE TO BE SO BLUNT ABOUT IT?!
YOINK
COME ON, SAY YOU'RE SORRY TO THE NICE LADY.
I'M SORRY.

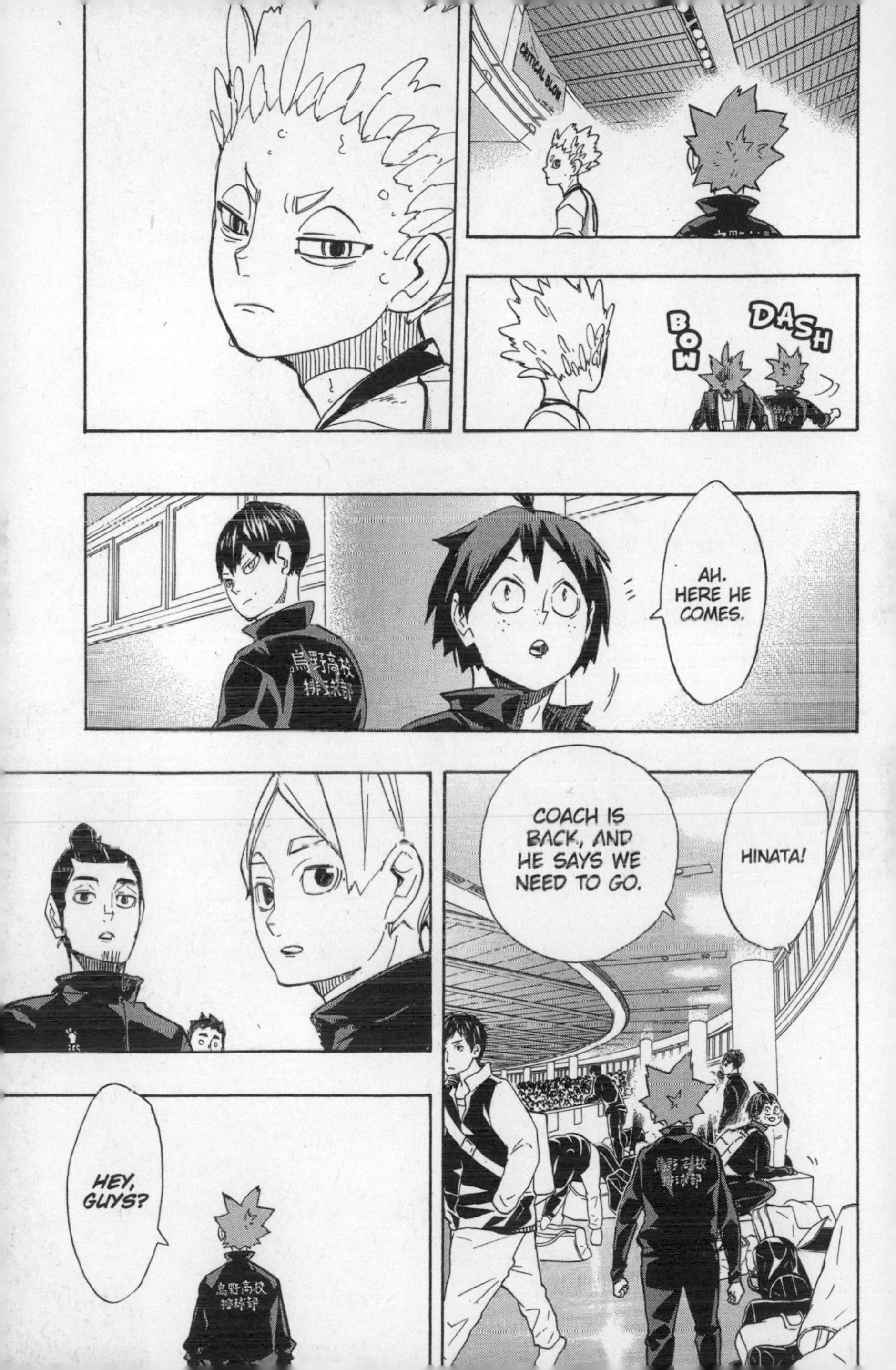
CRITICAL BLOW
DASH
BOW
AH. HERE HE COMES.
HINATA!
COACH IS BACK, AND HE SAYS WE NEED TO GO.
HEY, GUYS?

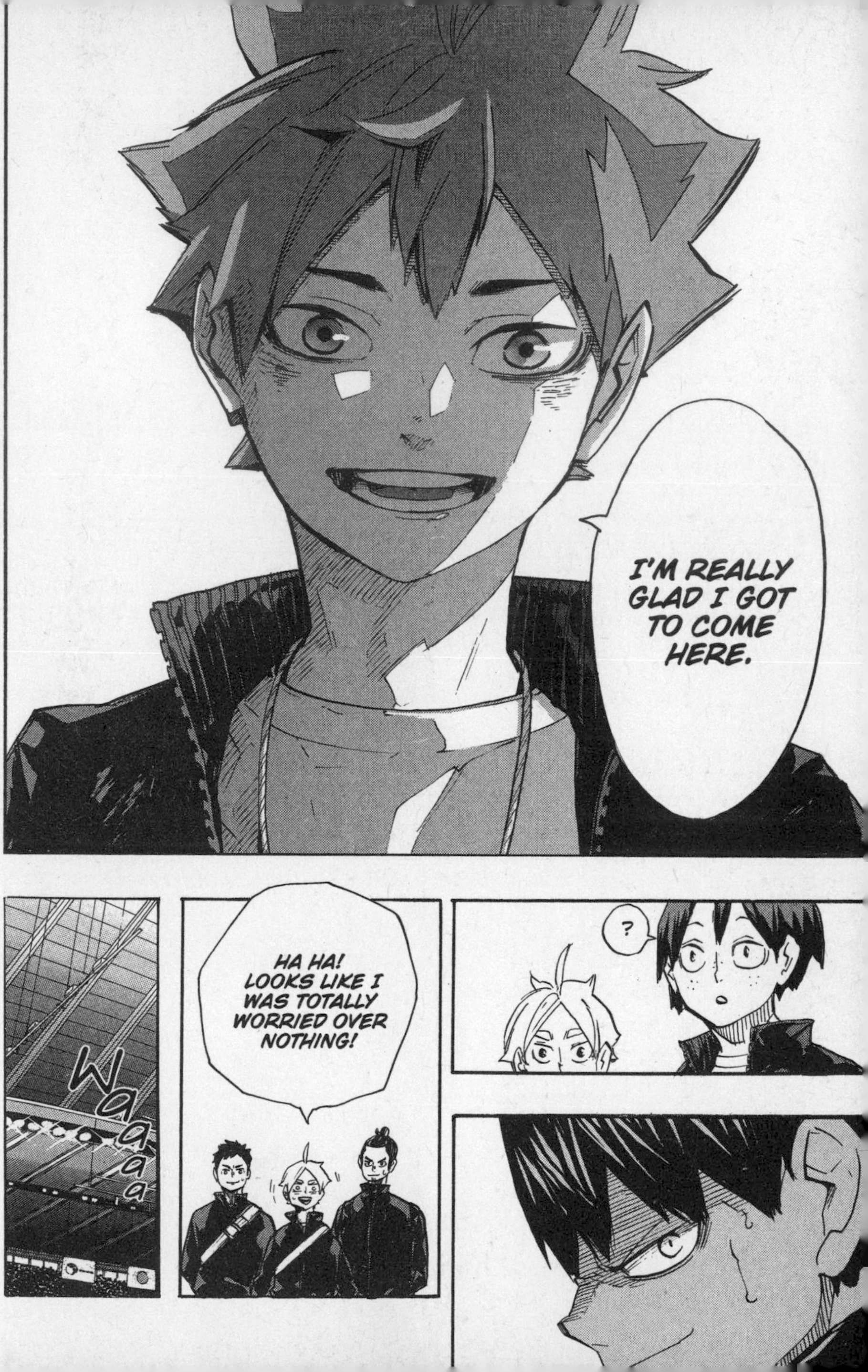
I'M REALLY GLAD I GOT TO COME HERE.
?
HA HA! LOOKS LIKE I WAS TOTALLY WORRIED OVER NOTHING!
Waaaa

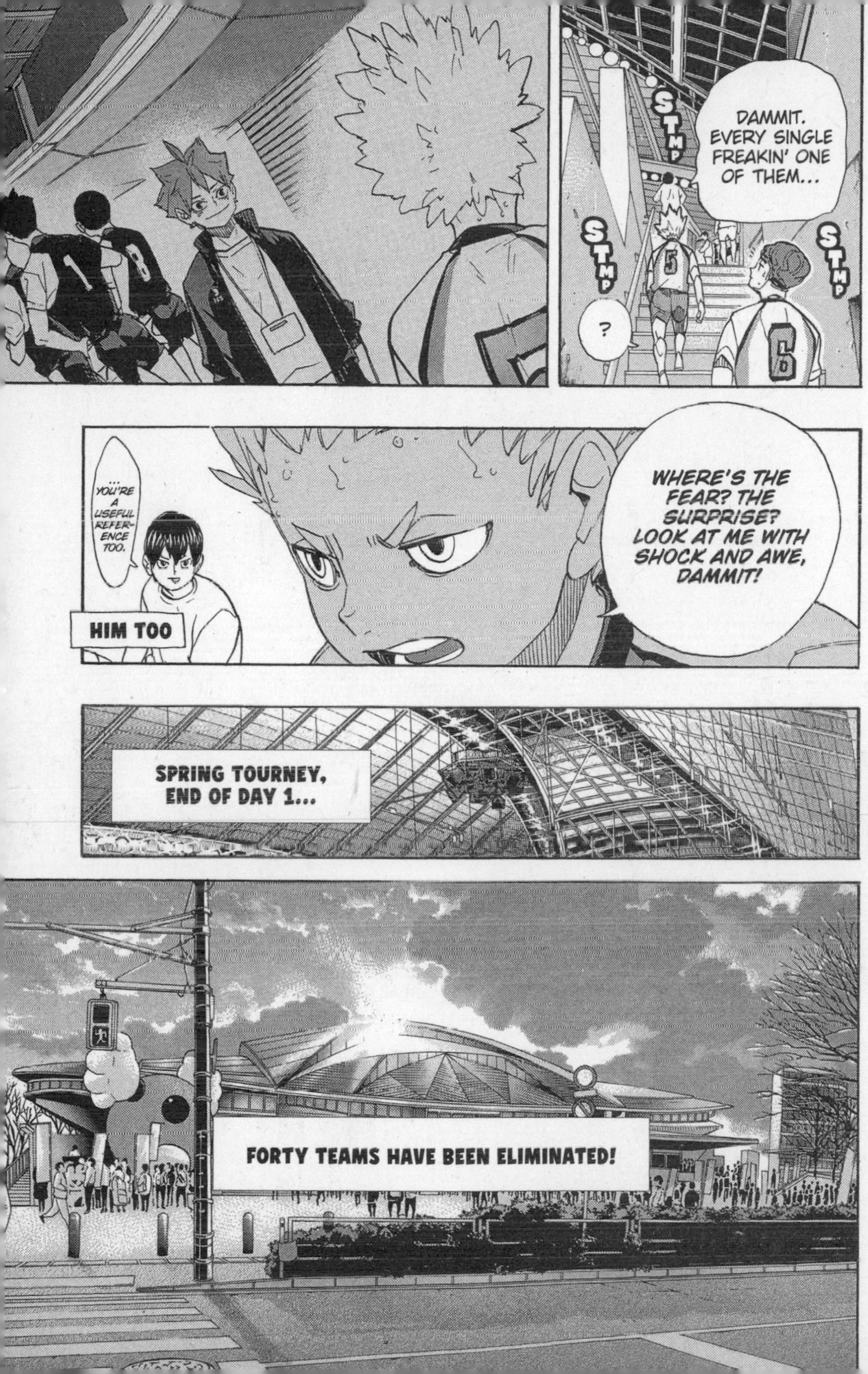

STMP
DAMMIT. EVERY SINGLE FREAKIN' ONE OF THEM...
STMP
STMP
?
WHERE'S THE FEAR? THE SURPRISE? LOOK AT ME WITH SHOCK AND AWE, DAMMIT!
...YOU'RE A USEFUL REFERENCE TOO.
HIM TOO
SPRING TOURNEY, END OF DAY 1...
FORTY TEAMS HAVE BEEN ELIMINATED!

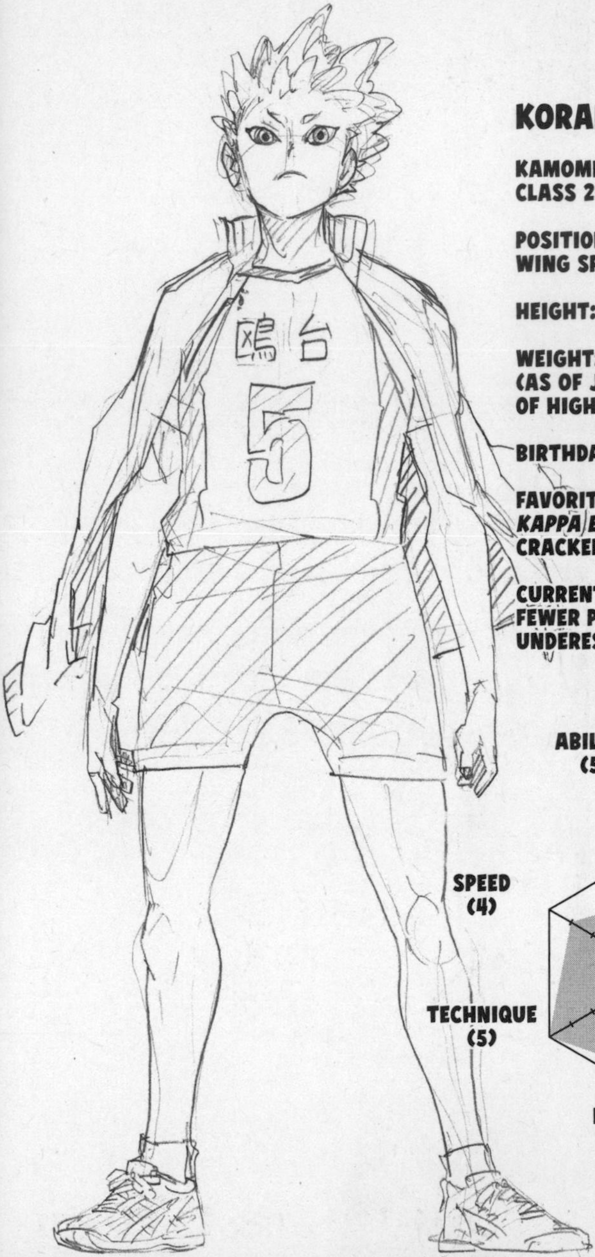
鴎台
5

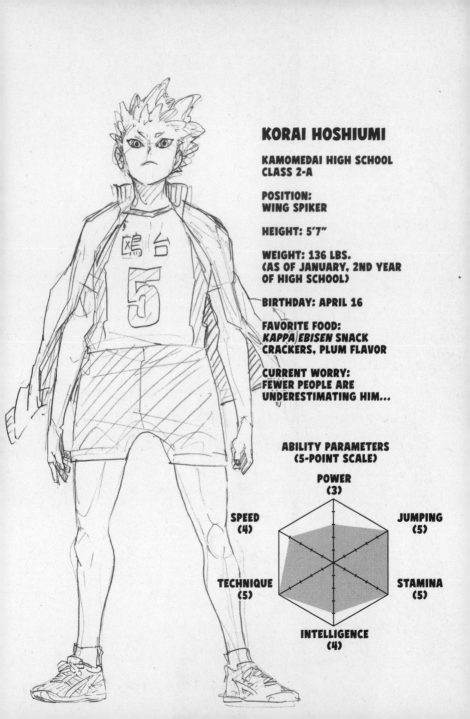

KORAI HOSHIUMI

KAMOMEDAI HIGH SCHOOL
CLASS 2-A

POSITION:
WING SPIKER

HEIGHT: 5'7"

WEIGHT: 136 LBS.
(AS OF JANUARY, 2ND YEAR OF HIGH SCHOOL)

BIRTHDAY: APRIL 16

FAVORITE FOOD:
***KAPPA EBISEN* SNACK CRACKERS, PLUM FLAVOR**

CURRENT WORRY:
FEWER PEOPLE ARE UNDERESTIMATING HIM...

ABILITY PARAMETERS
(5-POINT SCALE)

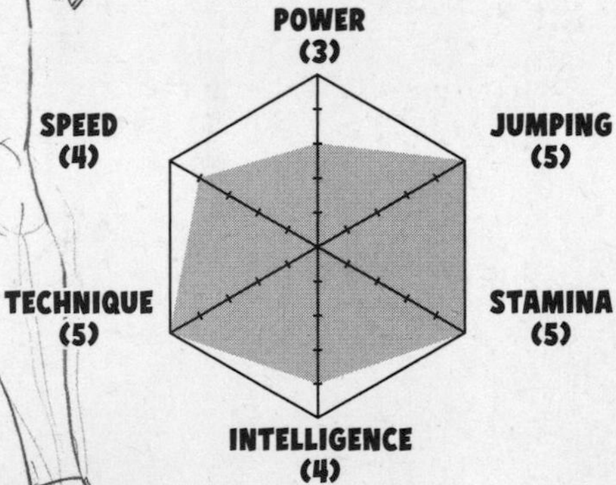
POWER
(3)
JUMPING
(5)
STAMINA
(5)
INTELLIGENCE
(4)
TECHNIQUE
(5)
SPEED
(4)

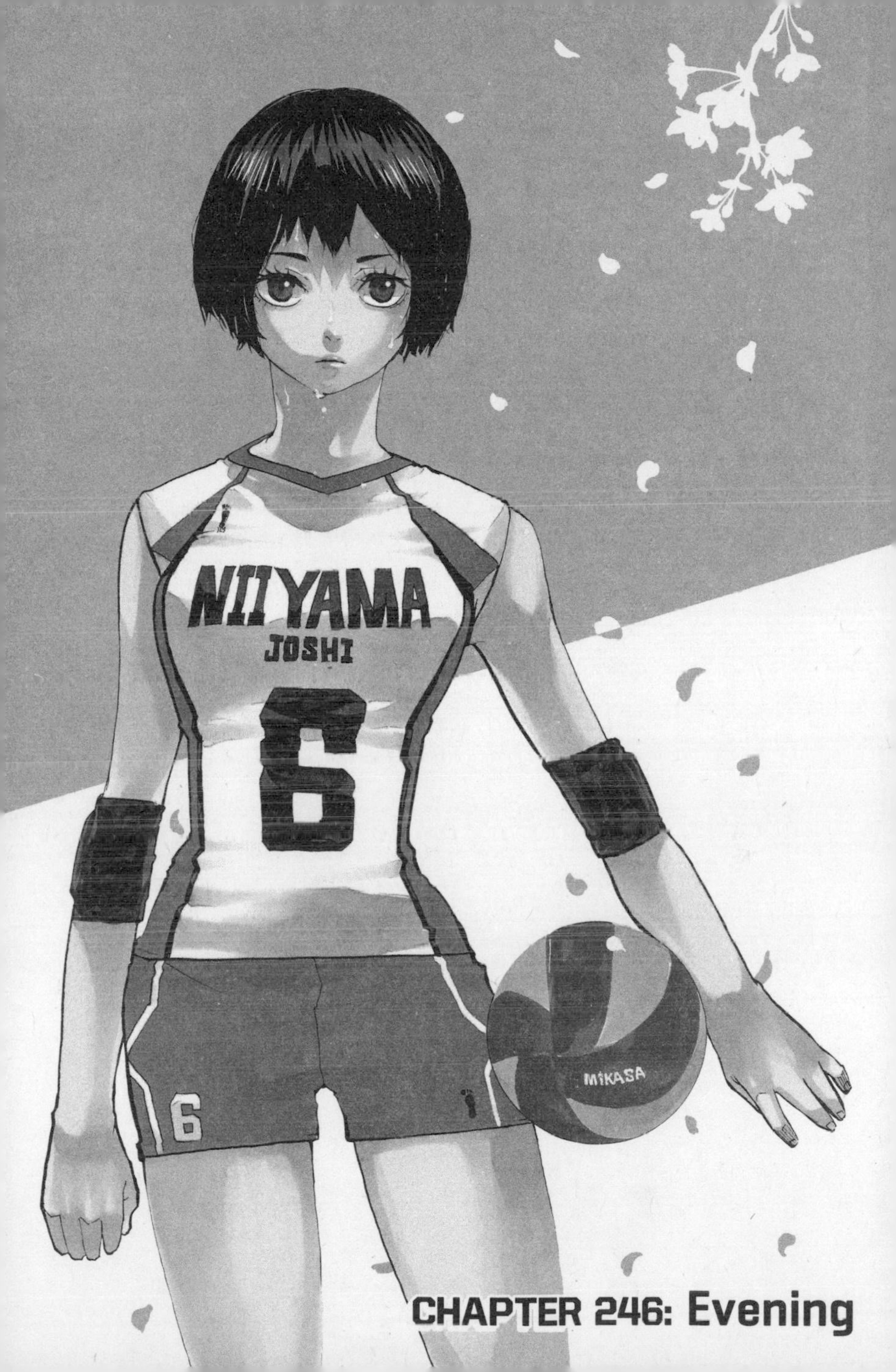
NIIYAMA
JOSHI
6
MIKASA
6

CHAPTER 246: Evening

HAIKYU!!

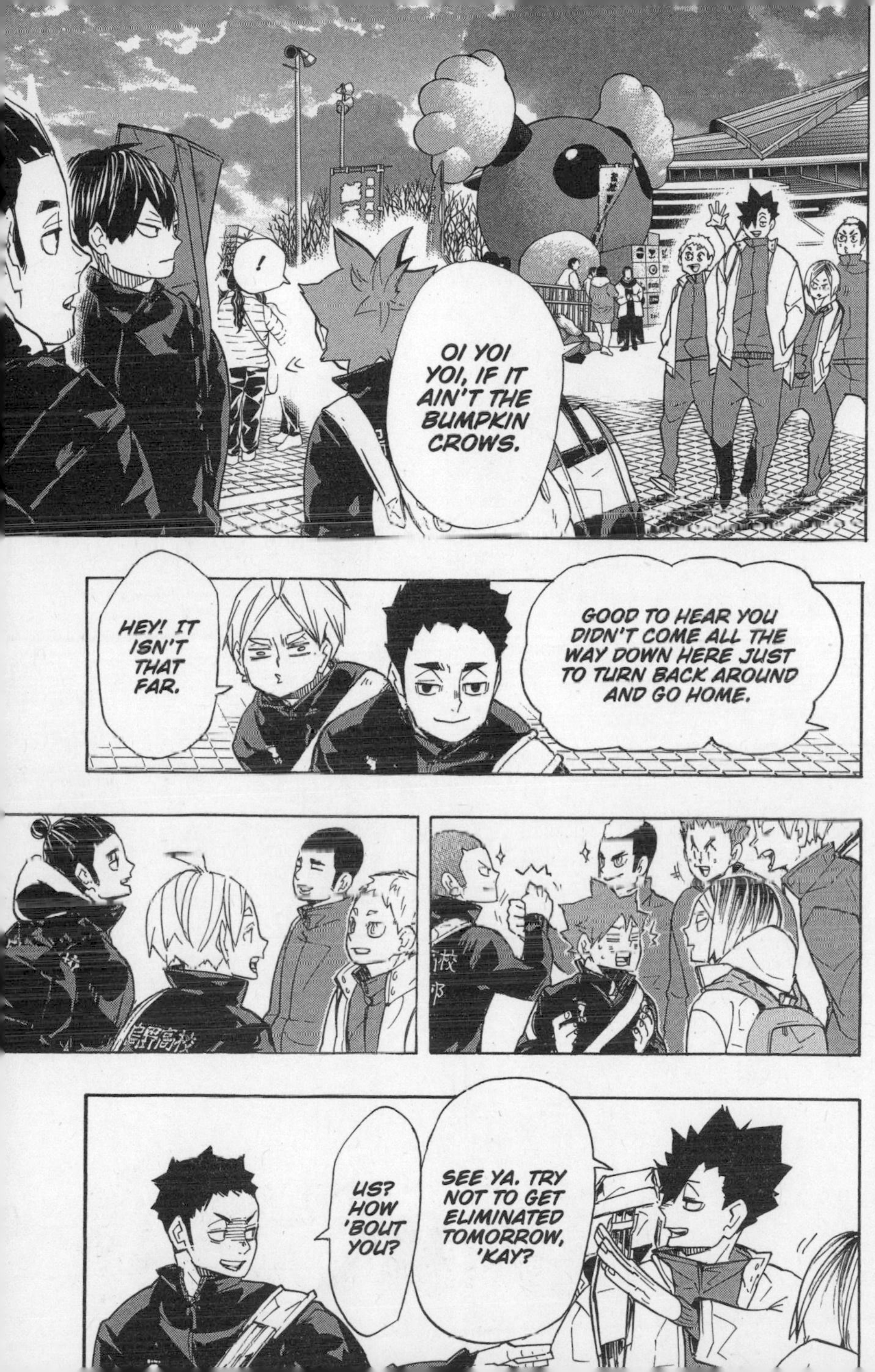
OI YOI YOI, IF IT AIN'T THE BUMPKIN CROWS.
!
GOOD TO HEAR YOU DIDN'T COME ALL THE WAY DOWN HERE JUST TO TURN BACK AROUND AND GO HOME.
HEY! IT ISN'T THAT FAR.
SEE YA. TRY NOT TO GET ELIMINATED TOMORROW, 'KAY?
US? HOW 'BOUT YOU?

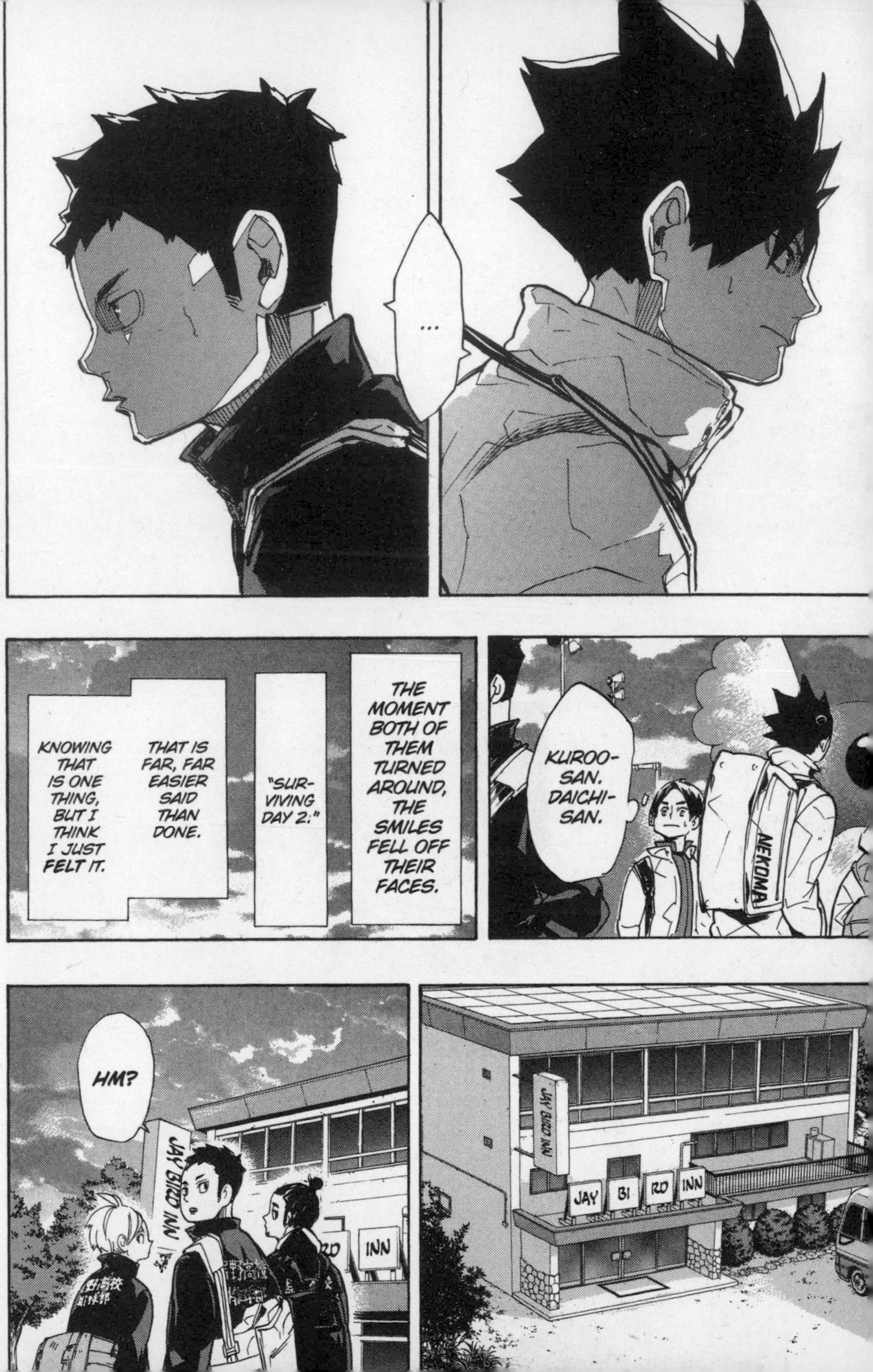
...
KUROO-SAN. DAICHI-SAN.
THE MOMENT BOTH OF THEM TURNED AROUND, THE SMILES FELL OFF THEIR FACES.
"SURVIVING DAY 2."
THAT IS FAR, FAR EASIER SAID THAN DONE.
KNOWING THAT IS ONE THING, BUT I THINK I JUST FELT IT.
NEKOMA
JAY BIRD INN
JAY BI RD INN
HM?
JAY BIRD INN
RD INN

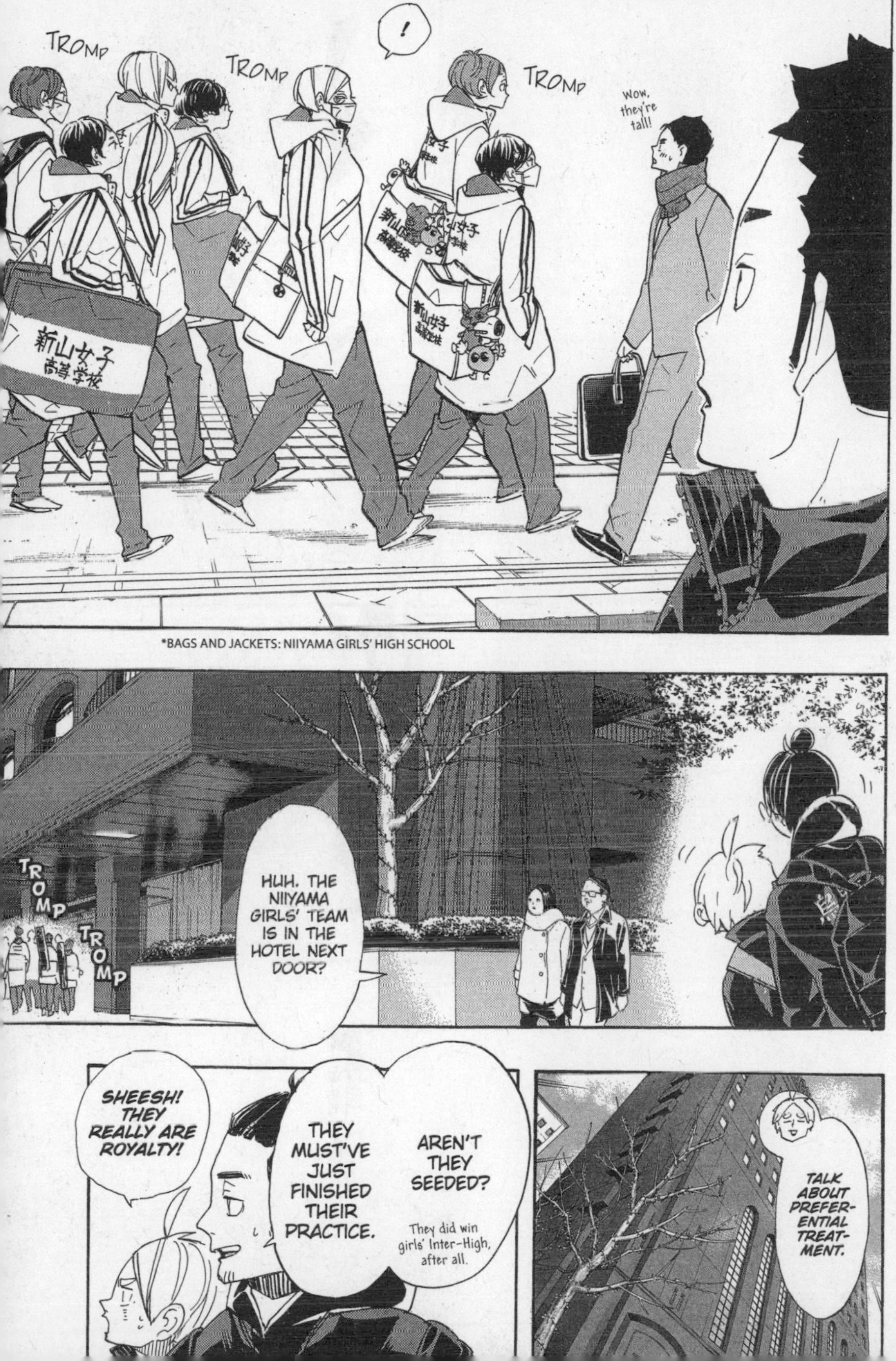
Wow, they're tall!
TROMP
!
TROMP
TROMP
*BAGS AND JACKETS: NIIYAMA GIRLS' HIGH SCHOOL
HUH. THE NIIYAMA GIRLS' TEAM IS IN THE HOTEL NEXT DOOR?
TROMP
TROMP
TALK ABOUT PREFERENTIAL TREATMENT.
AREN'T THEY SEEDED?
They did win girls' Inter-High, after all.
THEY MUST'VE JUST FINISHED THEIR PRACTICE.
SHEESH! THEY REALLY ARE ROYALTY!

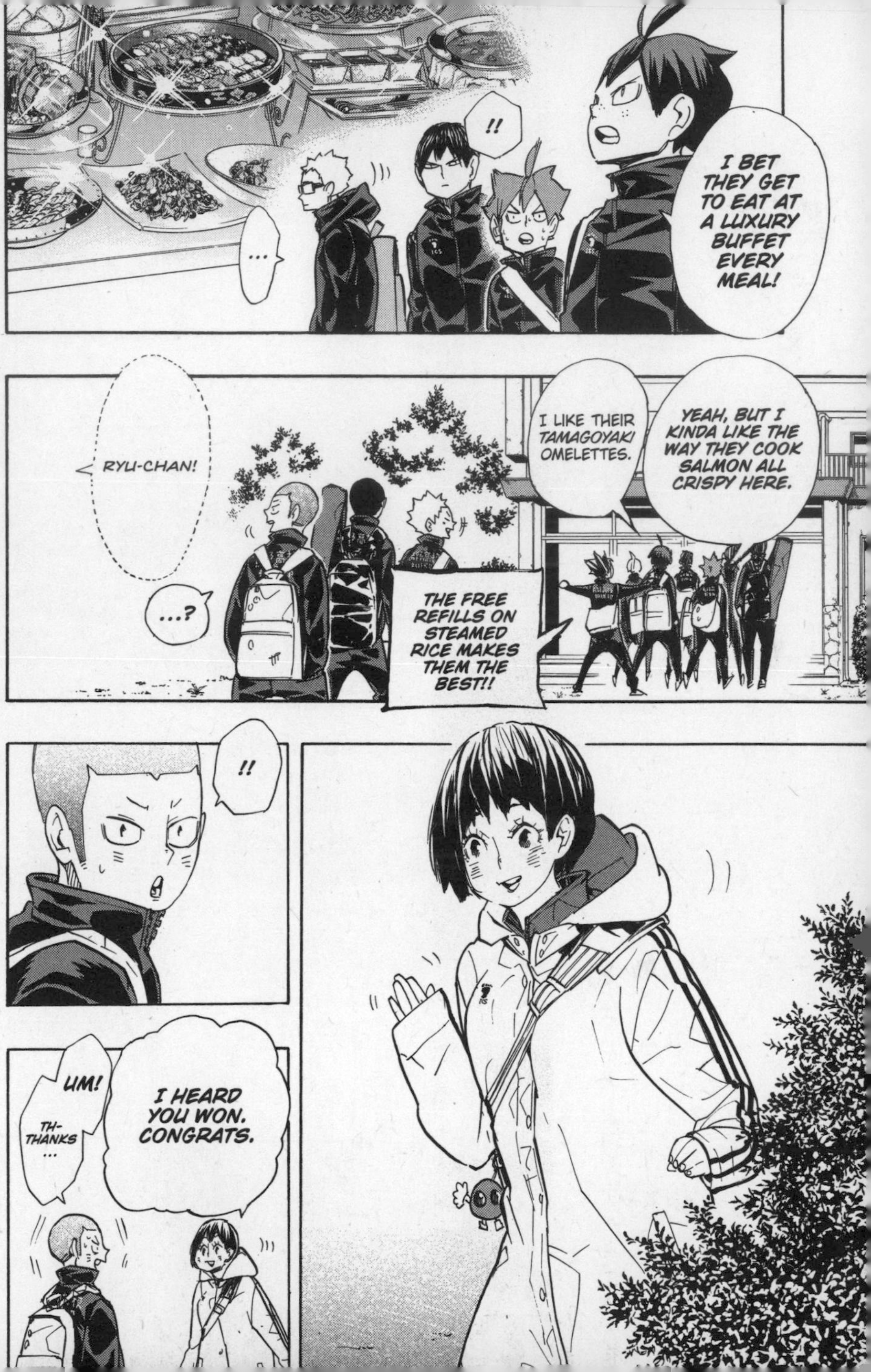
I BET THEY GET TO EAT AT A LUXURY BUFFET EVERY MEAL!
!!
...
YEAH, BUT I KINDA LIKE THE WAY THEY COOK SALMON ALL CRISPY HERE.
I LIKE THEIR TAMAGOYAKI OMELETTES.
THE FREE REFILLS ON STEAMED RICE MAKES THEM THE BEST!!
RYU-CHAN!
...?
!!
I HEARD YOU WON. CONGRATS.
UM!
TH-THANKS ...

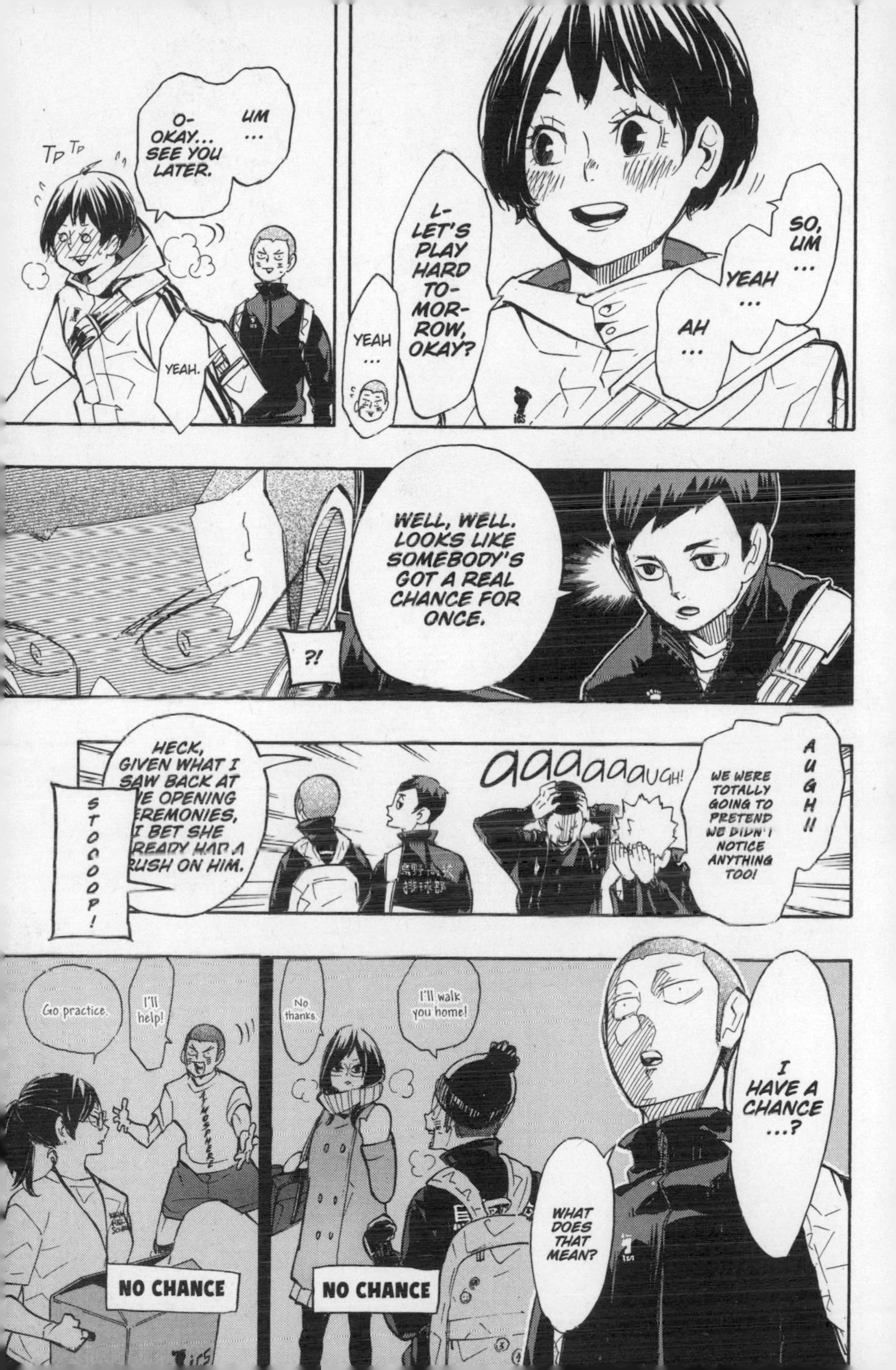
SO, UM ...
YEAH ...
AH ...
L-LET'S PLAY HARD TO-MORROW, OKAY?
YEAH ...
UM ...
O-OKAY... SEE YOU LATER.
TP TP
YEAH.
WELL, WELL. LOOKS LIKE SOMEBODY'S GOT A REAL CHANCE FOR ONCE.
?!
AUGH!!
WE WERE TOTALLY GOING TO PRETEND WE DIDN'T NOTICE ANYTHING TOO!
AAAAAAAUGH!
HECK, GIVEN WHAT I SAW BACK AT
STOOOOOP!
I HAVE A CHANCE ...?
WHAT DOES THAT MEAN?
I'll walk you home!
No thanks.
NO CHANCE
I'll help!
Go practice.
NO CHANCE

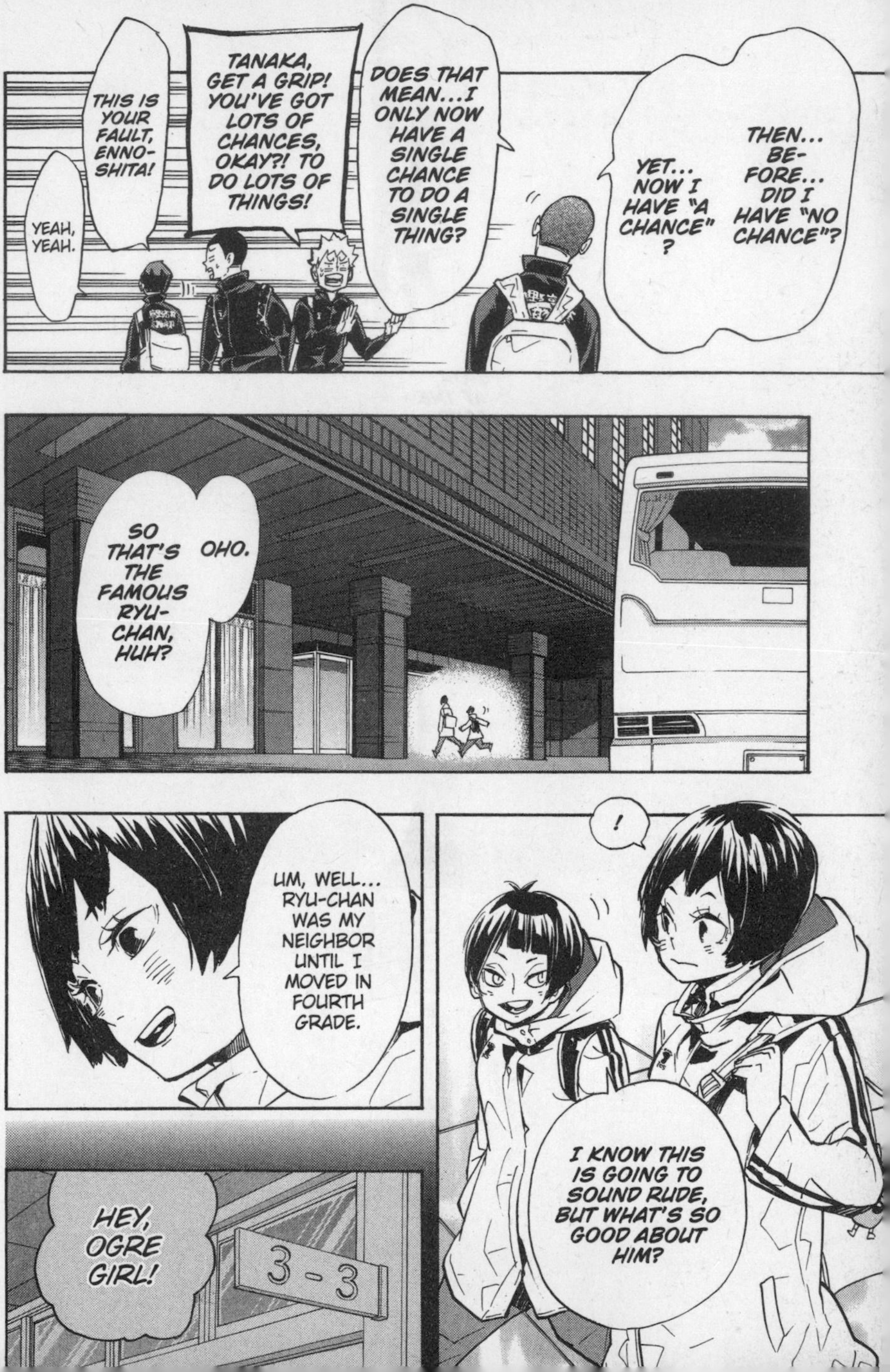
THEN... BE-FORE... DID I HAVE "NO CHANCE"?
YET... NOW I HAVE "A CHANCE"?
DOES THAT MEAN...I ONLY NOW HAVE A SINGLE CHANCE TO DO A SINGLE THING?
TANAKA, GET A GRIP! YOU'VE GOT LOTS OF CHANCES, OKAY?! TO DO LOTS OF THINGS!
THIS IS YOUR FAULT, ENNO-SHITA!
YEAH, YEAH.
OHO.
SO THAT'S THE FAMOUS RYU-CHAN, HUH?
!
I KNOW THIS IS GOING TO SOUND RUDE, BUT WHAT'S SO GOOD ABOUT HIM?
UM, WELL... RYU-CHAN WAS MY NEIGHBOR UNTIL I MOVED IN FOURTH GRADE.
3-3
HEY, OGRE GIRL!

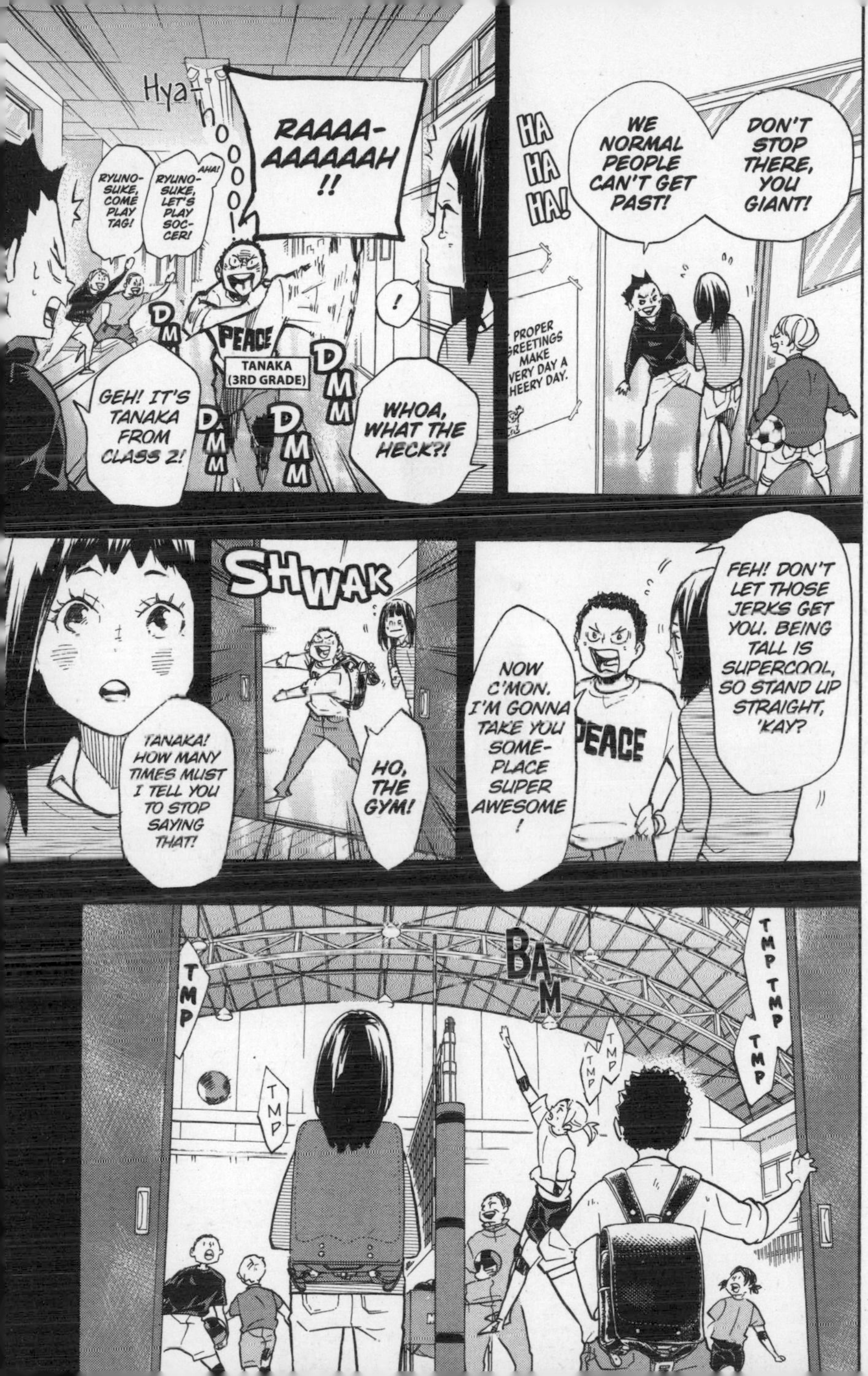
DON'T STOP THERE, YOU GIANT!
WE NORMAL PEOPLE CAN'T GET PAST!
HA HA HA!
PROPER GREETINGS MAKE VERY DAY A HEERY DAY.
RAAAA-AAAAAAH!!
Hya-hoooooo!
AHA! RYUNO-SUKE, LET'S PLAY SOC-CER!
RYUNO-SUKE, COME PLAY TAG!
!
PEACE
TANAKA (3RD GRADE)
DMM
DMM
DMM
DMM
WHOA, WHAT THE HECK?!
GEH! IT'S TANAKA FROM CLASS 2!
FEH! DON'T LET THOSE JERKS GET YOU. BEING TALL IS SUPERCOOL, SO STAND UP STRAIGHT, 'KAY?
NOW C'MON. I'M GONNA TAKE YOU SOME-PLACE SUPER AWESOME!
PEACE
SHWAK
HO, THE GYM!
TANAKA! HOW MANY TIMES MUST I TELL YOU TO STOP SAYING THAT!
TMP TMP TMP
BAM
TMP TMP
TMP
TMP

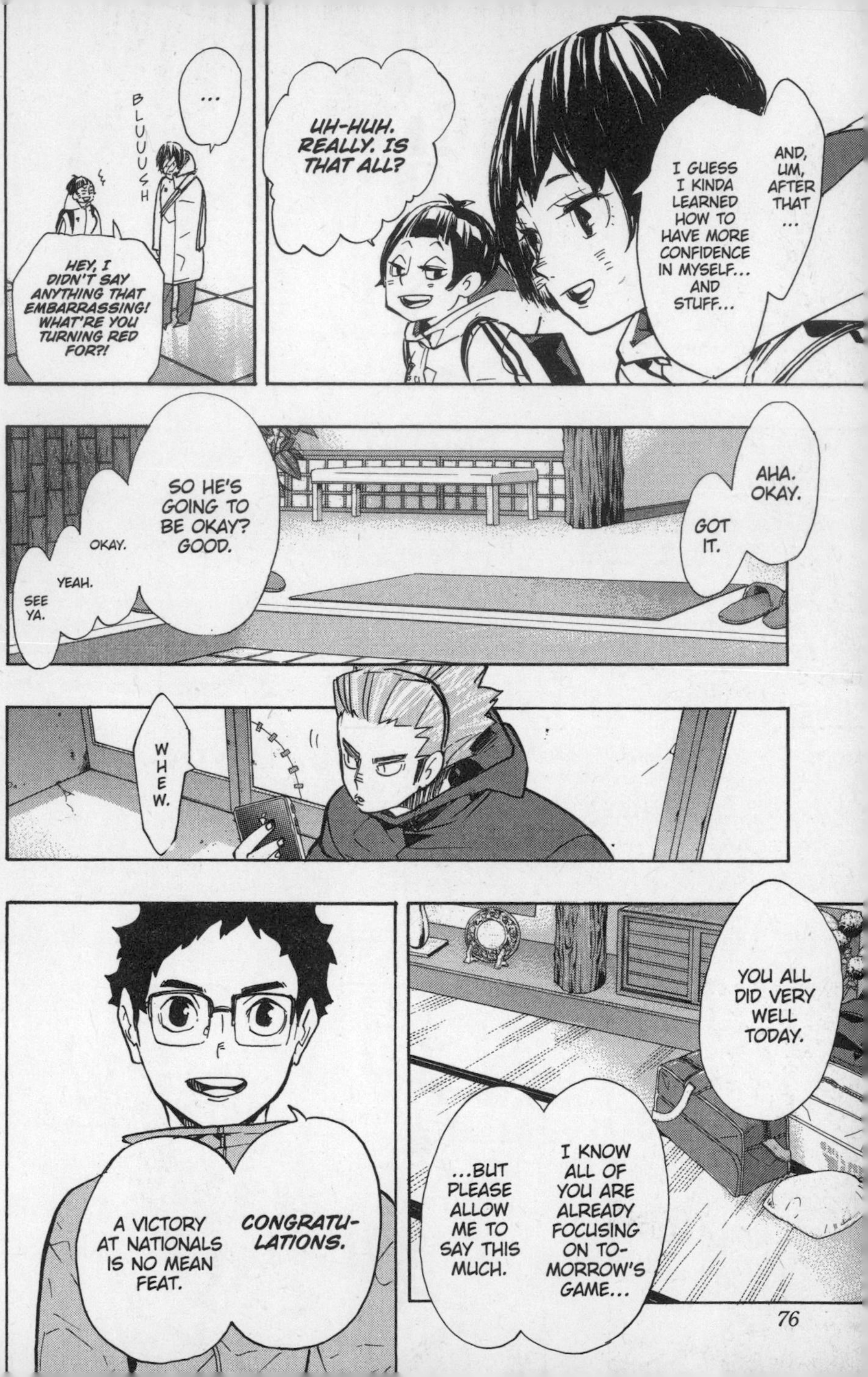
AND, UM, AFTER THAT...
I GUESS I KINDA LEARNED HOW TO HAVE MORE CONFIDENCE IN MYSELF... AND STUFF...
UH-HUH. REALLY. IS THAT ALL?
...
BLUUUSH
HEY, I DIDN'T SAY ANYTHING THAT EMBARRASSING! WHAT'RE YOU TURNING RED FOR?!
AHA. OKAY.
GOT IT.
SO HE'S GOING TO BE OKAY? GOOD.
OKAY.
YEAH.
SEE YA.
WHEW.
YOU ALL DID VERY WELL TODAY.
I KNOW ALL OF YOU ARE ALREADY FOCUSING ON TO-MORROW'S GAME...
...BUT PLEASE ALLOW ME TO SAY THIS MUCH.
CONGRATU-LATIONS.
A VICTORY AT NATIONALS IS NO MEAN FEAT.

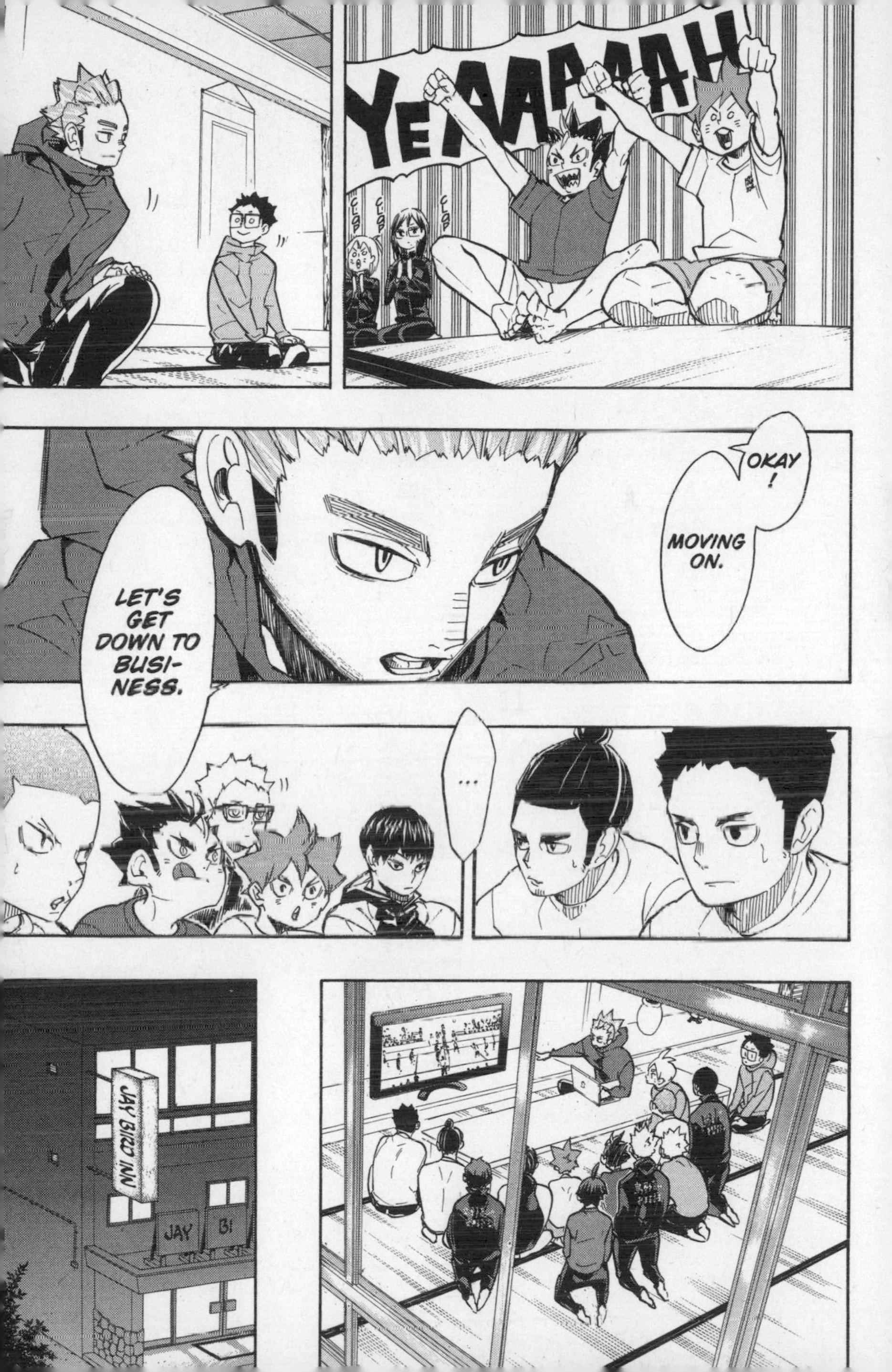
YEAAAAAH
OKAY!
MOVING ON.
LET'S GET DOWN TO BUSI-NESS.
...
JAY BIRD INN
JAY
BI

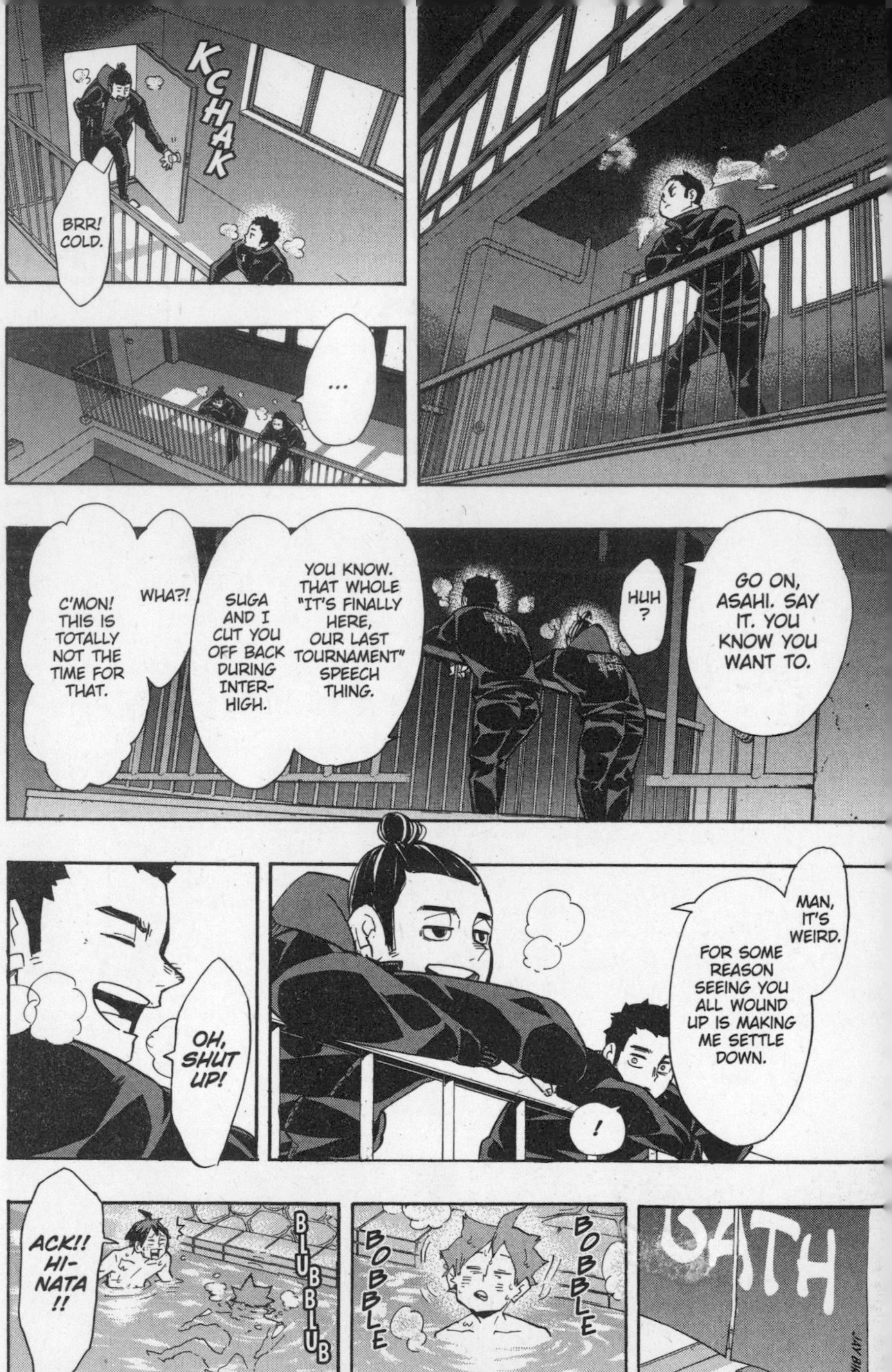
KCHAK
BRR! COLD.
...
GO ON, ASAHI. SAY IT. YOU KNOW YOU WANT TO.
HUH?
YOU KNOW. THAT WHOLE "IT'S FINALLY HERE, OUR LAST TOURNAMENT" SPEECH THING.
SUGA AND I CUT YOU OFF BACK DURING INTER-HIGH.
WHA?!
C'MON! THIS IS TOTALLY NOT THE TIME FOR THAT.
MAN, IT'S WEIRD.
FOR SOME REASON SEEING YOU ALL WOUND UP IS MAKING ME SETTLE DOWN.
!
OH, SHUT UP!
BOBBLE
BOBBLE
BLUBBLUB
ACK!! HI-NATA!!

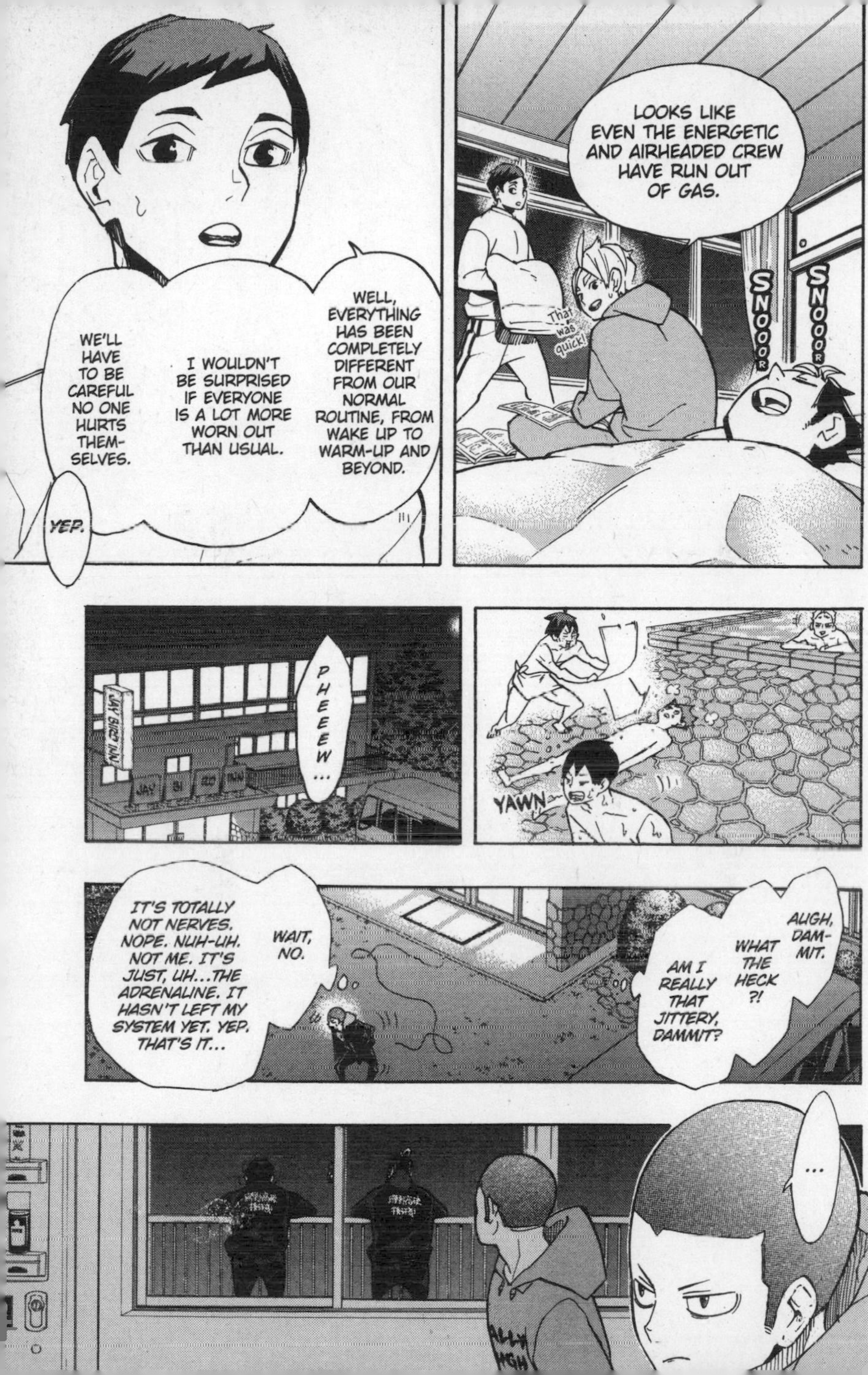

LOOKS LIKE EVEN THE ENERGETIC AND AIRHEADED CREW HAVE RUN OUT OF GAS.
That was quick!
SNOOOOR
SNOOOOR
WELL, EVERYTHING HAS BEEN COMPLETELY DIFFERENT FROM OUR NORMAL ROUTINE, FROM WAKE UP TO WARM-UP AND BEYOND.
I WOULDN'T BE SURPRISED IF EVERYONE IS A LOT MORE WORN OUT THAN USUAL.
WE'LL HAVE TO BE CAREFUL NO ONE HURTS THEMSELVES.
YEP.
YAWN
PHEEEW...
JAY BI RD INN
AUGH, DAMMIT.
WHAT THE HECK?!
AM I REALLY THAT JITTERY, DAMMIT?
WAIT, NO.
IT'S TOTALLY NOT NERVES. NOPE. NUH-UH. NOT ME. IT'S JUST, UH...THE ADRENALINE. IT HASN'T LEFT MY SYSTEM YET. YEP. THAT'S IT...
...

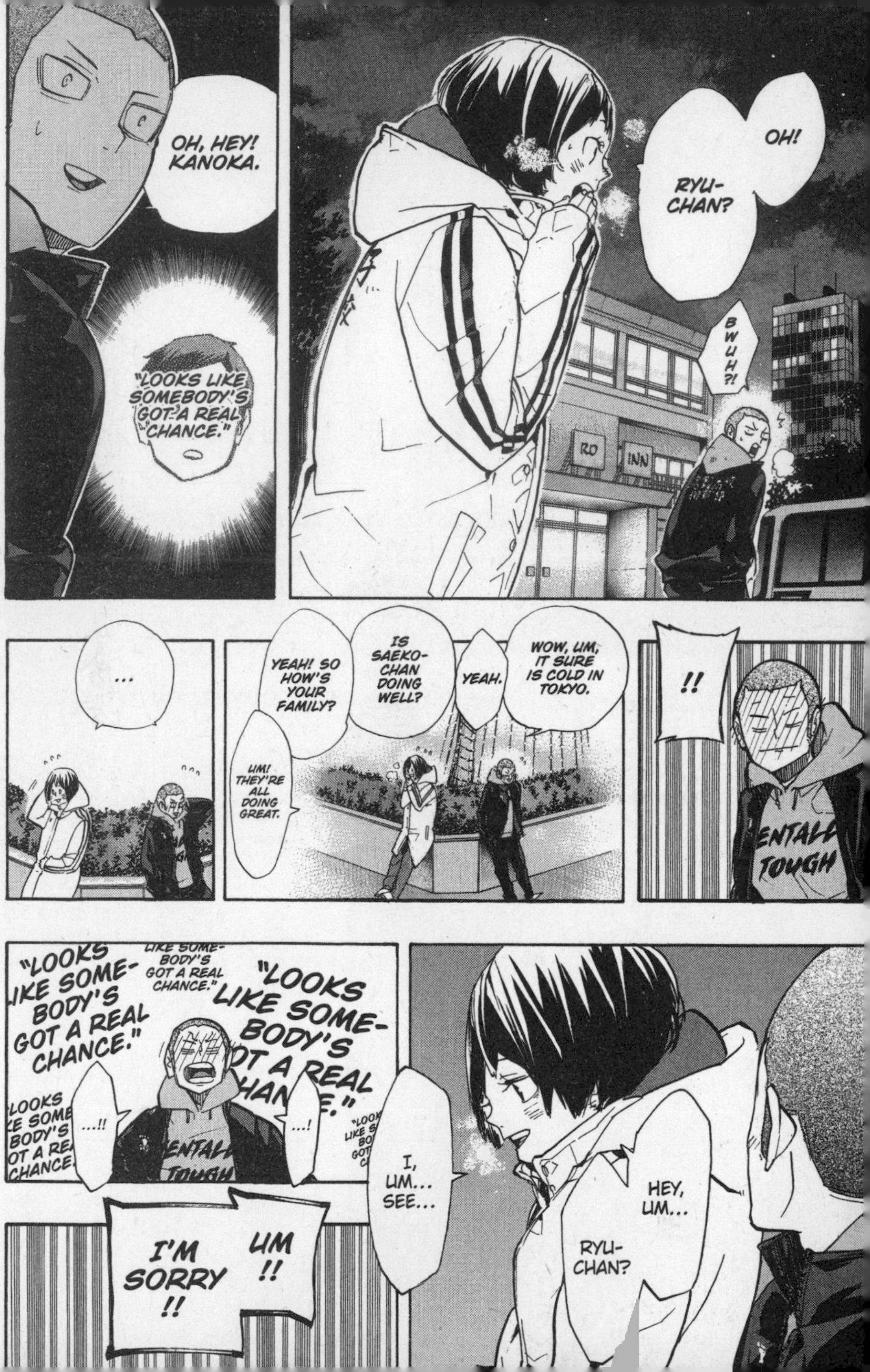
OH!
RYU-CHAN?
BWUH?!
RO
INN
OH, HEY! KANOKA.
"LOOKS LIKE SOMEBODY'S GOT A REAL CHANCE."
!!
WOW, UM, IT SURE IS COLD IN TOKYO.
YEAH.
IS SAEKO-CHAN DOING WELL?
YEAH! SO HOW'S YOUR FAMILY?
UM! THEY'RE ALL DOING GREAT.
...
HEY, UM...
RYU-CHAN?
I, UM... SEE...
"LOOKS LIKE SOME-BODY'S GOT A REAL CHANCE."
...!
...!!
"LOOKS LIKE SOME-BODY'S GOT A REAL CHANCE."
UM!!
I'M SORRY!!

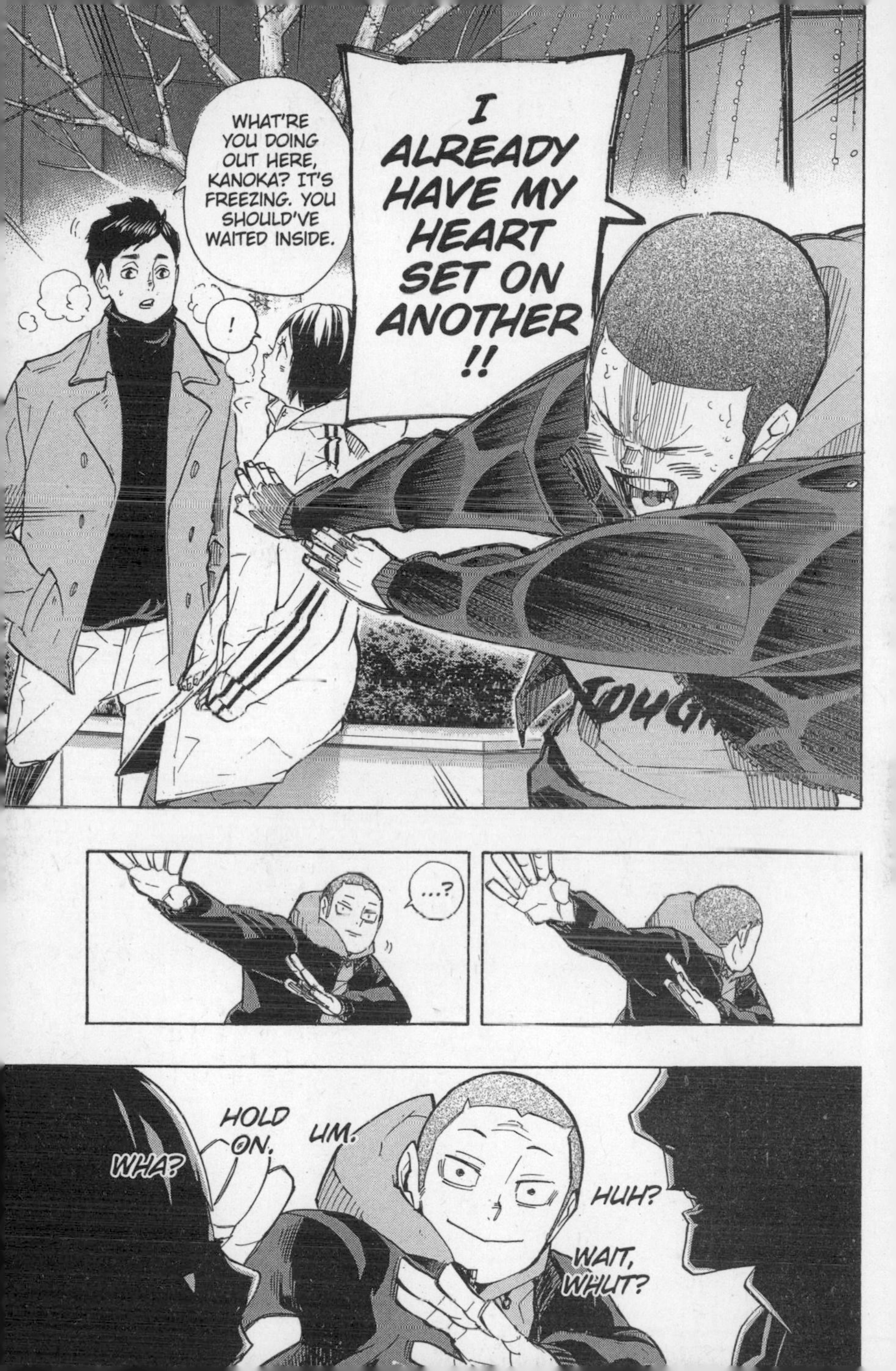
I ALREADY HAVE MY HEART SET ON ANOTHER!!
WHAT'RE YOU DOING OUT HERE, KANOKA? IT'S FREEZING. YOU SHOULD'VE WAITED INSIDE.
!
...?
HUH?
WAIT, WHUT?
UM.
HOLD ON.
WHA?

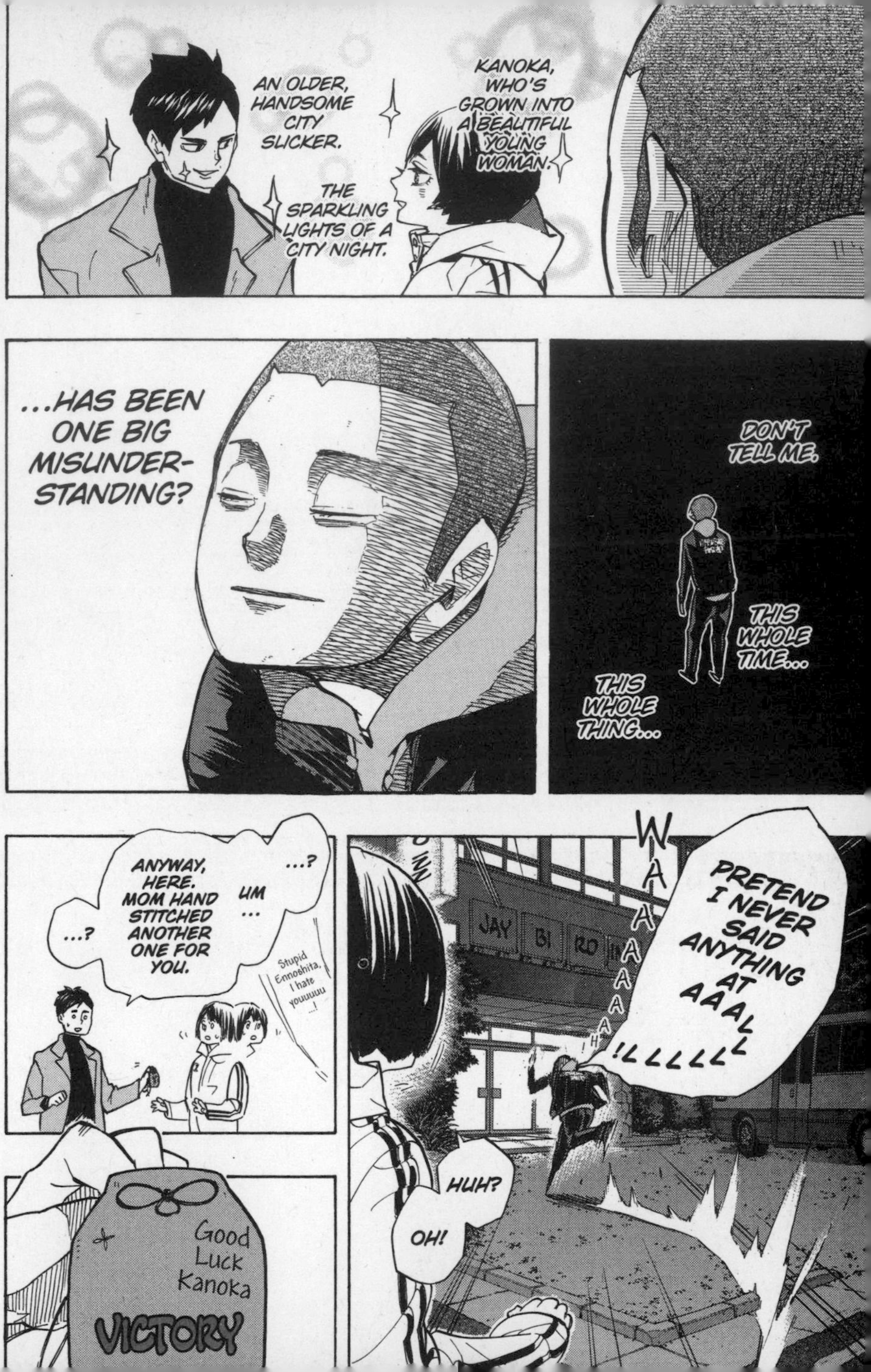
KANOKA, WHO'S GROWN INTO A BEAUTIFUL YOUNG WOMAN.
AN OLDER, HANDSOME CITY SLICKER.
THE SPARKLING LIGHTS OF A CITY NIGHT.
DON'T TELL ME.
THIS WHOLE TIME...
THIS WHOLE THING...
...HAS BEEN ONE BIG MISUNDER-STANDING?
WAAAAAAAH
PRETEND I NEVER SAID ANYTHING AT AAALLLLLLL!!
HUH?
OH!
...?
UM ...
ANYWAY, HERE. MOM HAND STITCHED ANOTHER ONE FOR YOU.
...?
Stupid Ennoshita, I hate youuuuu...!
Good Luck Kanoka
VICTORY

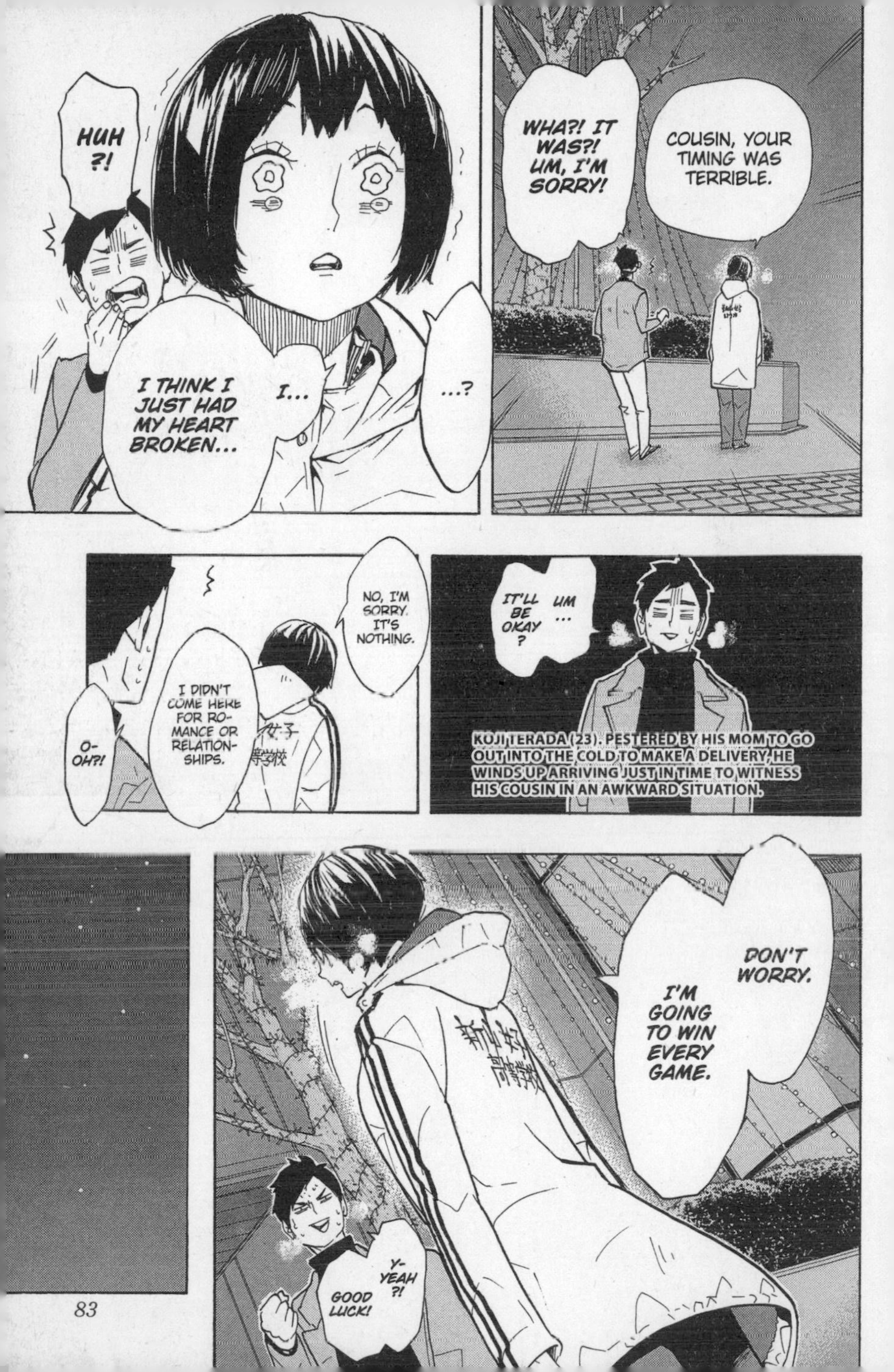
COUSIN, YOUR TIMING WAS TERRIBLE.
WHA?! IT WAS?! UM, I'M SORRY!
...?
I...
I THINK I JUST HAD MY HEART BROKEN...
HUH ?!
UM ...
IT'LL BE OKAY ?
KOJI TERADA (23). PESTERED BY HIS MOM TO GO OUT INTO THE COLD TO MAKE A DELIVERY, HE WINDS UP ARRIVING JUST IN TIME TO WITNESS HIS COUSIN IN AN AWKWARD SITUATION.
NO, I'M SORRY. IT'S NOTHING.
I DIDN'T COME HERE FOR RO-MANCE OR RELATION-SHIPS.
O-OH?!
DON'T WORRY.
I'M GOING TO WIN EVERY GAME.
Y-YEAH ?!
GOOD LUCK!

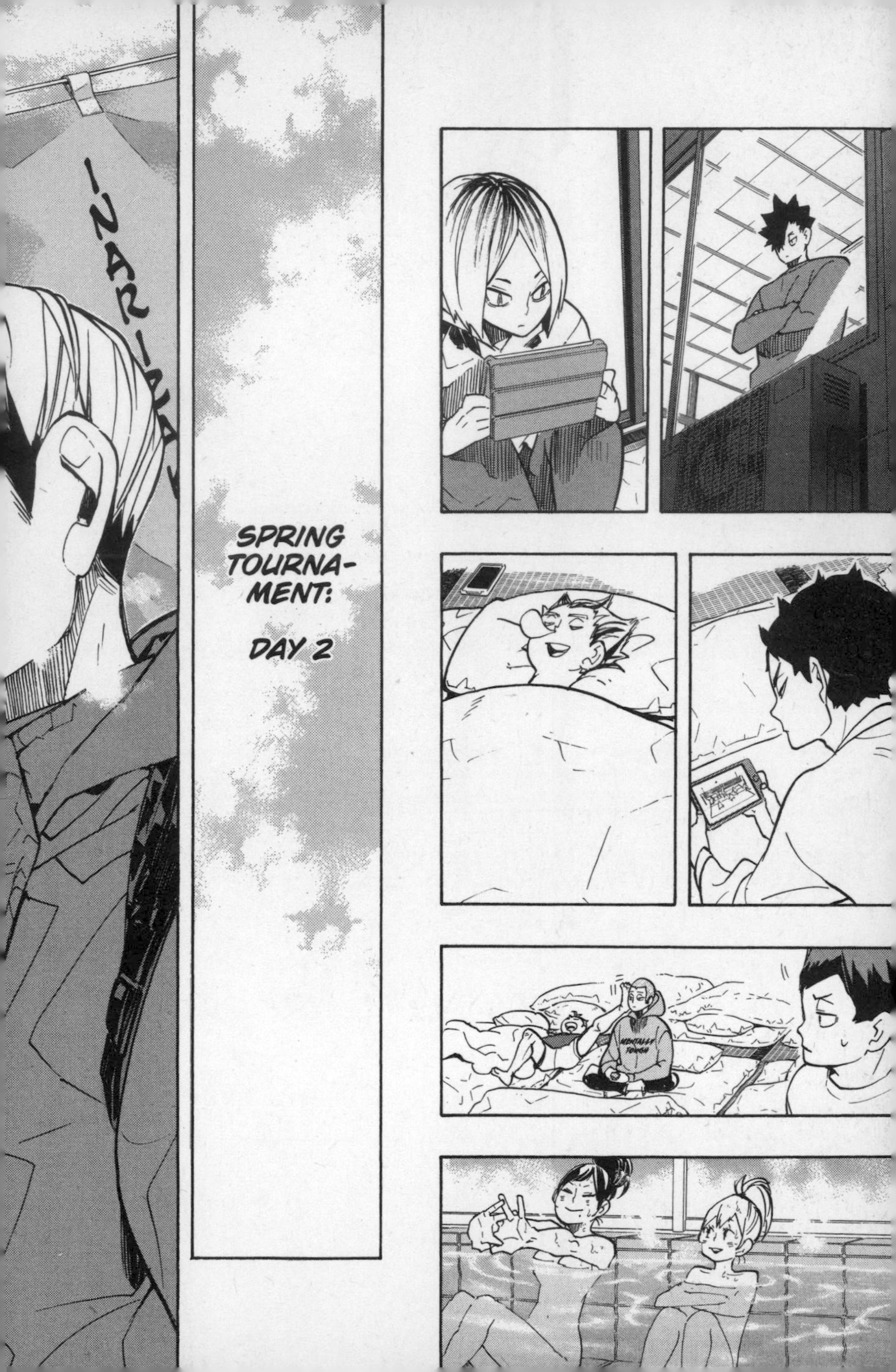
MENTALLY TOUGH
SPRING TOURNAMENT:
DAY 2
INARI

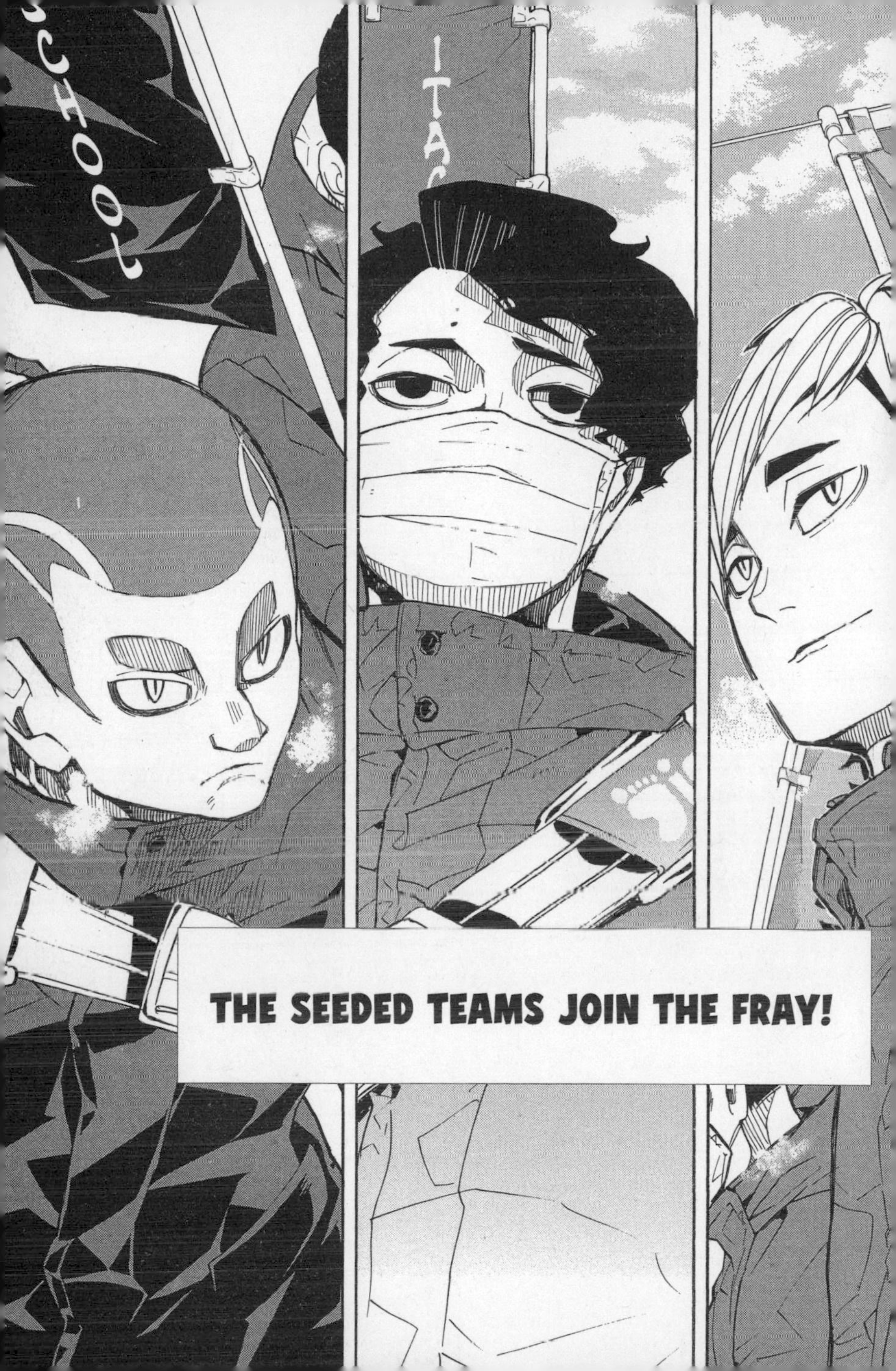
THE SEEDED TEAMS JOIN THE FRAY!

KANOKA AMANAI

NIIYAMA GIRLS' HIGH SCHOOL CLASS 2-7

POSITION:
WING SPIKER

HEIGHT: 5'9"

WEIGHT: 138 LBS.
(AS OF JANUARY, 2ND YEAR OF HIGH SCHOOL)

BIRTHDAY: OCTOBER 24

FAVORITE FOOD:
TUNA RICE BALLS

CURRENT WORRY:
SHE DOESN'T SEEM TO BE GETTING MUCH BETTER AT BUMPING SERVES, AND SHE CAN'T SEEM TO CONVINCE HERSELF THAT SHE'S ANY GOOD AT LINE SHOTS, AND SHE'S HAVING A HARD TIME GETTING OVER HER SHYNESS, OH, AND... (ETC.)

ABILITY PARAMETERS
(5-POINT SCALE)

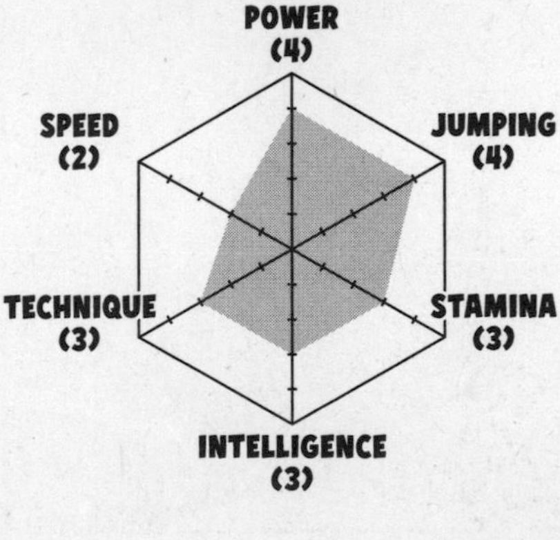
POWER (4)
JUMPING (4)
STAMINA (3)
INTELLIGENCE (3)
TECHNIQUE (3)
SPEED (2)

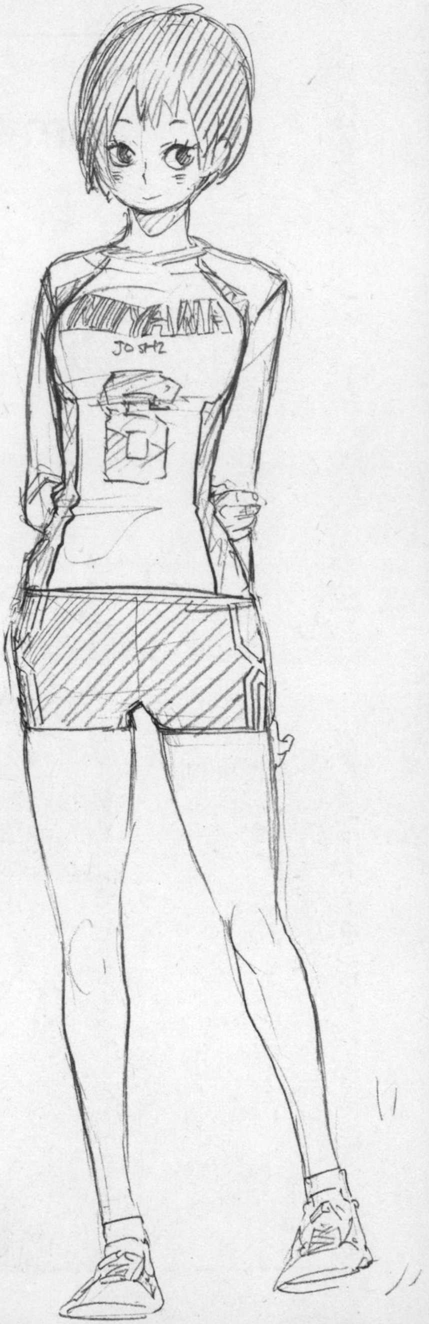
NIIYAMA

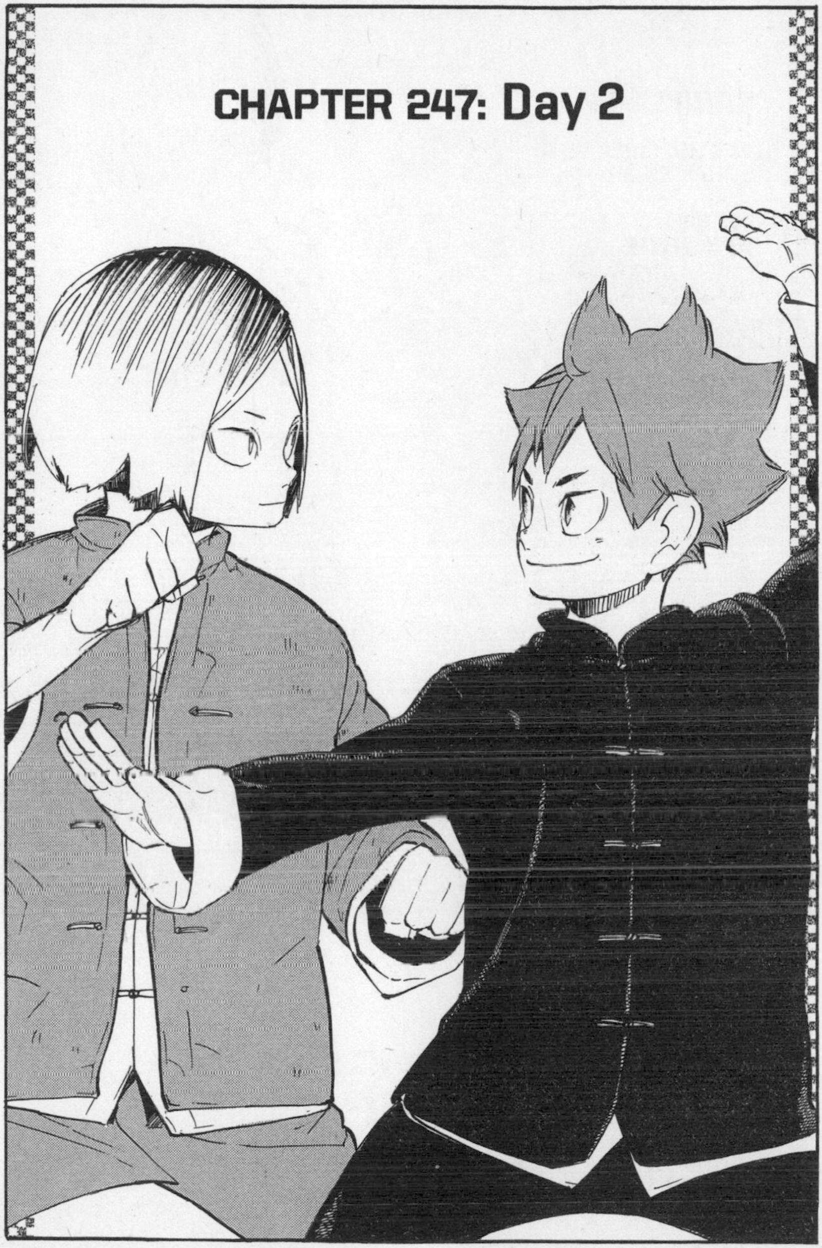
CHAPTER 247: Day 2

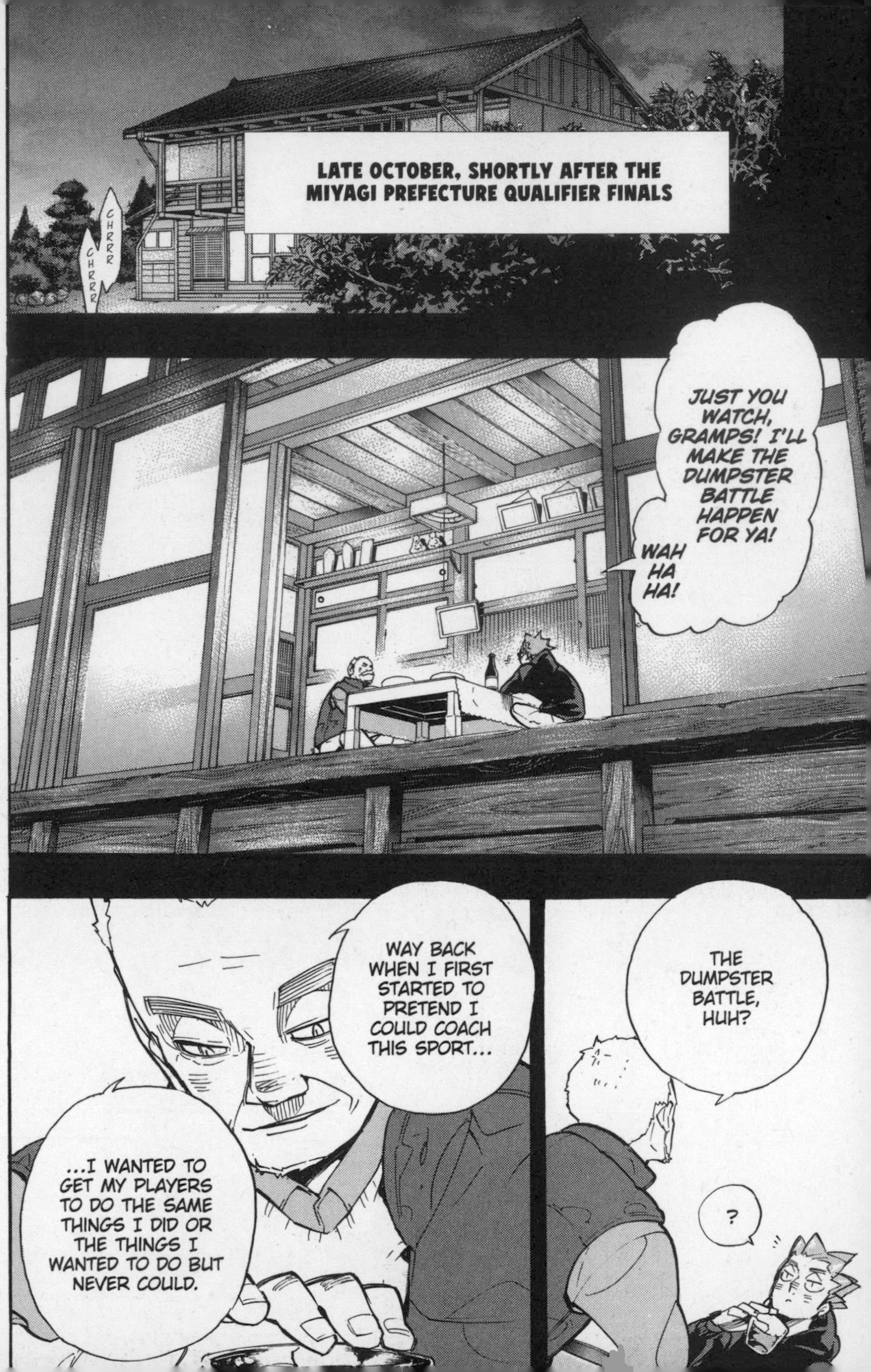
LATE OCTOBER, SHORTLY AFTER THE MIYAGI PREFECTURE QUALIFIER FINALS
CHRRR
CHRRR
JUST YOU WATCH, GRAMPS! I'LL MAKE THE DUMPSTER BATTLE HAPPEN FOR YA!
WAH HA HA!
THE DUMPSTER BATTLE, HUH?
?
WAY BACK WHEN I FIRST STARTED TO PRETEND I COULD COACH THIS SPORT...
...I WANTED TO GET MY PLAYERS TO DO THE SAME THINGS I DID OR THE THINGS I WANTED TO DO BUT NEVER COULD.

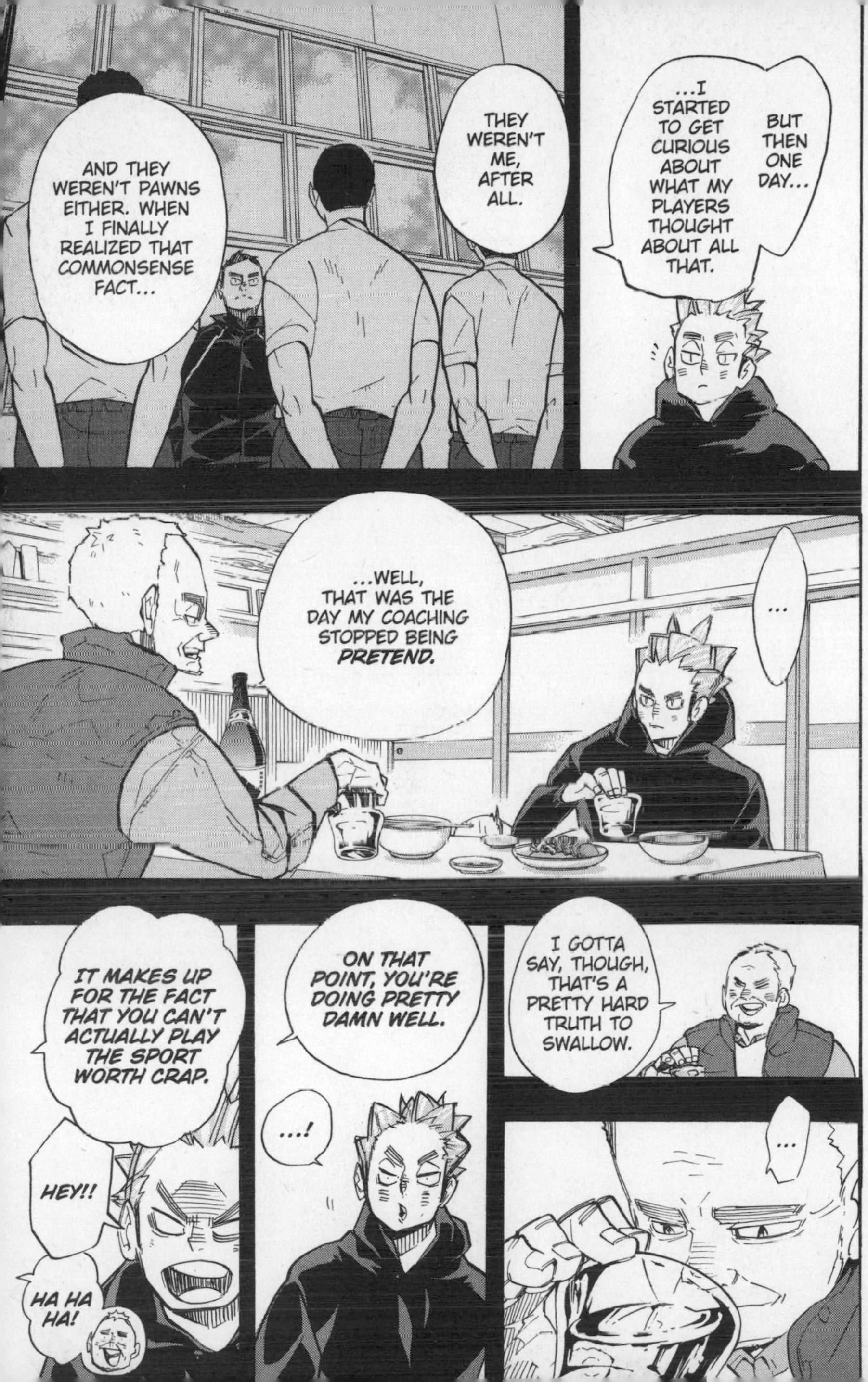
BUT THEN ONE DAY...
...I STARTED TO GET CURIOUS ABOUT WHAT MY PLAYERS THOUGHT ABOUT ALL THAT.
THEY WEREN'T ME, AFTER ALL.
AND THEY WEREN'T PAWNS EITHER. WHEN I FINALLY REALIZED THAT COMMONSENSE FACT...
...
...WELL, THAT WAS THE DAY MY COACHING STOPPED BEING *PRETEND.*
I GOTTA SAY, THOUGH, THAT'S A PRETTY HARD TRUTH TO SWALLOW.
ON THAT POINT, YOU'RE DOING PRETTY DAMN WELL.
IT MAKES UP FOR THE FACT THAT YOU CAN'T ACTUALLY PLAY THE SPORT WORTH CRAP.
...
...!
HEY!!
HA HA HA!

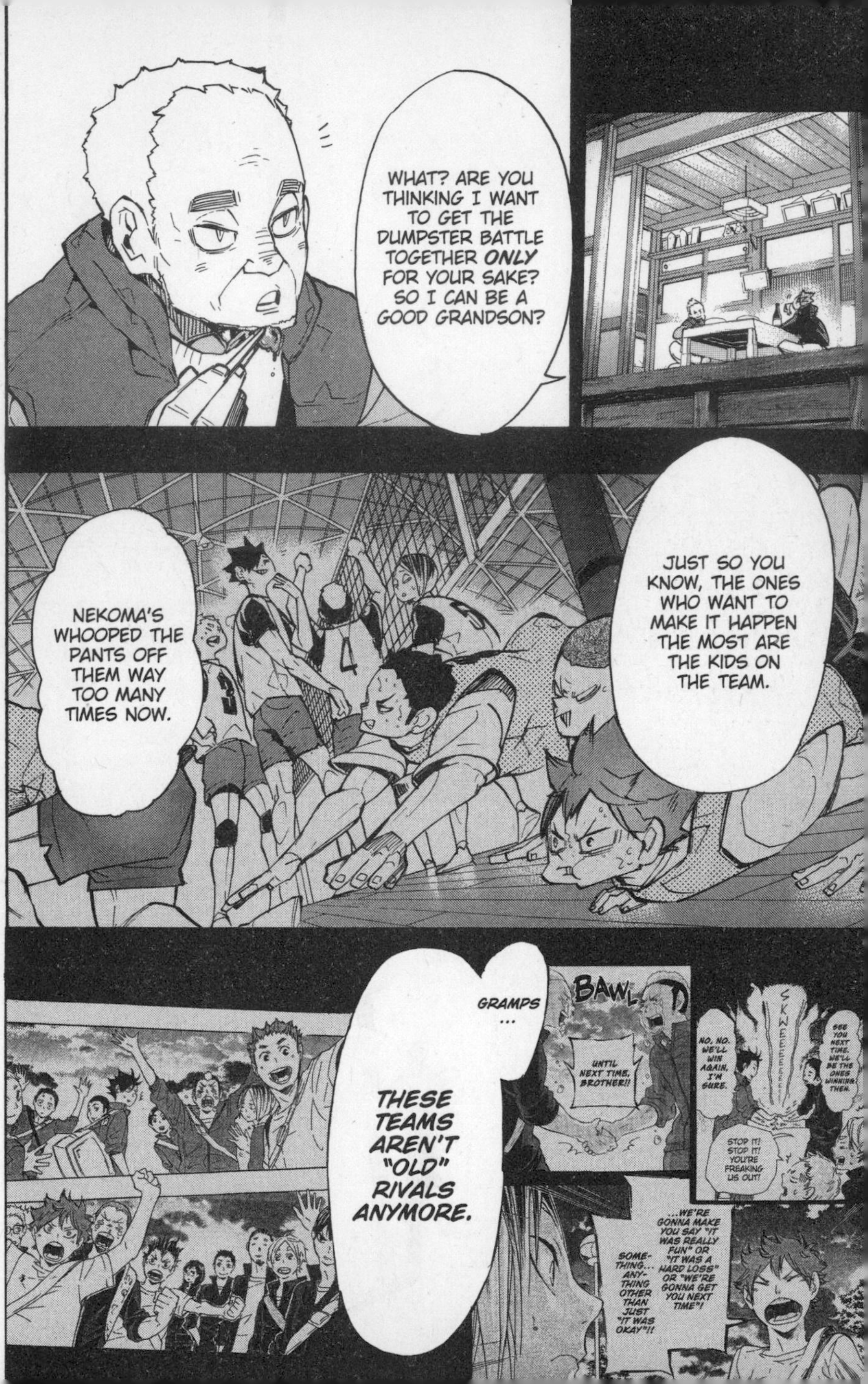
WHAT? ARE YOU THINKING I WANT TO GET THE DUMPSTER BATTLE TOGETHER ONLY FOR YOUR SAKE? SO I CAN BE A GOOD GRANDSON?
JUST SO YOU KNOW, THE ONES WHO WANT TO MAKE IT HAPPEN THE MOST ARE THE KIDS ON THE TEAM.
NEKOMA'S WHOOPED THE PANTS OFF THEM WAY TOO MANY TIMES NOW.
SEE YOU NEXT TIME. WE'LL BE THE ONES WINNING THEN.
SKWEEEEEEE
NO, NO. WE'LL WIN AGAIN, I'M SURE.
STOP IT! STOP IT! YOU'RE FREAKING US OUT!
BAWL
UNTIL NEXT TIME, BROTHER!!
GRAMPS...
THESE TEAMS AREN'T "OLD" RIVALS ANYMORE.
...WE'RE GONNA MAKE YOU SAY "IT WAS REALLY FUN" OR "IT WAS A HARD LOSS" OR "WE'RE GONNA GET YOU NEXT TIME"!
SOME-THING... ANY-THING OTHER THAN JUST "IT WAS OKAY"!!

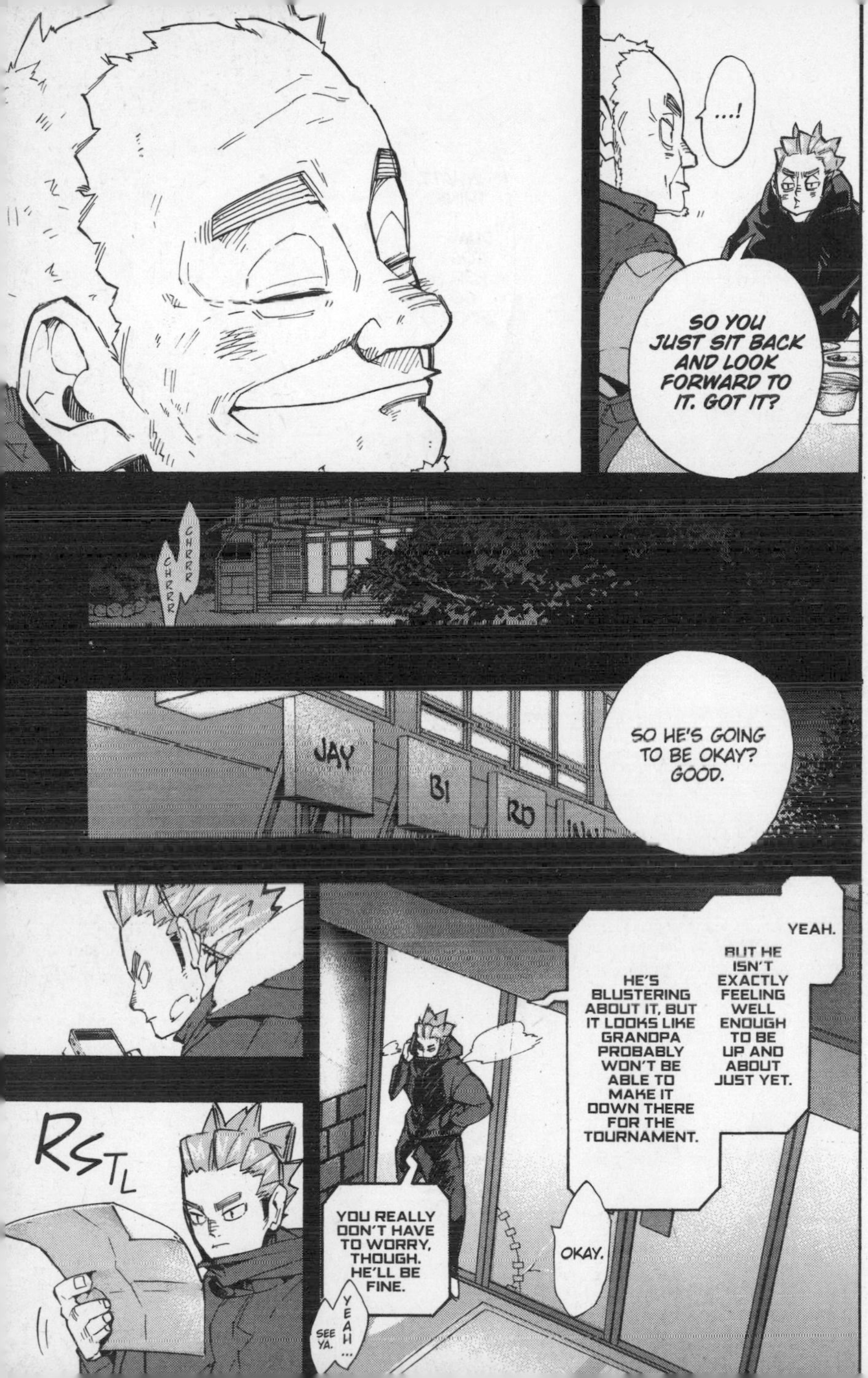
...!
SO YOU JUST SIT BACK AND LOOK FORWARD TO IT. GOT IT?
CHRRR CHRRR
JAY
BI
RD
SO HE'S GOING TO BE OKAY? GOOD.
YEAH.
BUT HE ISN'T EXACTLY FEELING WELL ENOUGH TO BE UP AND ABOUT JUST YET.
HE'S BLUSTERING ABOUT IT, BUT IT LOOKS LIKE GRANDPA PROBABLY WON'T BE ABLE TO MAKE IT DOWN THERE FOR THE TOURNAMENT.
OKAY.
YOU REALLY DON'T HAVE TO WORRY, THOUGH. HE'LL BE FINE.
YEAH...
SEE YA.
RSTL

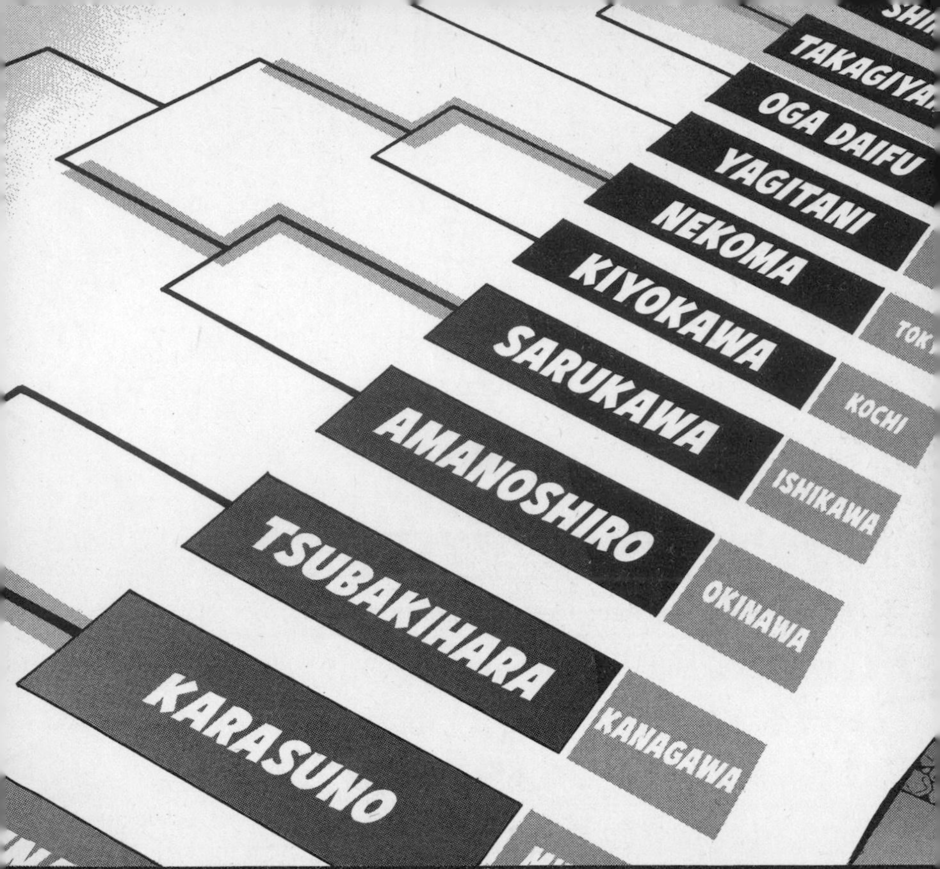
OGA DAIFU
YAGITANI
NEKOMA
KIYOKAWA
KOCHI
SARUKAWA
ISHIKAWA
AMANOSHIRO
OKINAWA
TSUBAKIHARA
KANAGAWA
KARASUNO

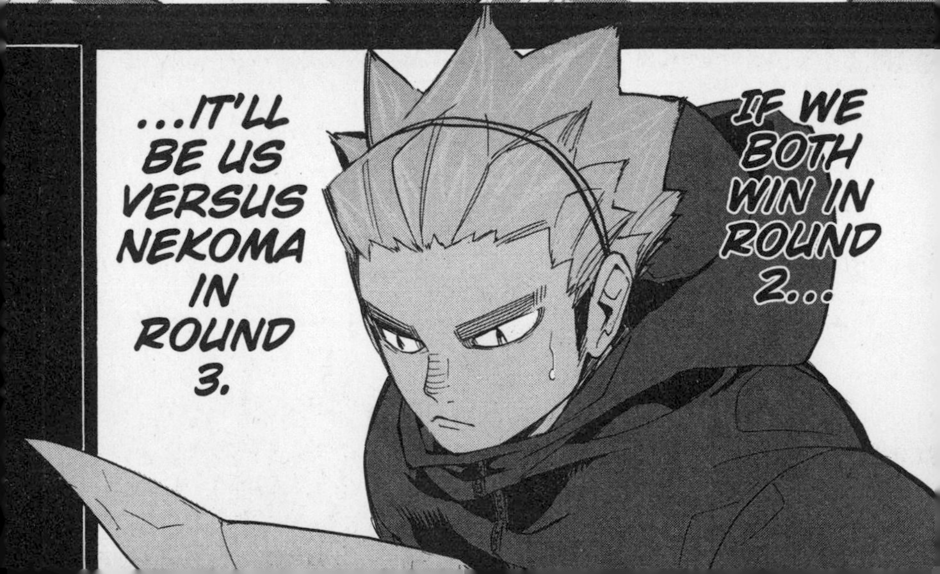
IF WE BOTH WIN IN ROUND 2...
...IT'LL BE US VERSUS NEKOMA IN ROUND 3.

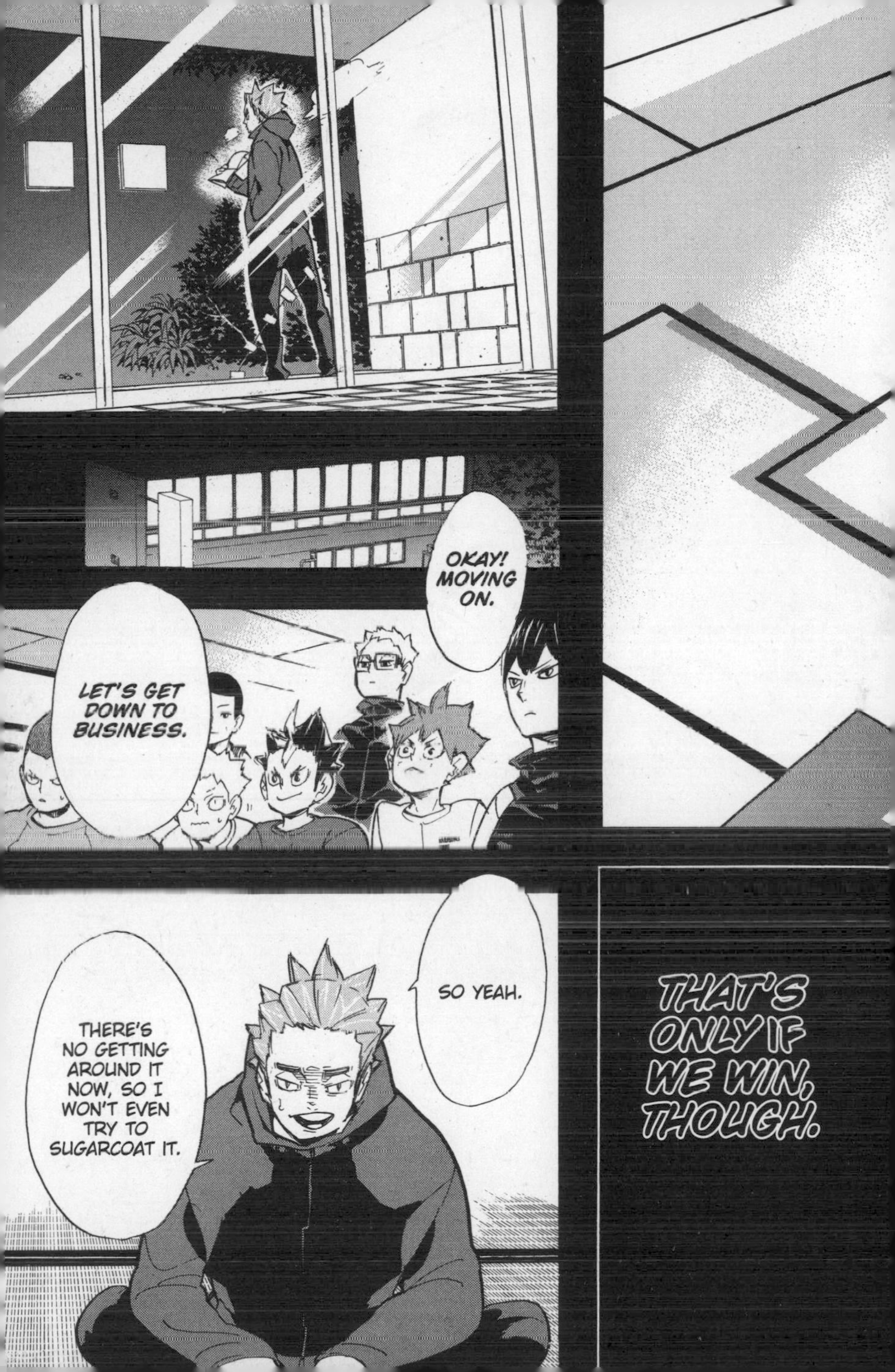
OKAY! MOVING ON.
LET'S GET DOWN TO BUSINESS.
THAT'S ONLY IF WE WIN, THOUGH.
SO YEAH.
THERE'S NO GETTING AROUND IT NOW, SO I WON'T EVEN TRY TO SUGARCOAT IT.

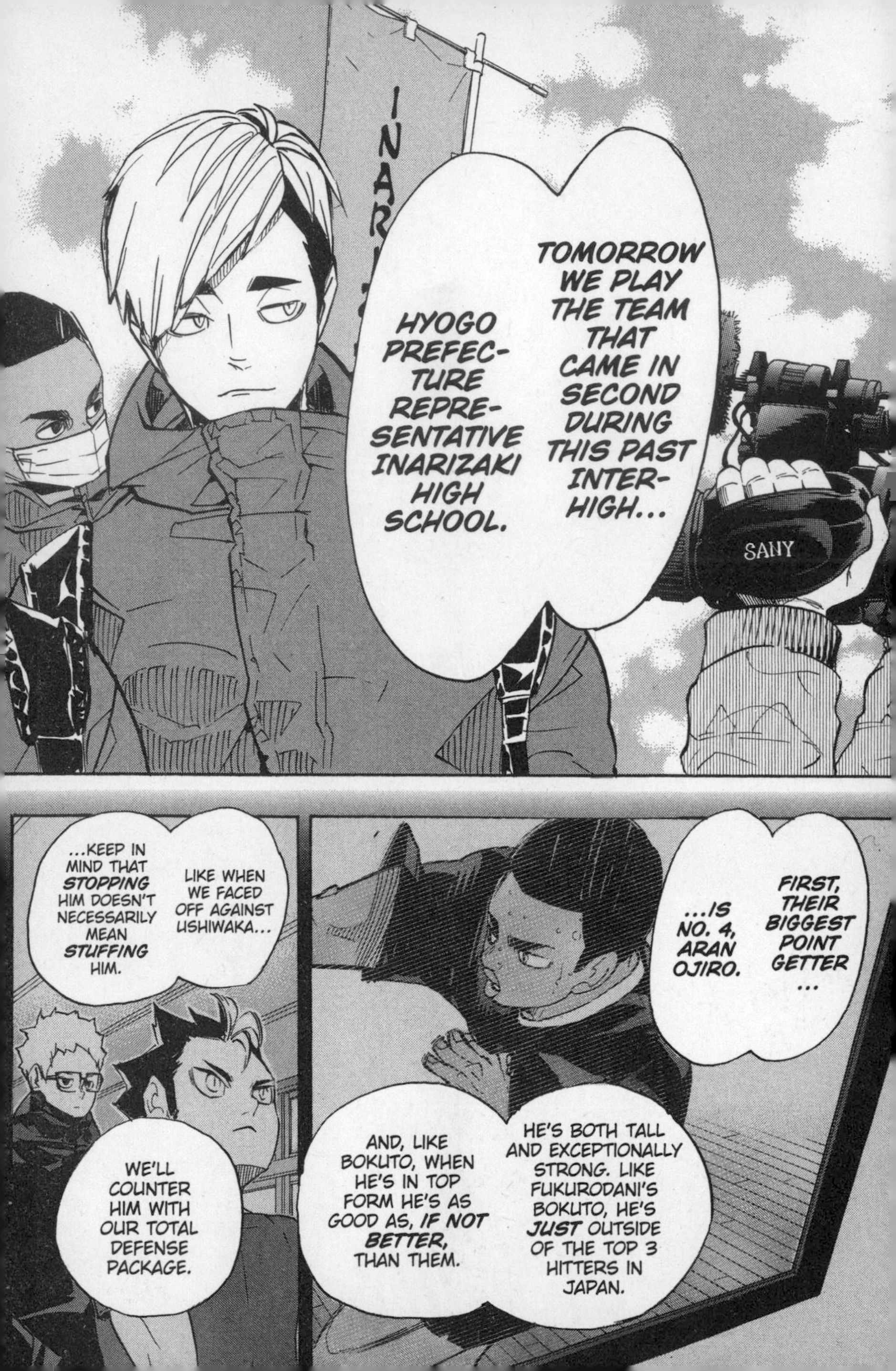
INARI
TOMORROW WE PLAY THE TEAM THAT CAME IN SECOND DURING THIS PAST INTER-HIGH...
HYOGO PREFECTURE REPRESENTATIVE INARIZAKI HIGH SCHOOL.
SANY
FIRST, THEIR BIGGEST POINT GETTER...
...IS NO. 4, ARAN OJIRO.
HE'S BOTH TALL AND EXCEPTIONALLY STRONG. LIKE FUKURODANI'S BOKUTO, HE'S JUST OUTSIDE OF THE TOP 3 HITTERS IN JAPAN.
AND, LIKE BOKUTO, WHEN HE'S IN TOP FORM HE'S AS GOOD AS, IF NOT BETTER, THAN THEM.
LIKE WHEN WE FACED OFF AGAINST USHIWAKA...
...KEEP IN MIND THAT STOPPING HIM DOESN'T NECESSARILY MEAN STUFFING HIM.
WE'LL COUNTER HIM WITH OUR TOTAL DEFENSE PACKAGE.

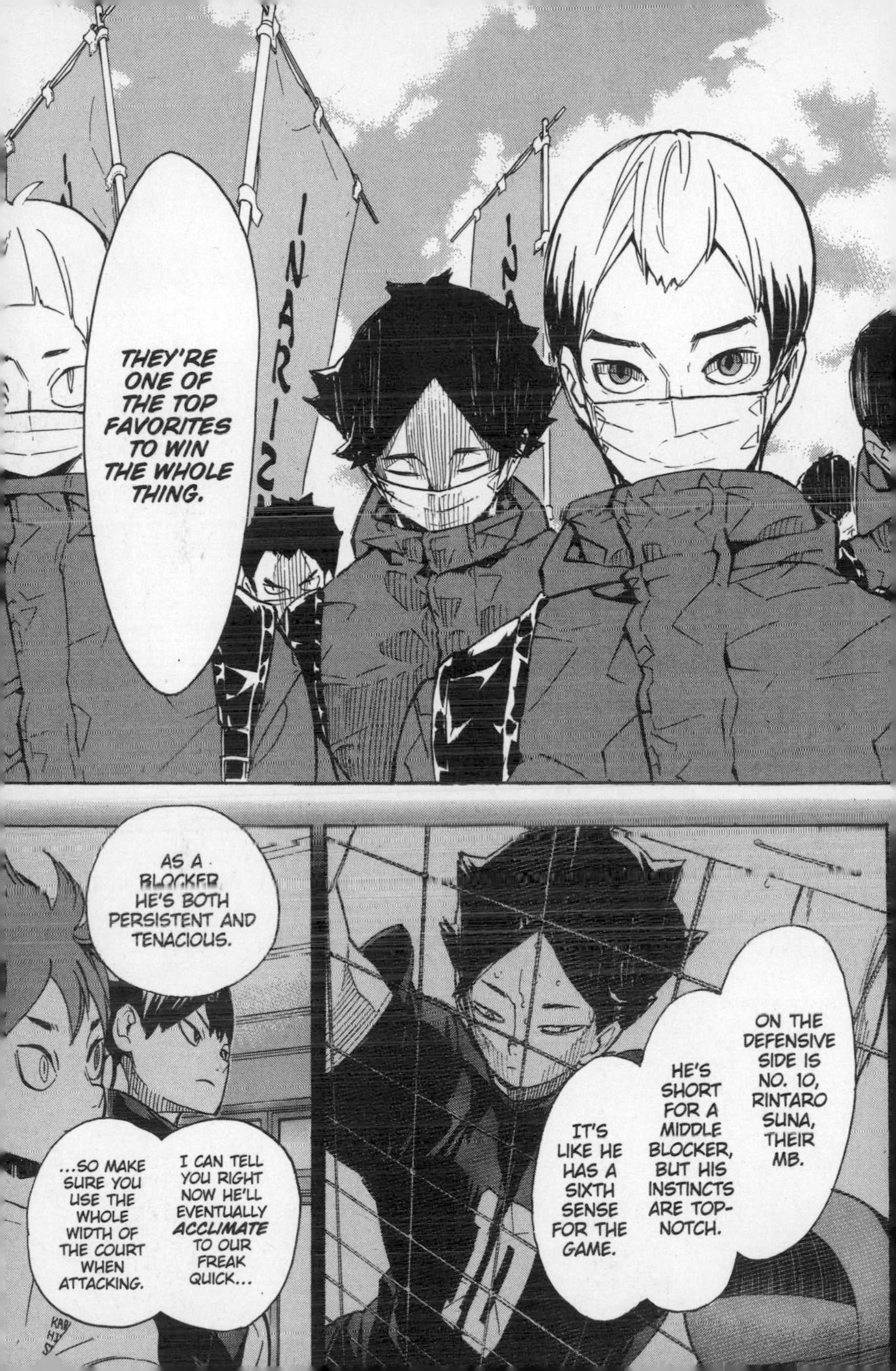
THEY'RE ONE OF THE TOP FAVORITES TO WIN THE WHOLE THING.
ON THE DEFENSIVE SIDE IS NO. 10, RINTARO SUNA, THEIR MB.
HE'S SHORT FOR A MIDDLE BLOCKER, BUT HIS INSTINCTS ARE TOP-NOTCH.
IT'S LIKE HE HAS A SIXTH SENSE FOR THE GAME.
AS A BLOCKER HE'S BOTH PERSISTENT AND TENACIOUS.
I CAN TELL YOU RIGHT NOW HE'LL EVENTUALLY ACCLIMATE TO OUR FREAK QUICK...
...SO MAKE SURE YOU USE THE WHOLE WIDTH OF THE COURT WHEN ATTACKING.

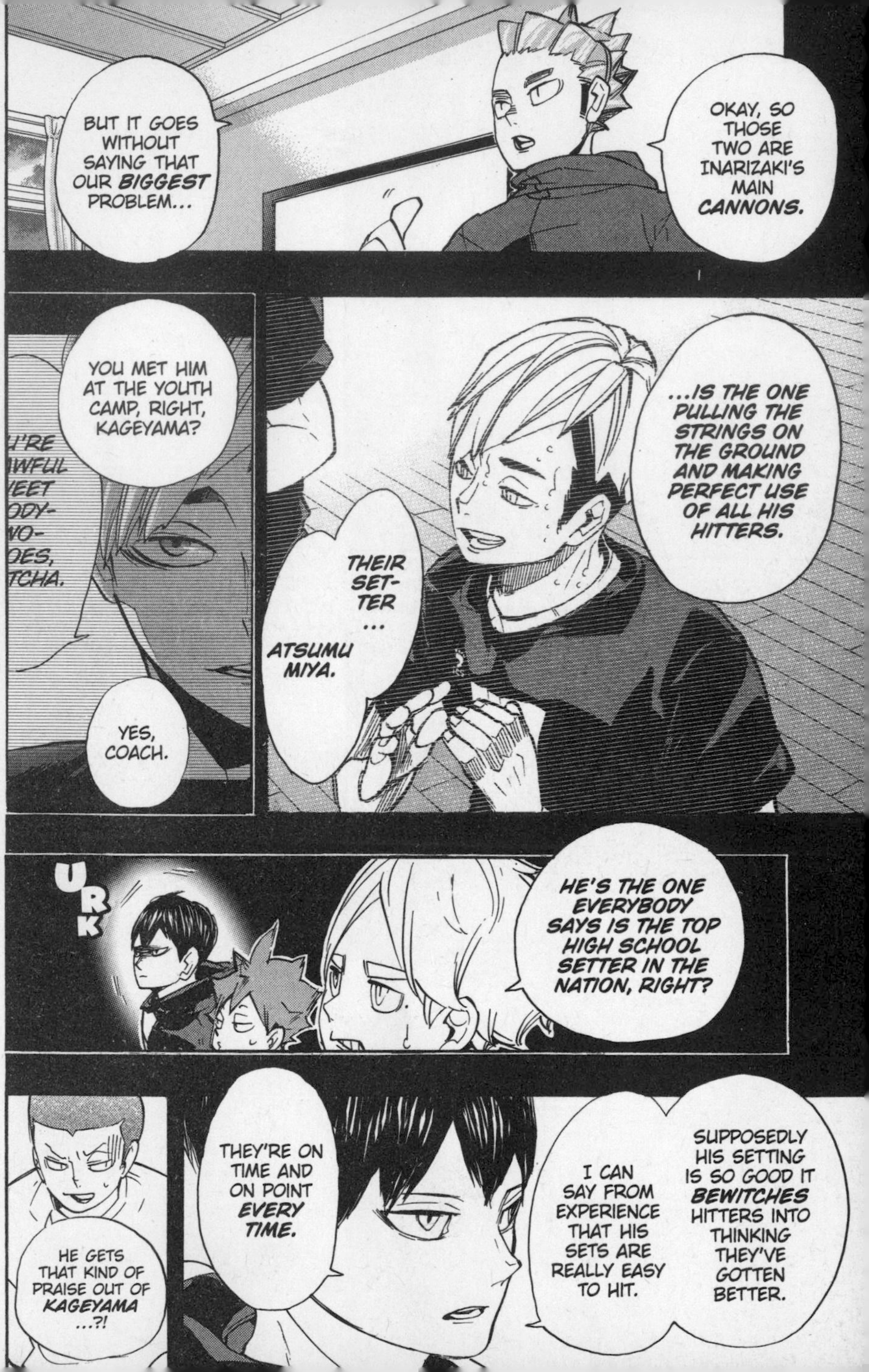
OKAY, SO THOSE TWO ARE INARIZAKI'S MAIN CANNONS.
BUT IT GOES WITHOUT SAYING THAT OUR BIGGEST PROBLEM...
...IS THE ONE PULLING THE STRINGS ON THE GROUND AND MAKING PERFECT USE OF ALL HIS HITTERS.
THEIR SETTER... ATSUMU MIYA.
YOU MET HIM AT THE YOUTH CAMP, RIGHT, KAGEYAMA?
YES, COACH.
HE'S THE ONE EVERYBODY SAYS IS THE TOP HIGH SCHOOL SETTER IN THE NATION, RIGHT?
URK
SUPPOSEDLY HIS SETTING IS SO GOOD IT BEWITCHES HITTERS INTO THINKING THEY'VE GOTTEN BETTER.
I CAN SAY FROM EXPERIENCE THAT HIS SETS ARE REALLY EASY TO HIT.
THEY'RE ON TIME AND ON POINT EVERY TIME.
HE GETS THAT KIND OF PRAISE OUT OF KAGEYAMA...?!

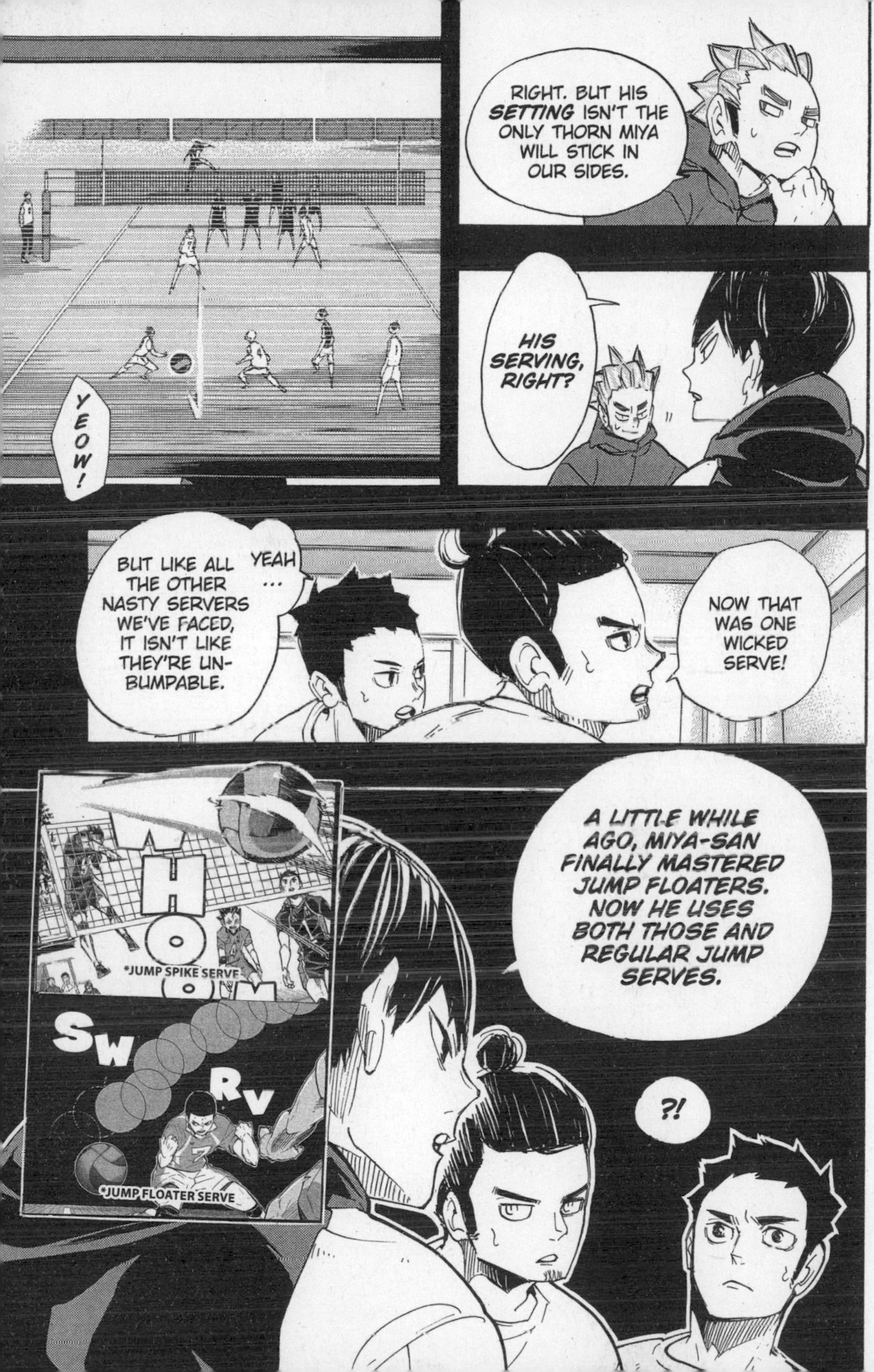
RIGHT. BUT HIS SETTING ISN'T THE ONLY THORN MIYA WILL STICK IN OUR SIDES.
HIS SERVING, RIGHT?
YEOW!
NOW THAT WAS ONE WICKED SERVE!
YEAH ...
BUT LIKE ALL THE OTHER NASTY SERVERS WE'VE FACED, IT ISN'T LIKE THEY'RE UN-BUMPABLE.
A LITTLE WHILE AGO, MIYA-SAN FINALLY MASTERED JUMP FLOATERS. NOW HE USES BOTH THOSE AND REGULAR JUMP SERVES.
WHOOM
*JUMP SPIKE SERVE
SWRV
*JUMP FLOATER SERVE
?!

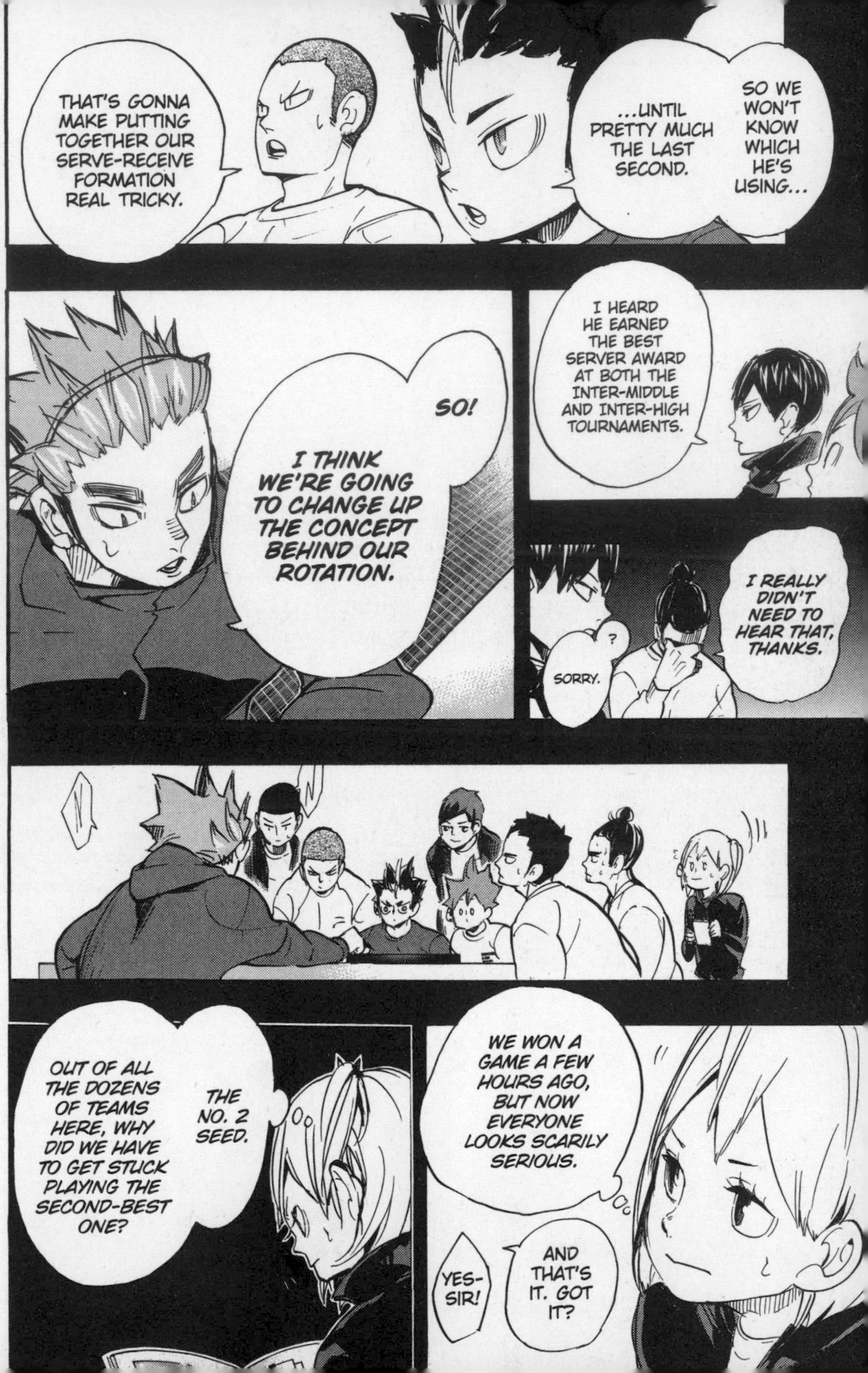
SO WE WON'T KNOW WHICH HE'S USING...
...UNTIL PRETTY MUCH THE LAST SECOND.
THAT'S GONNA MAKE PUTTING TOGETHER OUR SERVE-RECEIVE FORMATION REAL TRICKY.
I HEARD HE EARNED THE BEST SERVER AWARD AT BOTH THE INTER-MIDDLE AND INTER-HIGH TOURNAMENTS.
I REALLY DIDN'T NEED TO HEAR THAT, THANKS.
?
SORRY.
SO!
I THINK WE'RE GOING TO CHANGE UP THE CONCEPT BEHIND OUR ROTATION.
WE WON A GAME A FEW HOURS AGO, BUT NOW EVERYONE LOOKS SCARILY SERIOUS.
AND THAT'S IT. GOT IT?
YES-SIR!
THE NO. 2 SEED.
OUT OF ALL THE DOZENS OF TEAMS HERE, WHY DID WE HAVE TO GET STUCK PLAYING THE SECOND-BEST ONE?

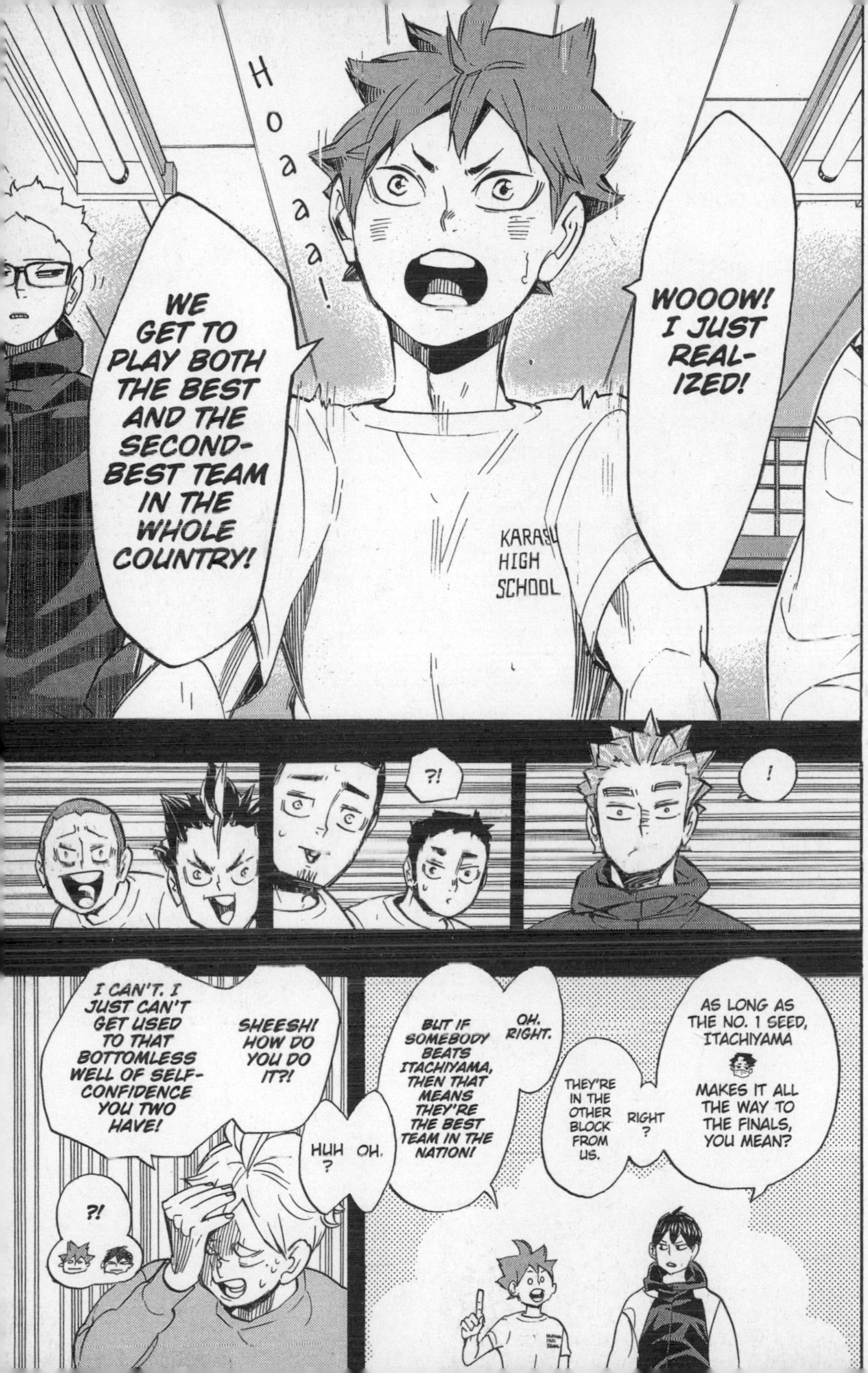

Hoaaa!
WOOOW! I JUST REAL-IZED!
WE GET TO PLAY BOTH THE BEST AND THE SECOND-BEST TEAM IN THE WHOLE COUNTRY!
KARASU HIGH SCHOOL
!
?!
AS LONG AS THE NO. 1 SEED, ITACHIYAMA MAKES IT ALL THE WAY TO THE FINALS, YOU MEAN?
THEY'RE IN THE OTHER BLOCK FROM US.
RIGHT?
OH. RIGHT.
BUT IF SOMEBODY BEATS ITACHIYAMA, THEN THAT MEANS THEY'RE THE BEST TEAM IN THE NATION!
HUH?
OH.
SHEESH! HOW DO YOU DO IT?!
I CAN'T. I JUST CAN'T GET USED TO THAT BOTTOMLESS WELL OF SELF-CONFIDENCE YOU TWO HAVE!
?!

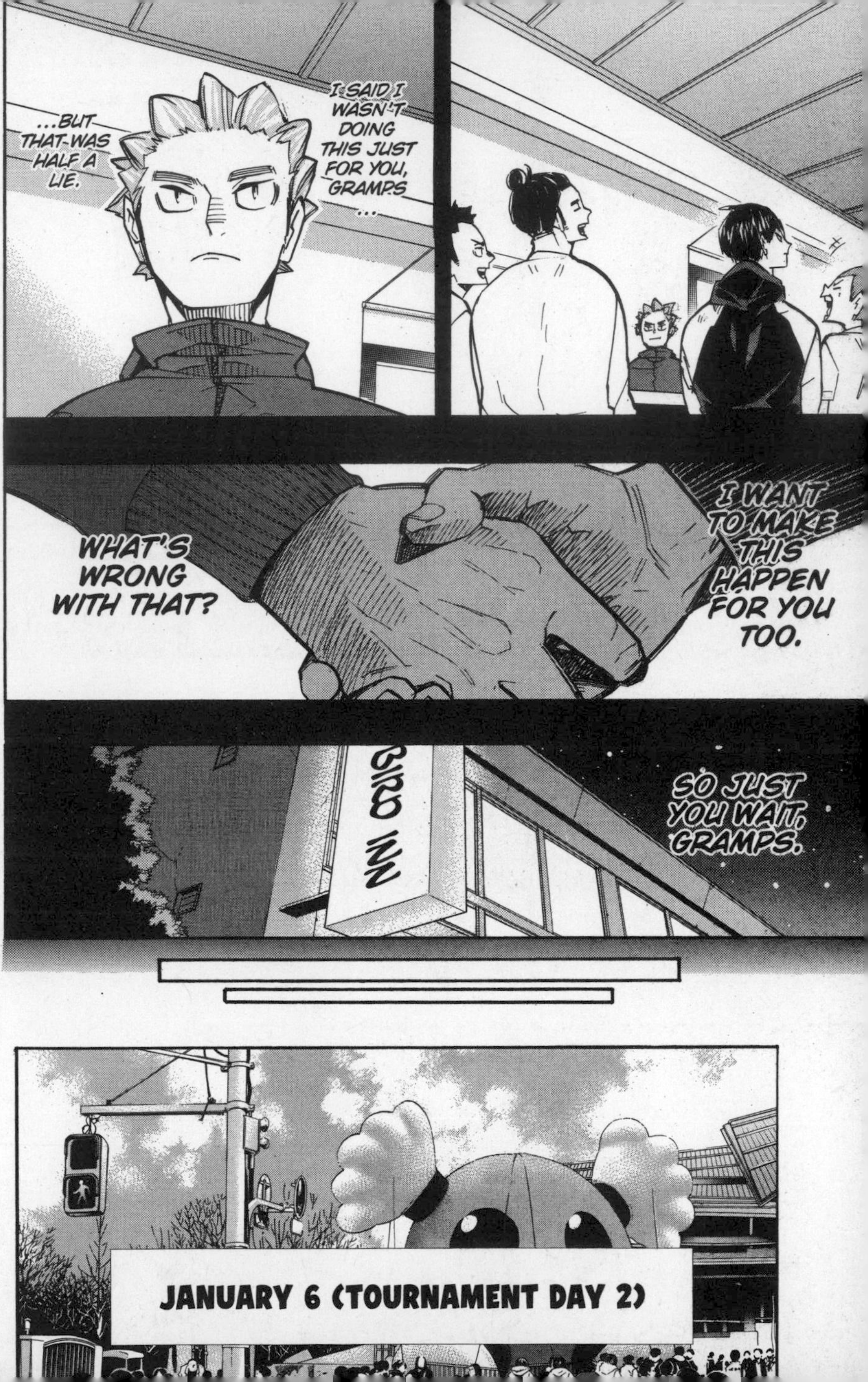
I SAID I WASN'T DOING THIS JUST FOR YOU, GRAMPS...
...BUT THAT WAS HALF A LIE.
I WANT TO MAKE THIS HAPPEN FOR YOU TOO.
WHAT'S WRONG WITH THAT?
SO JUST YOU WAIT, GRAMPS.
JANUARY 6 (TOURNAMENT DAY 2)

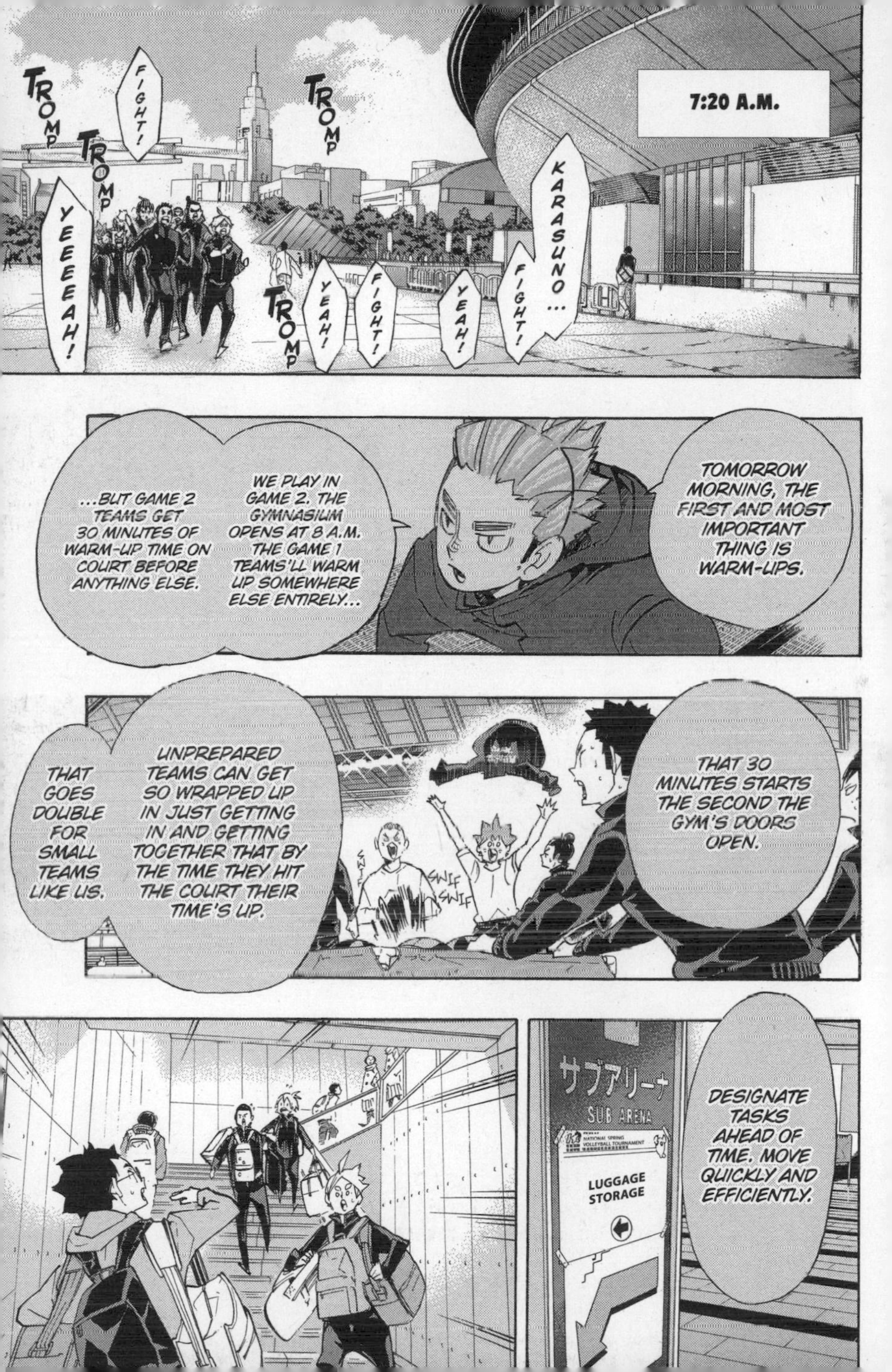
7:20 A.M.
KARASUNO...
FIGHT!
TROMP
YEAH!
FIGHT!
YEAH!
TROMP
FIGHT!
TROMP
TROMP
YEEEEAH!
TOMORROW MORNING, THE FIRST AND MOST IMPORTANT THING IS WARM-UPS.
WE PLAY IN GAME 2. THE GYMNASIUM OPENS AT 8 A.M. THE GAME 1 TEAMS'LL WARM UP SOMEWHERE ELSE ENTIRELY...
...BUT GAME 2 TEAMS GET 30 MINUTES OF WARM-UP TIME ON COURT BEFORE ANYTHING ELSE.
THAT 30 MINUTES STARTS THE SECOND THE GYM'S DOORS OPEN.
SWIF SWIF
SWIF
UNPREPARED TEAMS CAN GET SO WRAPPED UP IN JUST GETTING IN AND GETTING TOGETHER THAT BY THE TIME THEY HIT THE COURT THEIR TIME'S UP.
THAT GOES DOUBLE FOR SMALL TEAMS LIKE US.
サブアリーナ
SUB ARENA
NATIONAL SPRING VOLLEYBALL TOURNAMENT
LUGGAGE STORAGE
DESIGNATE TASKS AHEAD OF TIME. MOVE QUICKLY AND EFFICIENTLY.

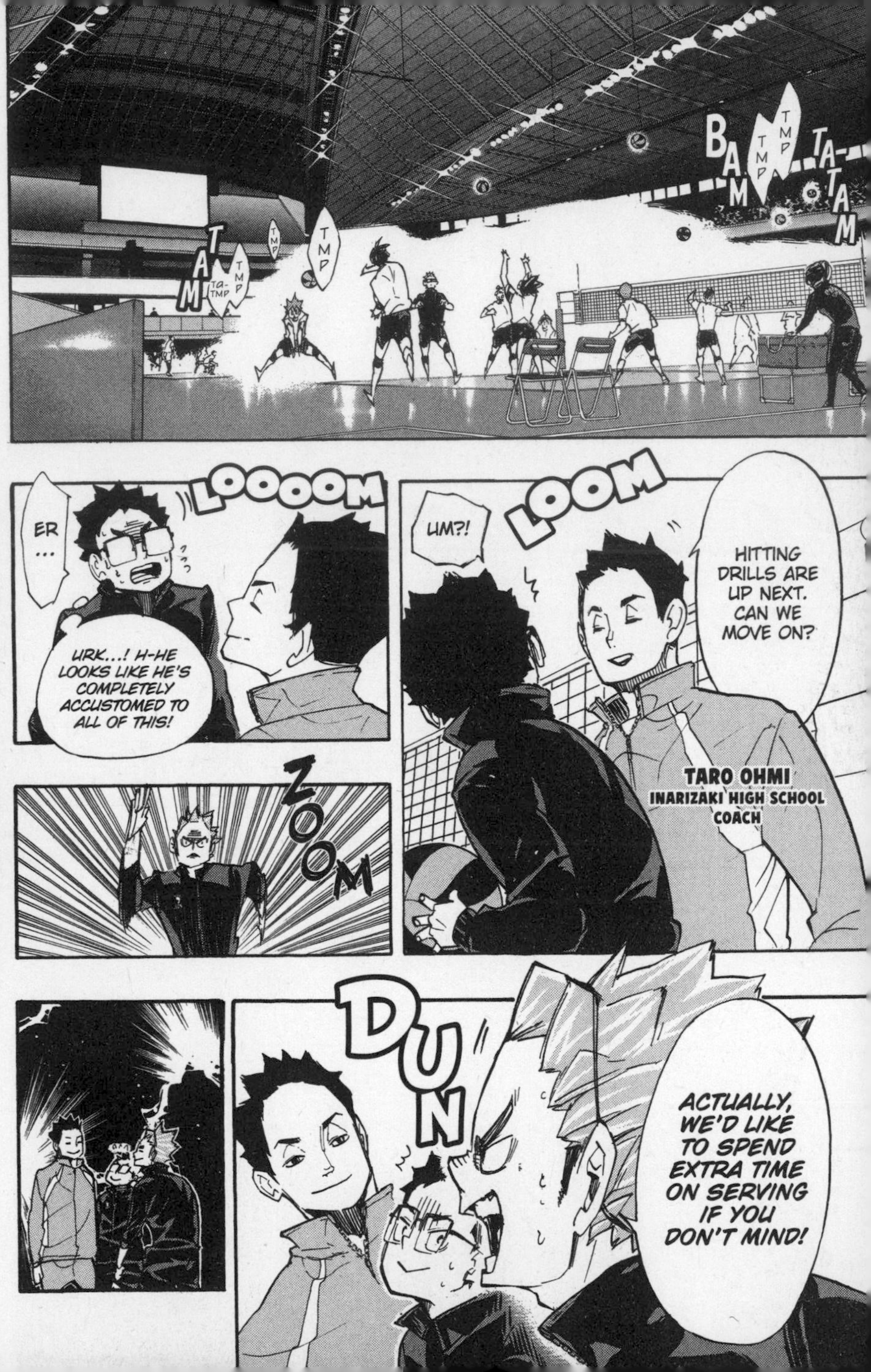
BAM
TMP
TMP
TA-TA-TAM
TMP
TMP
TAM
TA-TMP
TMP
HITTING DRILLS ARE UP NEXT. CAN WE MOVE ON?
LOOM
UM?!
TARO OHMI
INARIZAKI HIGH SCHOOL COACH
LOOOOM
ER ...
URK...! H-HE LOOKS LIKE HE'S COMPLETELY ACCUSTOMED TO ALL OF THIS!
ZOOM
ACTUALLY, WE'D LIKE TO SPEND EXTRA TIME ON SERVING IF YOU DON'T MIND!
DUN

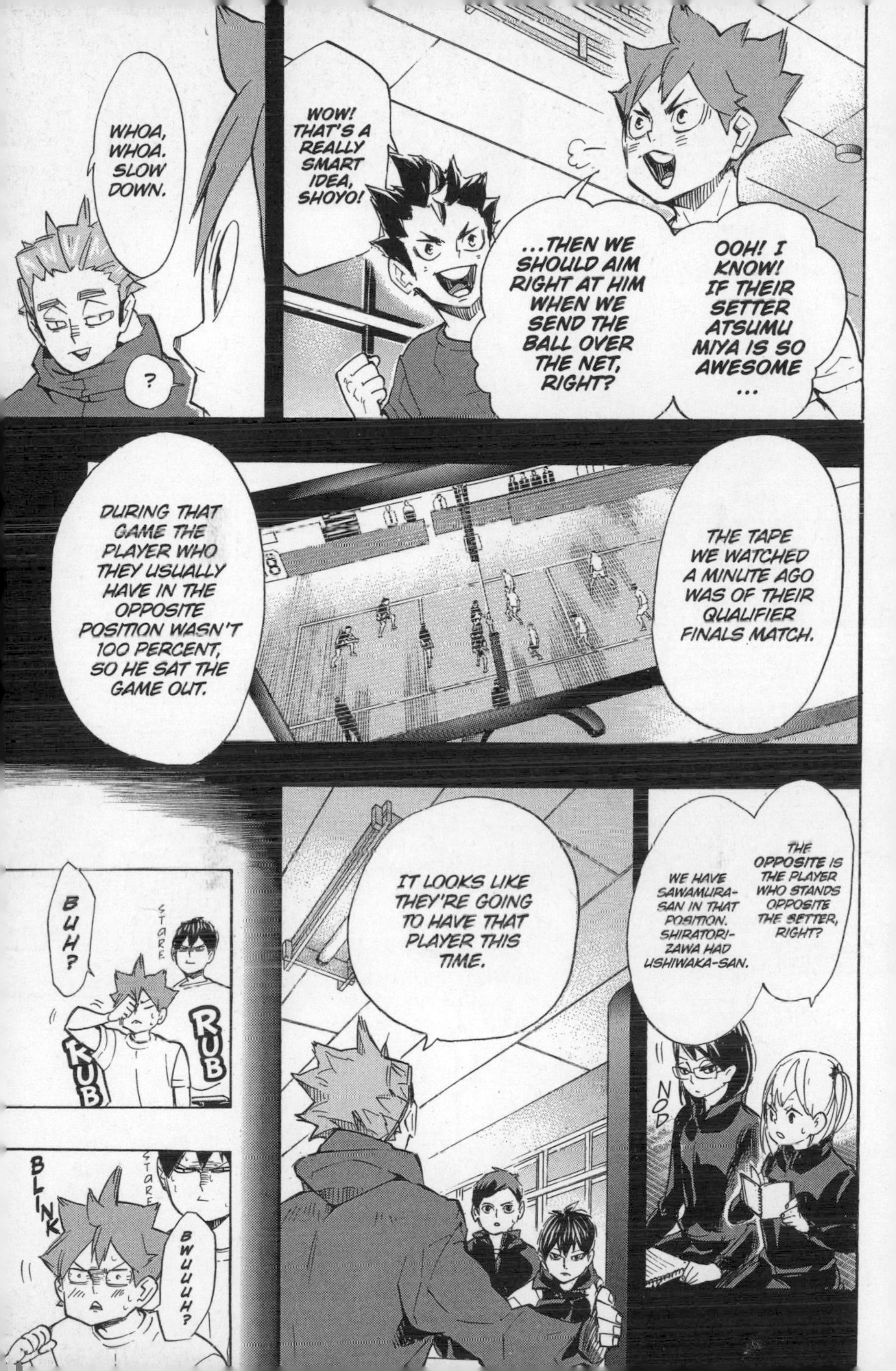
OOH! I KNOW! IF THEIR SETTER ATSUMU MIYA IS SO AWESOME ...
...THEN WE SHOULD AIM RIGHT AT HIM WHEN WE SEND THE BALL OVER THE NET, RIGHT?
WOW! THAT'S A REALLY SMART IDEA, SHOYO!
WHOA, WHOA. SLOW DOWN.
?
THE TAPE WE WATCHED A MINUTE AGO WAS OF THEIR QUALIFIER FINALS MATCH.
DURING THAT GAME THE PLAYER WHO THEY USUALLY HAVE IN THE OPPOSITE POSITION WASN'T 100 PERCENT, SO HE SAT THE GAME OUT.
THE OPPOSITE IS THE PLAYER WHO STANDS OPPOSITE THE SETTER, RIGHT?
WE HAVE SAWAMURA-SAN IN THAT POSITION. SHIRATORI-ZAWA HAD USHIWAKA-SAN.
NOD
IT LOOKS LIKE THEY'RE GOING TO HAVE THAT PLAYER THIS TIME.
BUH?
STARE
RUB
RUB
BLINK
STARE
BWUUUH?

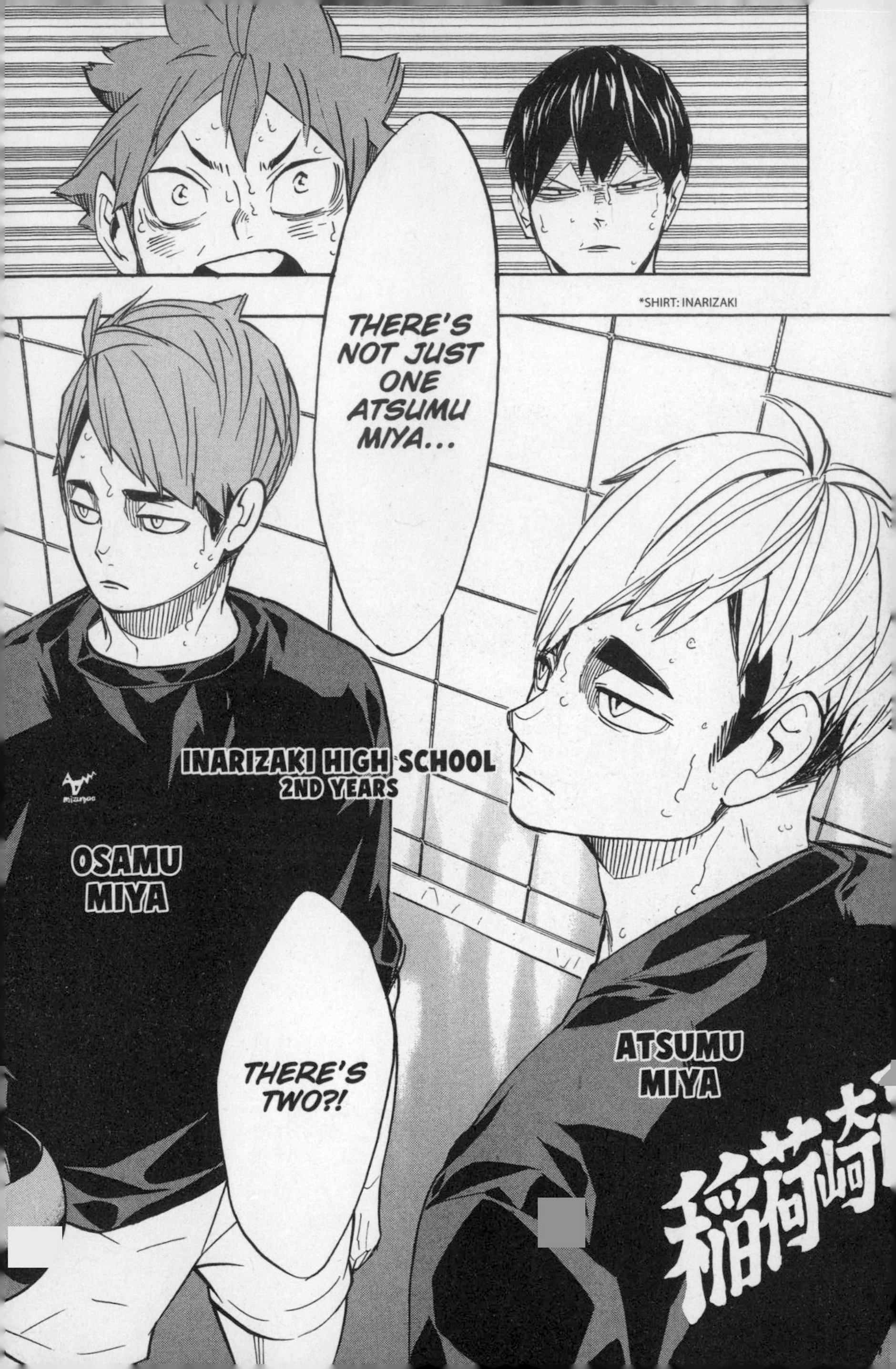
THERE'S NOT JUST ONE ATSUMU MIYA...
INARIZAKI HIGH SCHOOL
2ND YEARS
ATSUMU MIYA
OSAMU MIYA
THERE'S TWO?!
稲荷崎
*SHIRT: INARIZAKI

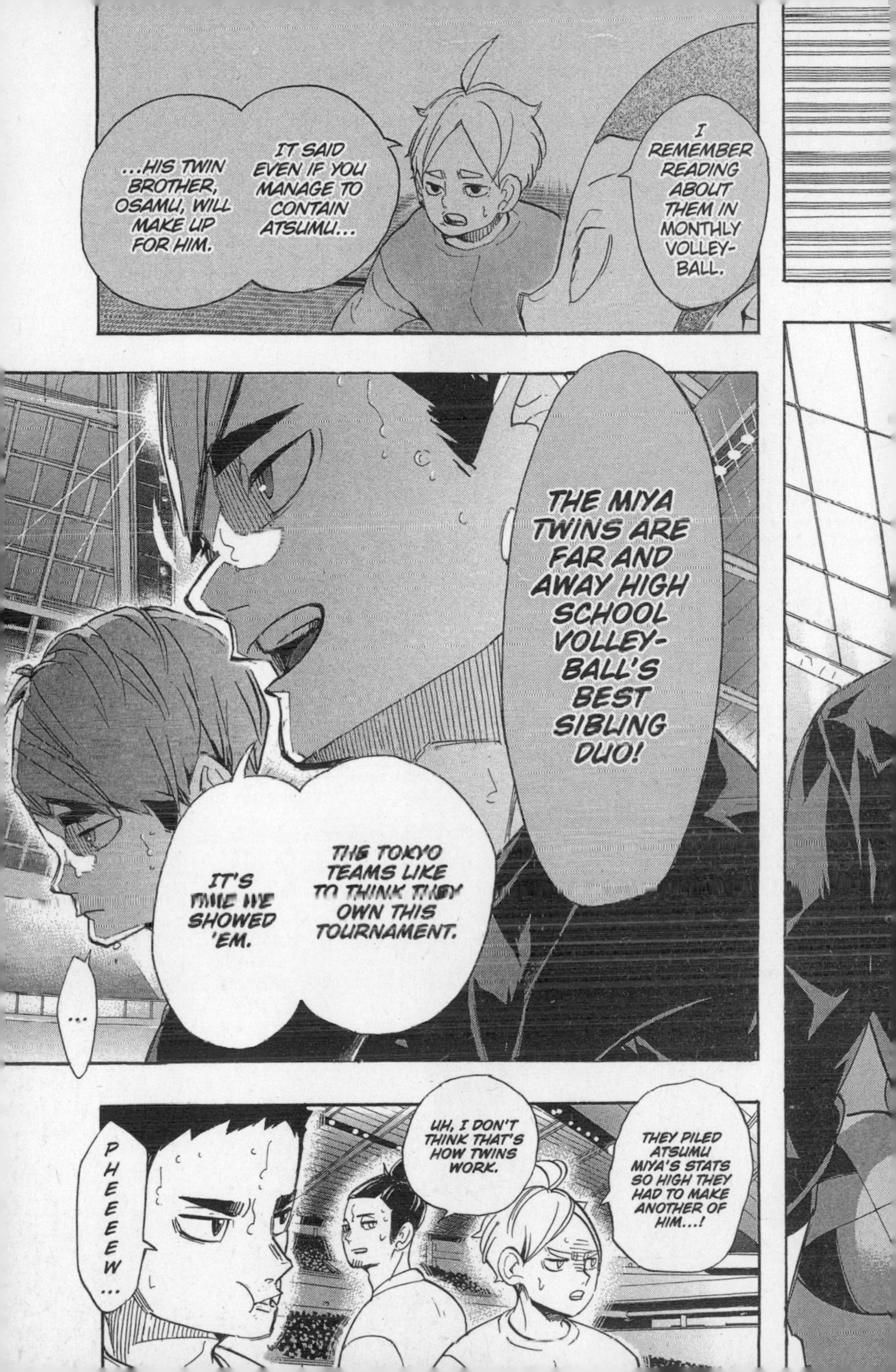
I REMEMBER READING ABOUT THEM IN MONTHLY VOLLEY-BALL.
IT SAID EVEN IF YOU MANAGE TO CONTAIN ATSUMU...
...HIS TWIN BROTHER, OSAMU, WILL MAKE UP FOR HIM.
THE MIYA TWINS ARE FAR AND AWAY HIGH SCHOOL VOLLEY-BALL'S BEST SIBLING DUO!
THE TOKYO TEAMS LIKE TO THINK THEY OWN THIS TOURNAMENT.
IT'S TIME WE SHOWED 'EM.
...
THEY PILED ATSUMU MIYA'S STATS SO HIGH THEY HAD TO MAKE ANOTHER OF HIM...!
UH, I DON'T THINK THAT'S HOW TWINS WORK.
PHEEEEEW...

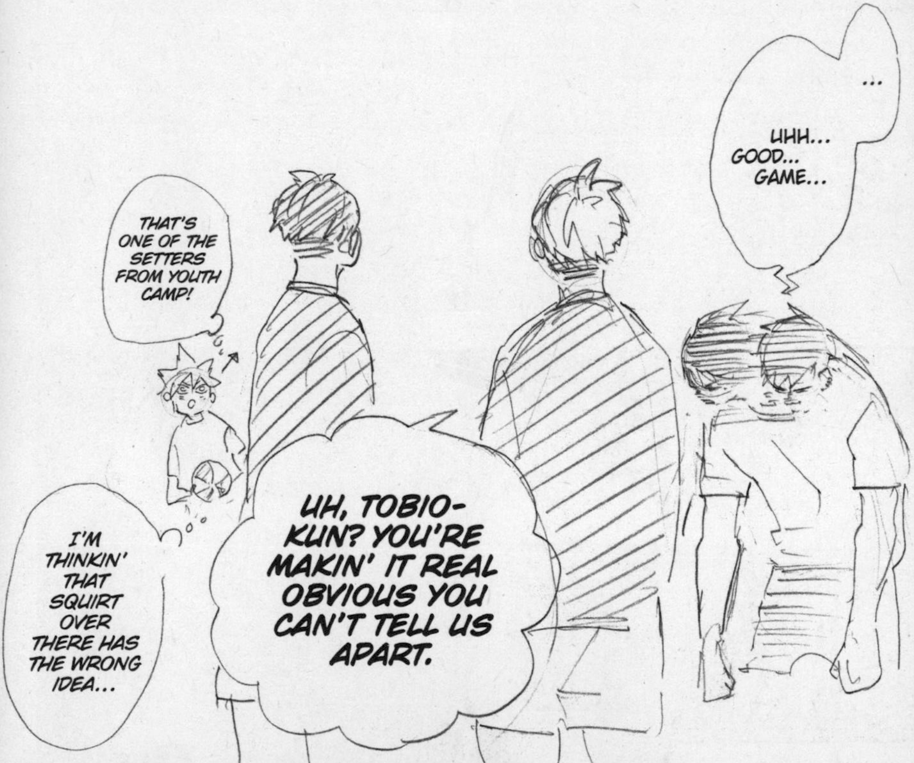
...
UHH... GOOD... GAME...
THAT'S ONE OF THE SETTERS FROM YOUTH CAMP!
UH, TOBIO-KUN? YOU'RE MAKIN' IT REAL OBVIOUS YOU CAN'T TELL US APART.
I'M THINKIN' THAT SQUIRT OVER THERE HAS THE WRONG IDEA...

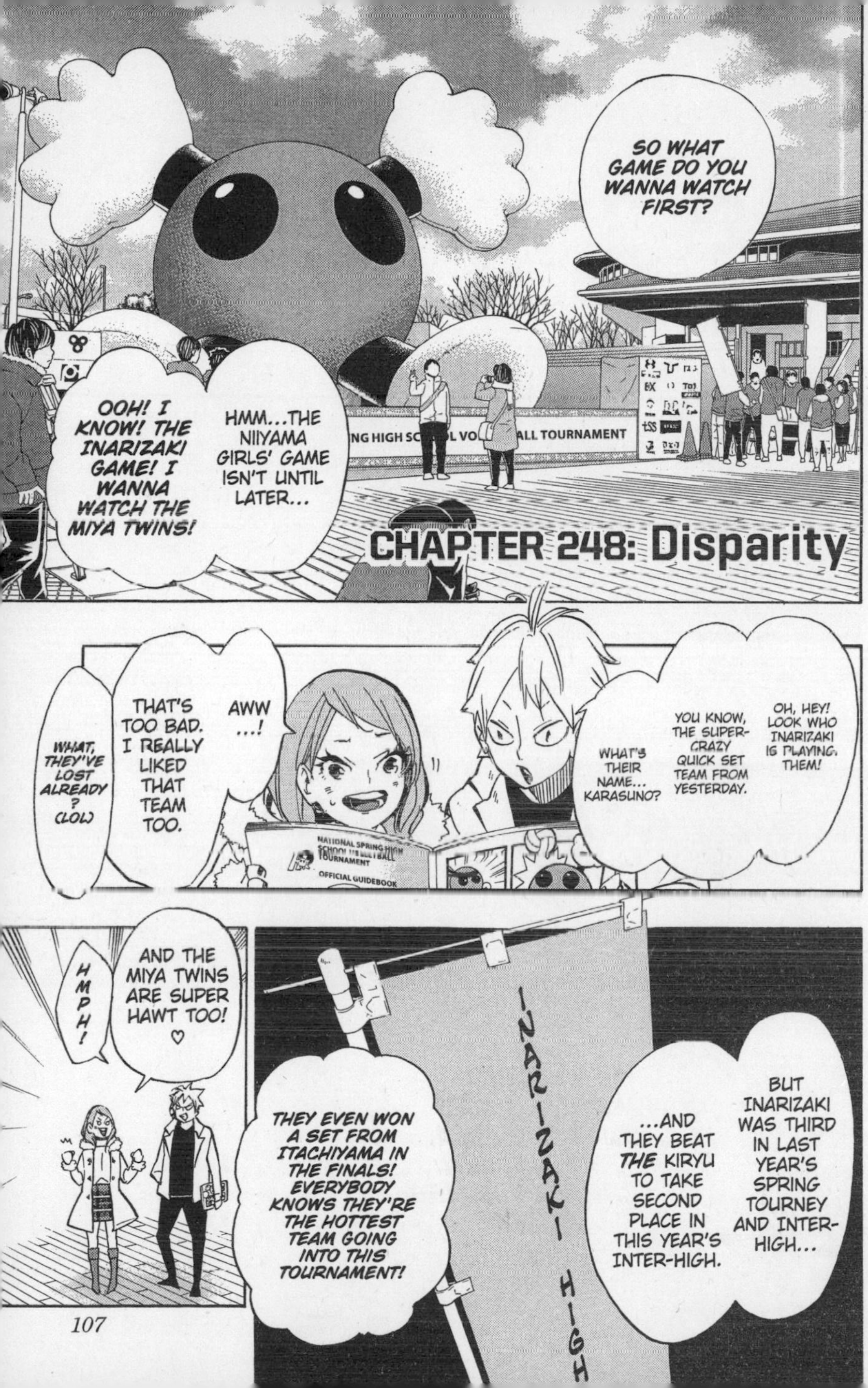
SO WHAT GAME DO YOU WANNA WATCH FIRST?
HMM...THE NIIYAMA GIRLS' GAME ISN'T UNTIL LATER...
OOH! I KNOW! THE INARIZAKI GAME! I WANNA WATCH THE MIYA TWINS!
CHAPTER 248: Disparity
OH, HEY! LOOK WHO INARIZAKI IS PLAYING. THEM!
YOU KNOW, THE SUPER-CRAZY QUICK SET TEAM FROM YESTERDAY.
WHAT'S THEIR NAME... KARASUNO?
AWW...!
THAT'S TOO BAD. I REALLY LIKED THAT TEAM TOO.
WHAT, THEY'VE LOST ALREADY? (LOL)
OFFICIAL GUIDEBOOK
INARIZAKI HIGH
BUT INARIZAKI WAS THIRD IN LAST YEAR'S SPRING TOURNEY AND INTER-HIGH...
...AND THEY BEAT THE KIRYU TO TAKE SECOND PLACE IN THIS YEAR'S INTER-HIGH.
THEY EVEN WON A SET FROM ITACHIYAMA IN THE FINALS! EVERYBODY KNOWS THEY'RE THE HOTTEST TEAM GOING INTO THIS TOURNAMENT!
AND THE MIYA TWINS ARE SUPER HAWT TOO! ♡
HMPH!

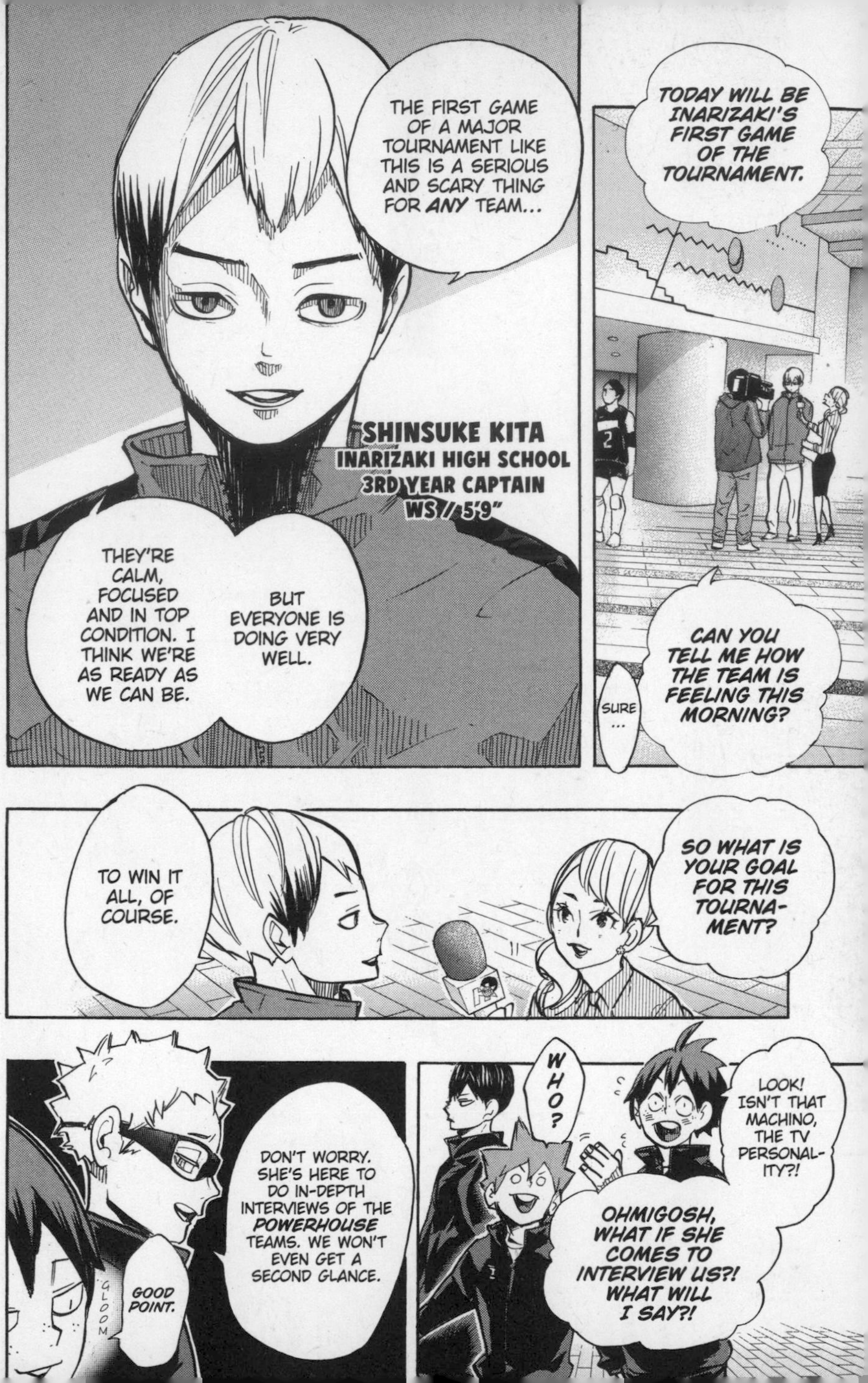

TODAY WILL BE INARIZAKI'S FIRST GAME OF THE TOURNAMENT.
CAN YOU TELL ME HOW THE TEAM IS FEELING THIS MORNING?
SURE...
THE FIRST GAME OF A MAJOR TOURNAMENT LIKE THIS IS A SERIOUS AND SCARY THING FOR ANY TEAM...
SHINSUKE KITA
INARIZAKI HIGH SCHOOL
3RD YEAR CAPTAIN
WS // 5'9"
BUT EVERYONE IS DOING VERY WELL.
THEY'RE CALM, FOCUSED AND IN TOP CONDITION. I THINK WE'RE AS READY AS WE CAN BE.
SO WHAT IS YOUR GOAL FOR THIS TOURNA-MENT?
TO WIN IT ALL, OF COURSE.
LOOK! ISN'T THAT MACHINO, THE TV PERSONAL-ITY?!
WHO?
OHMIGOSH, WHAT IF SHE COMES TO INTERVIEW US?! WHAT WILL I SAY?!
DON'T WORRY. SHE'S HERE TO DO IN-DEPTH INTERVIEWS OF THE POWERHOUSE TEAMS. WE WON'T EVEN GET A SECOND GLANCE.
GOOD POINT.
GLOOM

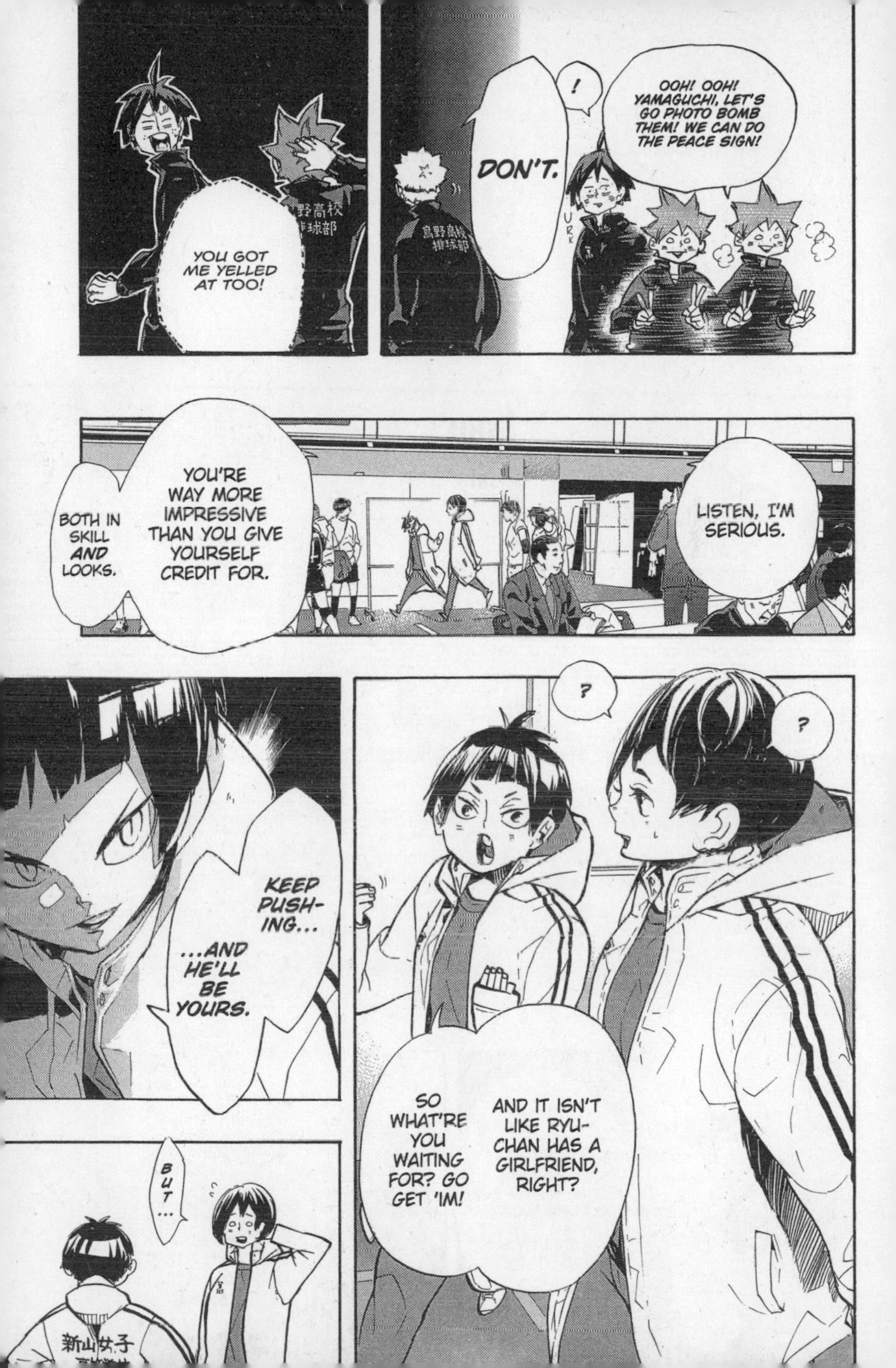
OOH! OOH! YAMAGUCHI, LET'S GO PHOTO BOMB THEM! WE CAN DO THE PEACE SIGN!
!
DON'T.
URK
鳥野高校
排球部
YOU GOT ME YELLED AT TOO!
LISTEN, I'M SERIOUS.
YOU'RE WAY MORE IMPRESSIVE THAN YOU GIVE YOURSELF CREDIT FOR.
BOTH IN SKILL AND LOOKS.
?
?
AND IT ISN'T LIKE RYU-CHAN HAS A GIRLFRIEND, RIGHT?
SO WHAT'RE YOU WAITING FOR? GO GET 'IM!
KEEP PUSHING...
...AND HE'LL BE YOURS.
BUT...
新山女子

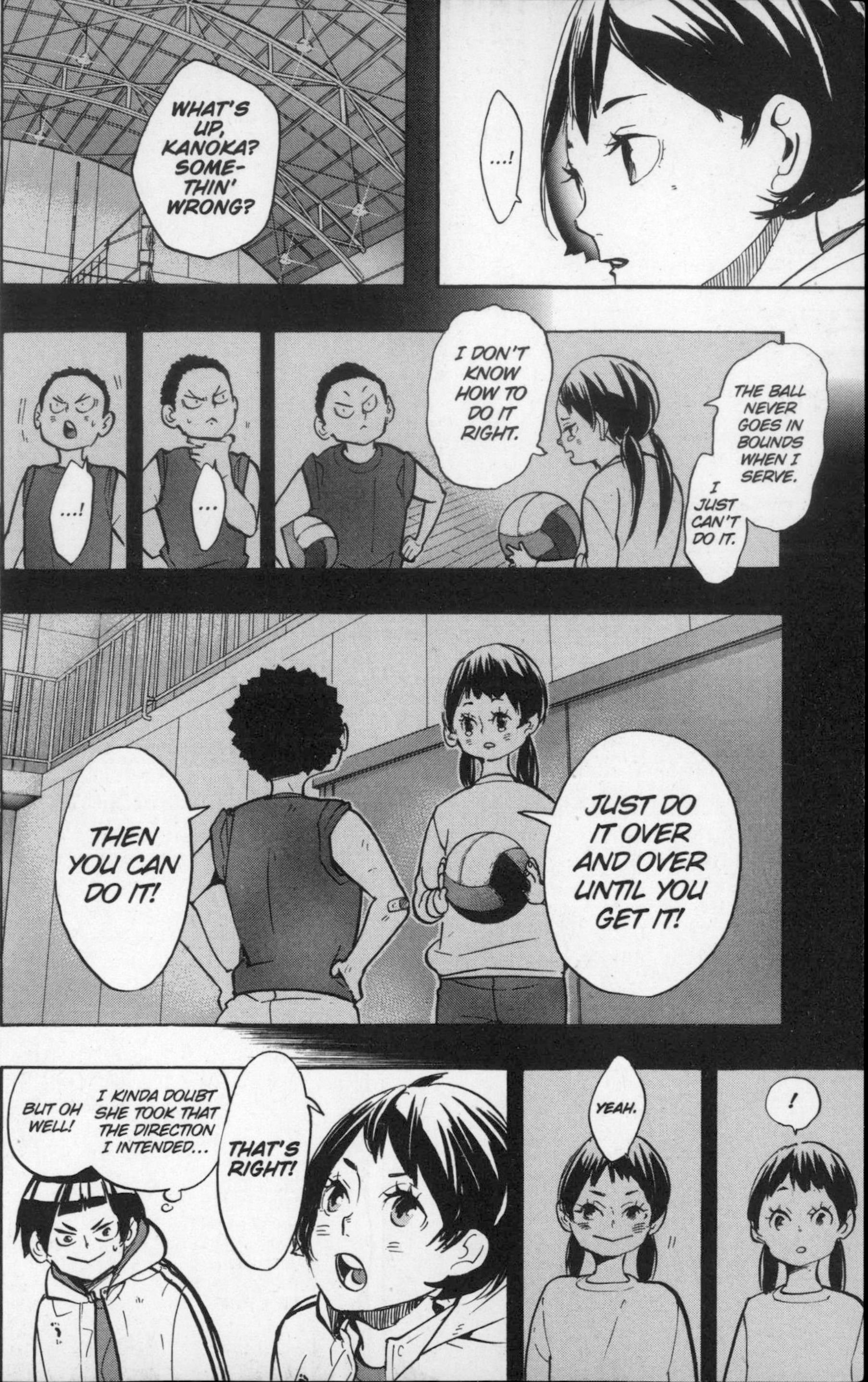
...!
WHAT'S UP, KANOKA? SOMETHIN' WRONG?
THE BALL NEVER GOES IN BOUNDS WHEN I SERVE.
I JUST CAN'T DO IT.
I DON'T KNOW HOW TO DO IT RIGHT.
...
...!
JUST DO IT OVER AND OVER UNTIL YOU GET IT!
THEN YOU CAN DO IT!
!
YEAH.
THAT'S RIGHT!
I KINDA DOUBT SHE TOOK THAT THE DIRECTION I INTENDED...
BUT OH WELL!

OH!

PSST!

KA-NOKA!

ZIIIP

!!

I'M REALLY SORRY ABOUT THAT.

I WASN'T EXPECT-ING MY COUSIN TO SHOW UP WHEN HE DID.

NO, NO!

JUST PRE-TEND IT NEVER HAP-PENED, 'KAY?

SORRY! I SAID A WHOLE BUNCHA WEIRD STUFF LAST NIGHT, DIDN'T I?

WOW, REALLY?

THAT'S REAL COOL OF THEM!

BUH?

COUSIN? YOU GOT FAMILY HERE?

UM, RYU-CHAN?

LISTEN.

THEN DOES THAT MEAN MY MISUN-DERSTANDING WAS JUST A MISUNDER-STANDING...?

HUH? WAIT A SEC...

WHENEVER I HAVE A GAME HERE, THEY ALWAYS SEND ME GOOD-LUCK CHARMS AND CARE PACKAGES AND STUFF.

YEAH, MY AUNT'S FAMILY LIVES HERE IN TOKYO.

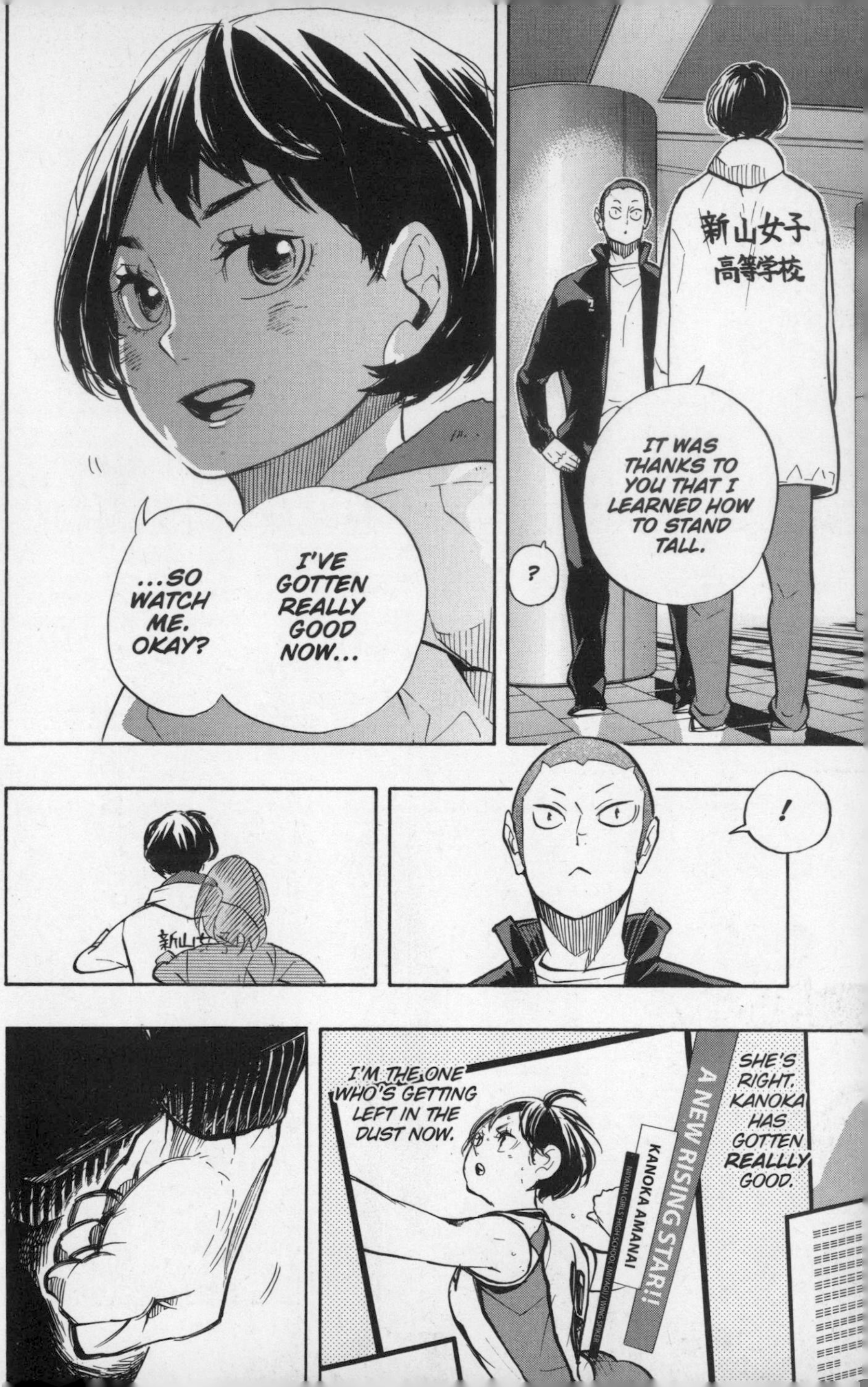
新山女子
高等学校
IT WAS THANKS TO YOU THAT I LEARNED HOW TO STAND TALL.
?
I'VE GOTTEN REALLY GOOD NOW...
...SO WATCH ME. OKAY?
!
SHE'S RIGHT. KANOKA HAS GOTTEN REALLLY GOOD.
A NEW RISING STAR!!
KANOKA AMANAI
NIIYAMA GIRLS' HIGH SCHOOL (MIYAGI) WING SPIKER
I'M THE ONE WHO'S GETTING LEFT IN THE DUST NOW.

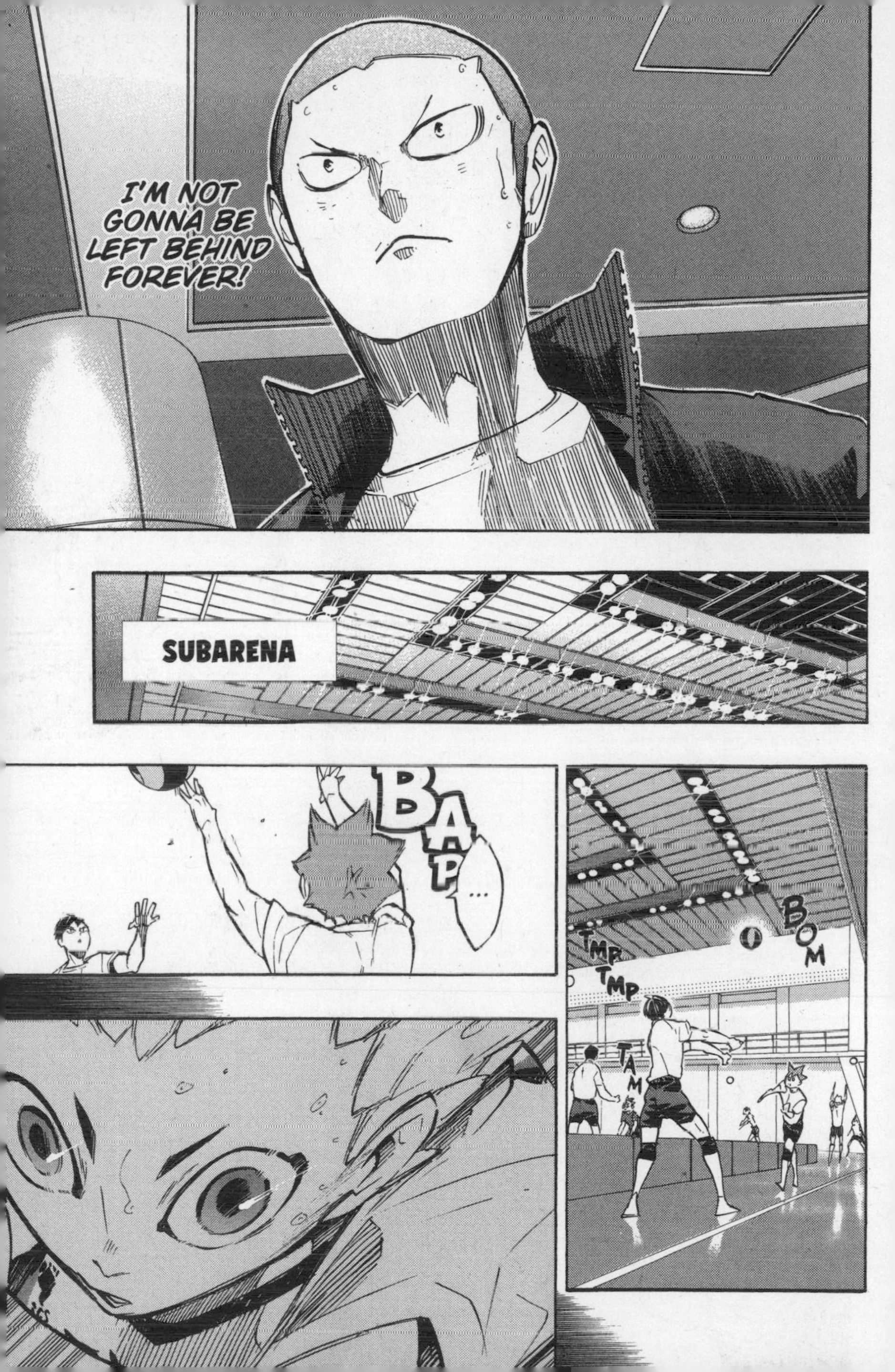
I'M NOT GONNA BE LEFT BEHIND FOREVER!
SUBARENA
BOM
TMP TMP
TAM
BAP...

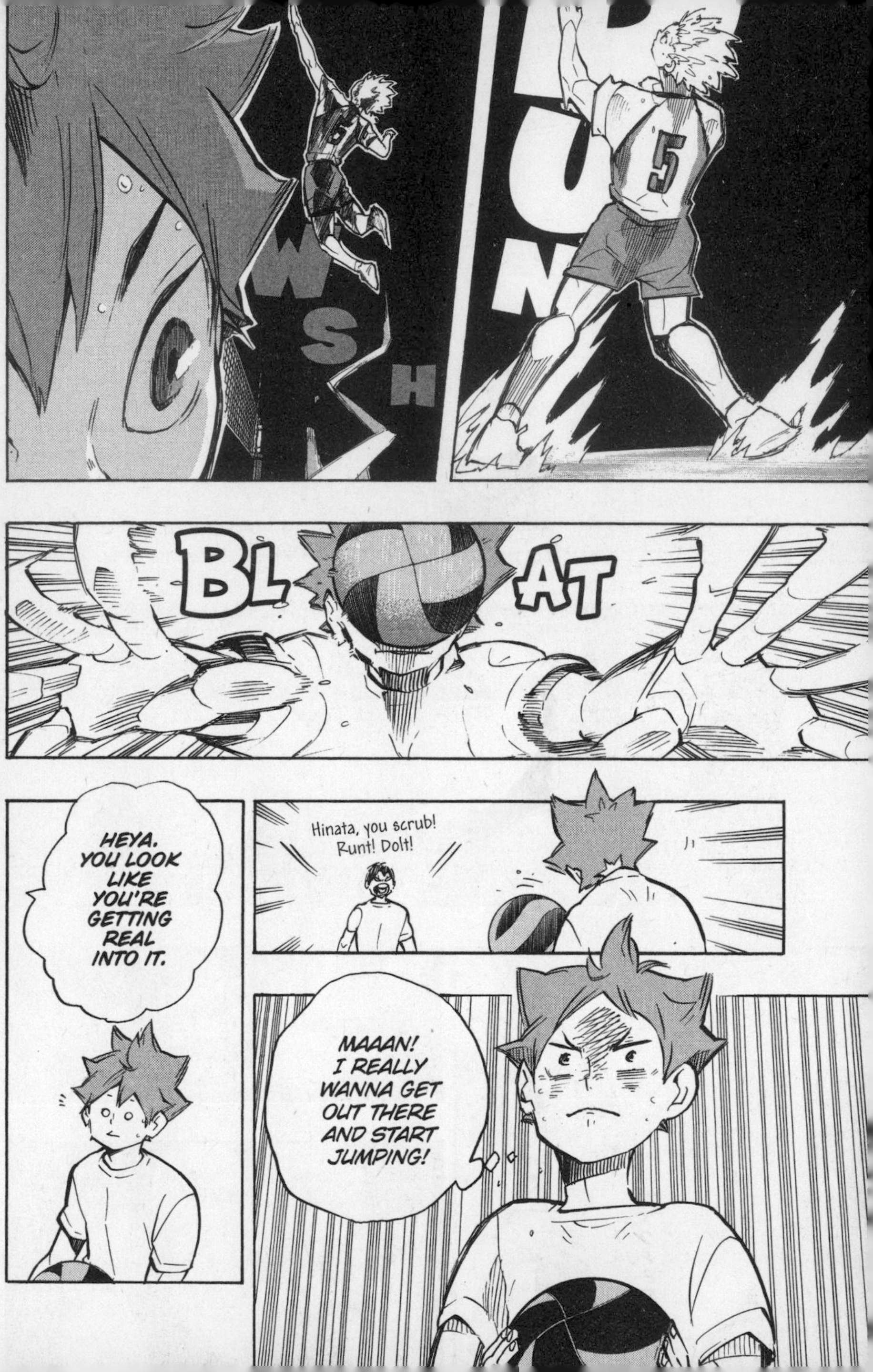
UN
WSH
BLAT
Hinata, you scrub! Runt! Dolt!
MAAAN! I REALLY WANNA GET OUT THERE AND START JUMPING!
HEYA. YOU LOOK LIKE YOU'RE GETTING REAL INTO IT.

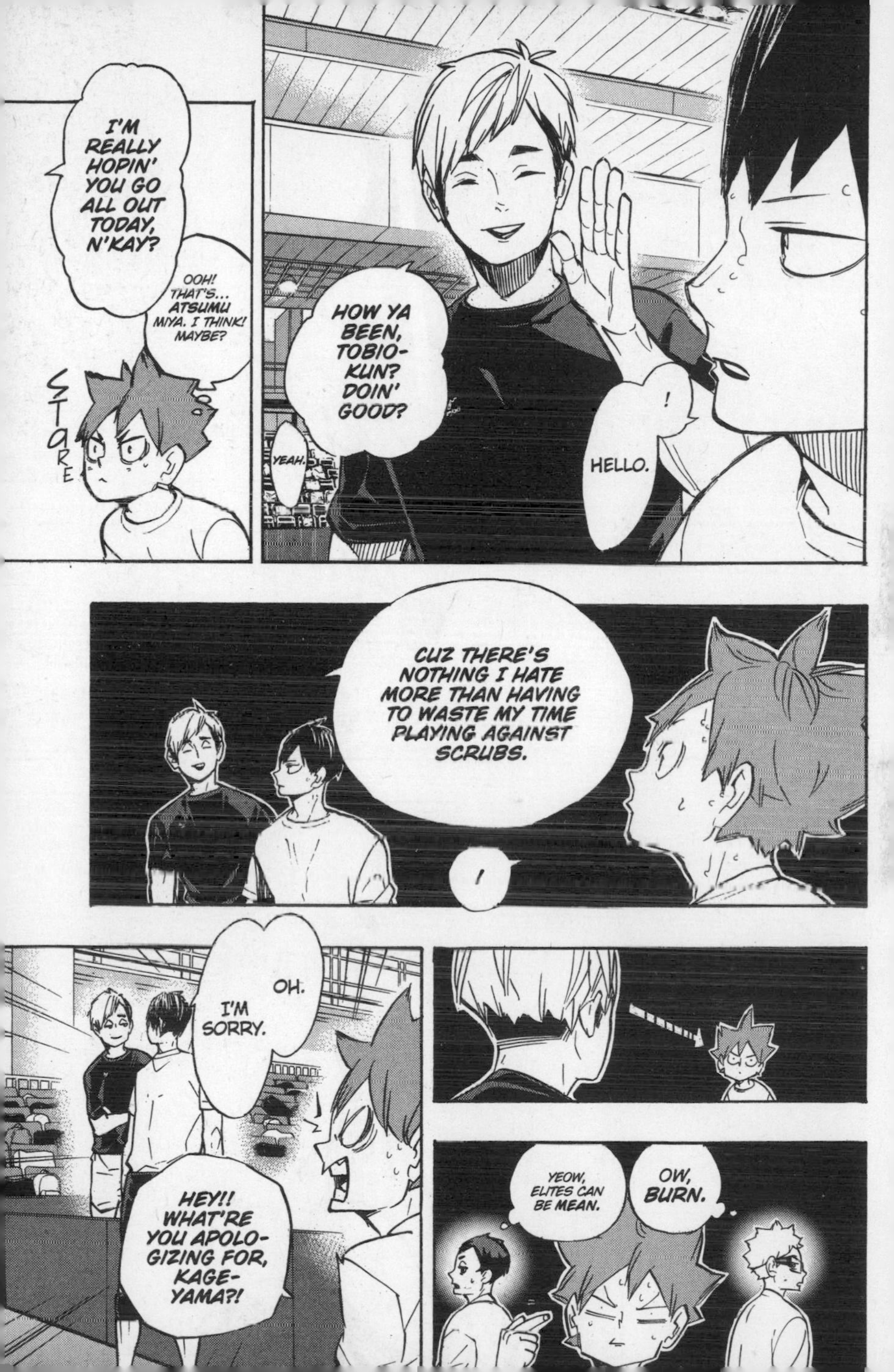
HOW YA BEEN, TOBIO-KUN? DOIN' GOOD?
!
HELLO.
YEAH.
I'M REALLY HOPIN' YOU GO ALL OUT TODAY, N'KAY?
OOH! THAT'S... ATSUMU MIYA. I THINK! MAYBE?
STARE
CUZ THERE'S NOTHING I HATE MORE THAN HAVING TO WASTE MY TIME PLAYING AGAINST SCRUBS.
!
OW, BURN.
YEOW, ELITES CAN BE MEAN.
OH. I'M SORRY.
HEY!! WHAT'RE YOU APOLOGIZING FOR, KAGEYAMA?!

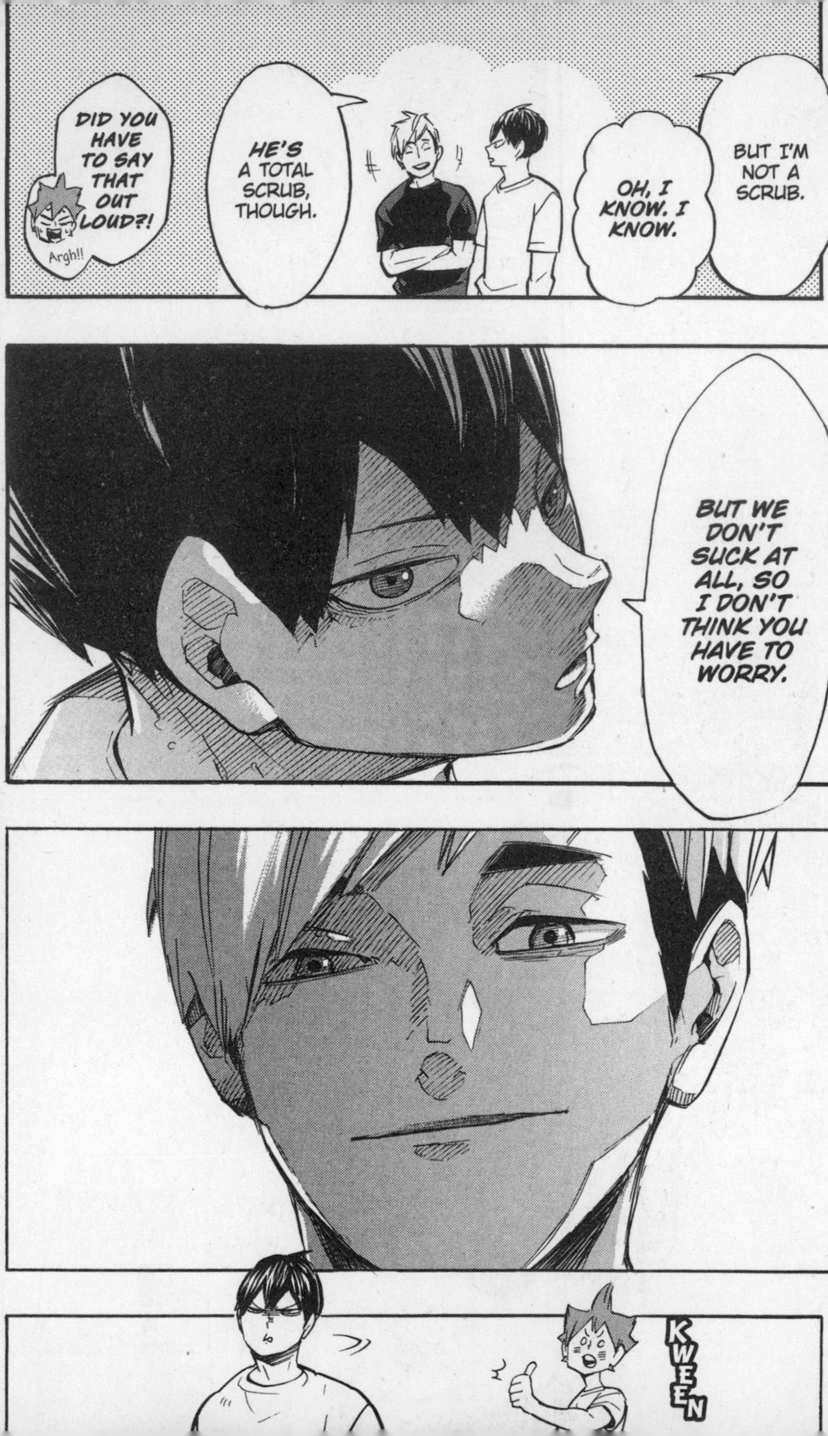
BUT I'M NOT A SCRUB.
OH, I KNOW. I KNOW.
HE'S A TOTAL SCRUB, THOUGH.
DID YOU HAVE TO SAY THAT OUT LOUD?!
Argh!!
BUT WE DON'T SUCK AT ALL, SO I DON'T THINK YOU HAVE TO WORRY.
KWEEN

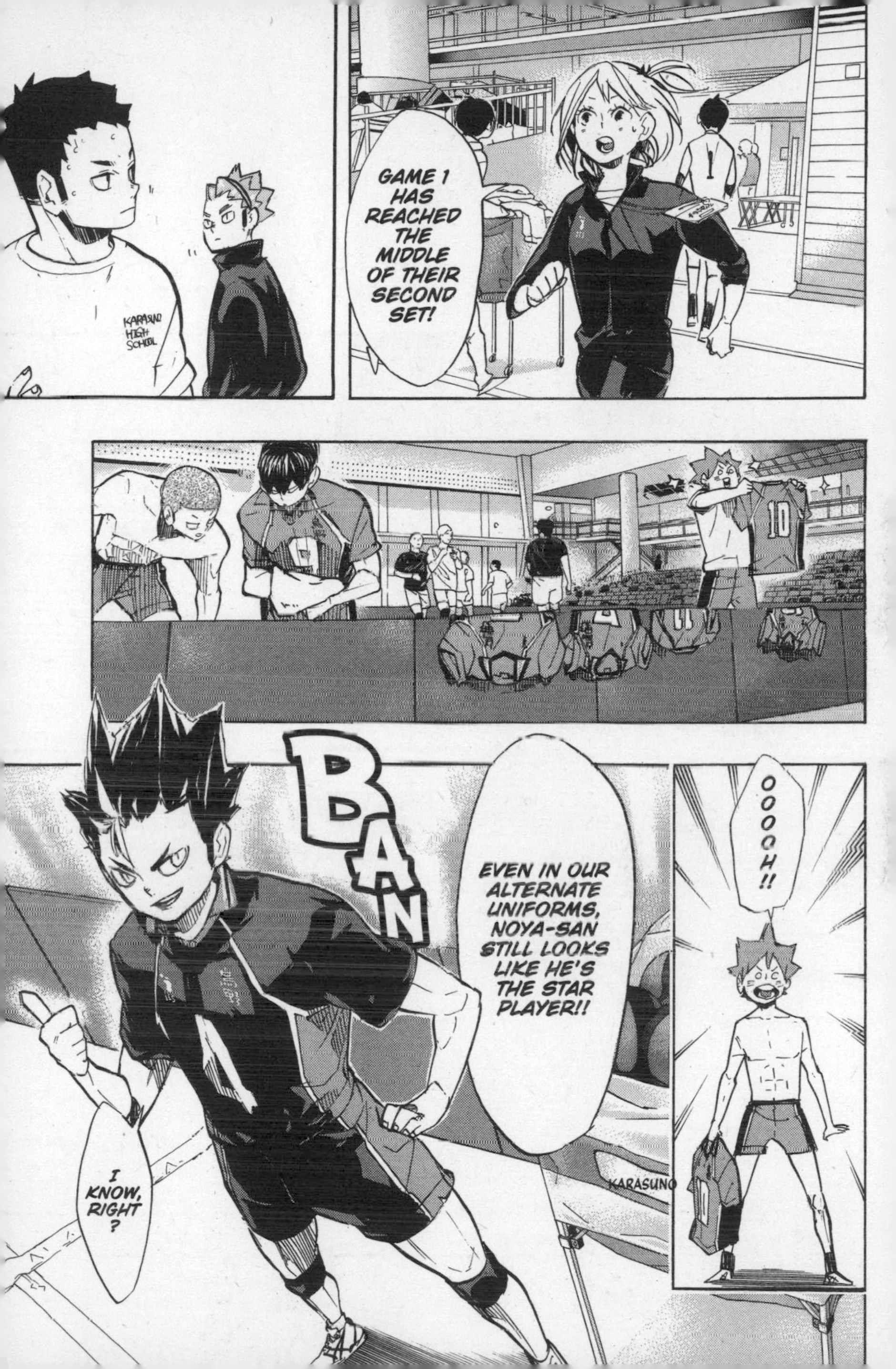
GAME 1 HAS REACHED THE MIDDLE OF THEIR SECOND SET!
KARASUNO HIGH SCHOOL
OOOOH!!
EVEN IN OUR ALTERNATE UNIFORMS, NOYA-SAN STILL LOOKS LIKE HE'S THE STAR PLAYER!!
BAN
I KNOW, RIGHT?
KARASUNO

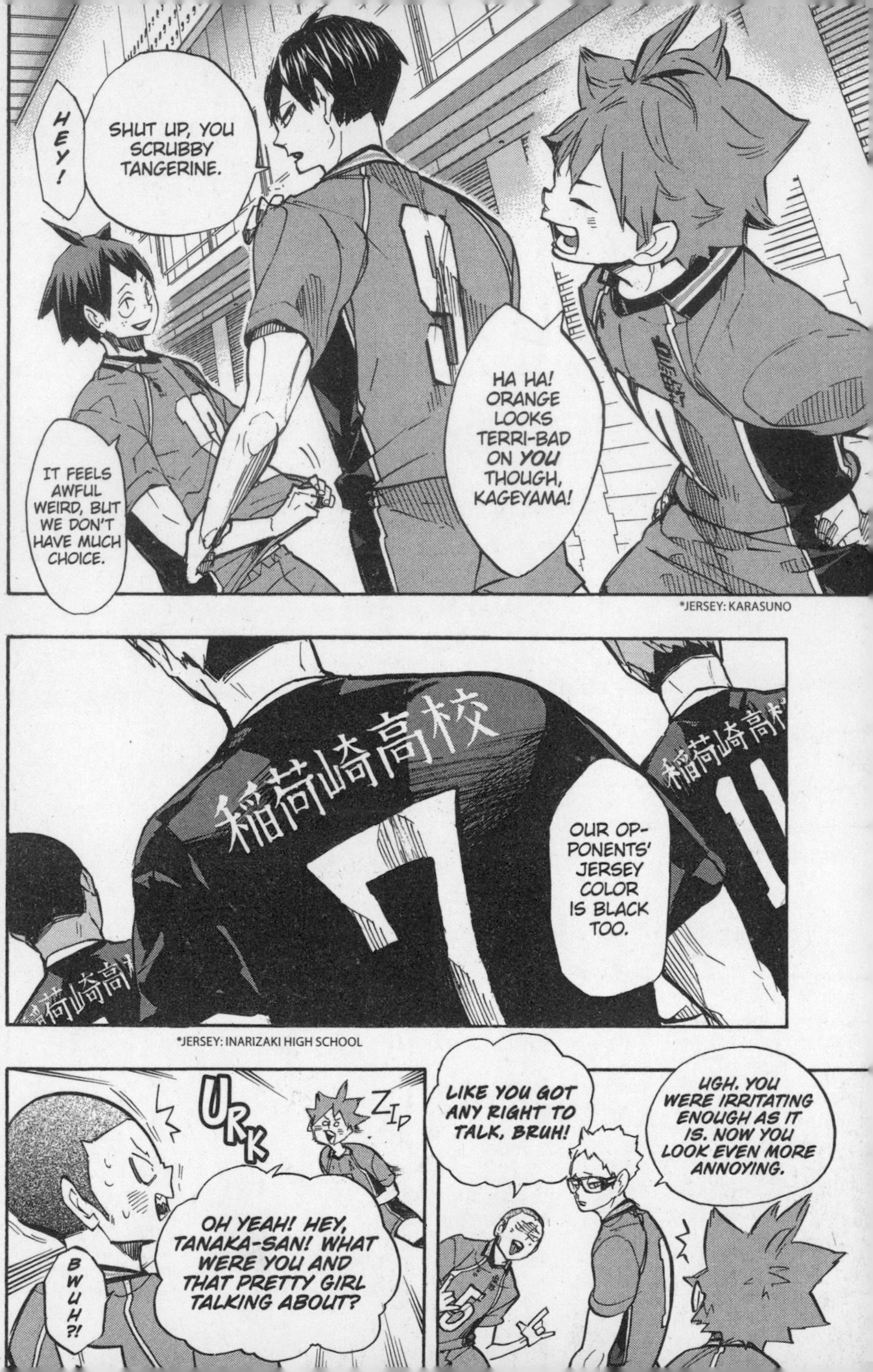
HA HA! ORANGE LOOKS TERRI-BAD ON *YOU* THOUGH, KAGEYAMA!
HEY!
SHUT UP, YOU SCRUBBY TANGERINE.
IT FEELS AWFUL WEIRD, BUT WE DON'T HAVE MUCH CHOICE.
*JERSEY: KARASUNO
稲荷崎高校
OUR OPPONENTS' JERSEY COLOR IS BLACK TOO.
*JERSEY: INARIZAKI HIGH SCHOOL
UGH. YOU WERE IRRITATING ENOUGH AS IT IS. NOW YOU LOOK EVEN MORE ANNOYING.
LIKE YOU GOT ANY RIGHT TO TALK, BRUH!
ZIP
OH YEAH! HEY, TANAKA-SAN! WHAT WERE YOU AND THAT PRETTY GIRL TALKING ABOUT?
URK
BWUH?!

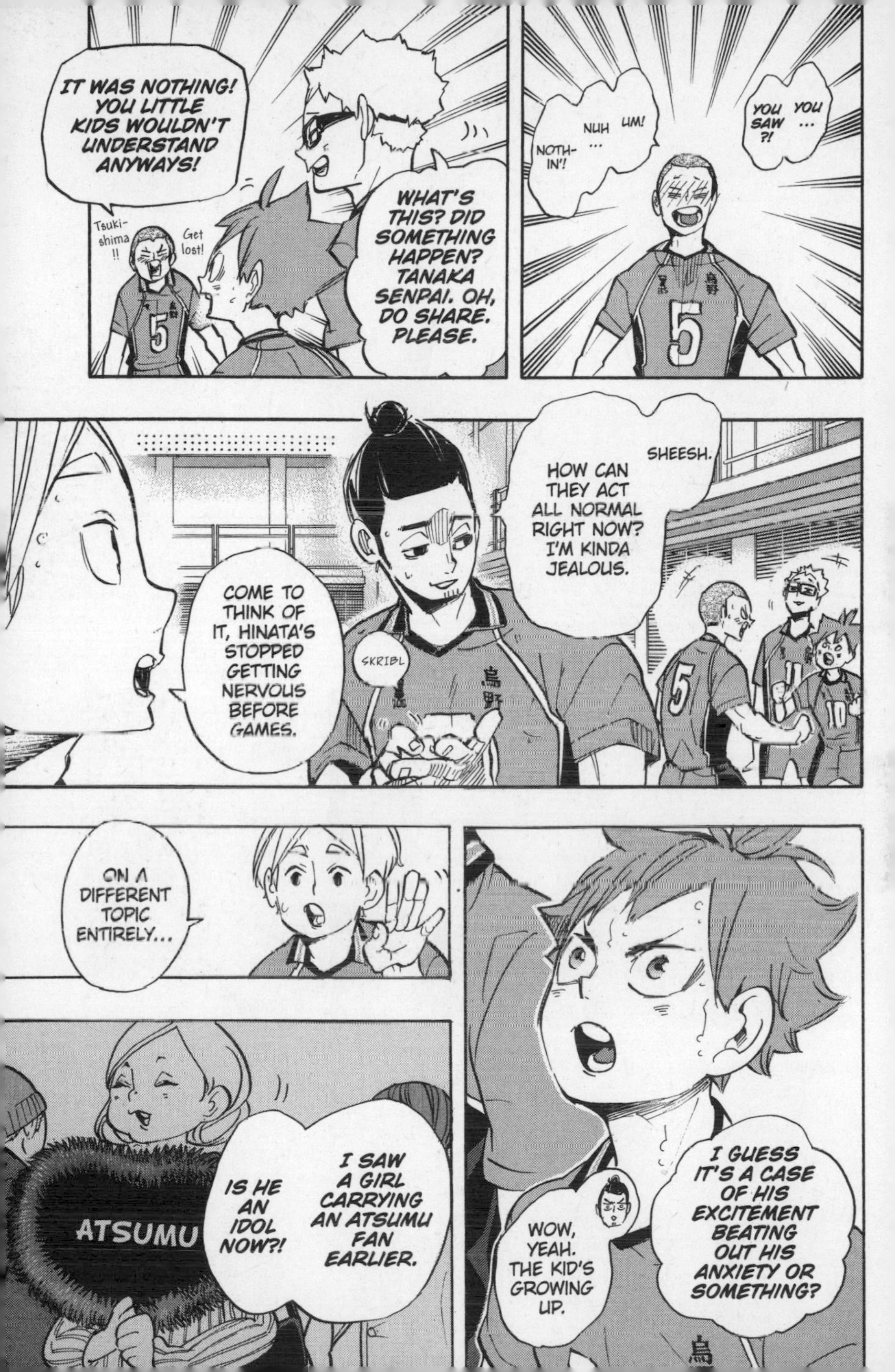

YOU ...
YOU SAW ?!
NUH ... UM!
NOTH-IN'!
WHAT'S THIS? DID SOMETHING HAPPEN? TANAKA SENPAI. OH, DO SHARE. PLEASE.
IT WAS NOTHING! YOU LITTLE KIDS WOULDN'T UNDERSTAND ANYWAYS!
Get lost!
Tsuki-shima !!
SHEESH.
HOW CAN THEY ACT ALL NORMAL RIGHT NOW? I'M KINDA JEALOUS.
SKRIBL
COME TO THINK OF IT, HINATA'S STOPPED GETTING NERVOUS BEFORE GAMES.
I GUESS IT'S A CASE OF HIS EXCITEMENT BEATING OUT HIS ANXIETY OR SOMETHING?
WOW, YEAH. THE KID'S GROWING UP.
ON A DIFFERENT TOPIC ENTIRELY...
I SAW A GIRL CARRYING AN ATSUMU FAN EARLIER.
IS HE AN IDOL NOW?!
ATSUMU

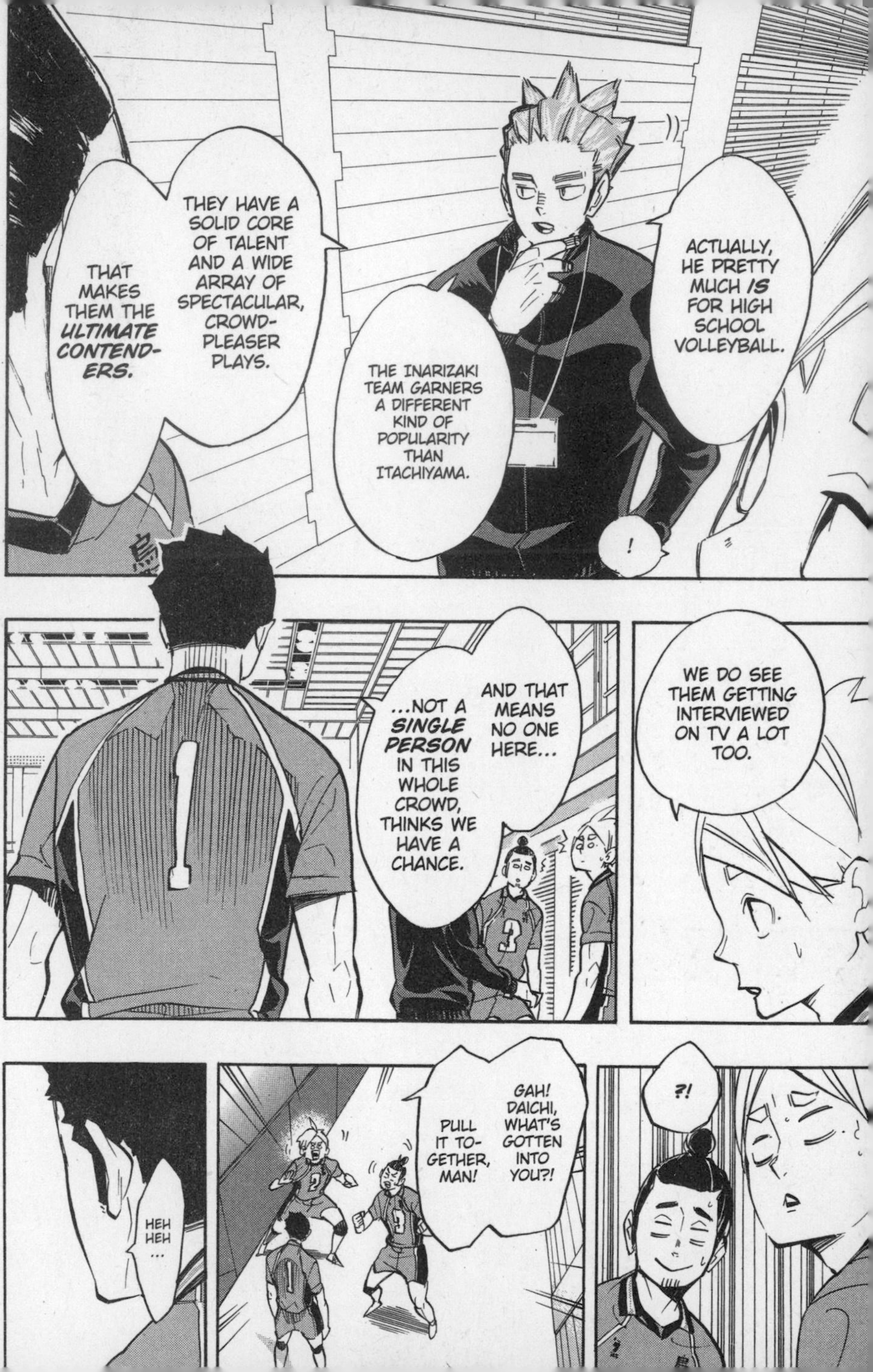
ACTUALLY, HE PRETTY MUCH *IS* FOR HIGH SCHOOL VOLLEYBALL.
!
THE INARIZAKI TEAM GARNERS A DIFFERENT KIND OF POPULARITY THAN ITACHIYAMA.
THEY HAVE A SOLID CORE OF TALENT AND A WIDE ARRAY OF SPECTACULAR, CROWD-PLEASER PLAYS.
THAT MAKES THEM THE ***ULTIMATE CONTENDERS.***
WE DO SEE THEM GETTING INTERVIEWED ON TV A LOT TOO.
AND THAT MEANS NO ONE HERE...
...NOT A ***SINGLE PERSON*** IN THIS WHOLE CROWD, THINKS WE HAVE A CHANCE.
?!
GAH! DAICHI, WHAT'S GOTTEN INTO YOU?!
PULL IT TO-GETHER, MAN!
HEH HEH ...

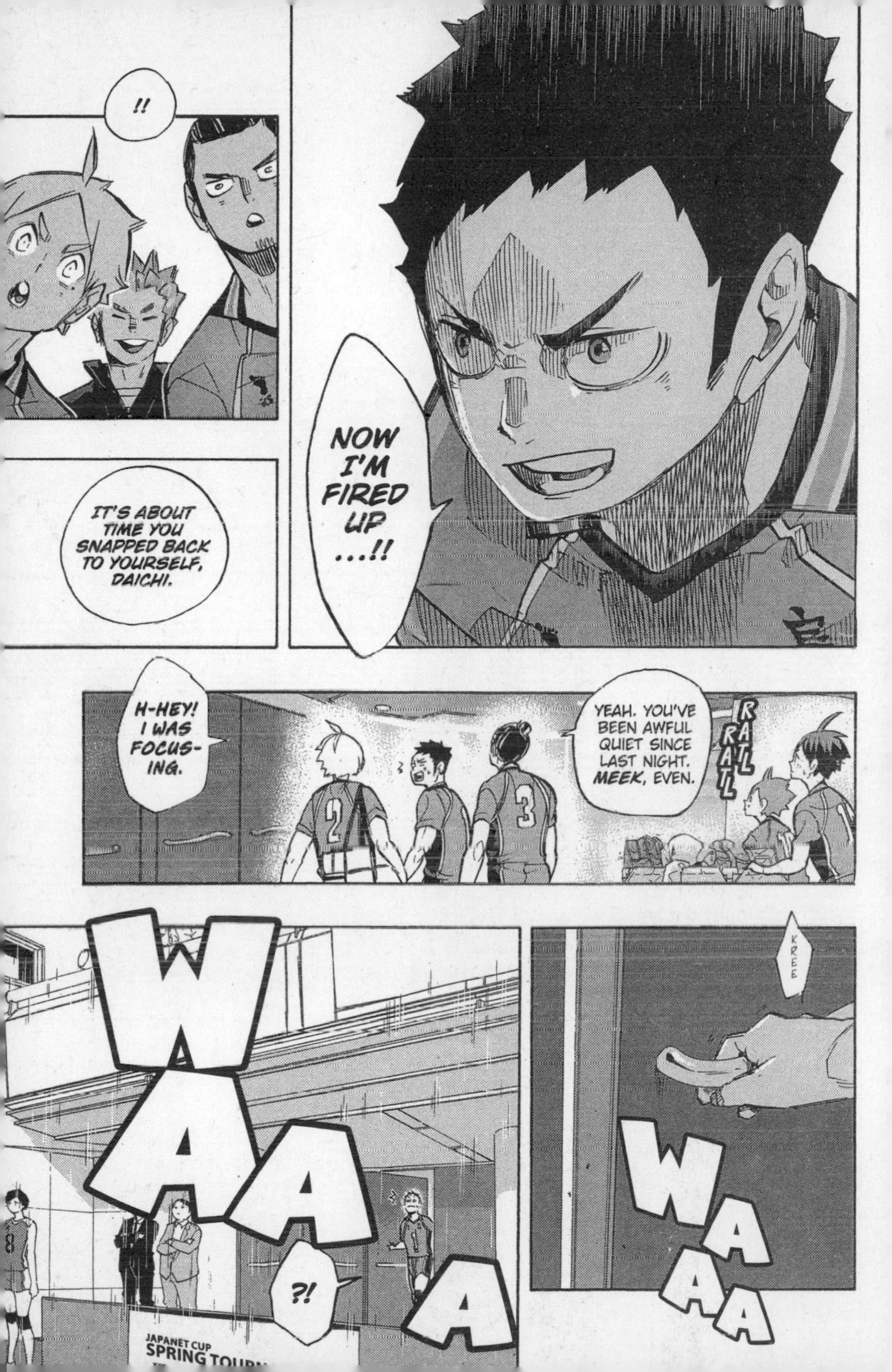

NOW I'M FIRED UP ...!!
!!
IT'S ABOUT TIME YOU SNAPPED BACK TO YOURSELF, DAICHI.
RATL
RATL
YEAH. YOU'VE BEEN AWFUL QUIET SINCE LAST NIGHT. MEEK, EVEN.
H-HEY! I WAS FOCUSING.
KREE
WAAAA
WAAAA
?!
JAPANET CUP
SPRING TOURN

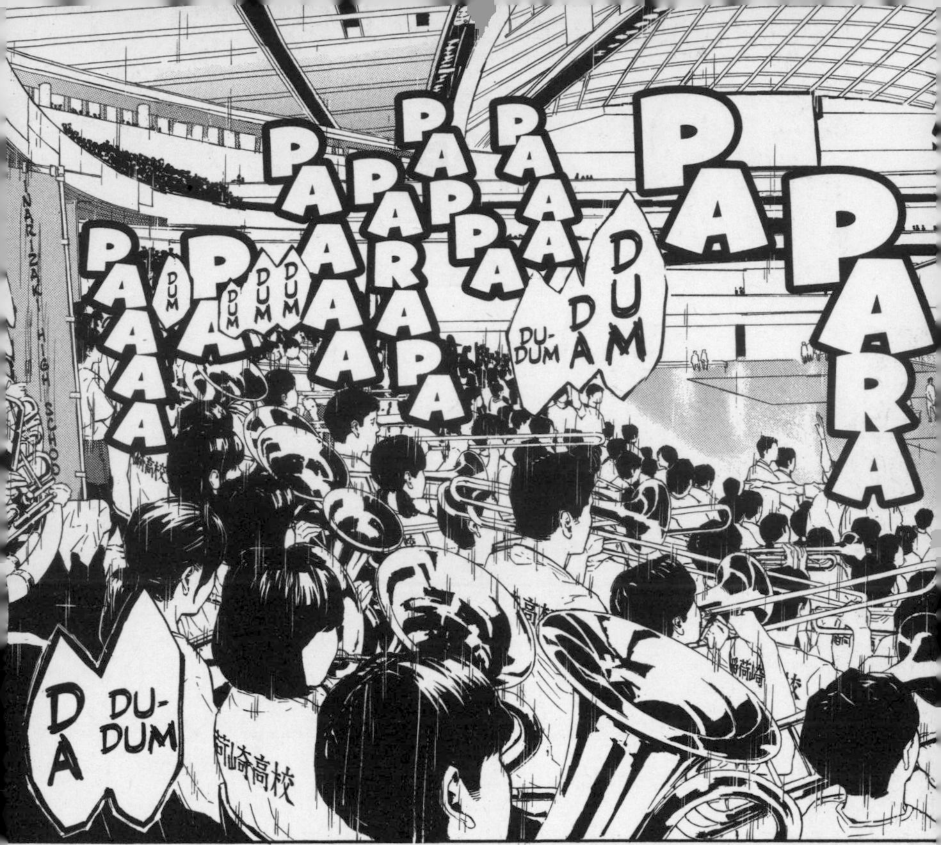
PA PA PARA
DU-DUM DA DUM
PAPAPAA
PAPAPA
PAPARAAAPA
DUM DUM DUM DUM
PAPAAAA
DA DU-DUM
INARIZAKI HIGH SCHOOL
稲荷崎高校
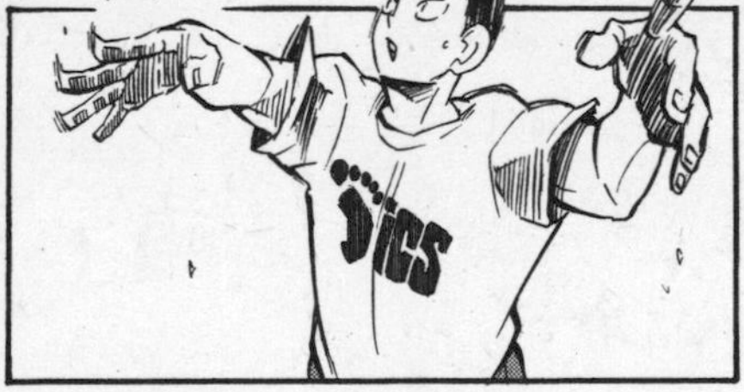
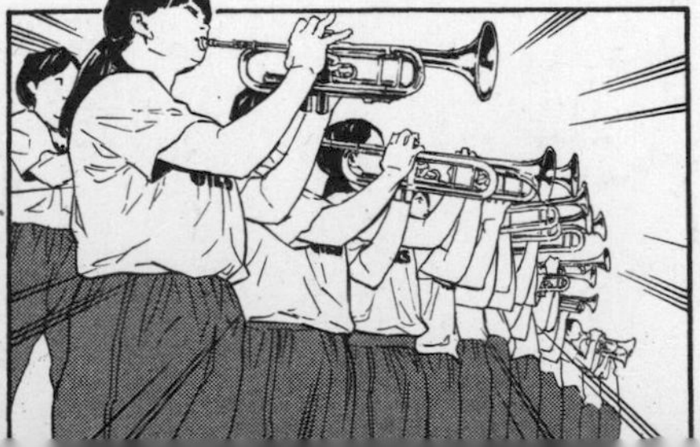
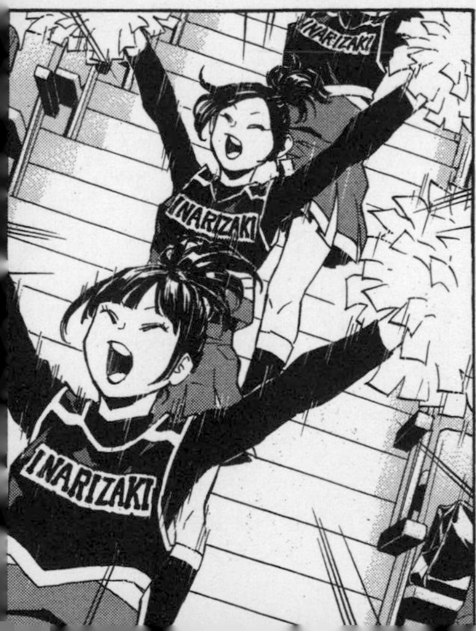
INARIZAKI
INARIZAKI
INARIZAKI

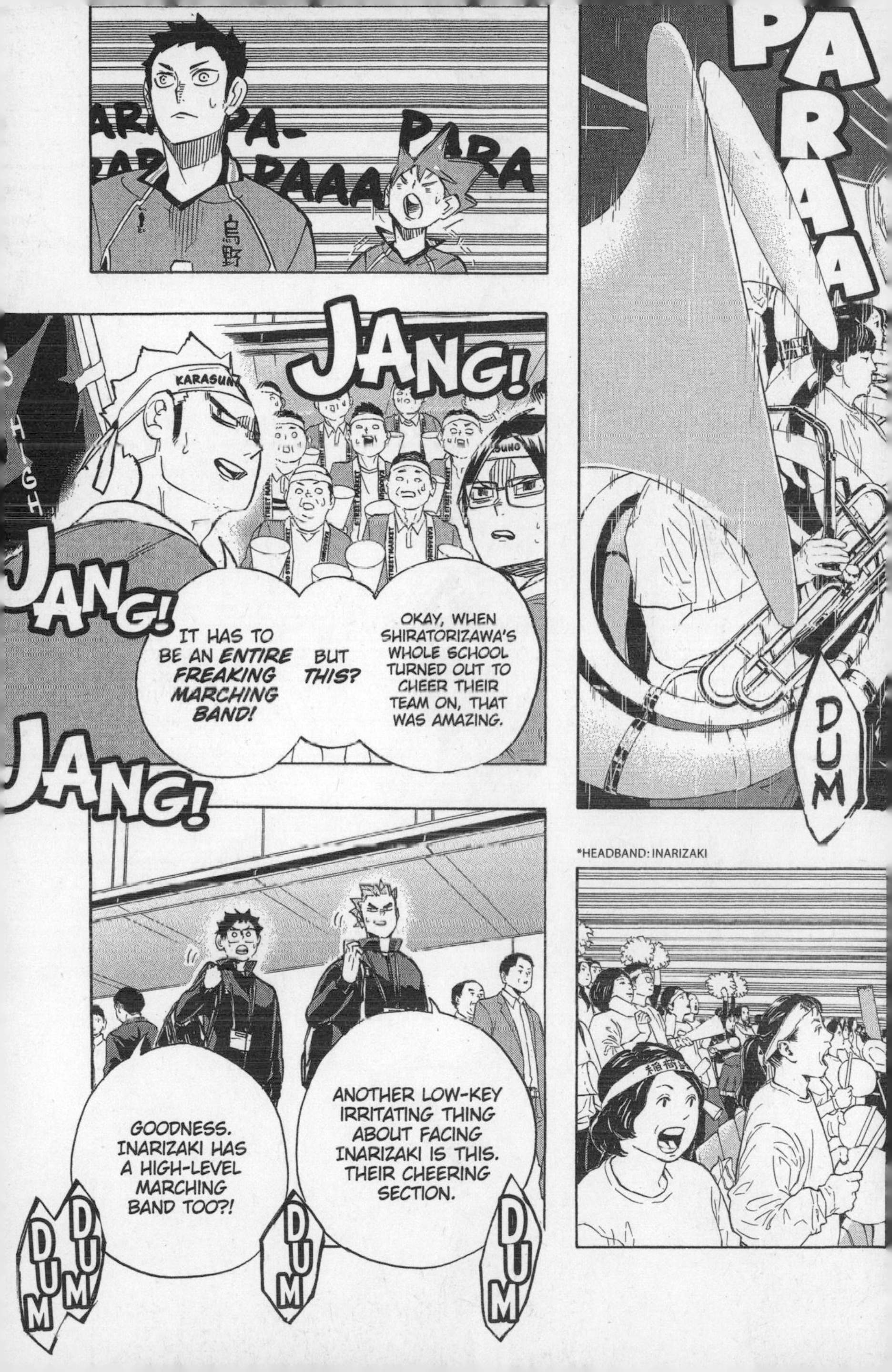
PARARAA
DUM
PARA
PAAA
JANG!
KARASUNO
JANG!
JANG!
OKAY, WHEN SHIRATORIZAWA'S WHOLE SCHOOL TURNED OUT TO CHEER THEIR TEAM ON, THAT WAS AMAZING.
BUT *THIS?*
IT HAS TO BE AN *ENTIRE FREAKING MARCHING BAND!*
*HEADBAND: INARIZAKI
ANOTHER LOW-KEY IRRITATING THING ABOUT FACING INARIZAKI IS THIS. THEIR CHEERING SECTION.
DUM
GOODNESS. INARIZAKI HAS A HIGH-LEVEL MARCHING BAND TOO?!
DUM
DUM
DUM

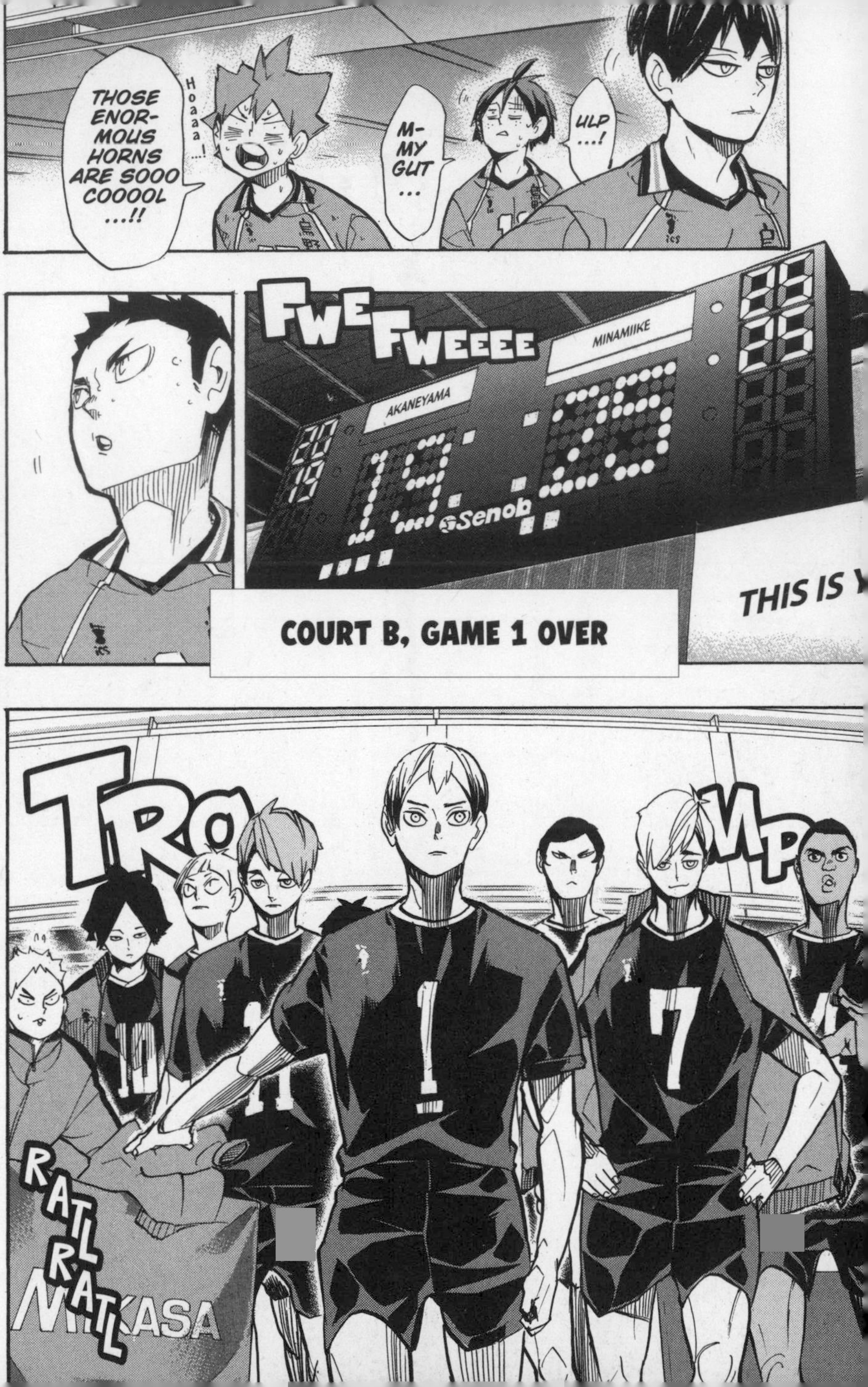
ULP ...!
M-MY GUT ...
Hoaaa...!
THOSE ENORMOUS HORNS ARE SOOO COOOOL ...!!
FWEFWEEEE
MINAMIIKE
AKANEYAMA
Senob
THIS IS
COURT B, GAME 1 OVER
TRO
MP
RATTL RATTL

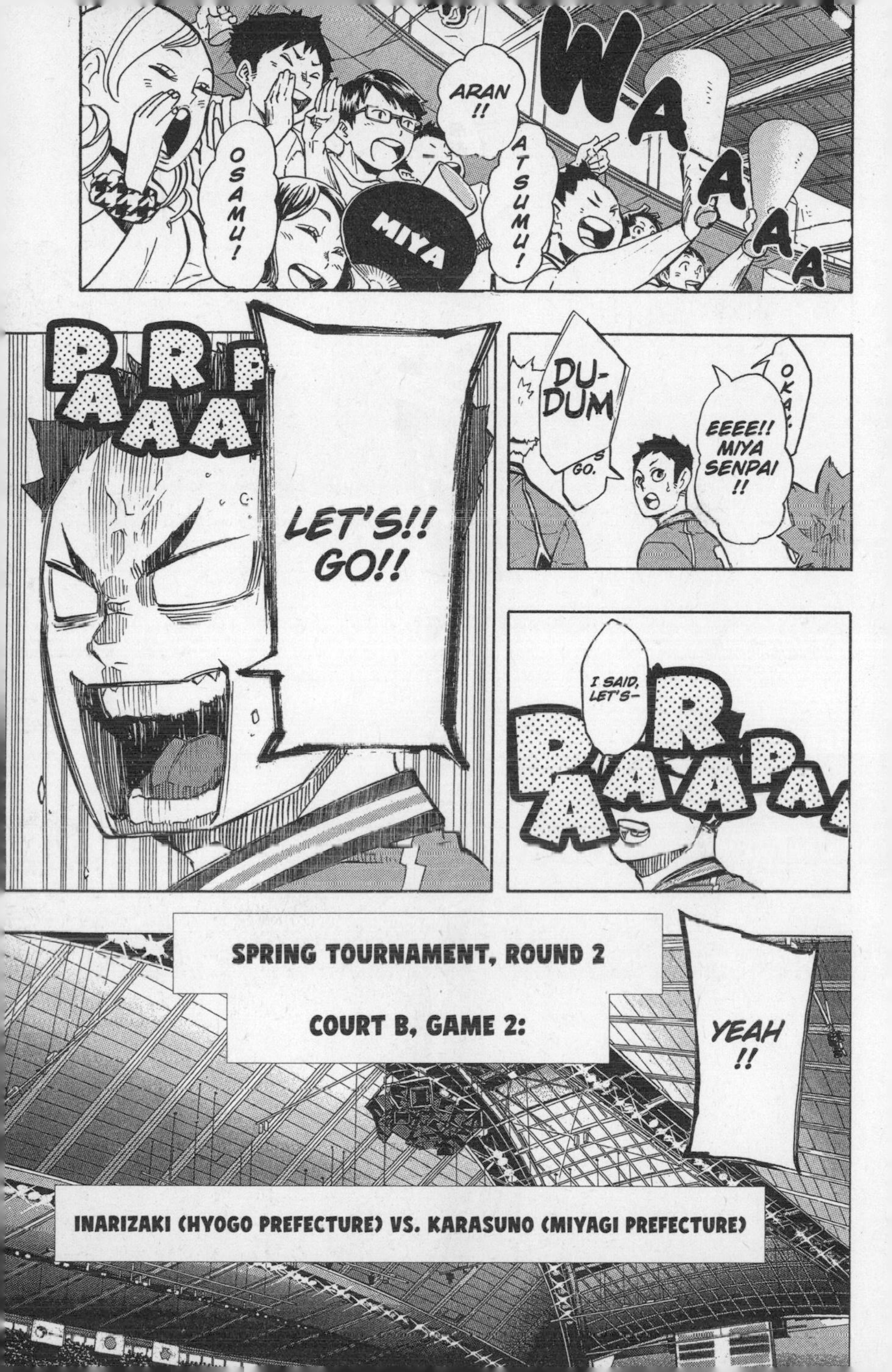
WAAAAA
ATSUMU!
ARAN!!
MIYA
OSAMU!
EEEE!! MIYA SENPAI!!
DU-DUM
I SAID, LET'S—
LET'S!! GO!!
YEAH!!
SPRING TOURNAMENT, ROUND 2
COURT B, GAME 2:
INARIZAKI (HYOGO PREFECTURE) VS. KARASUNO (MIYAGI PREFECTURE)

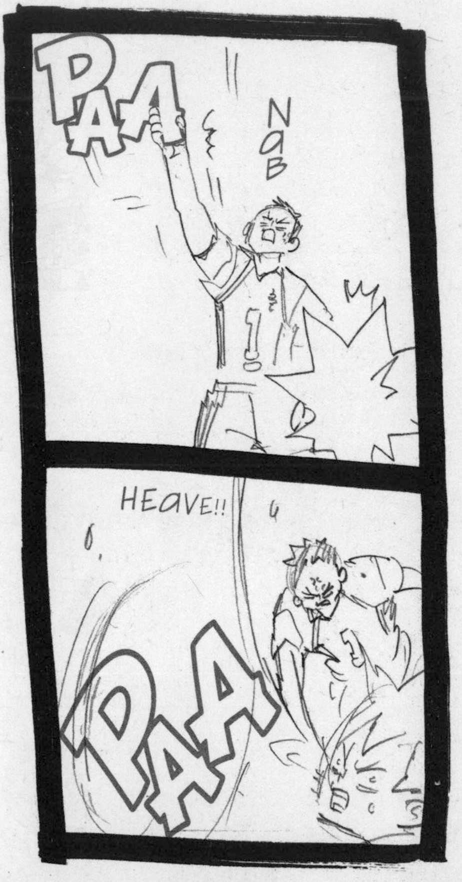
NAB
PAA
HEAVE!!
PAA

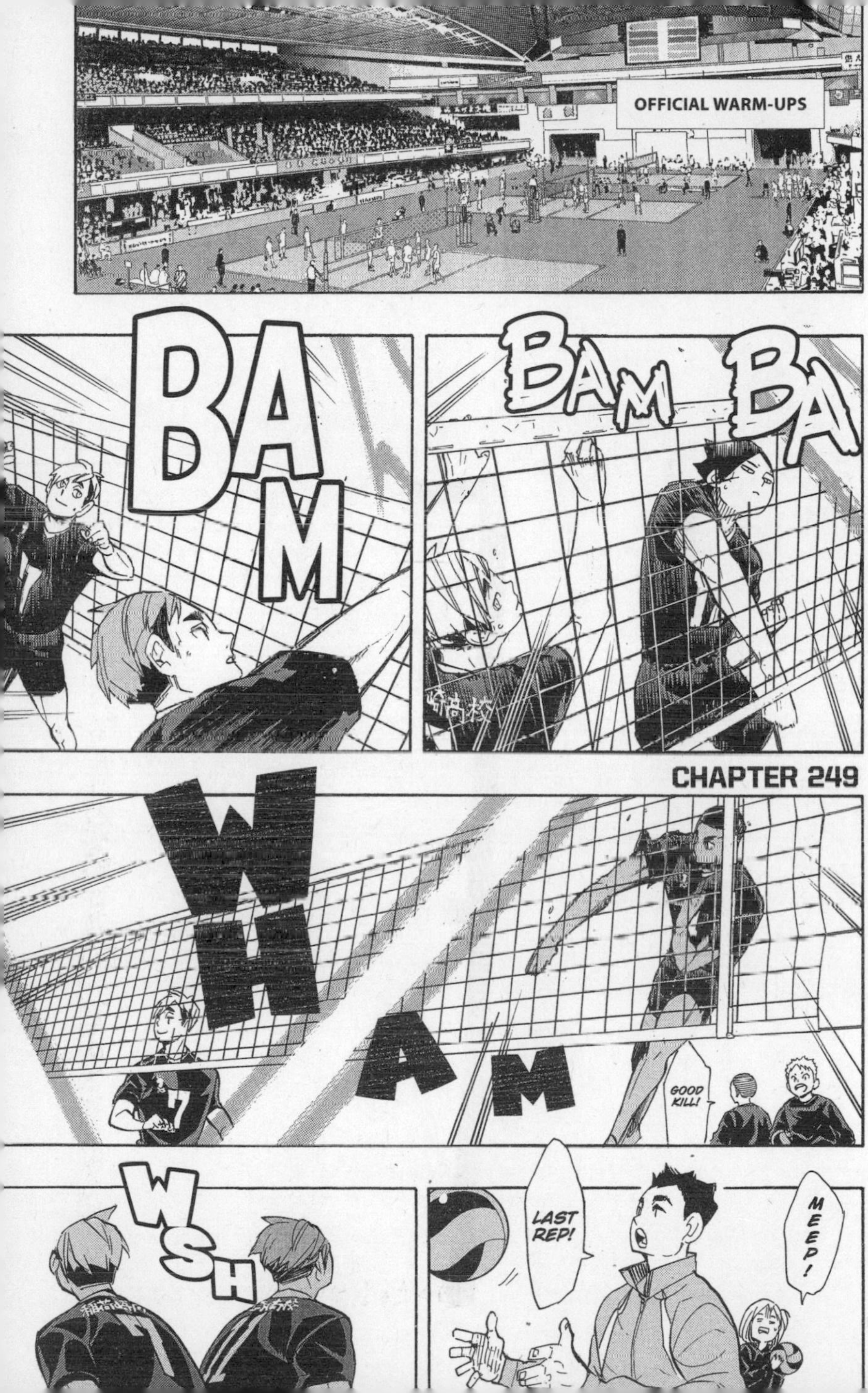
OFFICIAL WARM-UPS
BAM BA
BAM
CHAPTER 249
WHAM
GOOD KILL!
MEEP!
LAST REP!
WSH

CHAPTER 249: Silence and Clamor

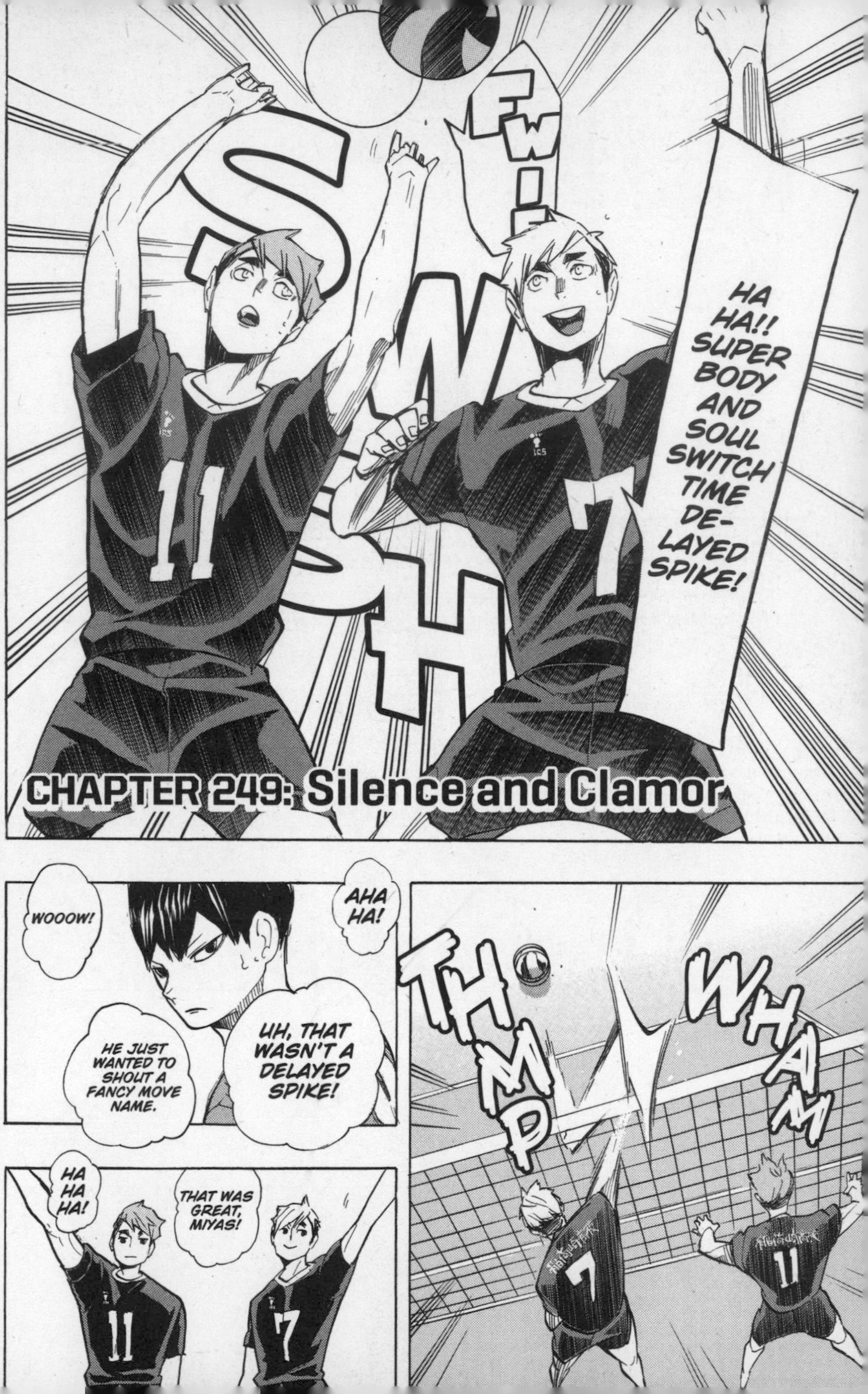
HA HA!! SUPER BODY AND SOUL SWITCH TIME DE-LAYED SPIKE!
WHAM
THMP
AHA HA!
WOOOW!
UH, THAT WASN'T A DELAYED SPIKE!
HE JUST WANTED TO SHOUT A FANCY MOVE NAME.
THAT WAS GREAT, MIYAS!
HA HA HA!

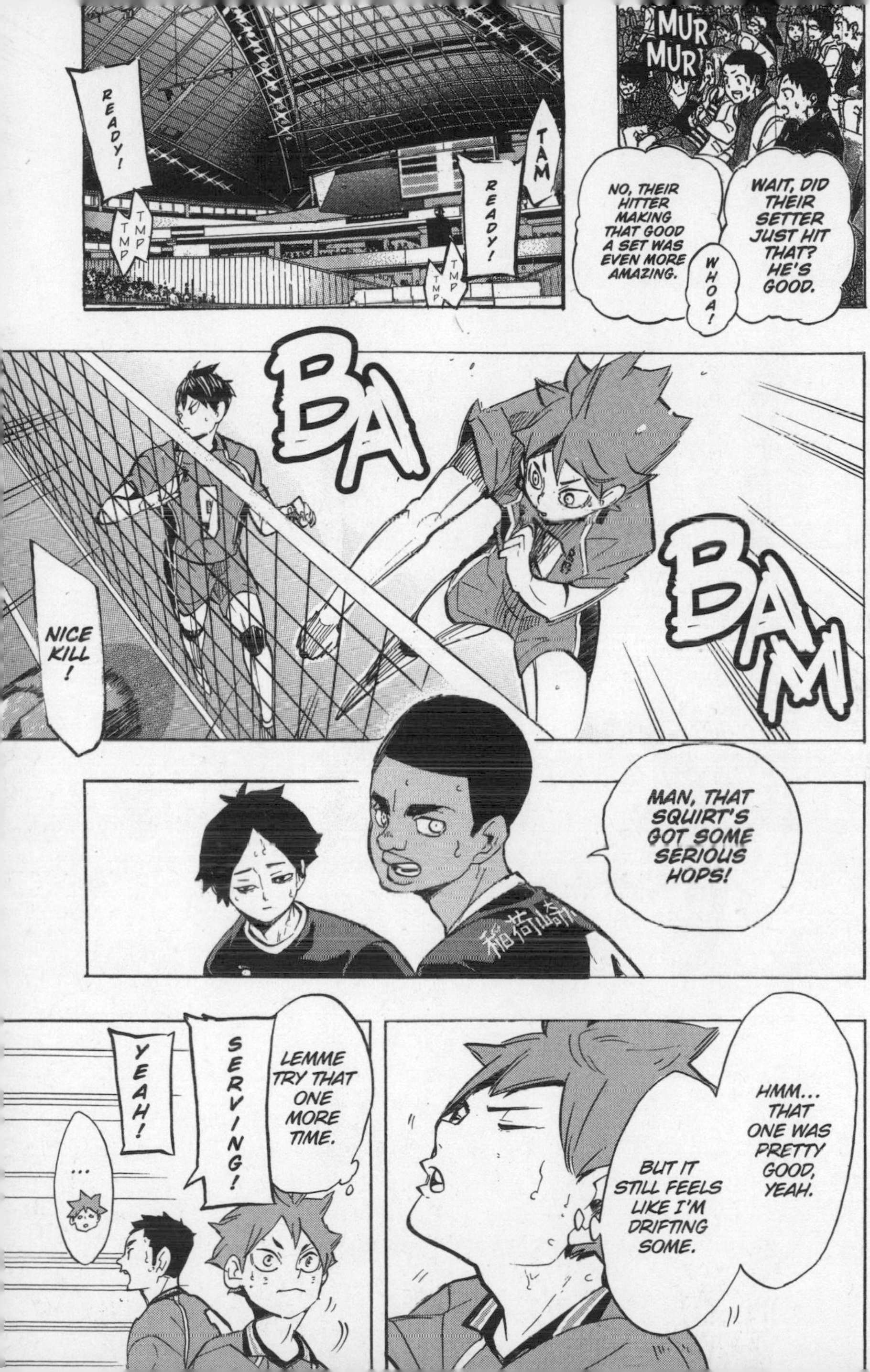
MUR MUR
WAIT, DID THEIR SETTER JUST HIT THAT? HE'S GOOD.
WHOA!
NO, THEIR HITTER MAKING THAT GOOD A SET WAS EVEN MORE AMAZING.
TAM
READY!
TMP TMP
READY!
TMP TMP
BA
BAM
NICE KILL!
MAN, THAT SQUIRT'S GOT SOME SERIOUS HOPS!
HMM... THAT ONE WAS PRETTY GOOD, YEAH.
BUT IT STILL FEELS LIKE I'M DRIFTING SOME.
LEMME TRY THAT ONE MORE TIME.
SERVING!
YEAH!
...

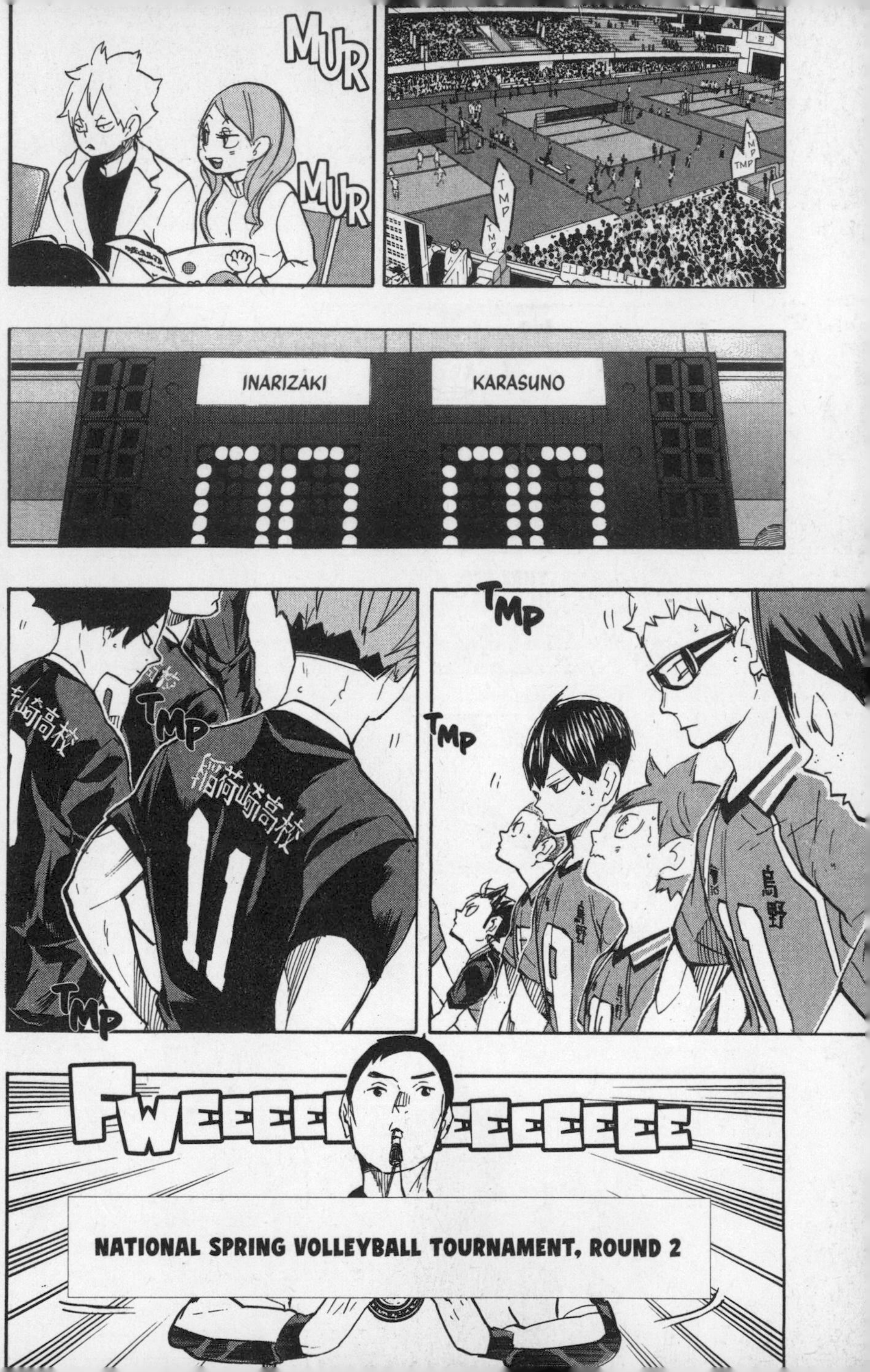
TMP
TMP
TMP
TMP
MUR
MUR
INARIZAKI
KARASUNO
TMP
TMP
TMP
TMP
FWEEEEEEEEEEEEE
NATIONAL SPRING VOLLEYBALL TOURNAMENT, ROUND 2

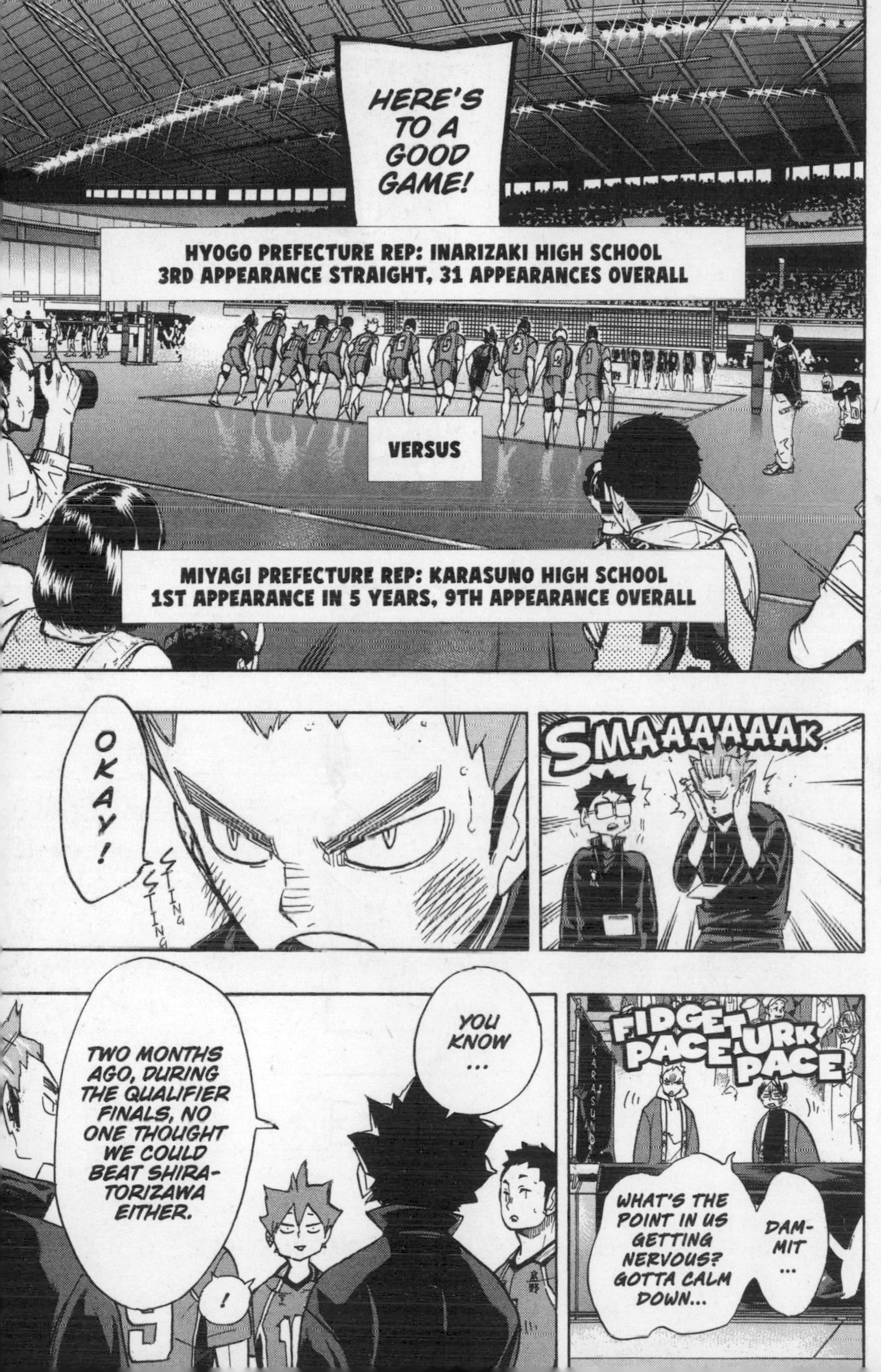
HERE'S TO A GOOD GAME!
HYOGO PREFECTURE REP: INARIZAKI HIGH SCHOOL
3RD APPEARANCE STRAIGHT, 31 APPEARANCES OVERALL
VERSUS
MIYAGI PREFECTURE REP: KARASUNO HIGH SCHOOL
1ST APPEARANCE IN 5 YEARS, 9TH APPEARANCE OVERALL
SMAAAAAAK
OKAY!
STING STING
FIDGET
PACE
TURK
PACE
DAM-MIT...
WHAT'S THE POINT IN US GETTING NERVOUS? GOTTA CALM DOWN...
YOU KNOW...
TWO MONTHS AGO, DURING THE QUALIFIER FINALS, NO ONE THOUGHT WE COULD BEAT SHIRA-TORIZAWA EITHER.
!

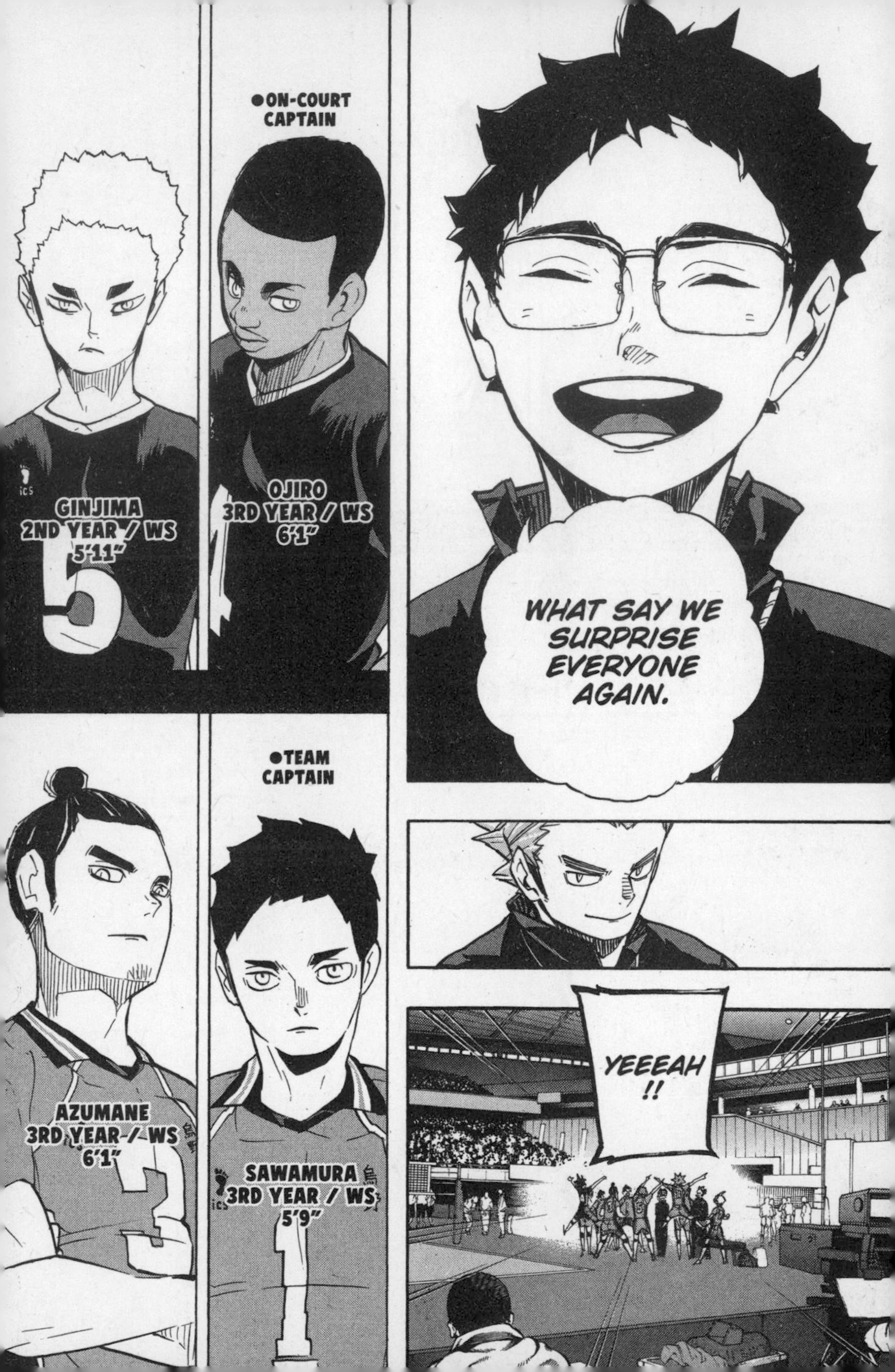
WHAT SAY WE SURPRISE EVERYONE AGAIN.
YEEEAH !!
●ON-COURT CAPTAIN
OJIRO 3RD YEAR / WS 6'1"
GINJIMA 2ND YEAR / WS 5'11"
●TEAM CAPTAIN
SAWAMURA 3RD YEAR / WS 5'9"
AZUMANE 3RD YEAR / WS 6'1"

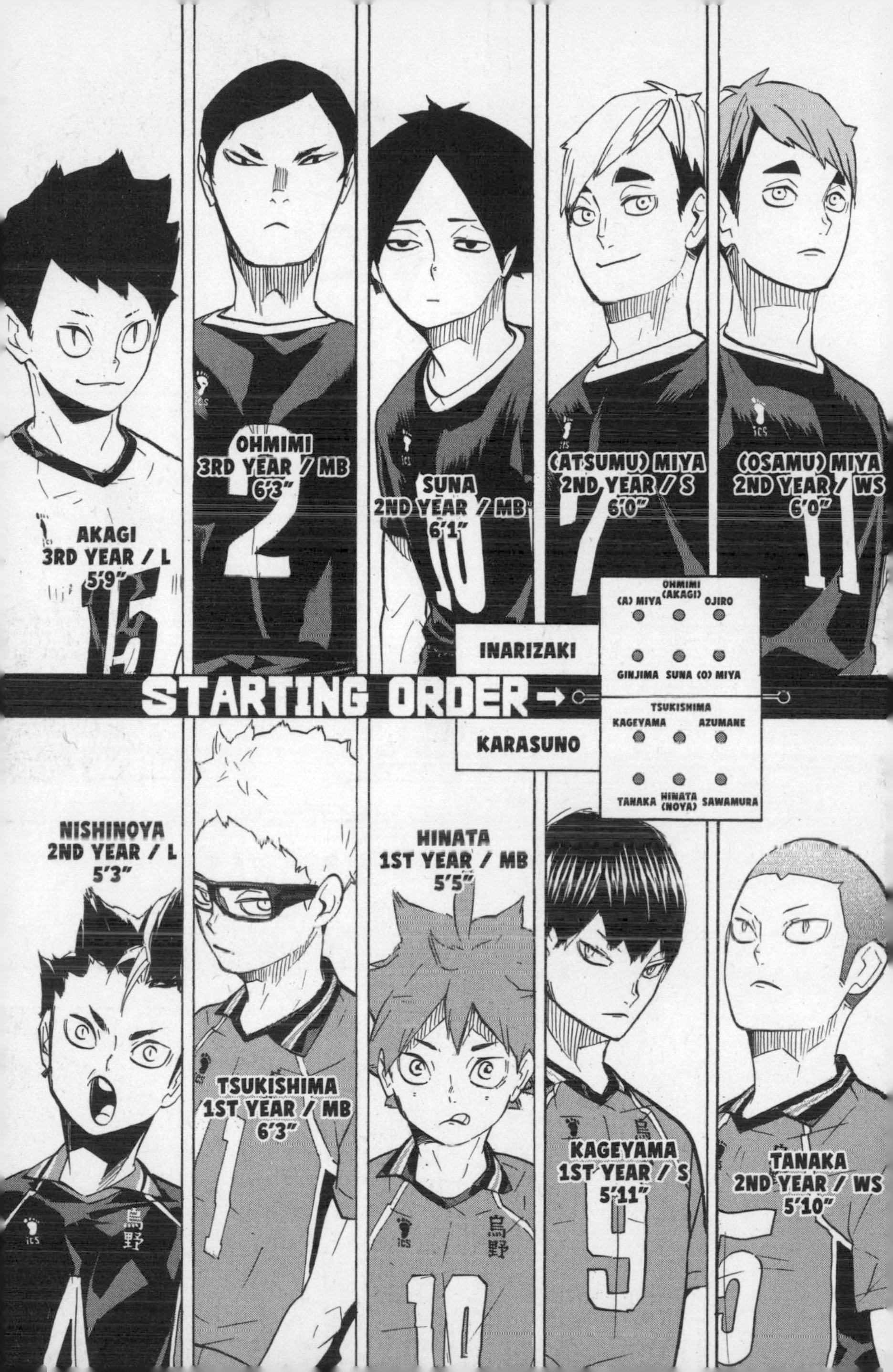
(OSAMU) MIYA
2ND YEAR / WS
6'0"
(ATSUMU) MIYA
2ND YEAR / S
6'0"
SUNA
2ND YEAR / MB
6'1"
OHMIMI
3RD YEAR / MB
6'3"
AKAGI
3RD YEAR / L
5'9"
INARIZAKI
(A) MIYA
OHMIMI (AKAGI)
OJIRO
GINJIMA
SUNA
(O) MIYA
STARTING ORDER →
KARASUNO
KAGEYAMA
TSUKISHIMA
AZUMANE
TANAKA
HINATA (NOYA)
SAWAMURA
TANAKA
2ND YEAR / WS
5'10"
KAGEYAMA
1ST YEAR / S
5'11"
HINATA
1ST YEAR / MB
5'5"
TSUKISHIMA
1ST YEAR / MB
6'3"
NISHINOYA
2ND YEAR / L
5'3"

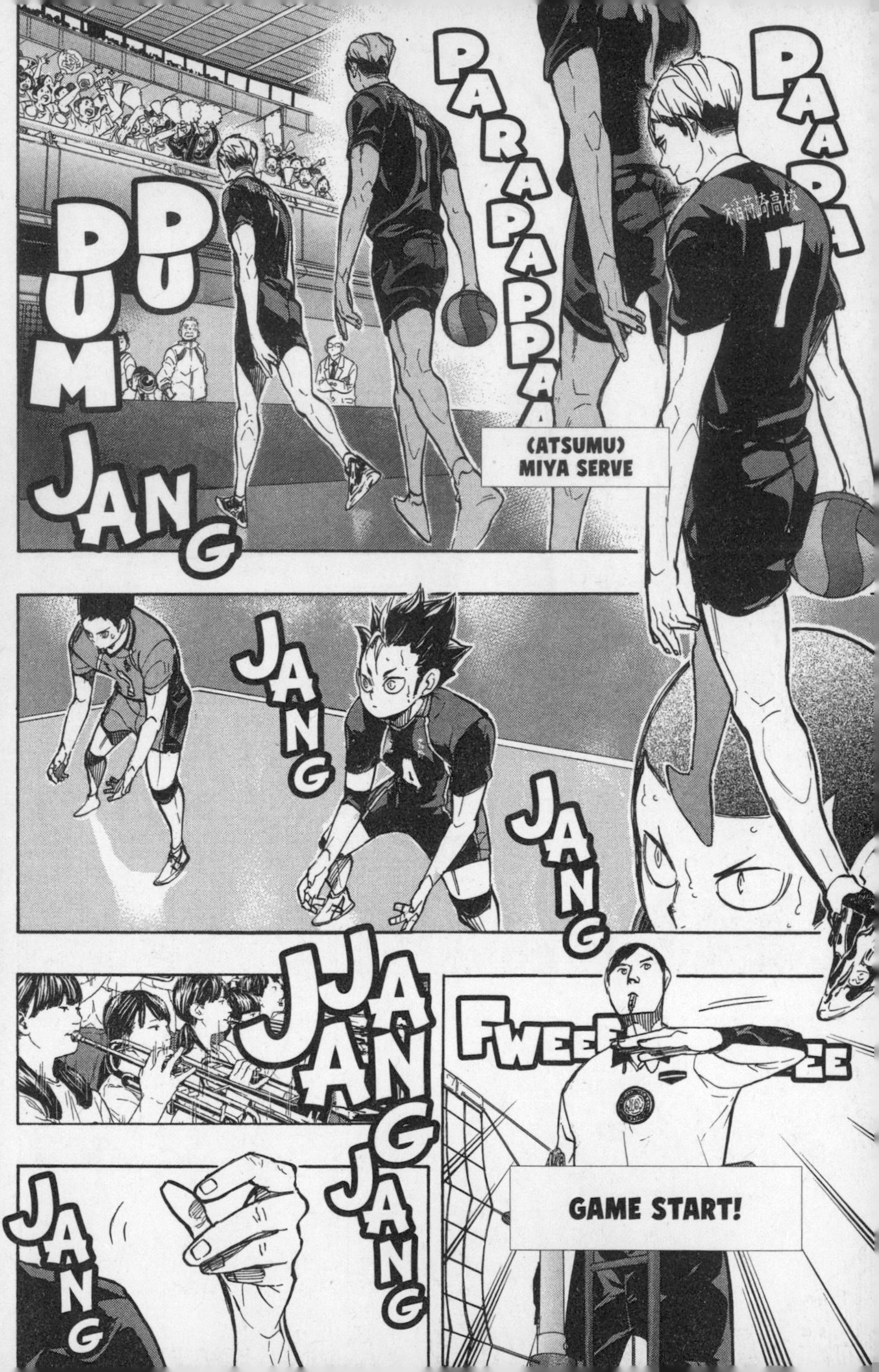
PAAPA
稲荷崎高校
PARAPAPPAA
(ATSUMU) MIYA SERVE
DUM DUM
JANG
JANG
JANG
FWEEE
EE
GAME START!
JAJANG
JANG
JANG

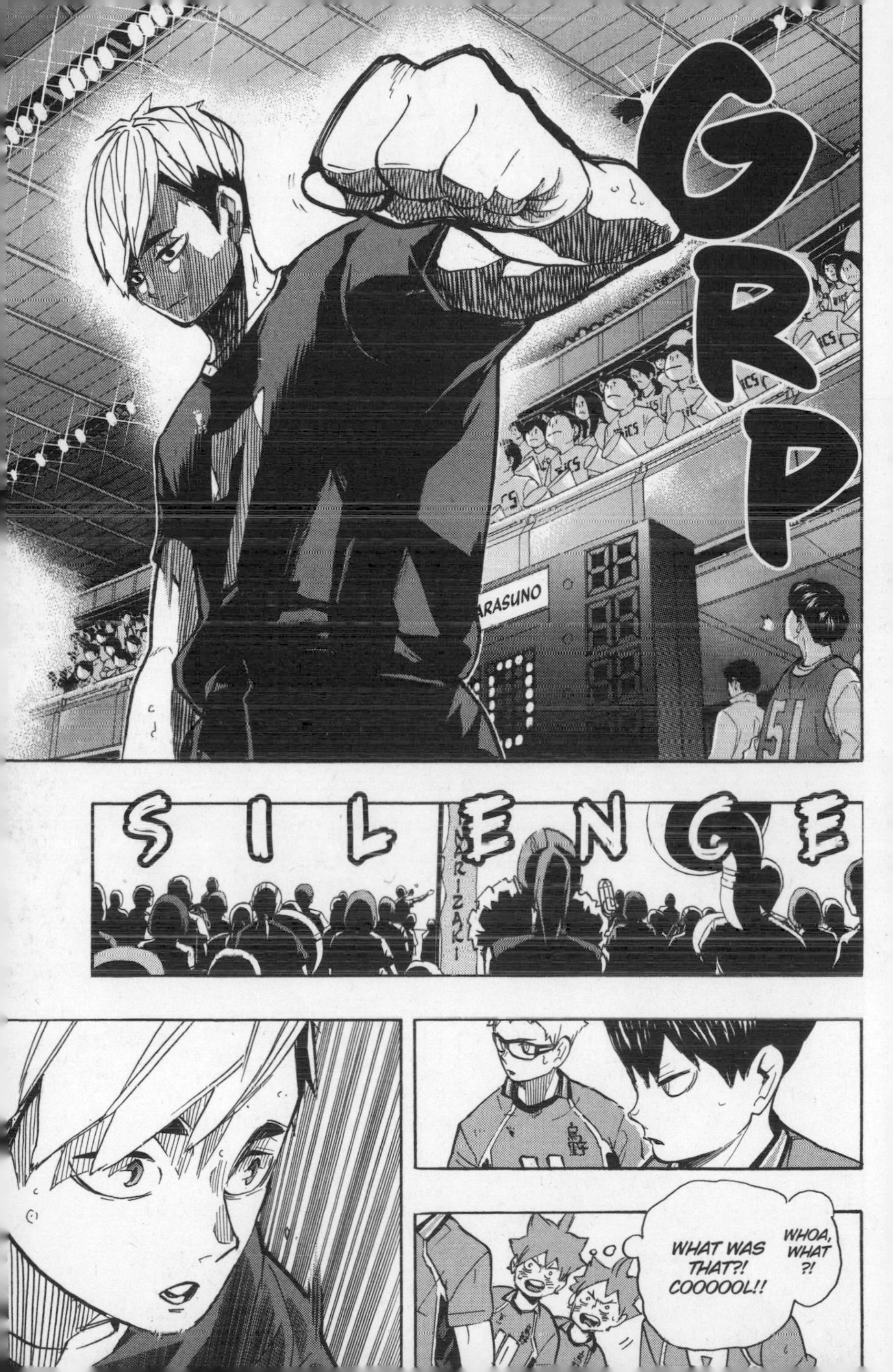
GRP
ARASUNO
SILENCE
WHOA, WHAT?!
WHAT WAS THAT?! COOOOOL!!

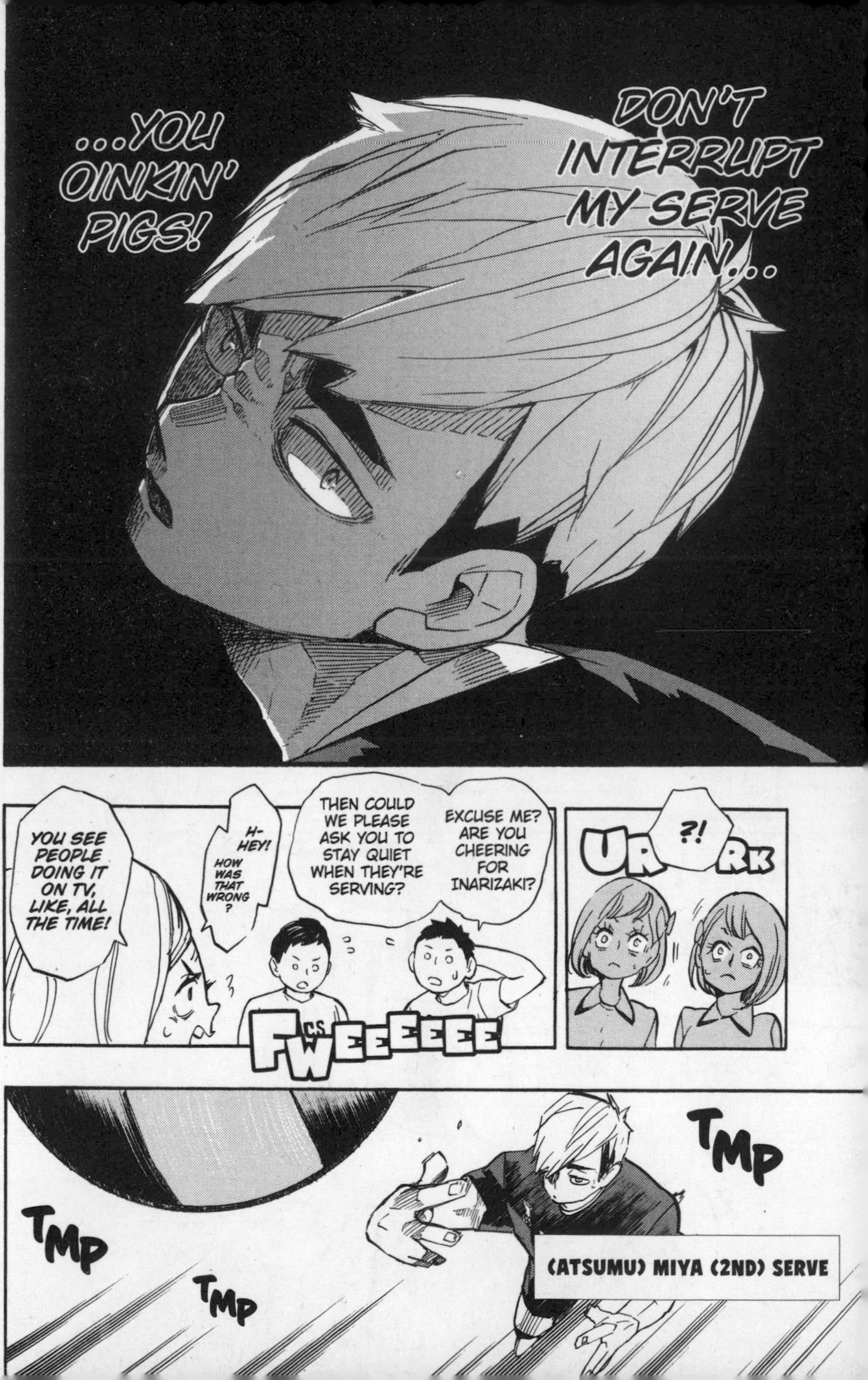
DON'T INTERRUPT MY SERVE AGAIN...
...YOU OINKIN' PIGS!
?!
UR RK
EXCUSE ME? ARE YOU CHEERING FOR INARIZAKI?
THEN COULD WE PLEASE ASK YOU TO STAY QUIET WHEN THEY'RE SERVING?
H-HEY! HOW WAS THAT WRONG?
YOU SEE PEOPLE DOING IT ON TV, LIKE, ALL THE TIME!
FWEEEEEE
C.S.
TMP
(ATSUMU) MIYA (2ND) SERVE
TMP
TMP

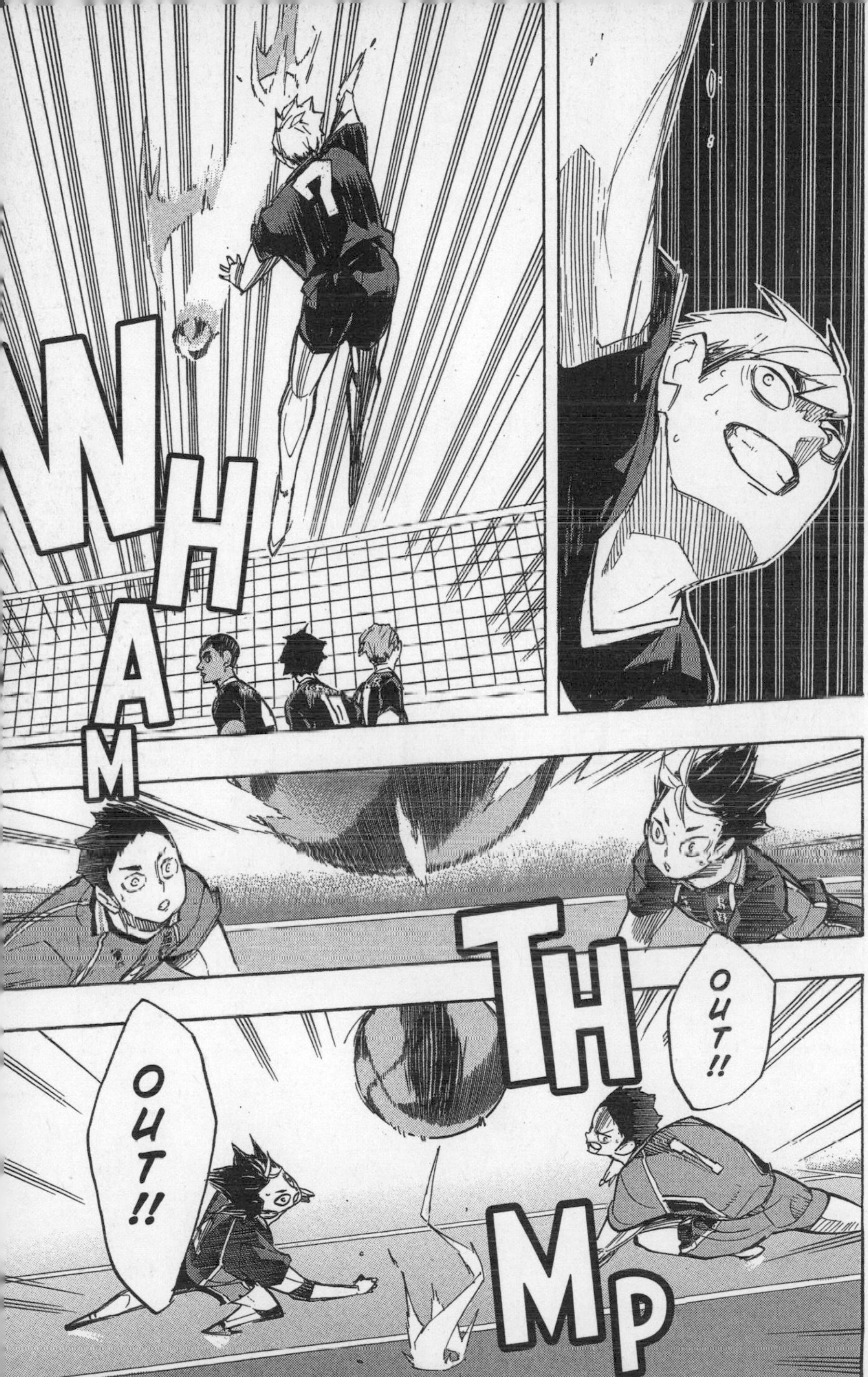
WHAM
THMP
OUT!!
OUT!!

CAN IT!

LAAAME...

GAAAAAAH!!

FEH! MY SERVE TOSS GOT AWAY FROM ME.

TMP

AZUMANE SERVE

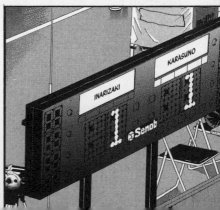

INARIZAKI

KARASUNO

Senob

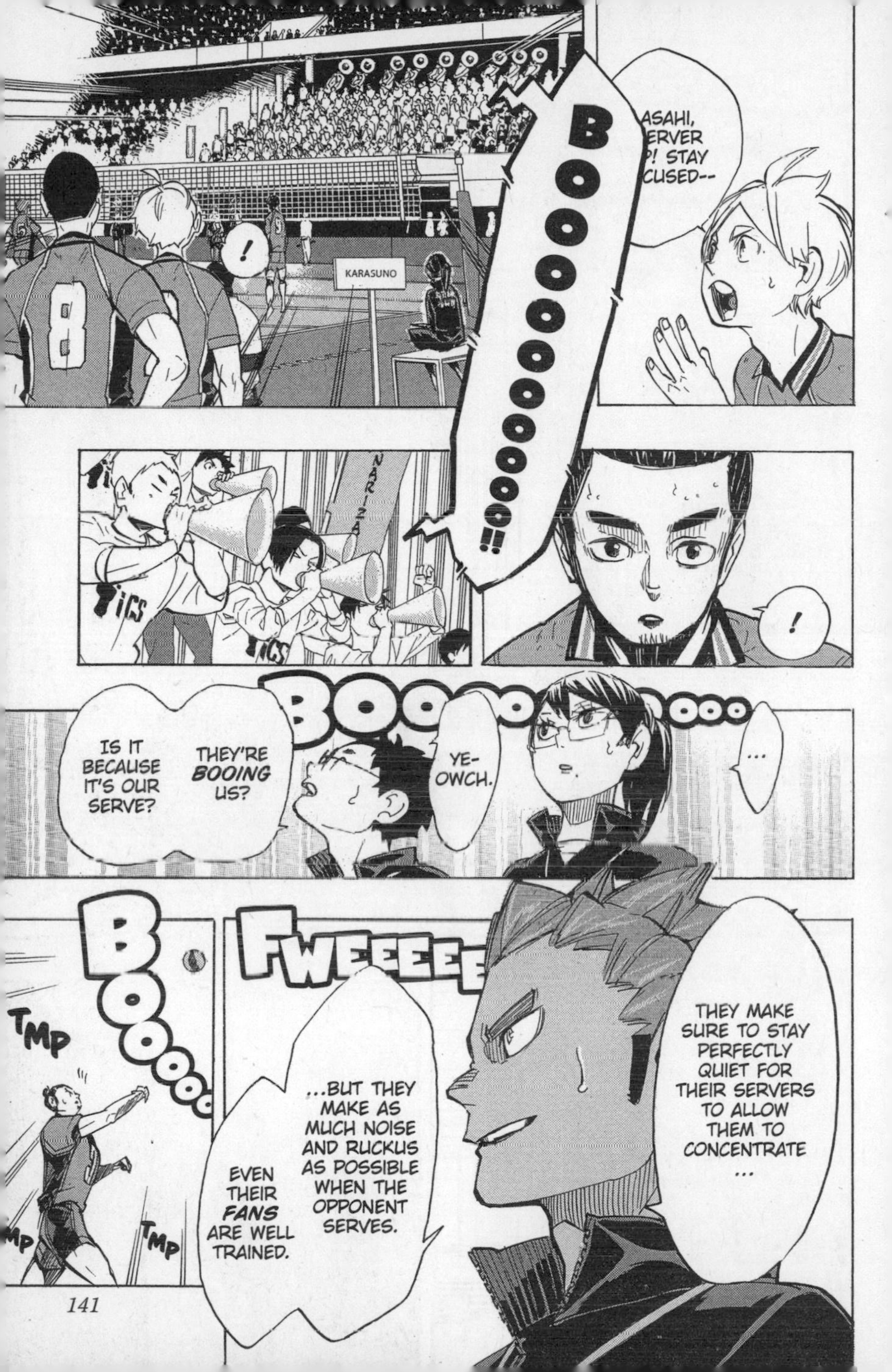
ASAHI, ERVER P! STAY CUSED--
BOOOOOOOOOOOOO!!
!
KARASUNO
!
...
YE-OWCH.
BOOooooo...
THEY'RE *BOOING* US?
IS IT BECAUSE IT'S OUR SERVE?
THEY MAKE SURE TO STAY PERFECTLY QUIET FOR THEIR SERVERS TO ALLOW THEM TO CONCENTRATE...
...BUT THEY MAKE AS MUCH NOISE AND RUCKUS AS POSSIBLE WHEN THE OPPONENT SERVES.
EVEN THEIR *FANS* ARE WELL TRAINED.
FWEEEEE
BOOOOO
TMP
TMP
MP

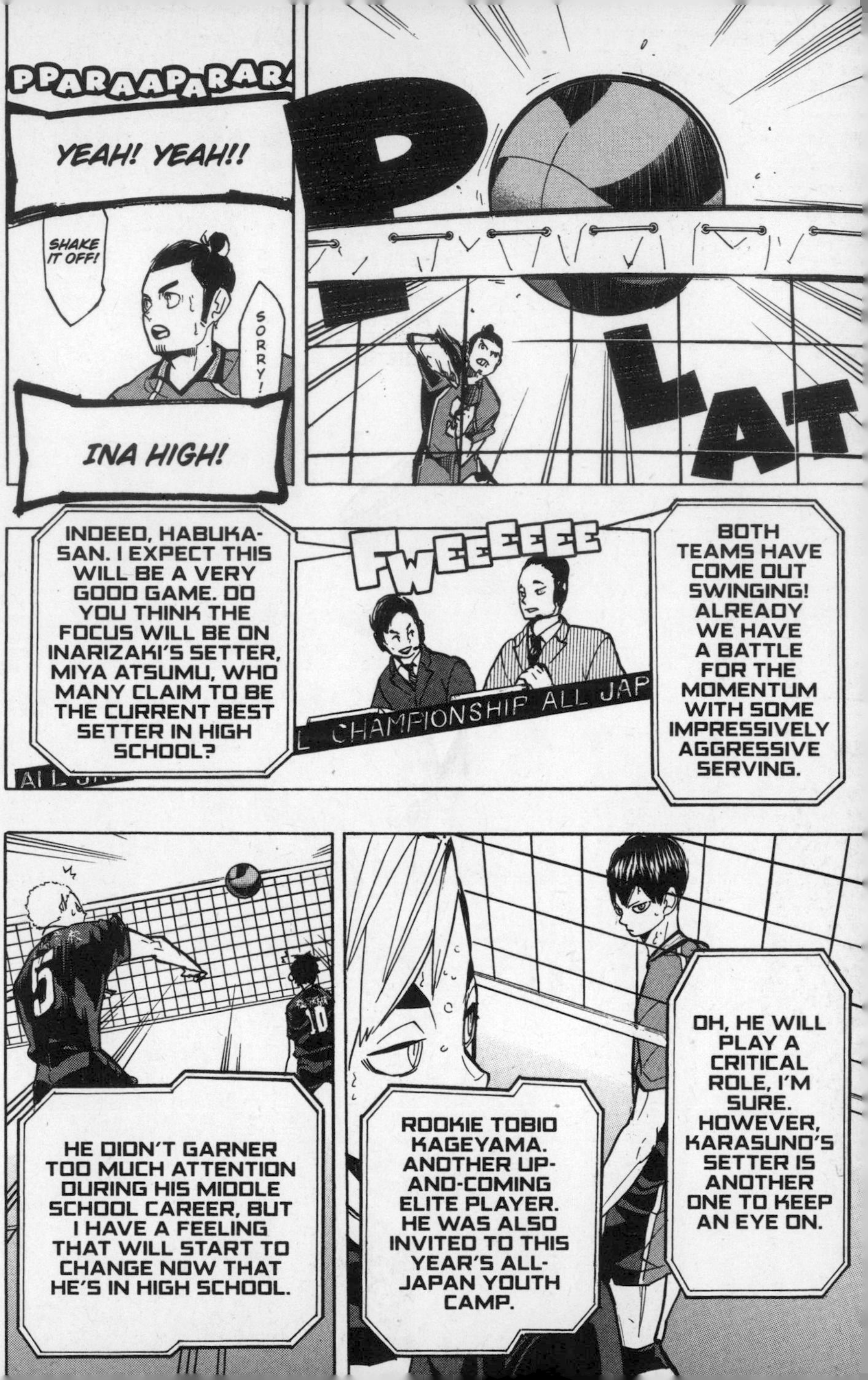
POLAT
PPARAAPARARA
YEAH! YEAH!!
SHAKE IT OFF!
SORRY!
INA HIGH!
BOTH TEAMS HAVE COME OUT SWINGING! ALREADY WE HAVE A BATTLE FOR THE MOMENTUM WITH SOME IMPRESSIVELY AGGRESSIVE SERVING.
FWEEEEEE
CHAMPIONSHIP ALL JAP
INDEED, HABUKA-SAN. I EXPECT THIS WILL BE A VERY GOOD GAME. DO YOU THINK THE FOCUS WILL BE ON INARIZAKI'S SETTER, MIYA ATSUMU, WHO MANY CLAIM TO BE THE CURRENT BEST SETTER IN HIGH SCHOOL?
OH, HE WILL PLAY A CRITICAL ROLE, I'M SURE. HOWEVER, KARASUNO'S SETTER IS ANOTHER ONE TO KEEP AN EYE ON.
ROOKIE TOBIO KAGEYAMA. ANOTHER UP-AND-COMING ELITE PLAYER. HE WAS ALSO INVITED TO THIS YEAR'S ALL-JAPAN YOUTH CAMP.
HE DIDN'T GARNER TOO MUCH ATTENTION DURING HIS MIDDLE SCHOOL CAREER, BUT I HAVE A FEELING THAT WILL START TO CHANGE NOW THAT HE'S IN HIGH SCHOOL.

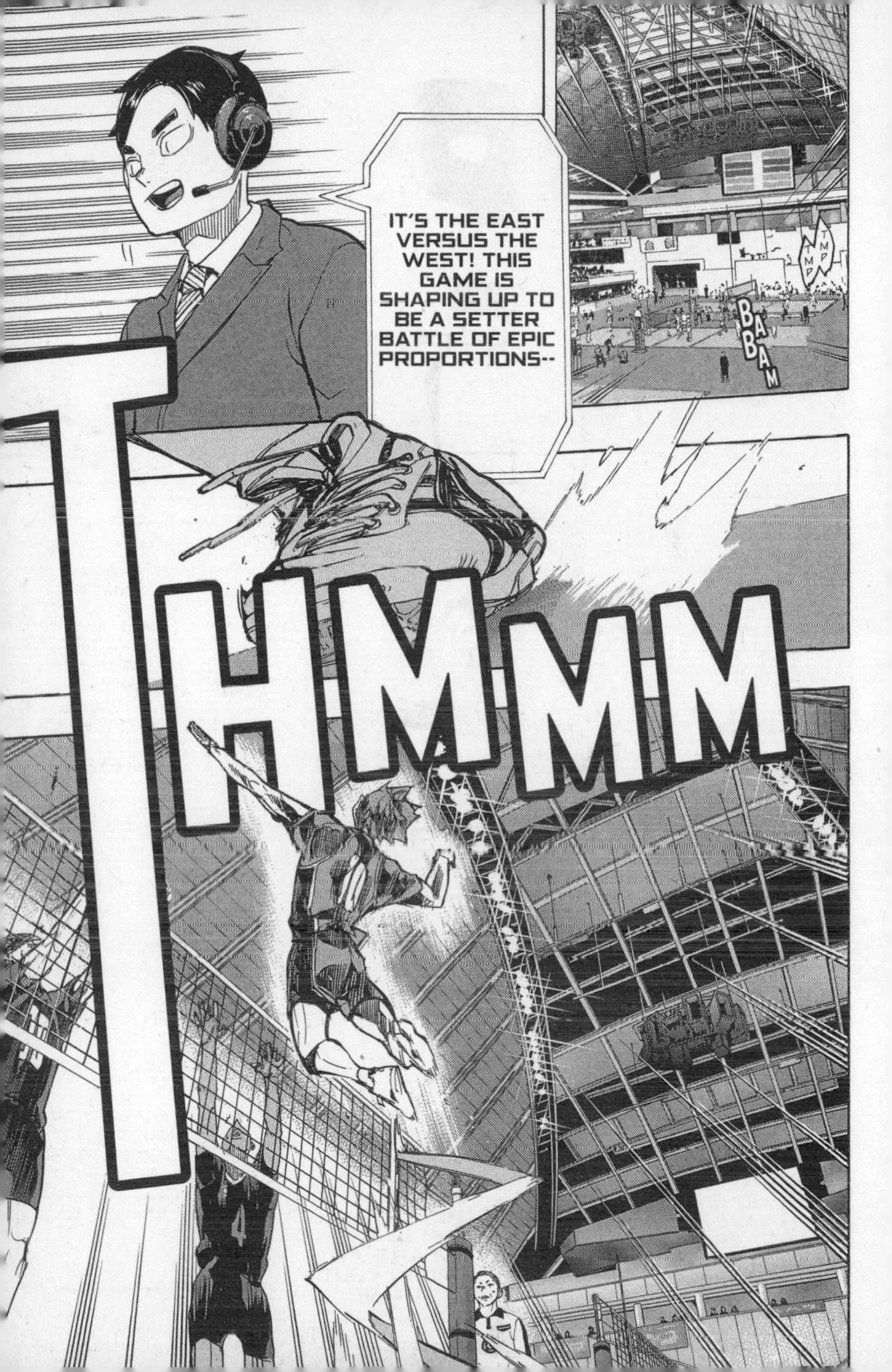
TMP TMP
BABAM
IT'S THE EAST VERSUS THE WEST! THIS GAME IS SHAPING UP TO BE A SETTER BATTLE OF EPIC PROPORTIONS--
HMMM

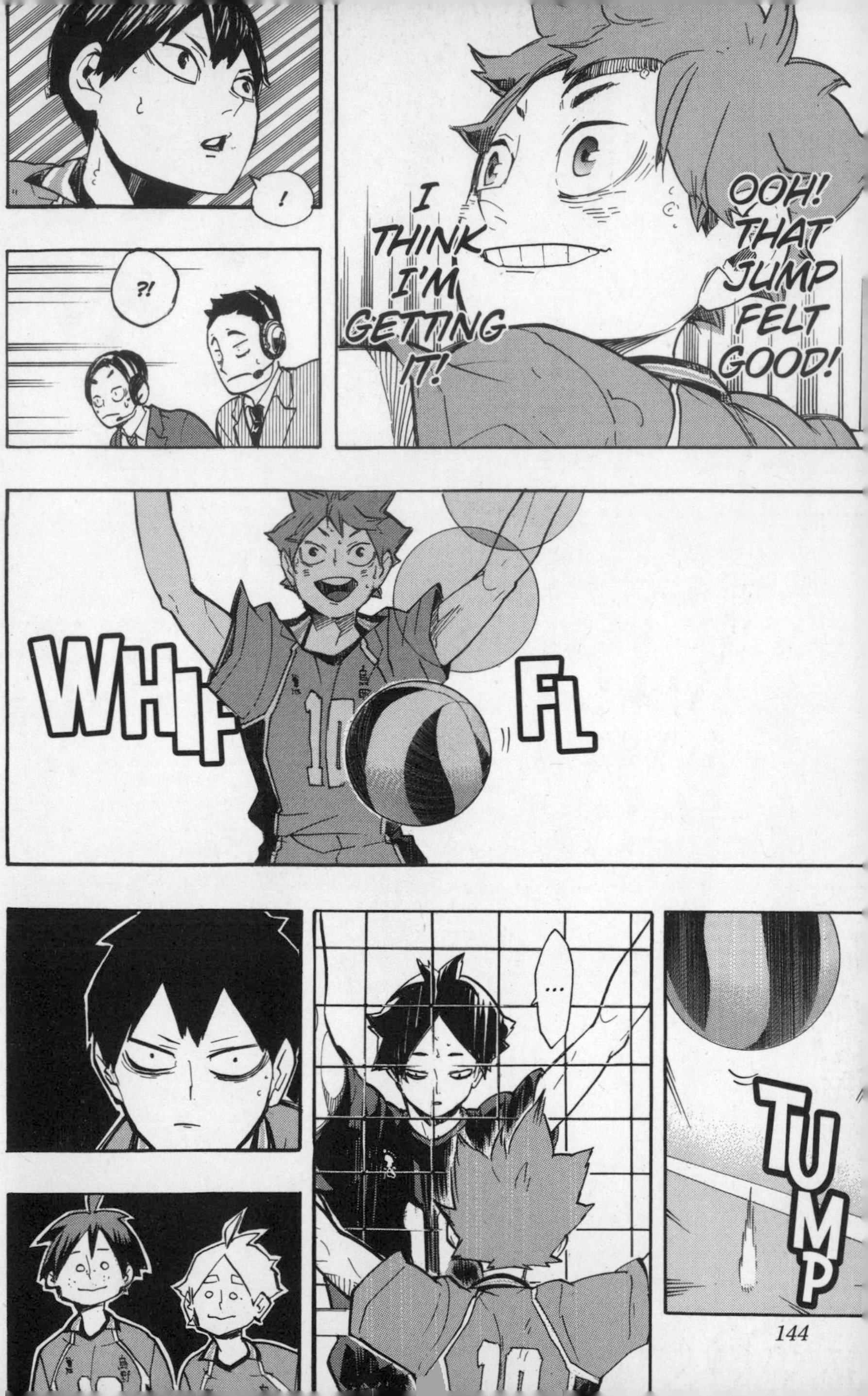

OOH! THAT JUMP FELT GOOD!
I THINK I'M GETTING IT!
!
?!
FL
WHIF
TUMP
...

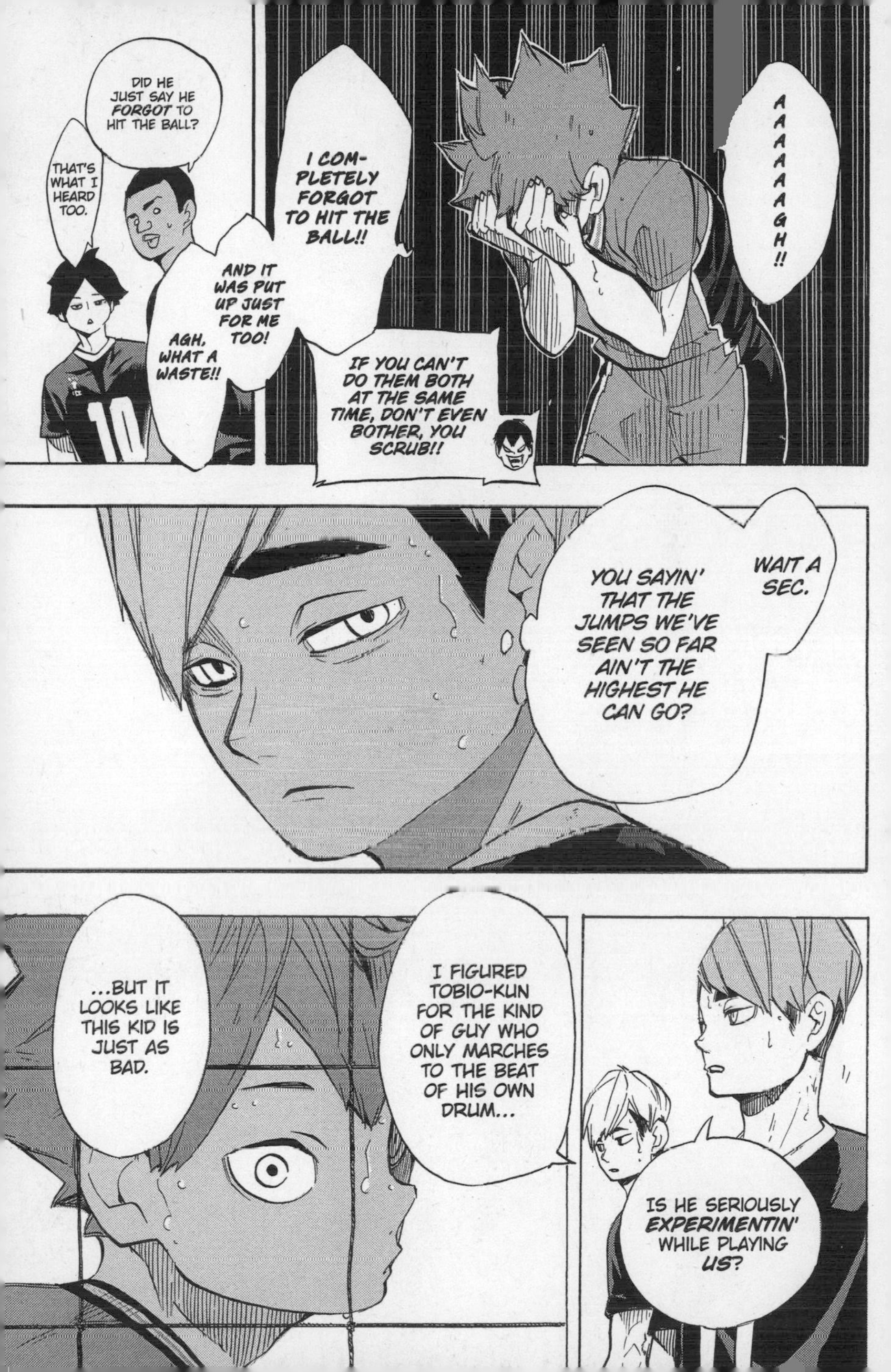
AAAAAAGH!!
I COMPLETELY FORGOT TO HIT THE BALL!!
AND IT WAS PUT UP JUST FOR ME TOO!
AGH, WHAT A WASTE!!
IF YOU CAN'T DO THEM BOTH AT THE SAME TIME, DON'T EVEN BOTHER, YOU SCRUB!!
DID HE JUST SAY HE *FORGOT* TO HIT THE BALL?
THAT'S WHAT I HEARD TOO.
WAIT A SEC.
YOU SAYIN' THAT THE JUMPS WE'VE SEEN SO FAR AIN'T THE HIGHEST HE CAN GO?
IS HE SERIOUSLY *EXPERIMENTIN'* WHILE PLAYING *US*?
I FIGURED TOBIO-KUN FOR THE KIND OF GUY WHO ONLY MARCHES TO THE BEAT OF HIS OWN DRUM...
...BUT IT LOOKS LIKE THIS KID IS JUST AS BAD.

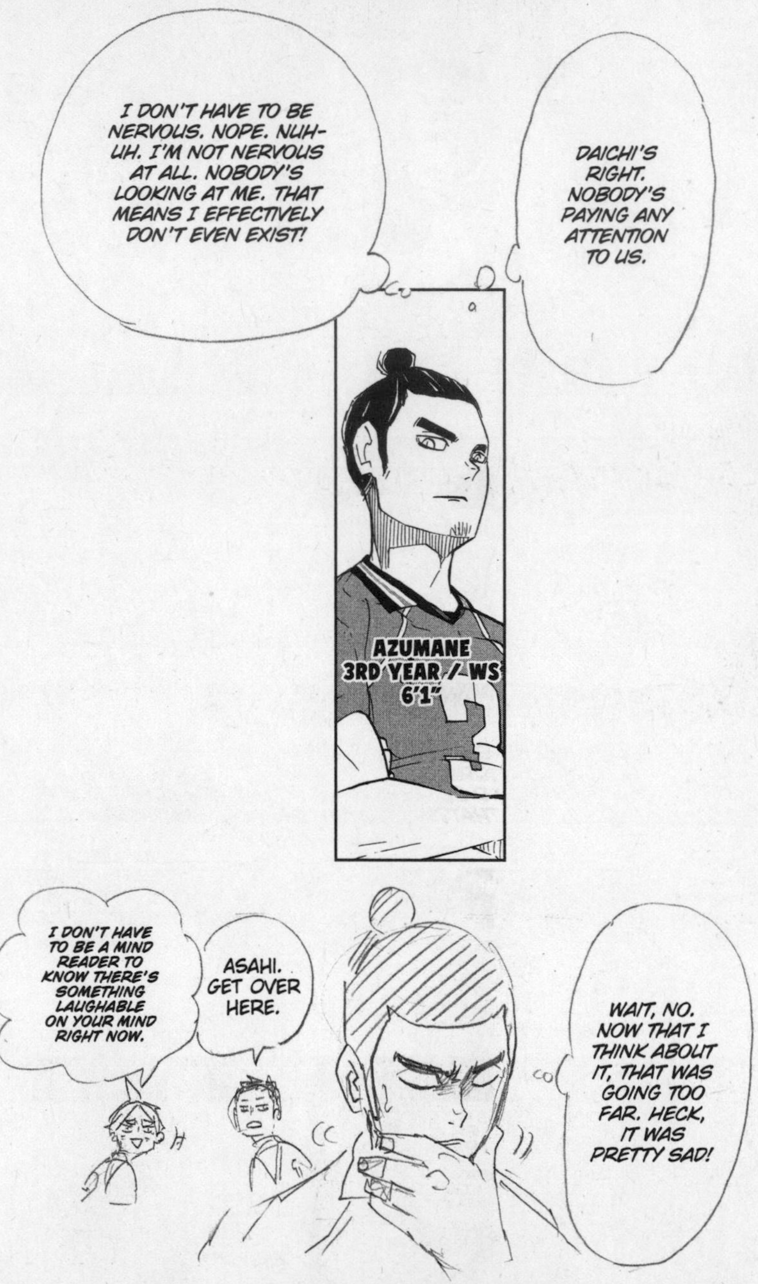
DAICHI'S RIGHT. NOBODY'S PAYING ANY ATTENTION TO US.
I DON'T HAVE TO BE NERVOUS. NOPE. NUH-UH. I'M NOT NERVOUS AT ALL. NOBODY'S LOOKING AT ME. THAT MEANS I EFFECTIVELY DON'T EVEN EXIST!
AZUMANE 3RD YEAR / WS 6'1"
WAIT, NO. NOW THAT I THINK ABOUT IT, THAT WAS GOING TOO FAR. HECK, IT WAS PRETTY SAD!
ASAHI. GET OVER HERE.
I DON'T HAVE TO BE A MIND READER TO KNOW THERE'S SOMETHING LAUGHABLE ON YOUR MIND RIGHT NOW.

CHAPTER 250

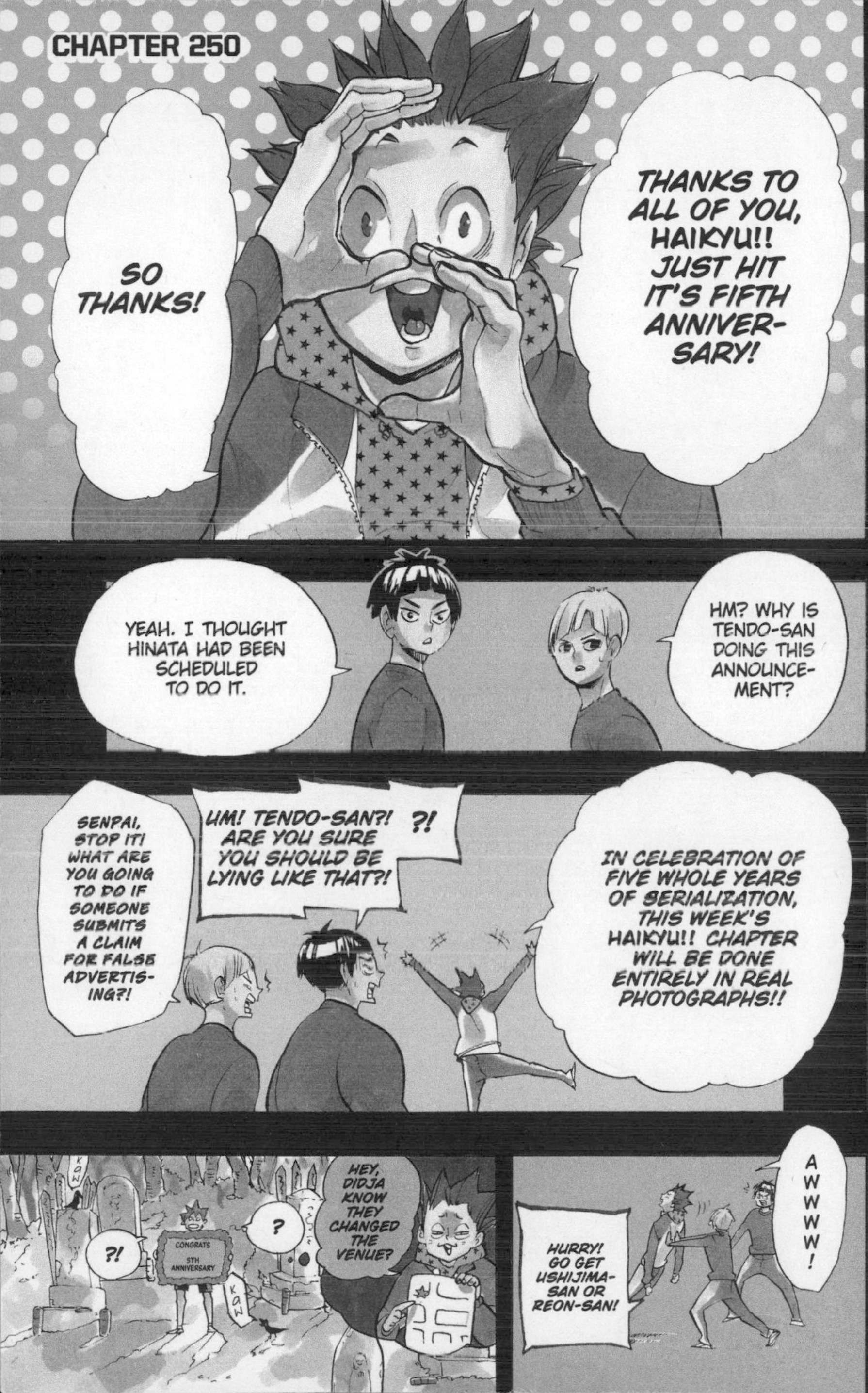
THANKS TO ALL OF YOU, HAIKYU!! JUST HIT IT'S FIFTH ANNIVERSARY!
SO THANKS!
HM? WHY IS TENDO-SAN DOING THIS ANNOUNCEMENT?
YEAH. I THOUGHT HINATA HAD BEEN SCHEDULED TO DO IT.
IN CELEBRATION OF FIVE WHOLE YEARS OF SERIALIZATION, THIS WEEK'S HAIKYU!! CHAPTER WILL BE DONE ENTIRELY IN REAL PHOTOGRAPHS!!
?!
UM! TENDO-SAN?! ARE YOU SURE YOU SHOULD BE LYING LIKE THAT?!
SENPAI, STOP IT! WHAT ARE YOU GOING TO DO IF SOMEONE SUBMITS A CLAIM FOR FALSE ADVERTISING?!
AWWWW!
HURRY! GO GET USHIJIMA-SAN OR REON-SAN!
HEY, DIDJA KNOW THEY CHANGED THE VENUE?
KAW
?
CONGRATS 5TH ANNIVERSARY
?!
KAW

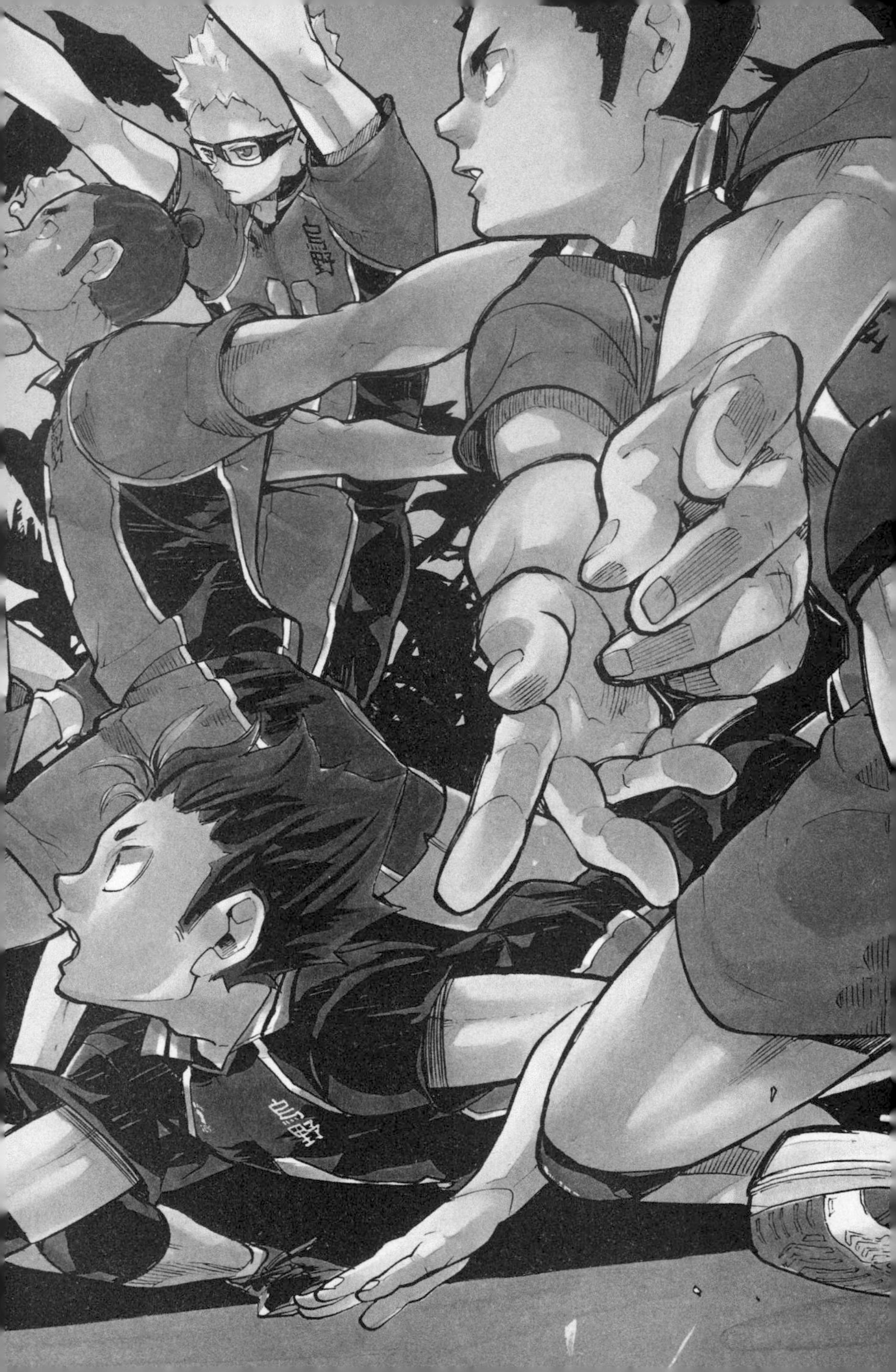

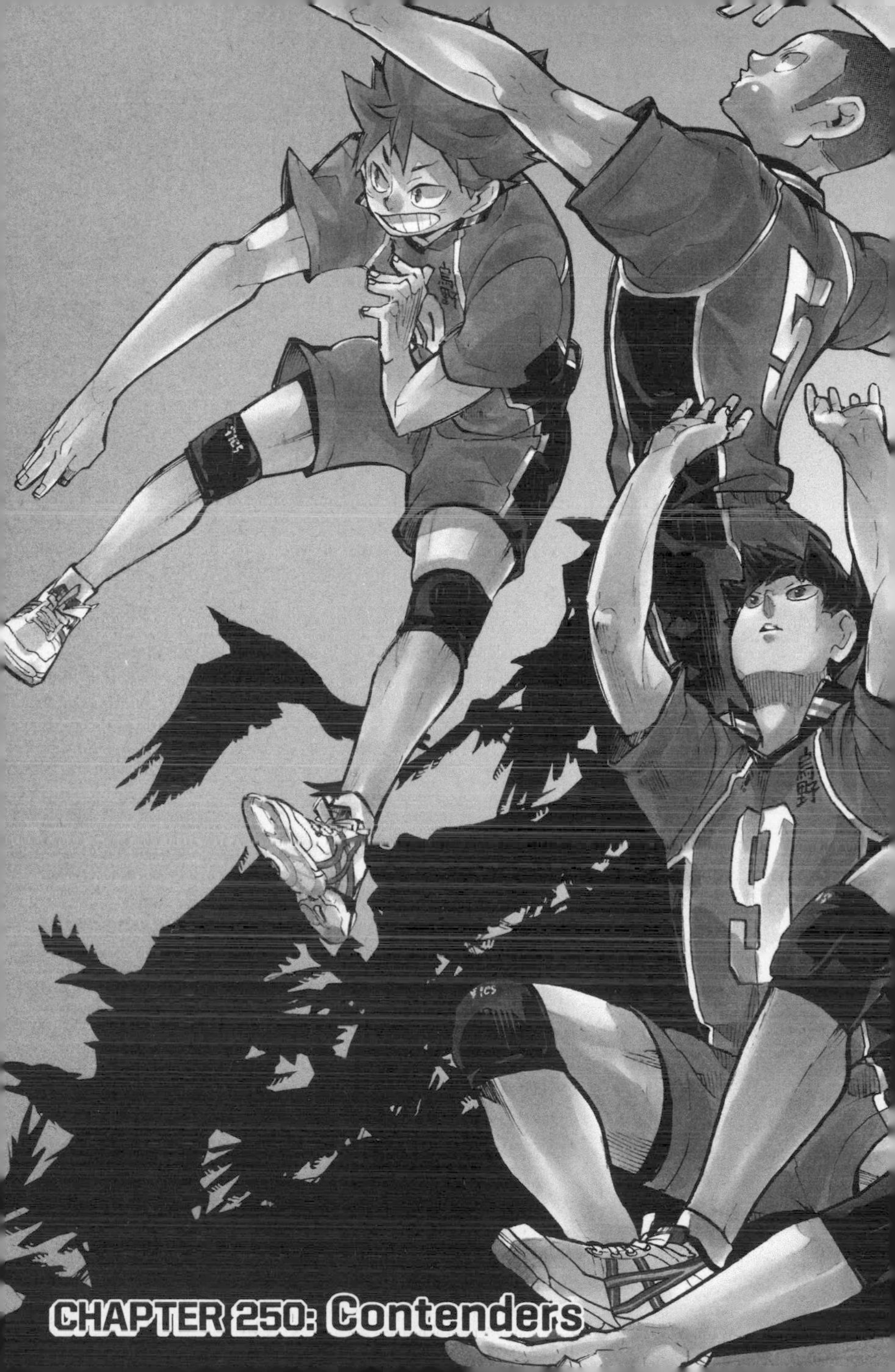
CHAPTER 250: Contenders

HAIKYU!!

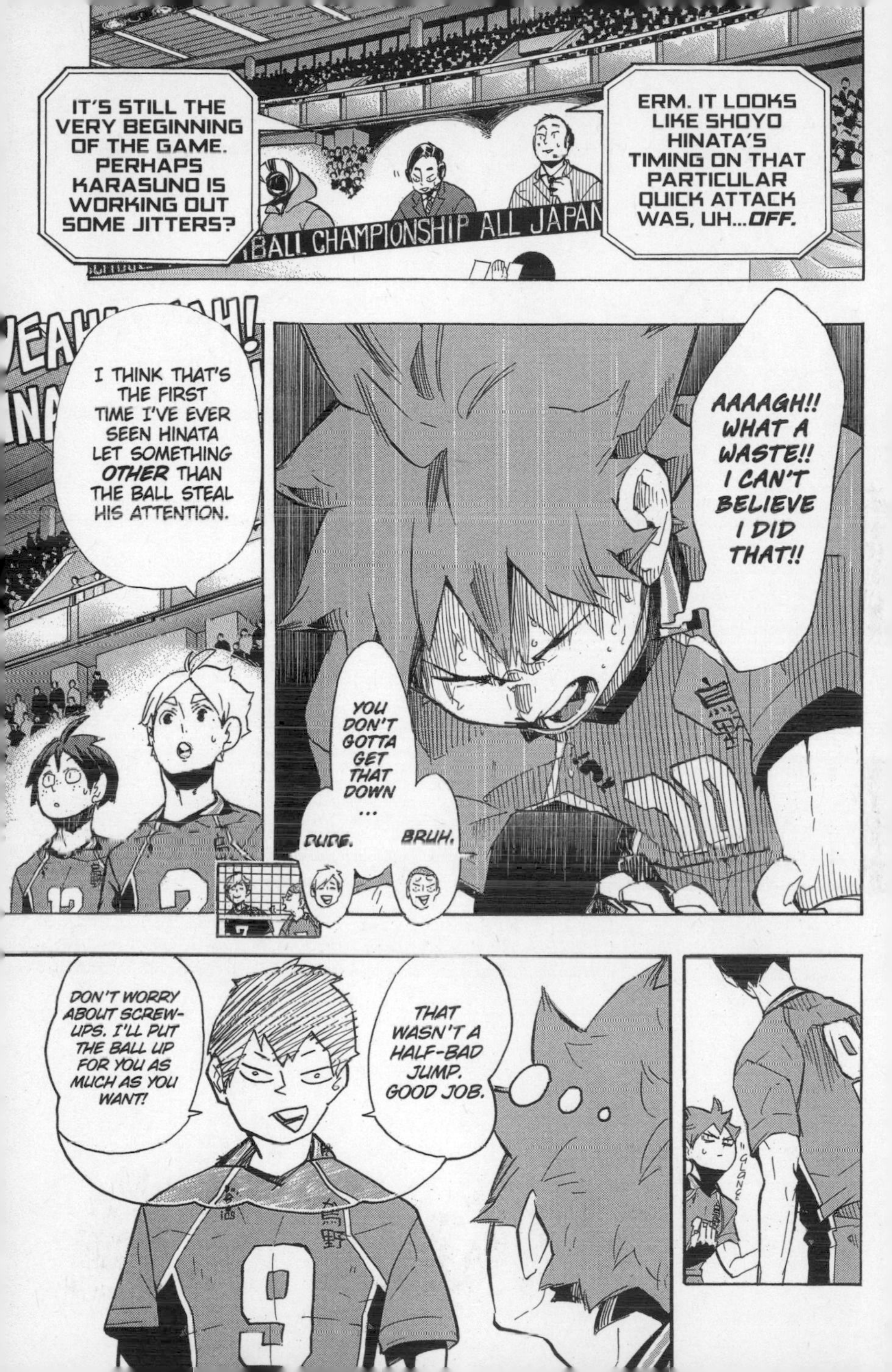
ERM. IT LOOKS LIKE SHOYO HINATA'S TIMING ON THAT PARTICULAR QUICK ATTACK WAS, UH...*OFF.*
IT'S STILL THE VERY BEGINNING OF THE GAME. PERHAPS KARASUNO IS WORKING OUT SOME JITTERS?
CHAMPIONSHIP ALL JAPAN
AAAAGH!! WHAT A WASTE!! I CAN'T BELIEVE I DID THAT!!
YOU DON'T GOTTA GET THAT DOWN...
BRUH.
DUDE.
I THINK THAT'S THE FIRST TIME I'VE EVER SEEN HINATA LET SOMETHING ***OTHER*** THAN THE BALL STEAL HIS ATTENTION.
GLANCE
THAT WASN'T A HALF-BAD JUMP. GOOD JOB.
DON'T WORRY ABOUT SCREW-UPS. I'LL PUT THE BALL UP FOR YOU AS MUCH AS YOU WANT!

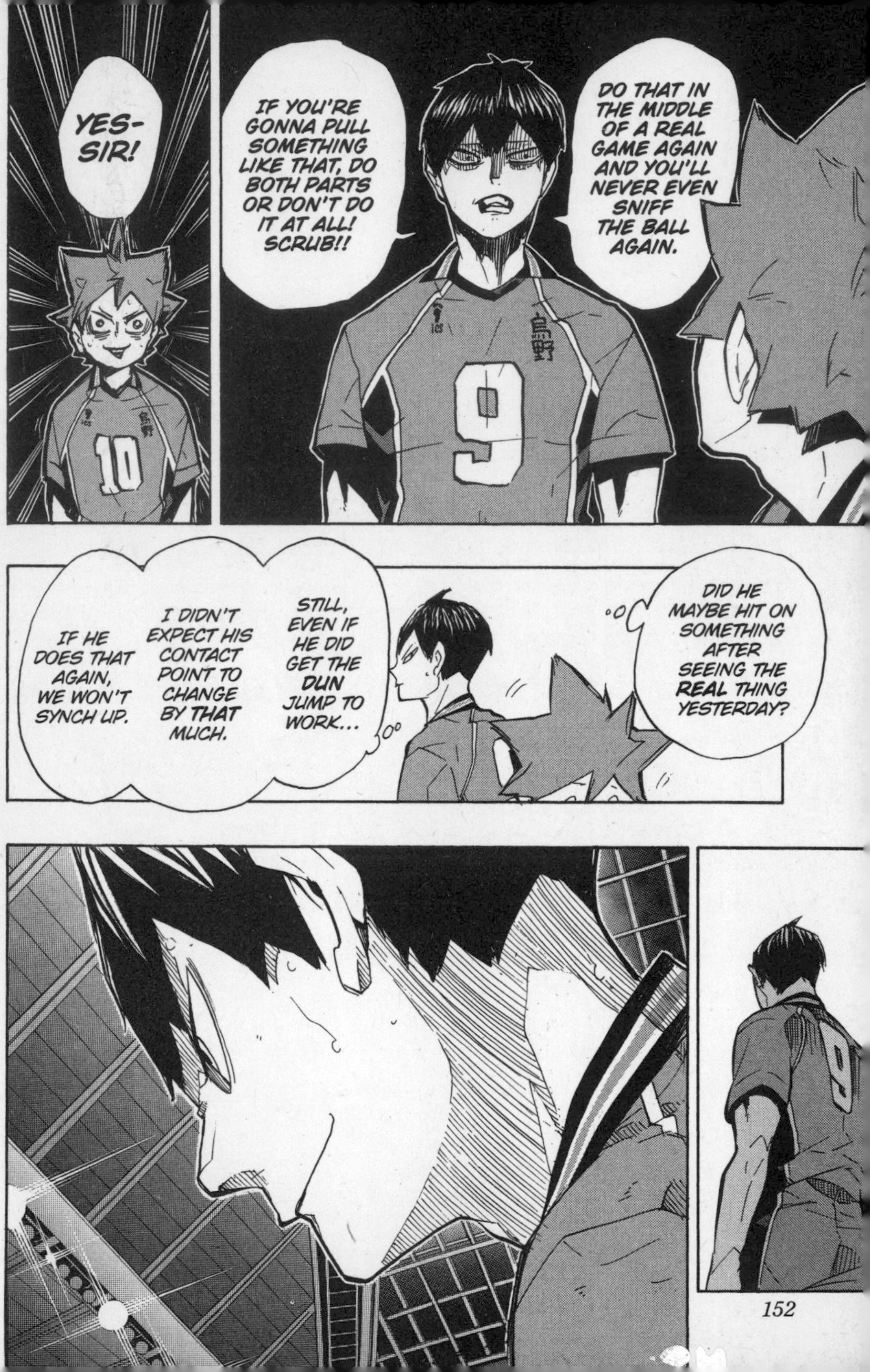

DO THAT IN THE MIDDLE OF A REAL GAME AGAIN AND YOU'LL NEVER EVEN SNIFF THE BALL AGAIN.
IF YOU'RE GONNA PULL SOMETHING LIKE THAT, DO BOTH PARTS OR DON'T DO IT AT ALL! SCRUB!!
YES-SIR!
DID HE MAYBE HIT ON SOMETHING AFTER SEEING THE REAL THING YESTERDAY?
STILL, EVEN IF HE DID GET THE DUN JUMP TO WORK...
I DIDN'T EXPECT HIS CONTACT POINT TO CHANGE BY THAT MUCH.
IF HE DOES THAT AGAIN, WE WON'T SYNCH UP.

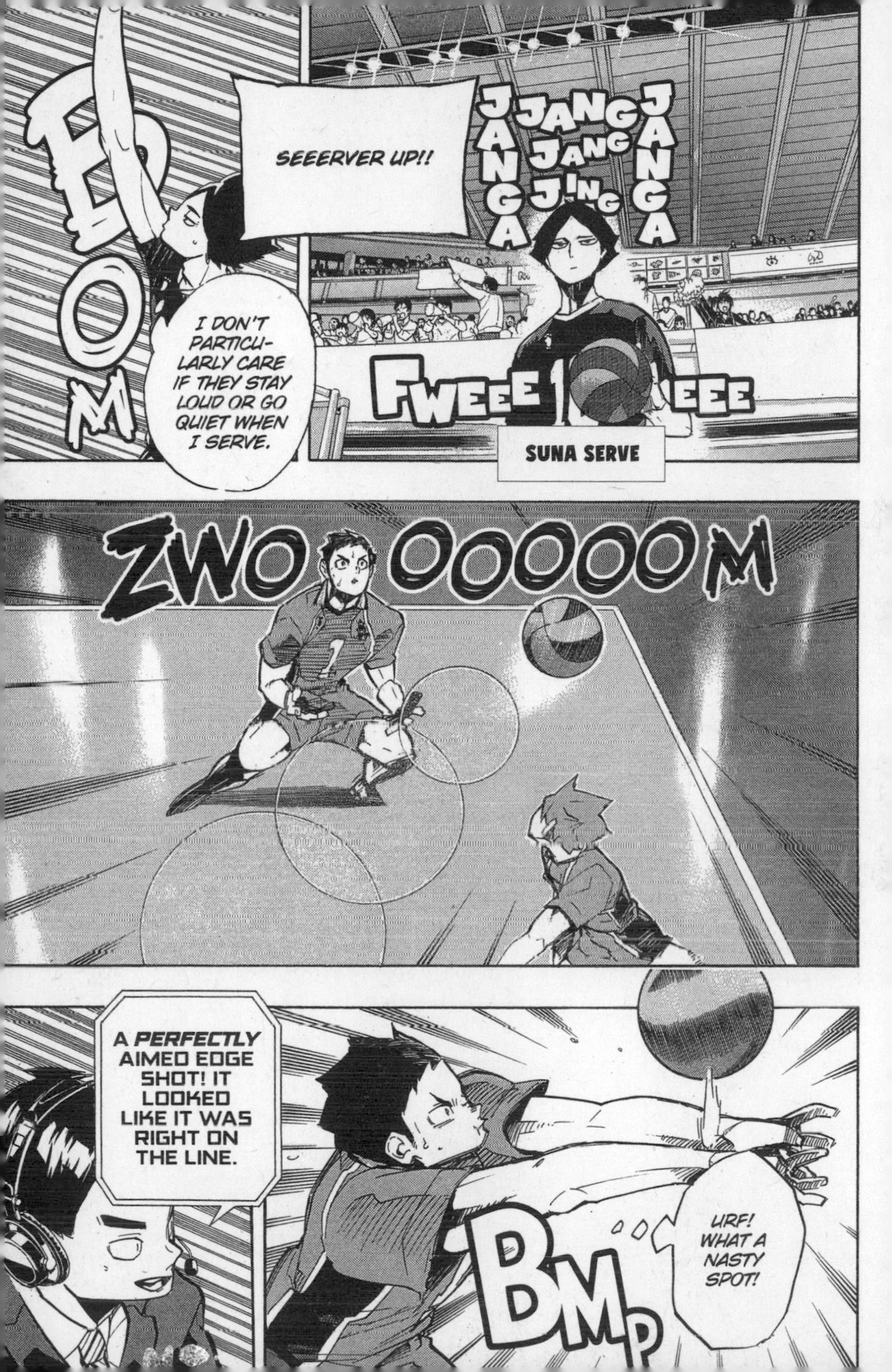
JANGA
JANG
JANG
JING
JANGA
FWEEE EEE
SUNA SERVE
SEEERVER UP!!
BOOM
I DON'T PARTICULARLY CARE IF THEY STAY LOUD OR GO QUIET WHEN I SERVE.
ZWOOOOOOOM
URF! WHAT A NASTY SPOT!
BMP
A *PERFECTLY* AIMED EDGE SHOT! IT LOOKED LIKE IT WAS RIGHT ON THE LINE.

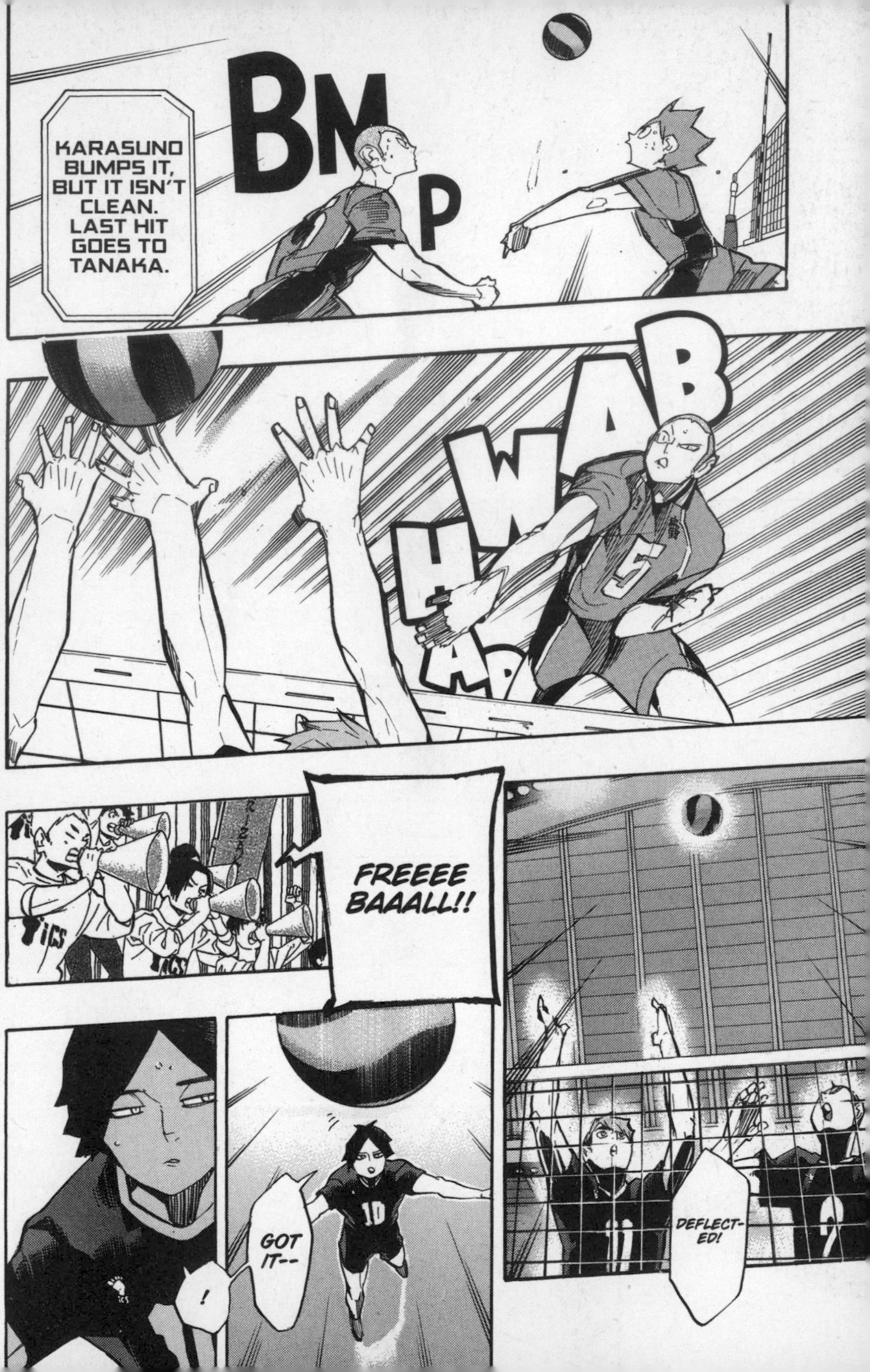
BMP
KARASUNO BUMPS IT, BUT IT ISN'T CLEAN. LAST HIT GOES TO TANAKA.
HWAB
DEFLECT-ED!
FREEEE BAAALL!!
GOT IT--
!

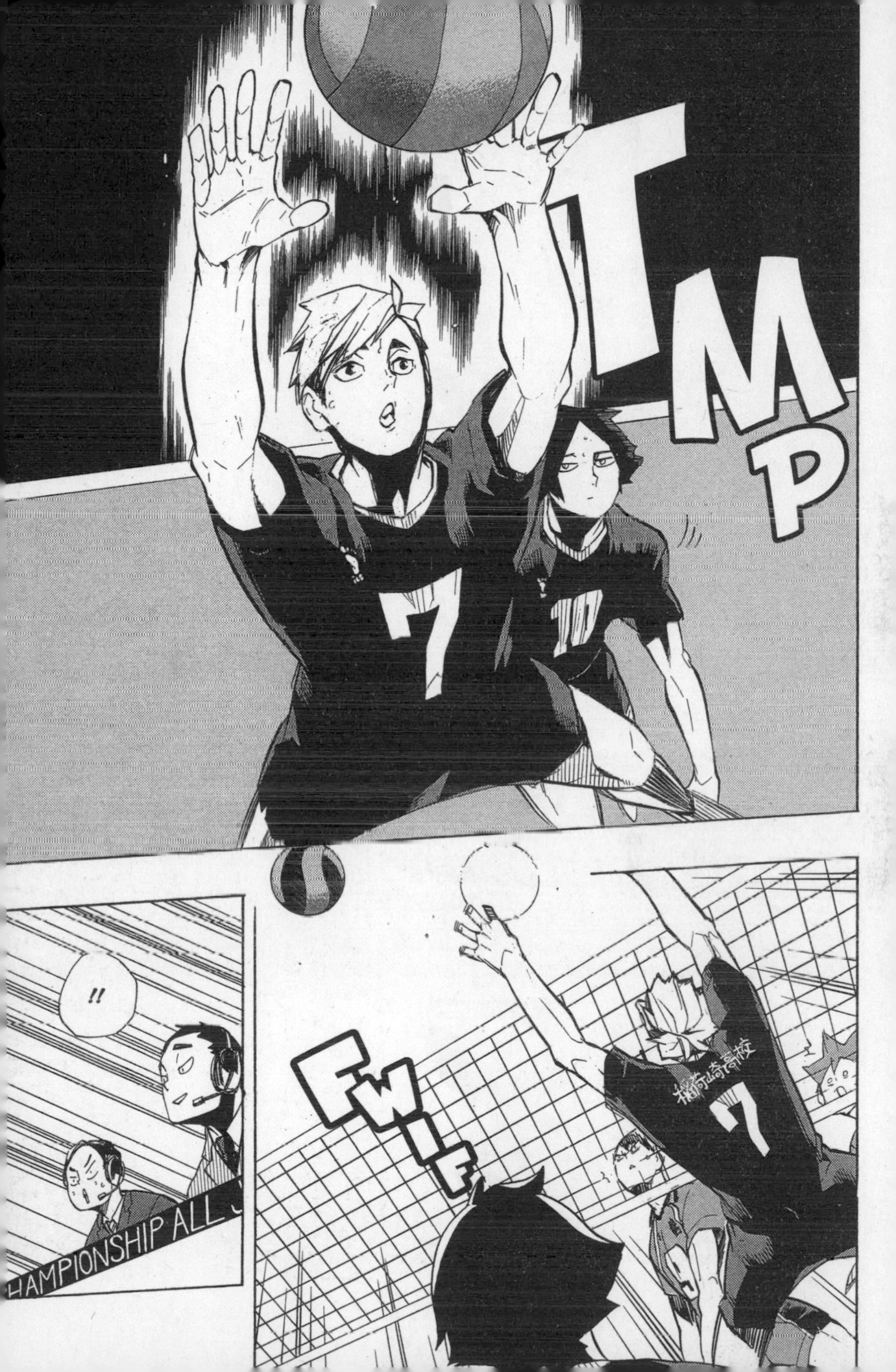
TMP
FWIF
!!
HAMPIONSHIP ALL

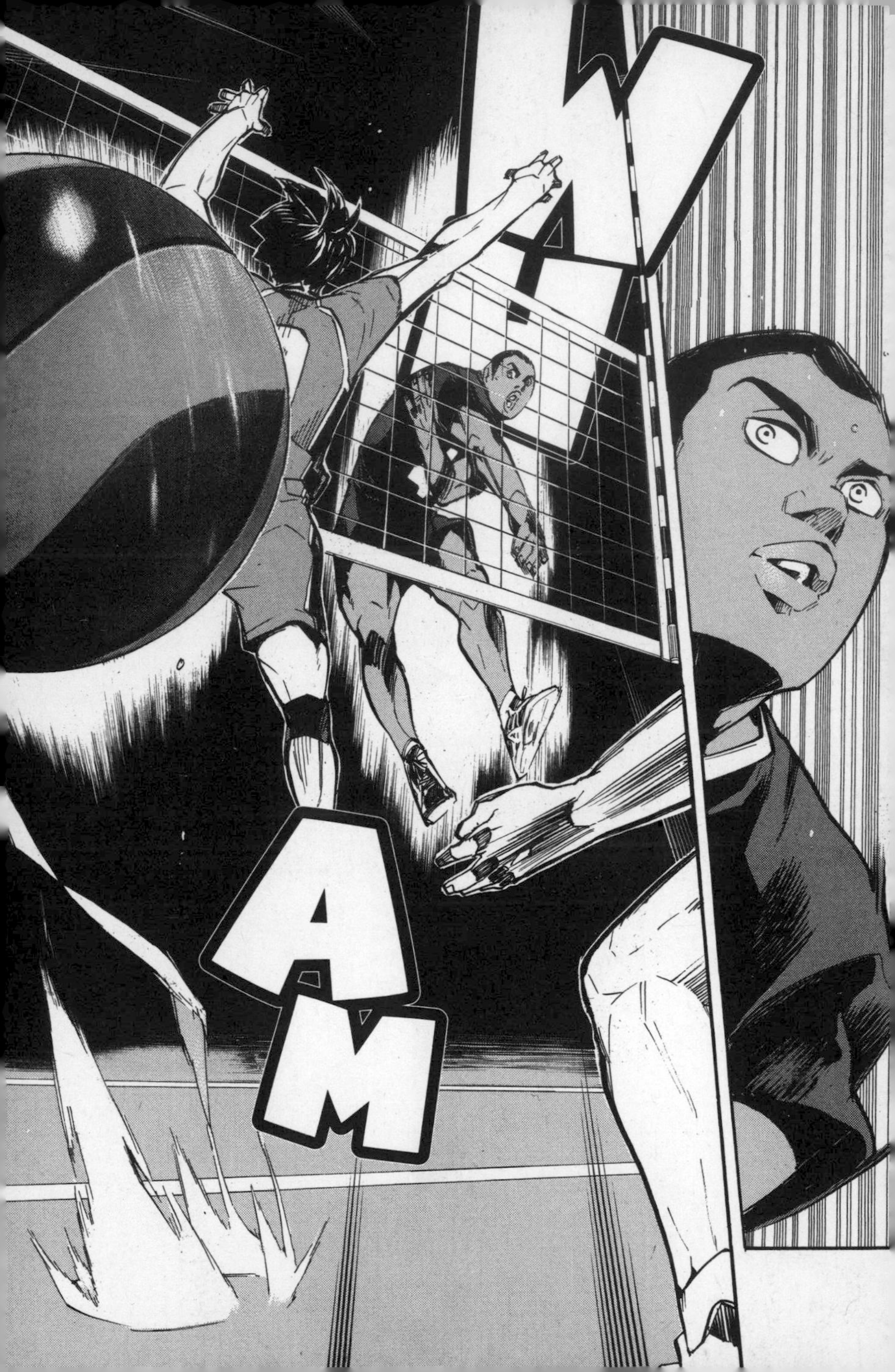
AM

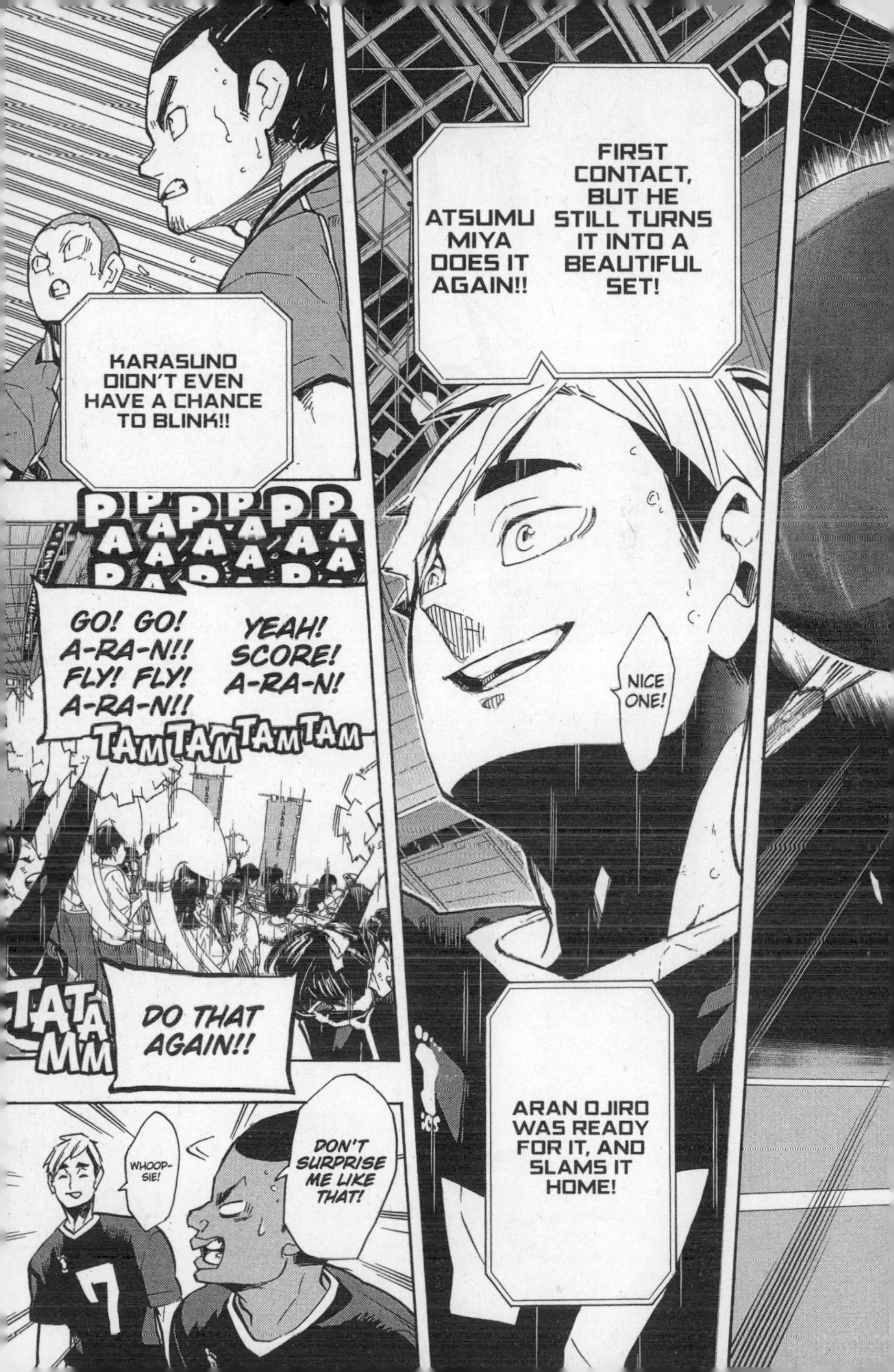
FIRST CONTACT, BUT HE STILL TURNS IT INTO A BEAUTIFUL SET!
ATSUMU MIYA DOES IT AGAIN!!
NICE ONE!
ARAN OJIRO WAS READY FOR IT, AND SLAMS IT HOME!
KARASUNO DIDN'T EVEN HAVE A CHANCE TO BLINK!!
PPPPPP AAAAAA AAAAAA
YEAH! SCORE! A-RA-N!
GO! GO! A-RA-N!! FLY! FLY! A-RA-N!!
TAM TAM TAM TAM
DO THAT AGAIN!!
TATAMM
DON'T SURPRISE ME LIKE THAT!
WHOOPSIE!

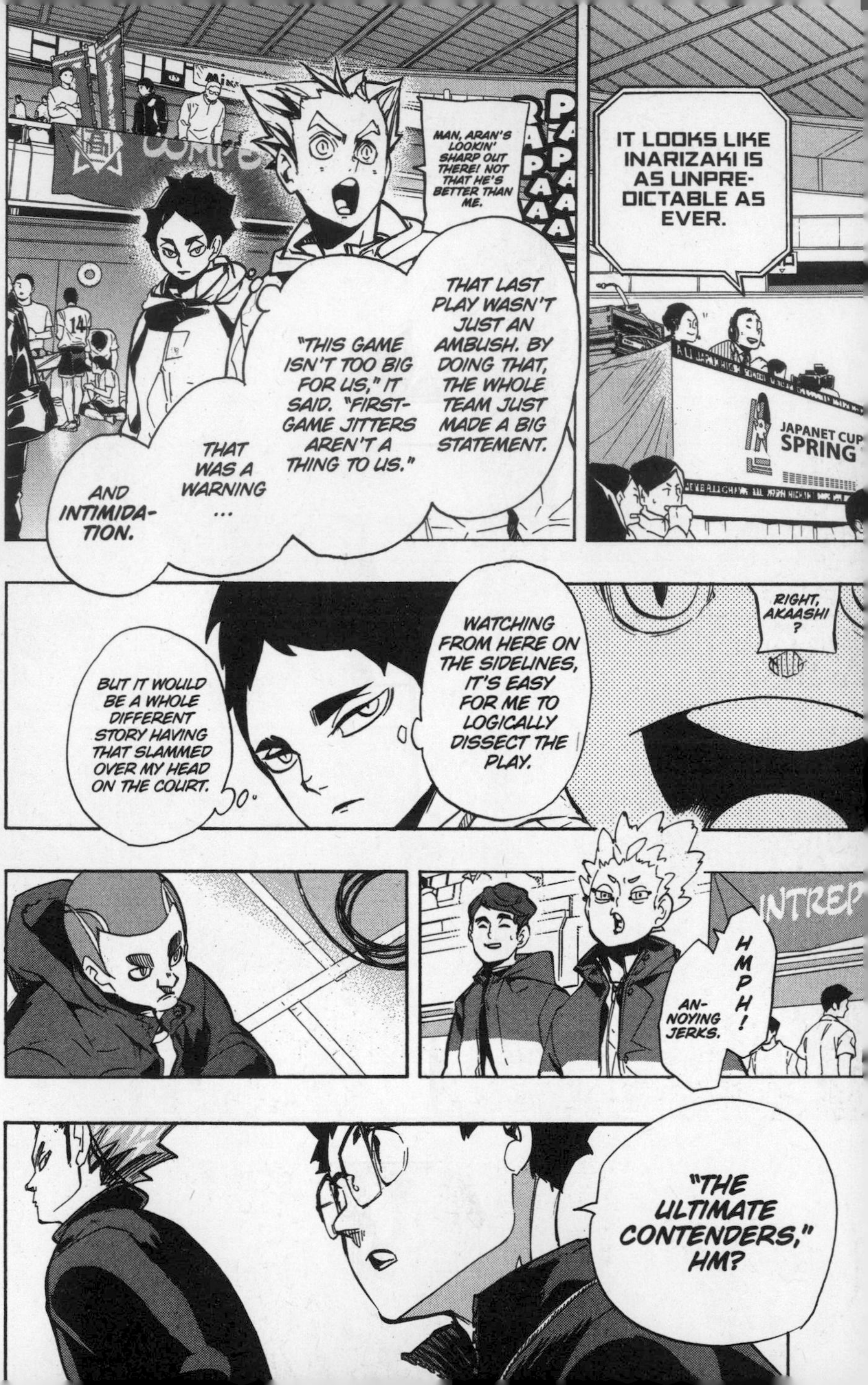

IT LOOKS LIKE INARIZAKI IS AS UNPRE-DICTABLE AS EVER.
JAPANET CUP SPRING
MAN, ARAN'S LOOKIN' SHARP OUT THERE! NOT THAT HE'S BETTER THAN ME.
THAT LAST PLAY WASN'T JUST AN AMBUSH. BY DOING THAT, THE WHOLE TEAM JUST MADE A BIG STATEMENT.
"THIS GAME ISN'T TOO BIG FOR US," IT SAID. "FIRST-GAME JITTERS AREN'T A THING TO US."
THAT WAS A WARNING...
AND INTIMIDA-TION.
RIGHT, AKAASHI?
WATCHING FROM HERE ON THE SIDELINES, IT'S EASY FOR ME TO LOGICALLY DISSECT THE PLAY.
BUT IT WOULD BE A WHOLE DIFFERENT STORY HAVING THAT SLAMMED OVER MY HEAD ON THE COURT.
HMPH!
AN-NOYING JERKS.
"THE ULTIMATE CONTENDERS," HM?

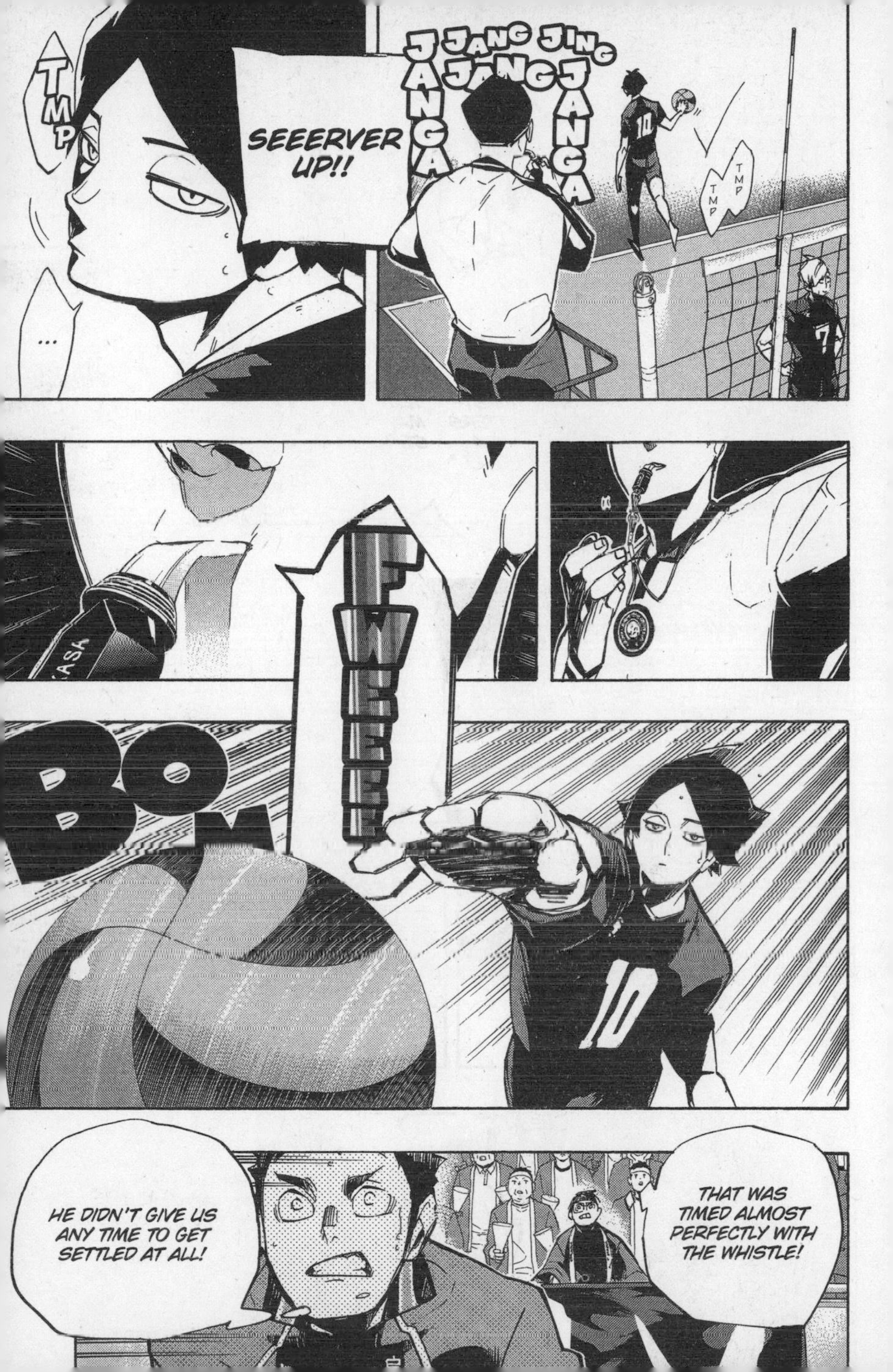
JANGA JANG JANG JING JANGA
TMP TMP
SEEERVER UP!!
TMP
...
FWEEEE
BOOM
THAT WAS TIMED ALMOST PERFECTLY WITH THE WHISTLE!
HE DIDN'T GIVE US ANY TIME TO GET SETTLED AT ALL!

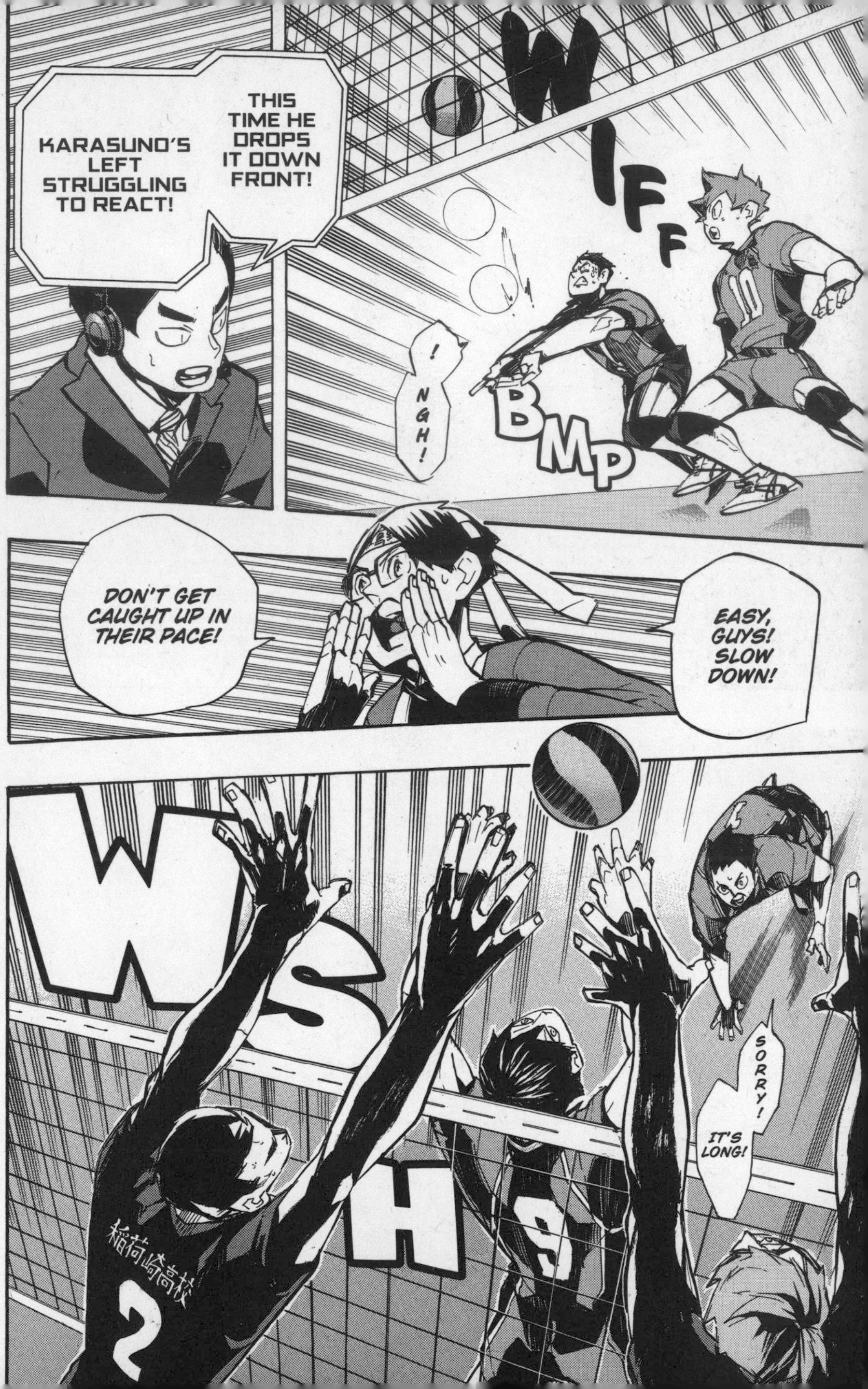
WIFF
!
NGH!
BMP
THIS TIME HE DROPS IT DOWN FRONT!
KARASUNO'S LEFT STRUGGLING TO REACT!
EASY, GUYS! SLOW DOWN!
DON'T GET CAUGHT UP IN THEIR PACE!
SORRY!
IT'S LONG!
WSH
稲荷崎高校

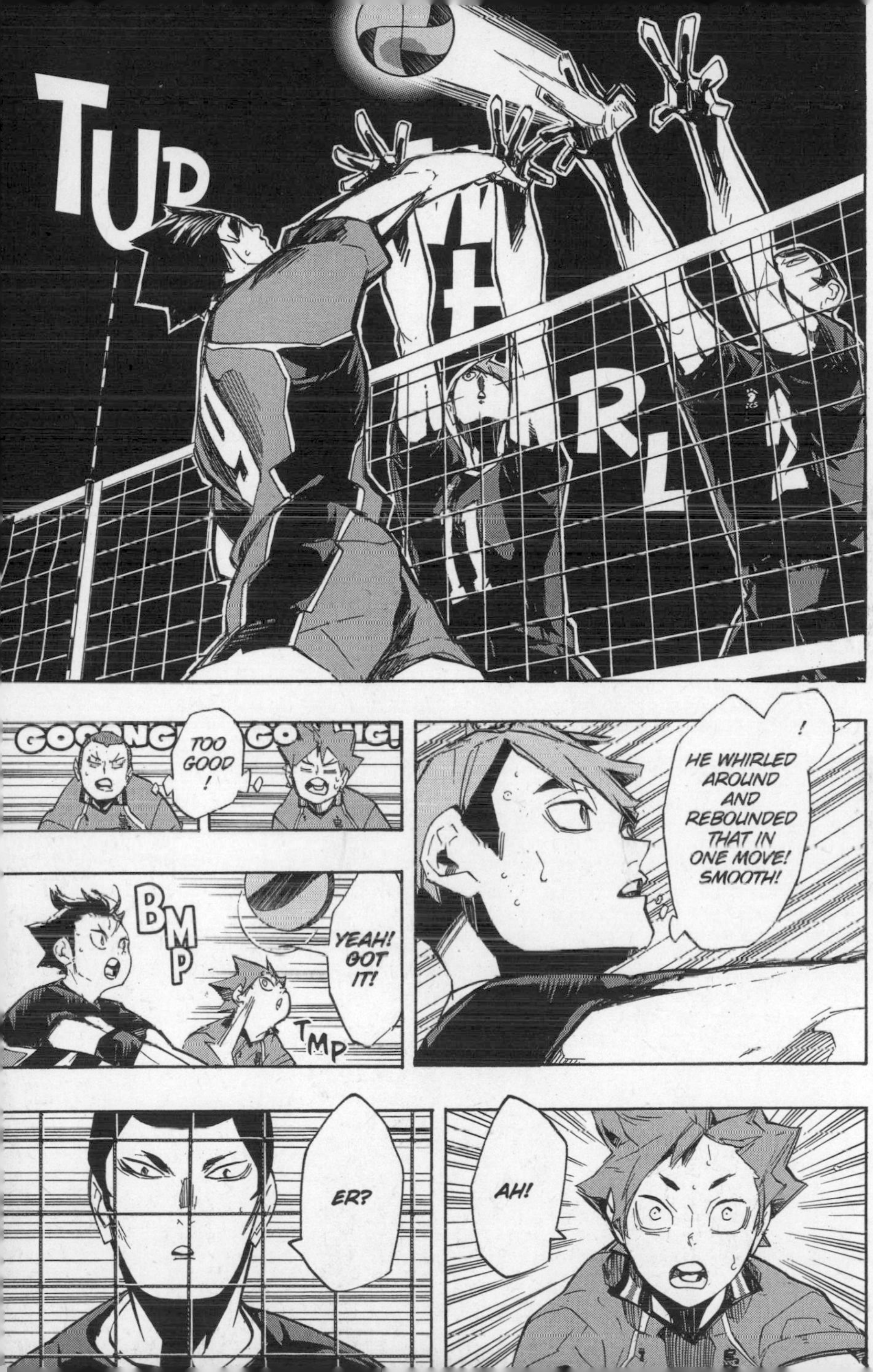

TUD
!
HE WHIRLED AROUND AND REBOUNDED THAT IN ONE MOVE! SMOOTH!
TOO GOOD!
YEAH! GOT IT!
BMP
TMP
AH!
ER?

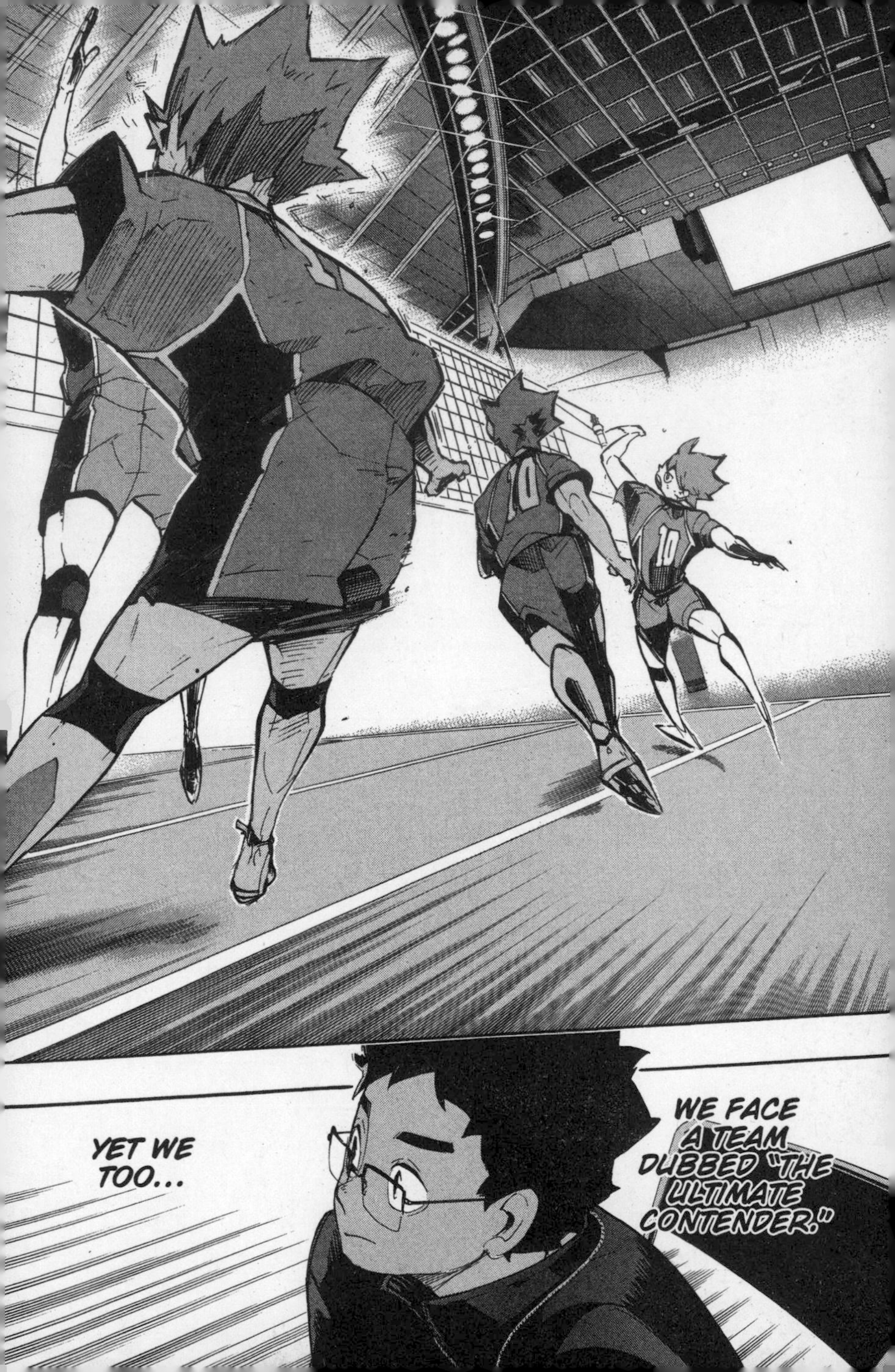
WE FACE A TEAM DUBBED "THE ULTIMATE CONTENDER."
YET WE TOO...

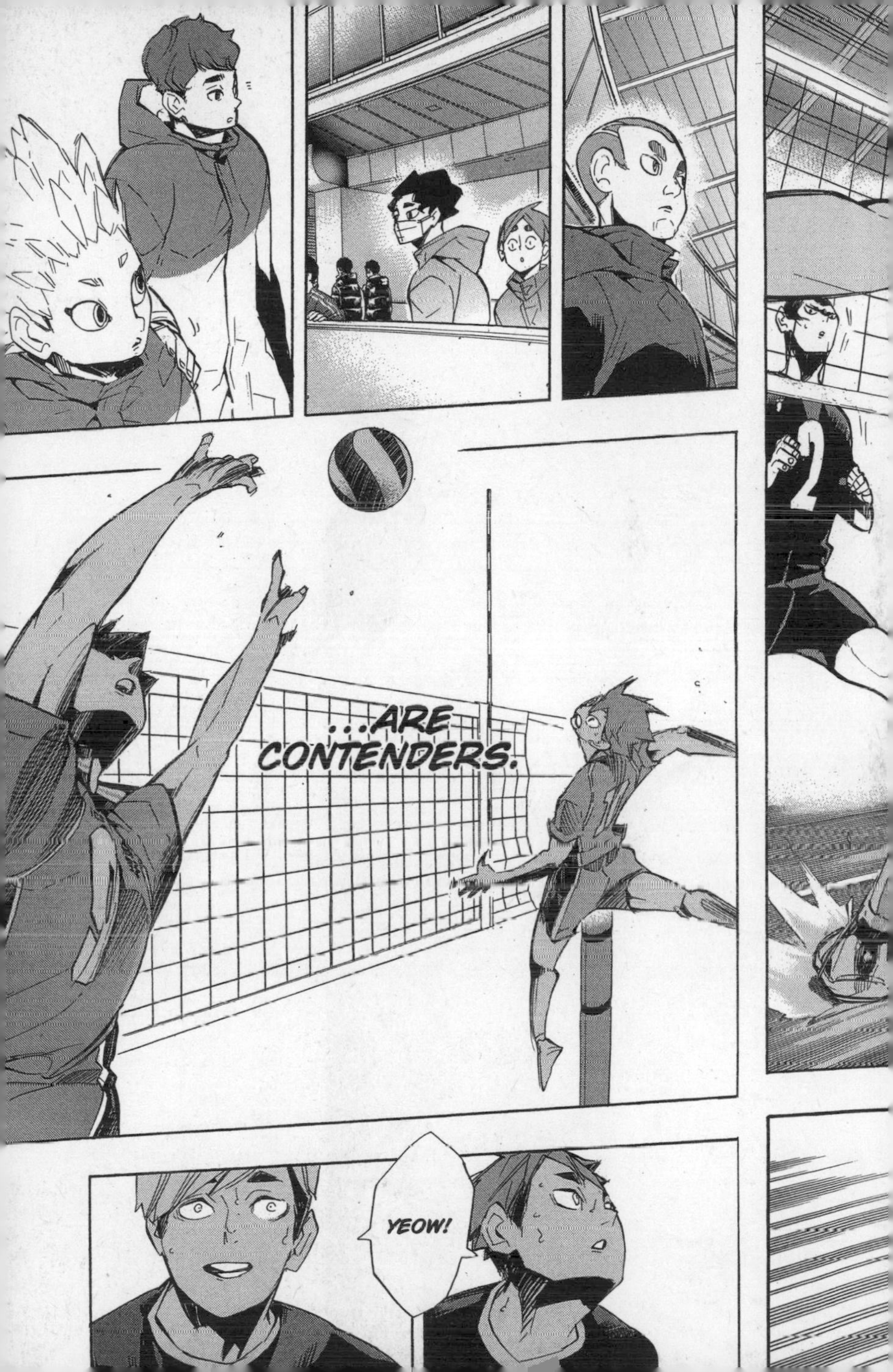
...ARE CONTENDERS.
YEOW!

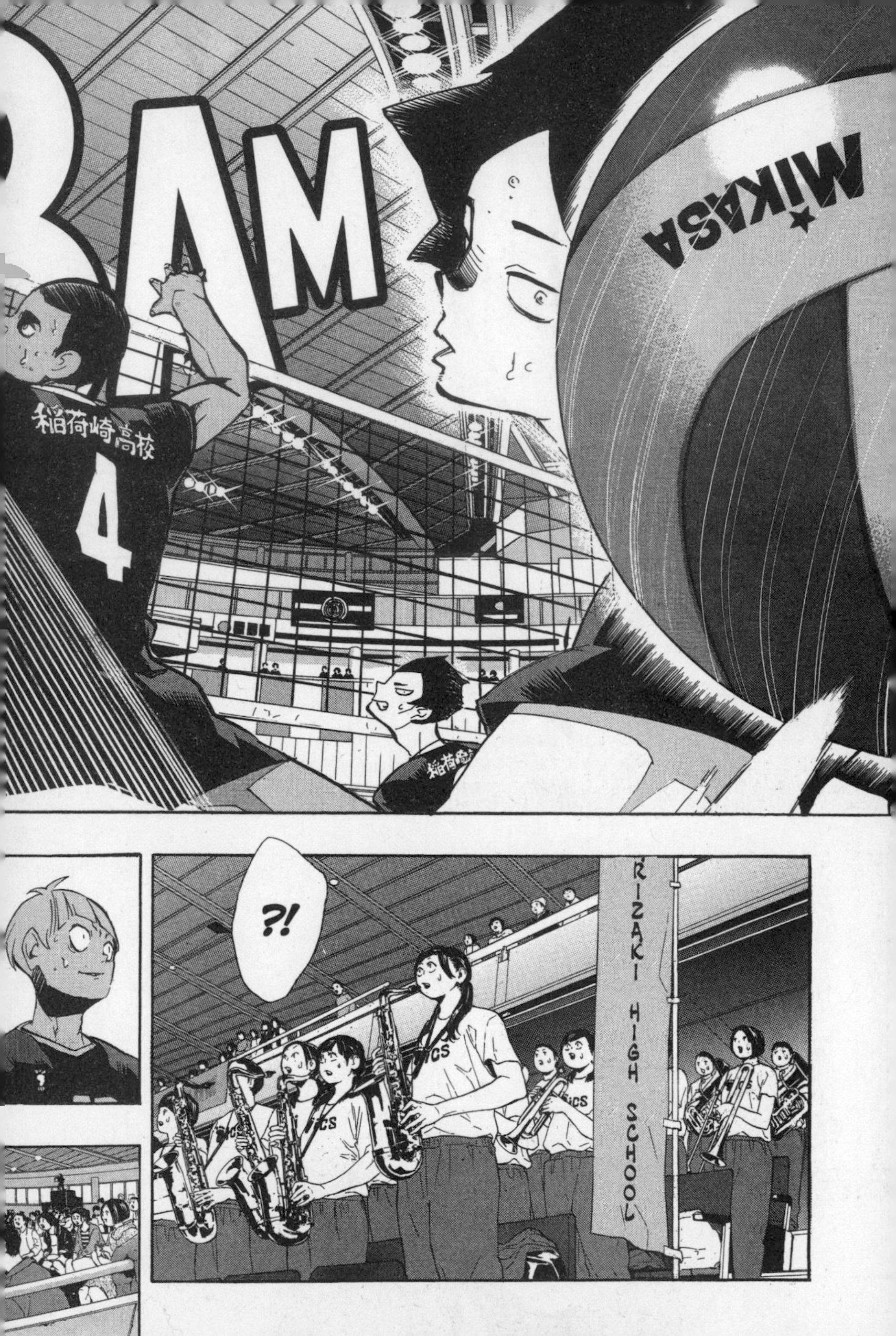

AM
MIKASA
稲荷崎高校
4
稲荷崎
?!
RIZAKI HIGH SCHOOL

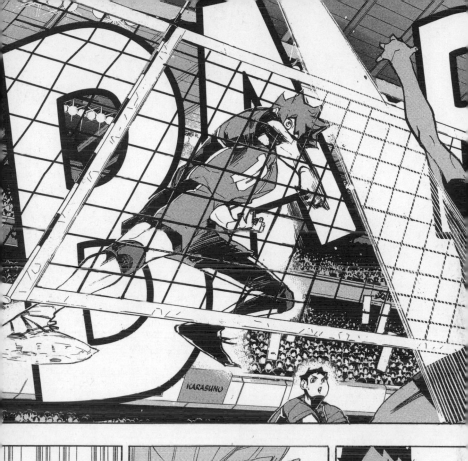

KARASUNO

?!

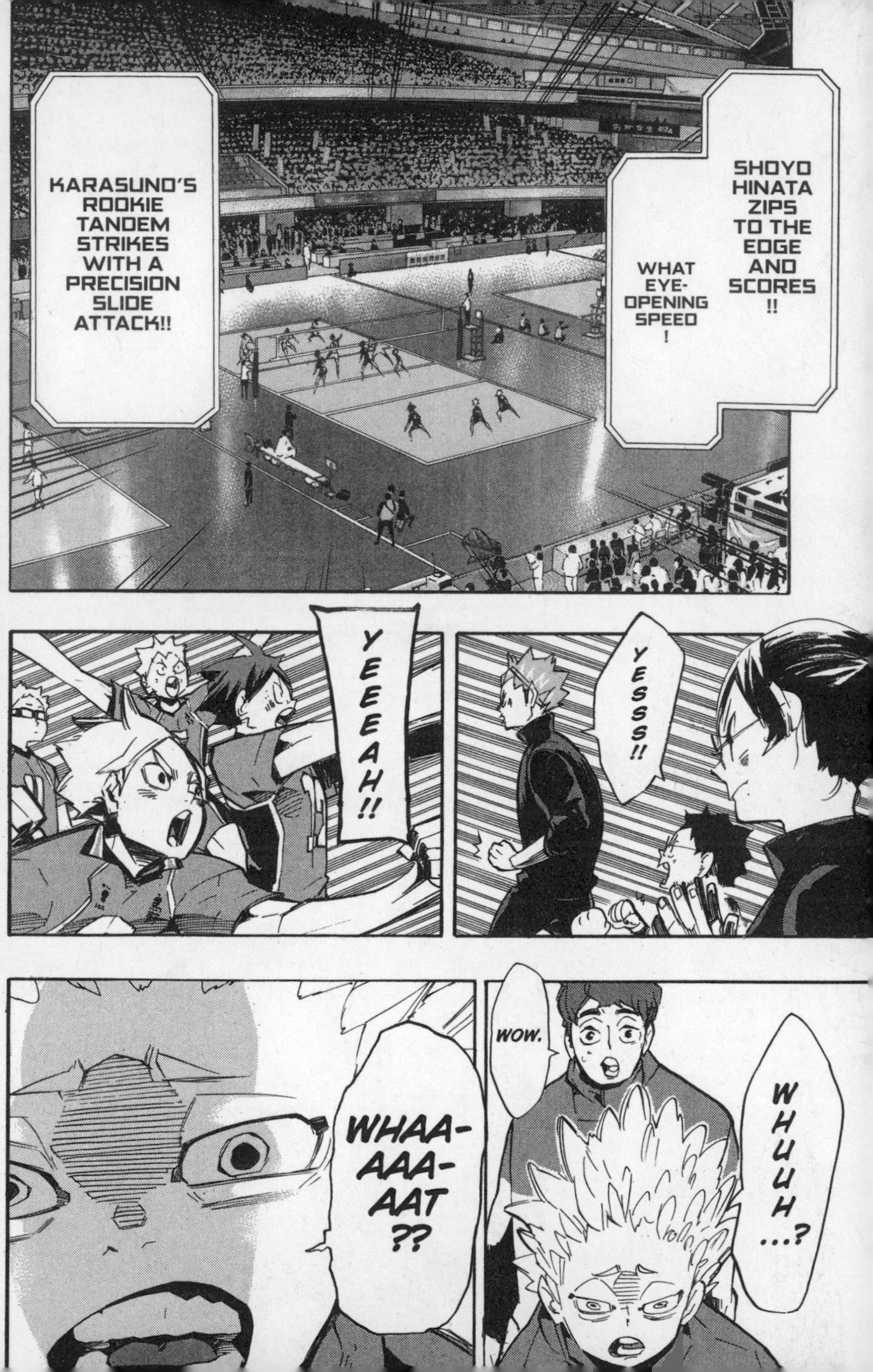
SHOYO HINATA ZIPS TO THE EDGE AND SCORES!!
WHAT EYE-OPENING SPEED!
KARASUNO'S ROOKIE TANDEM STRIKES WITH A PRECISION SLIDE ATTACK!!
YESSS!!
YEEEEAH!!
WHUUH...?
WOW.
WHAA-AAA-AAT??

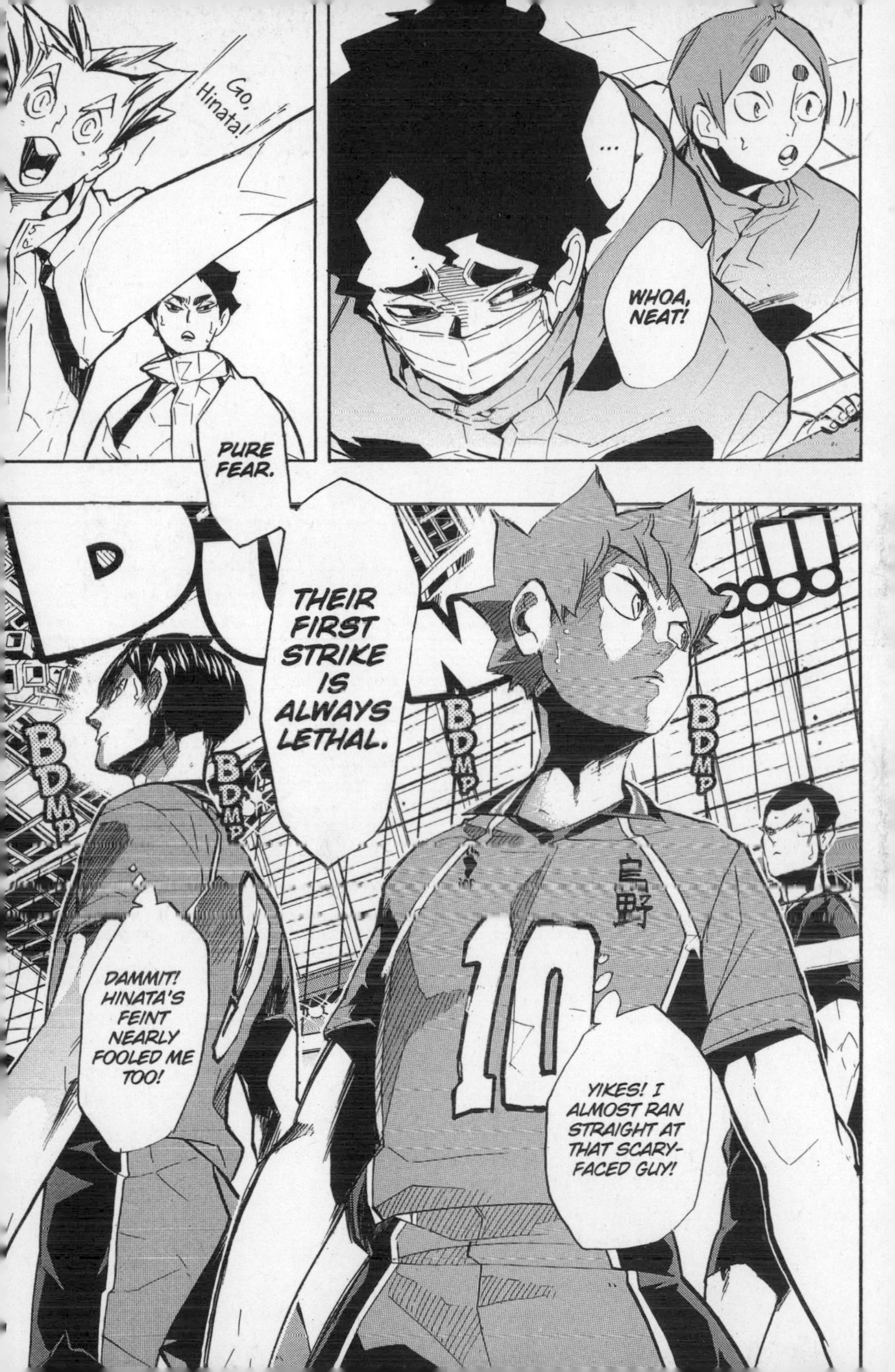
...
WHOA, NEAT!
Go, Hinata!
PURE FEAR.
!!
BDMP
BDMP
THEIR FIRST STRIKE IS ALWAYS LETHAL.
BDMP
BDMP
YIKES! I ALMOST RAN STRAIGHT AT THAT SCARY-FACED GUY!
DAMMIT! HINATA'S FEINT NEARLY FOOLED ME TOO!

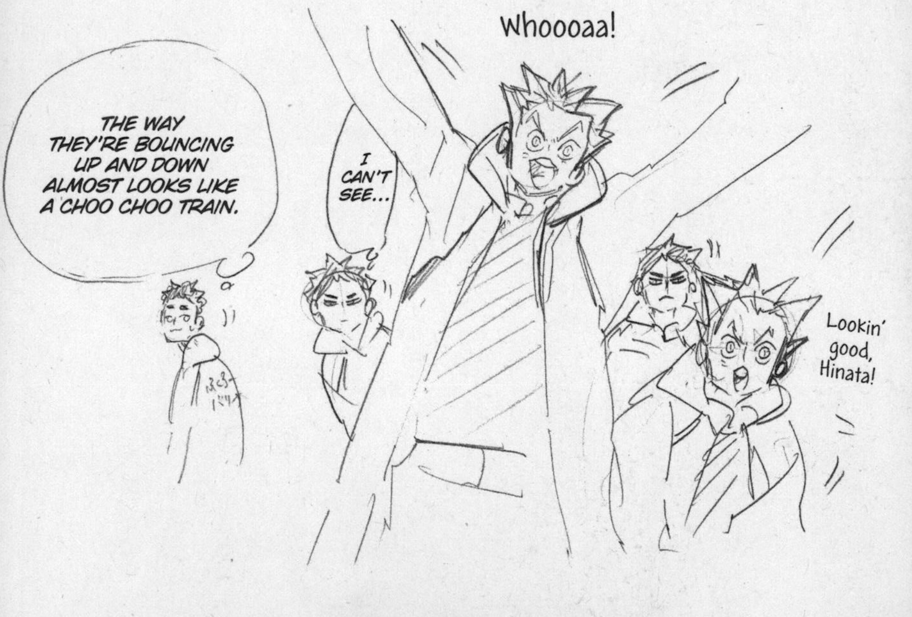
Whoooaa!
Lookin' good, Hinata!
I CAN'T SEE...
THE WAY THEY'RE BOUNCING UP AND DOWN ALMOST LOOKS LIKE A CHOO CHOO TRAIN.

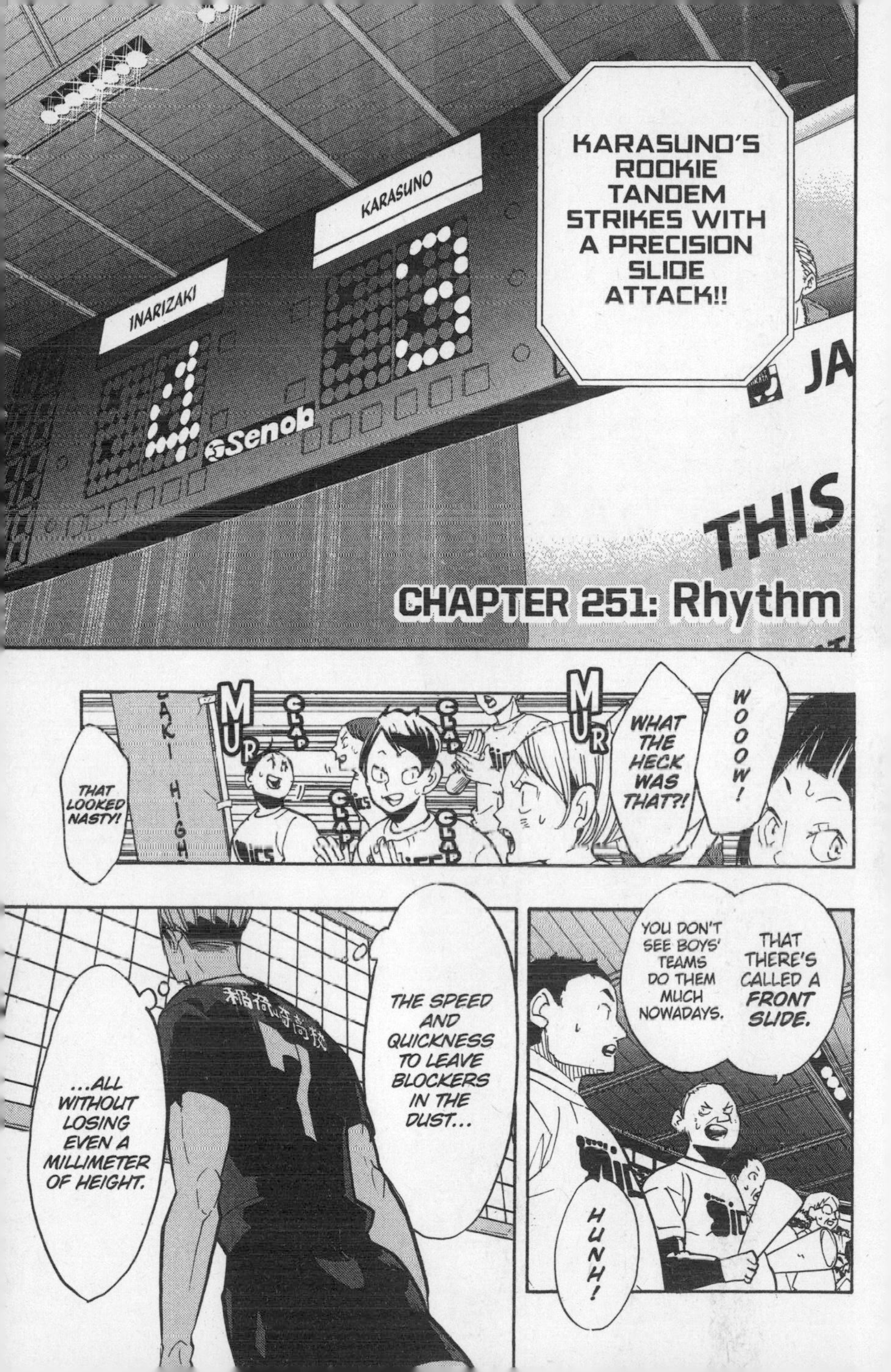
KARASUNO'S ROOKIE TANDEM STRIKES WITH A PRECISION SLIDE ATTACK!!
JA
THIS
KARASUNO
INARIZAKI
Senoh
CHAPTER 251: Rhythm
WOOOOW!
WHAT THE HECK WAS THAT?!
MUR
CLAP
CLAP
CLAP
CLAP
MUR
THAT LOOKED NASTY!
THAT THERE'S CALLED A FRONT SLIDE.
YOU DON'T SEE BOYS' TEAMS DO THEM MUCH NOWADAYS.
HUNH!
THE SPEED AND QUICKNESS TO LEAVE BLOCKERS IN THE DUST...
稲荷崎高校
...ALL WITHOUT LOSING EVEN A MILLIMETER OF HEIGHT.

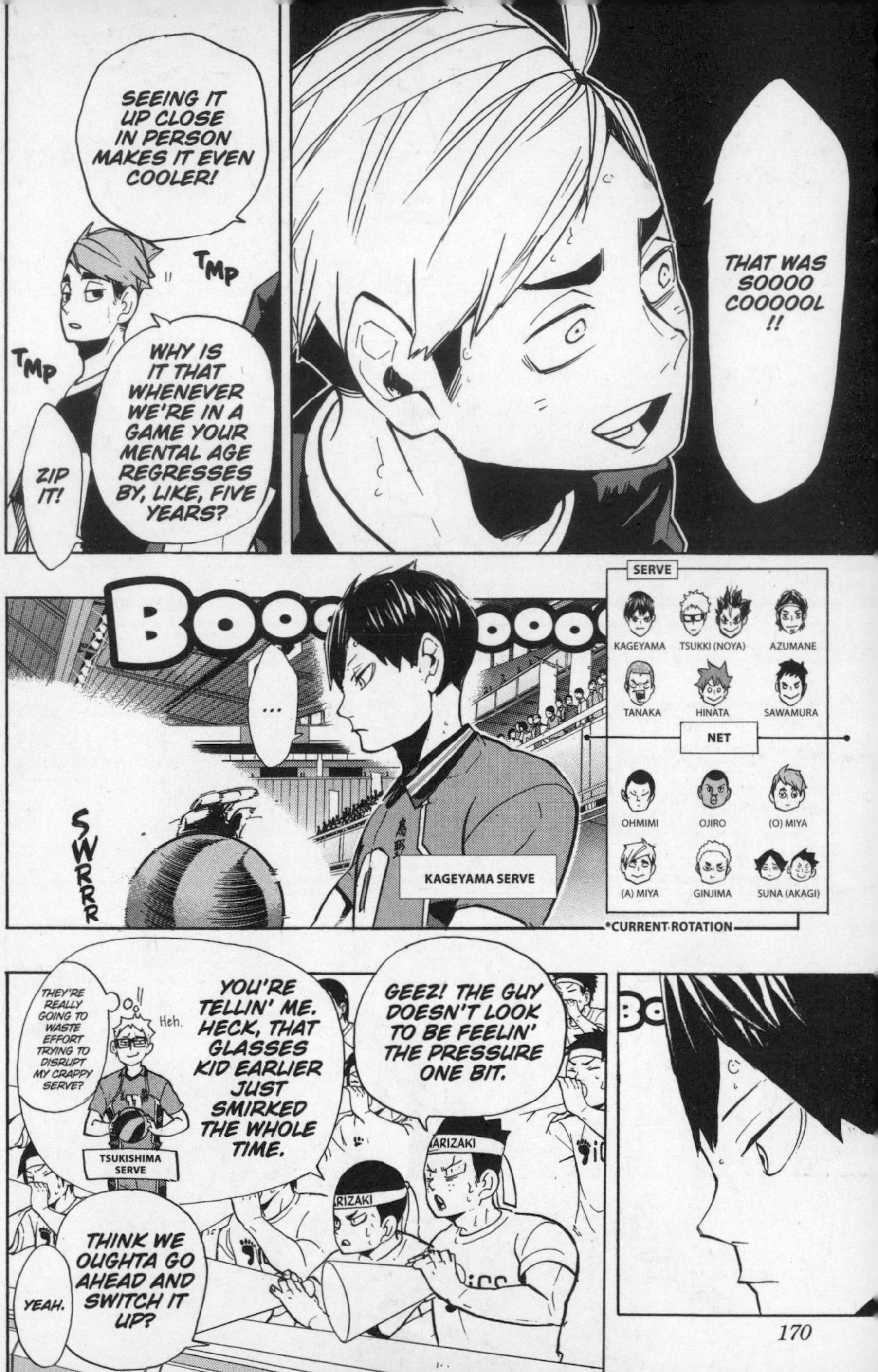
THAT WAS SOOOO COOOOOL !!
SEEING IT UP CLOSE IN PERSON MAKES IT EVEN COOLER!
TMP
WHY IS IT THAT WHENEVER WE'RE IN A GAME YOUR MENTAL AGE REGRESSES BY, LIKE, FIVE YEARS?
TMP
ZIP IT!
BOOOOOOO
...
SWRRR
KAGEYAMA SERVE
SERVE
KAGEYAMA
TSUKKI (NOYA)
AZUMANE
TANAKA
HINATA
SAWAMURA
NET
OHMIMI
OJIRO
(O) MIYA
(A) MIYA
GINJIMA
SUNA (AKAGI)
*CURRENT ROTATION
BO
GEEZ! THE GUY DOESN'T LOOK TO BE FEELIN' THE PRESSURE ONE BIT.
YOU'RE TELLIN' ME. HECK, THAT GLASSES KID EARLIER JUST SMIRKED THE WHOLE TIME.
THEY'RE REALLY GOING TO WASTE EFFORT TRYING TO DISRUPT MY CRAPPY SERVE?
Heh.
TSUKISHIMA SERVE
ARIZAKI
ARIZAKI
THINK WE OUGHTA GO AHEAD AND SWITCH IT UP?
YEAH.

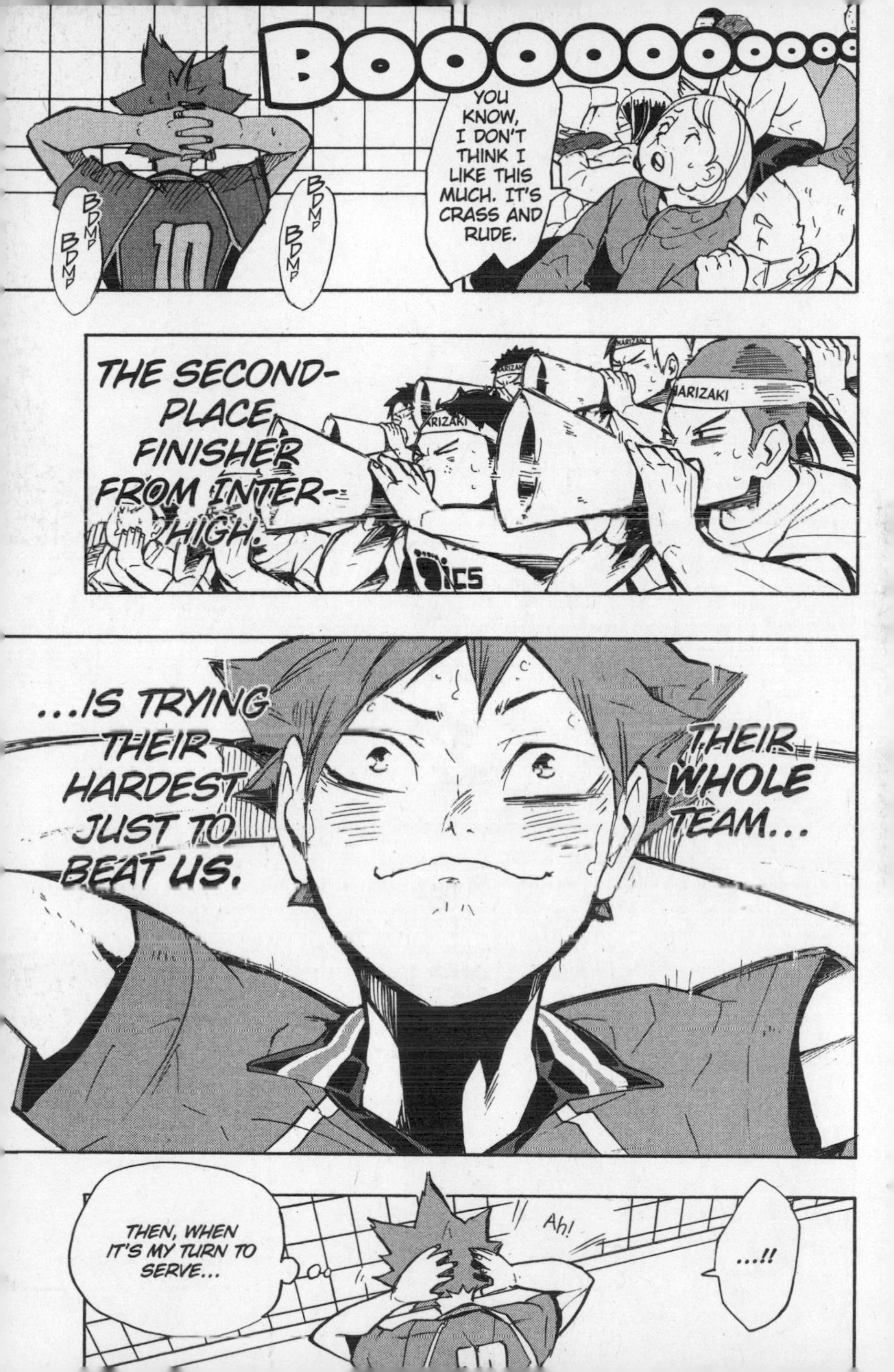
BOOOOOOOOOO
YOU KNOW, I DON'T THINK I LIKE THIS MUCH. IT'S CRASS AND RUDE.
BDMP BDMP
BDMP BDMP
HARIZAKI
THE SECOND-PLACE FINISHER FROM INTER-HIGH.
THEIR WHOLE TEAM...
...IS TRYING THEIR HARDEST JUST TO BEAT US.
...!!
Ah!
THEN, WHEN IT'S MY TURN TO SERVE...

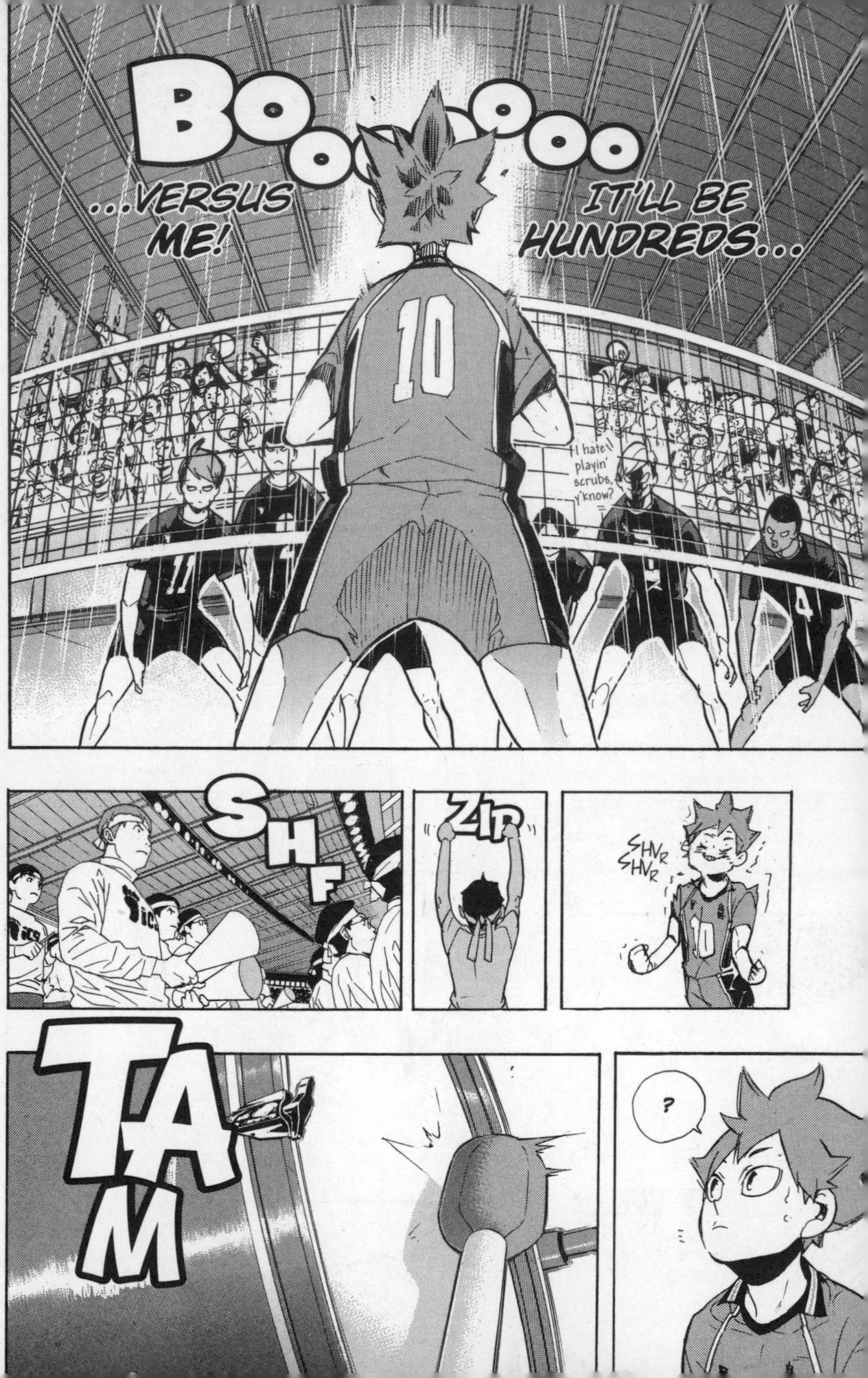
BOOOOOOO
IT'LL BE HUNDREDS...
...VERSUS ME!
I hate playin' scrubs, y'know?
SHVR SHVR
ZIP
SHF
?
TAM

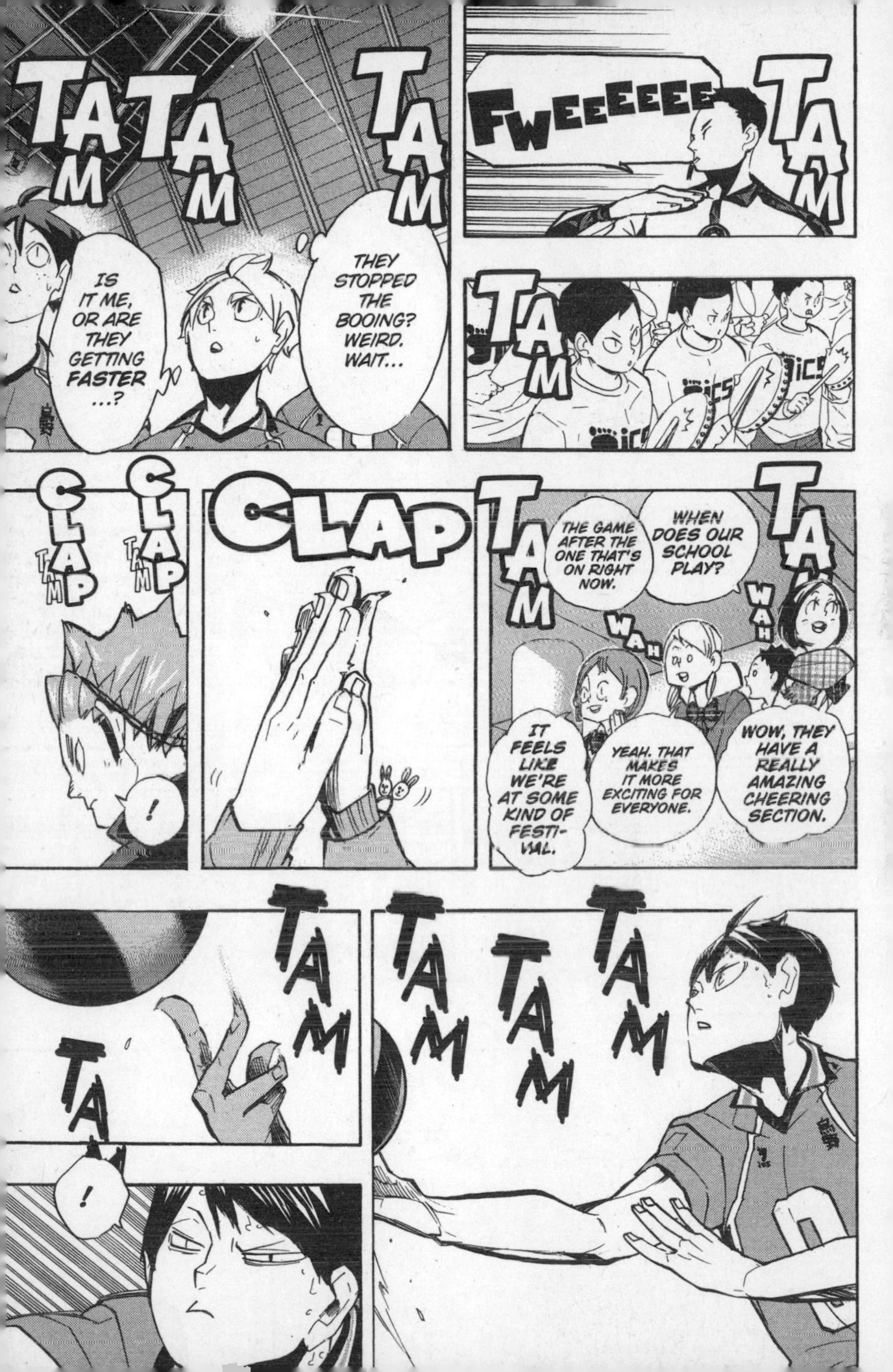
FWEEEEEE
TAM
TAM
TATAM TAM
TAM
THEY STOPPED THE BOOING? WEIRD. WAIT...
IS IT ME, OR ARE THEY GETTING FASTER ...?
TAM
TAM
WHEN DOES OUR SCHOOL PLAY?
THE GAME AFTER THE ONE THAT'S ON RIGHT NOW.
WAH
WAH
WOW, THEY HAVE A REALLY AMAZING CHEERING SECTION.
YEAH. THAT MAKES IT MORE EXCITING FOR EVERYONE.
IT FEELS LIKE WE'RE AT SOME KIND OF FESTI-VAL.
CLAP
CLAP
TAMP
CLAP
TAMP
!
TAM
TAM
TAM
TAM
TAM
!

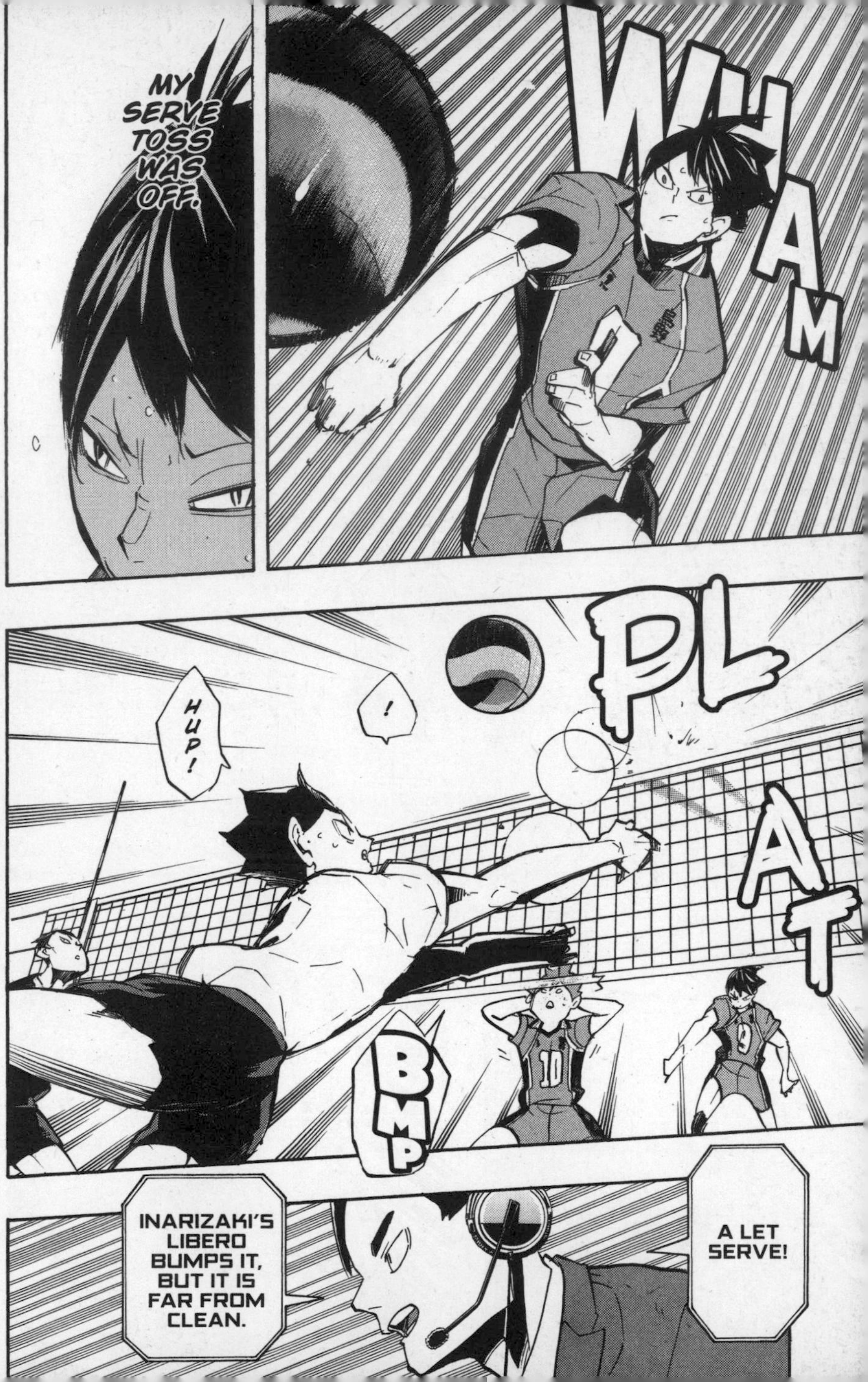
WHAM
MY SERVE TOSS WAS OFF.
PLAT
!
HUP!
BUMP
A LET SERVE!
INARIZAKI'S LIBERO BUMPS IT, BUT IT IS FAR FROM CLEAN.

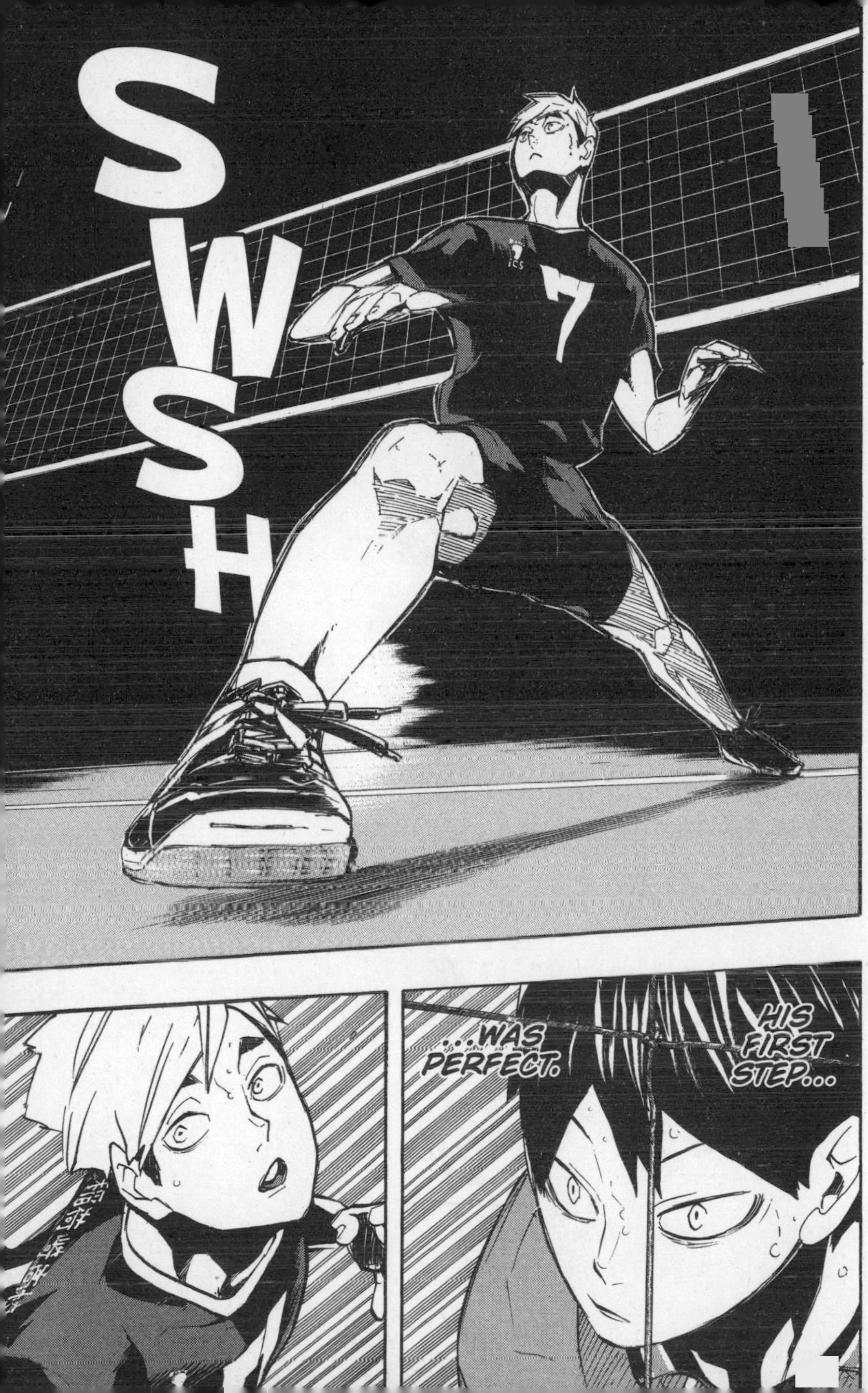
SWSH
HIS FIRST STEP...
...WAS PERFECT.

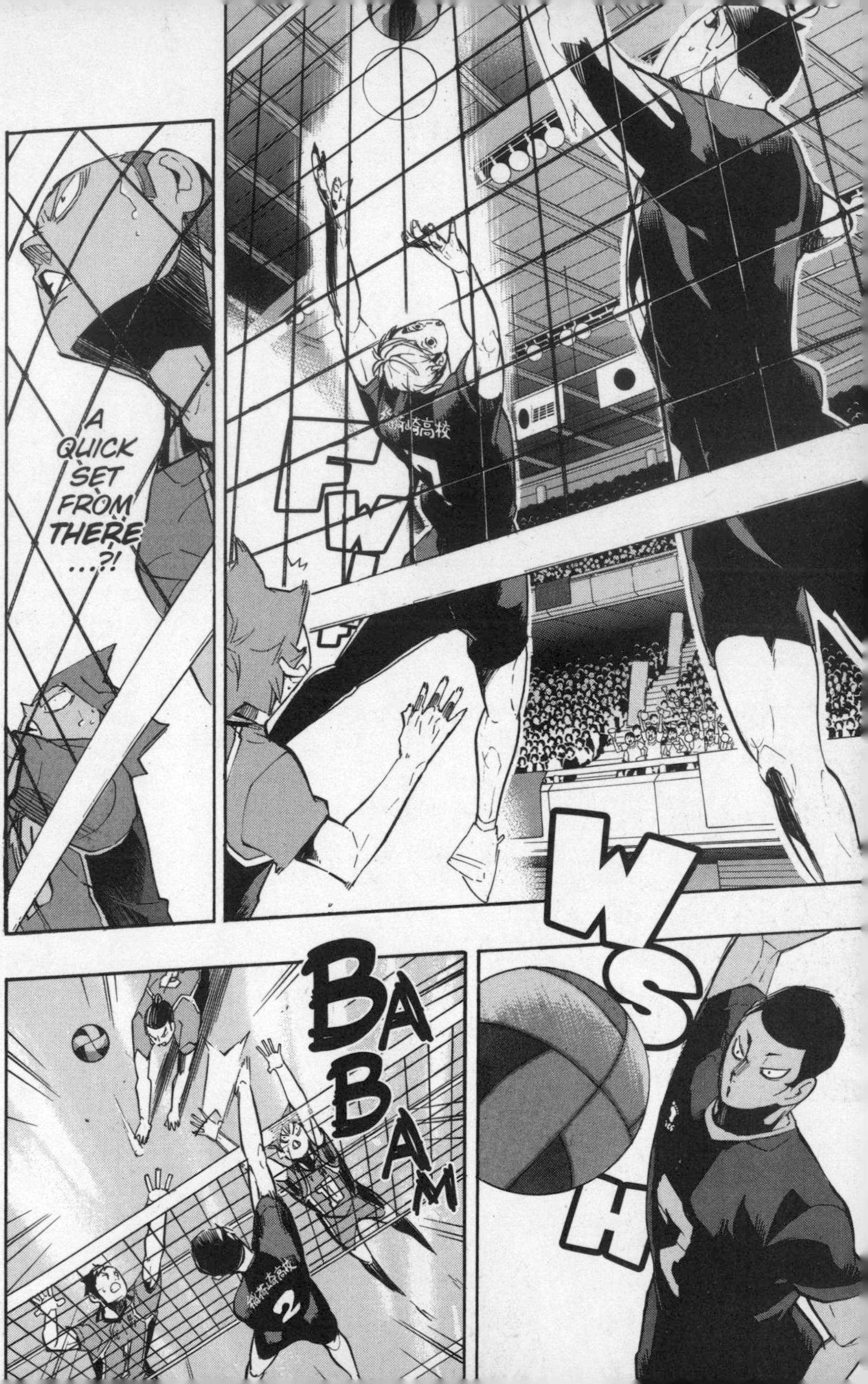
A QUICK SET FROM THERE...?!
WHSH
BABAM

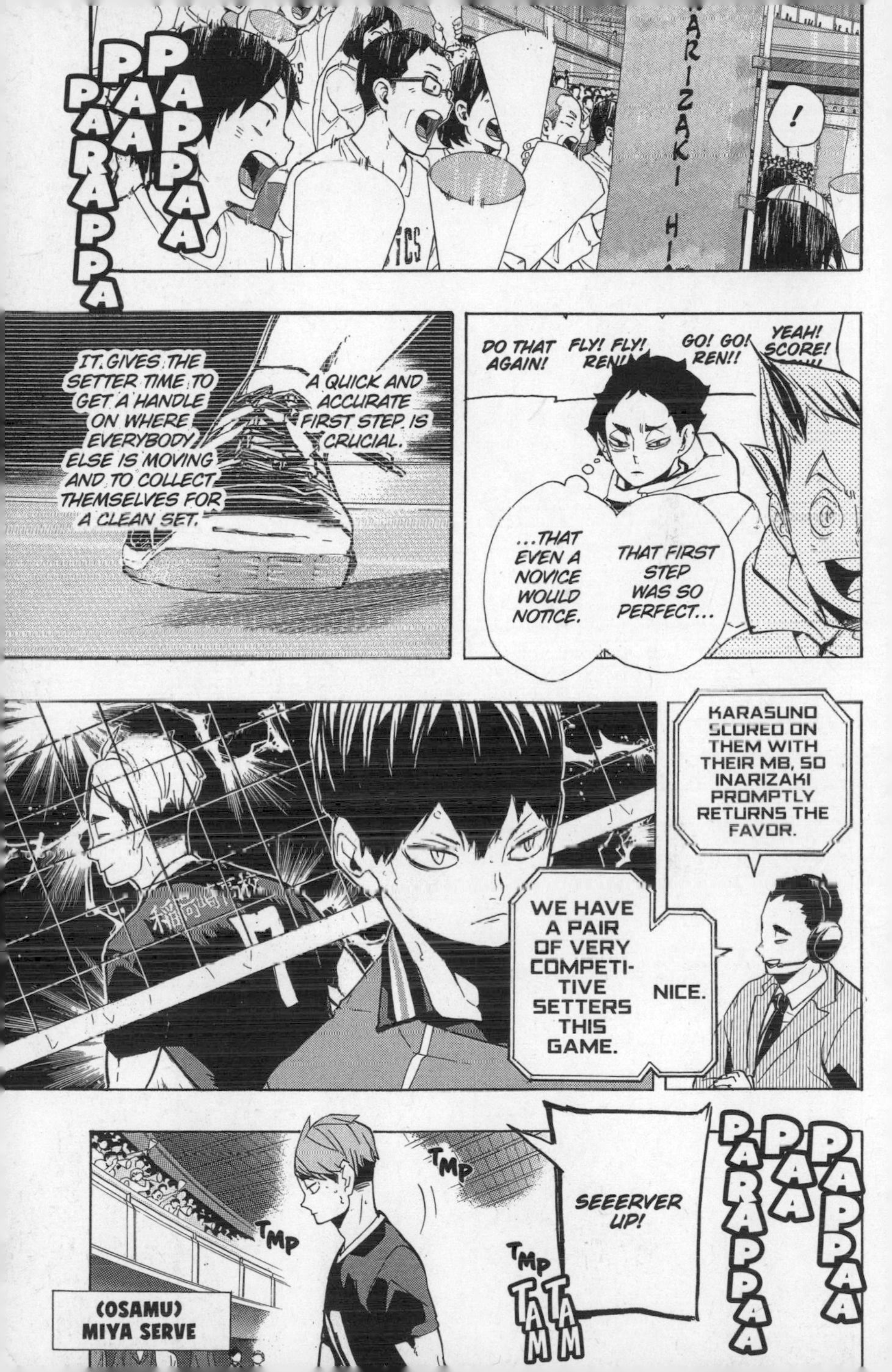
!
ARIZAKI HI
PAPPAA
PAA
PARAPPAPA
YEAH! SCORE!
GO! GO! REN!!
FLY! FLY! REN!
DO THAT AGAIN!
THAT FIRST STEP WAS SO PERFECT...
...THAT EVEN A NOVICE WOULD NOTICE.
A QUICK AND ACCURATE FIRST STEP IS CRUCIAL.
IT GIVES THE SETTER TIME TO GET A HANDLE ON WHERE EVERYBODY ELSE IS MOVING AND TO COLLECT THEMSELVES FOR A CLEAN SET.
KARASUNO SCORED ON THEM WITH THEIR MB, SO INARIZAKI PROMPTLY RETURNS THE FAVOR.
NICE.
WE HAVE A PAIR OF VERY COMPETI- TIVE SETTERS THIS GAME.
PAPPAA
PAA
PARAPPAA
SEEERVER UP!
TMP
TMP
TMP
TAM TAM
(OSAMU) MIYA SERVE

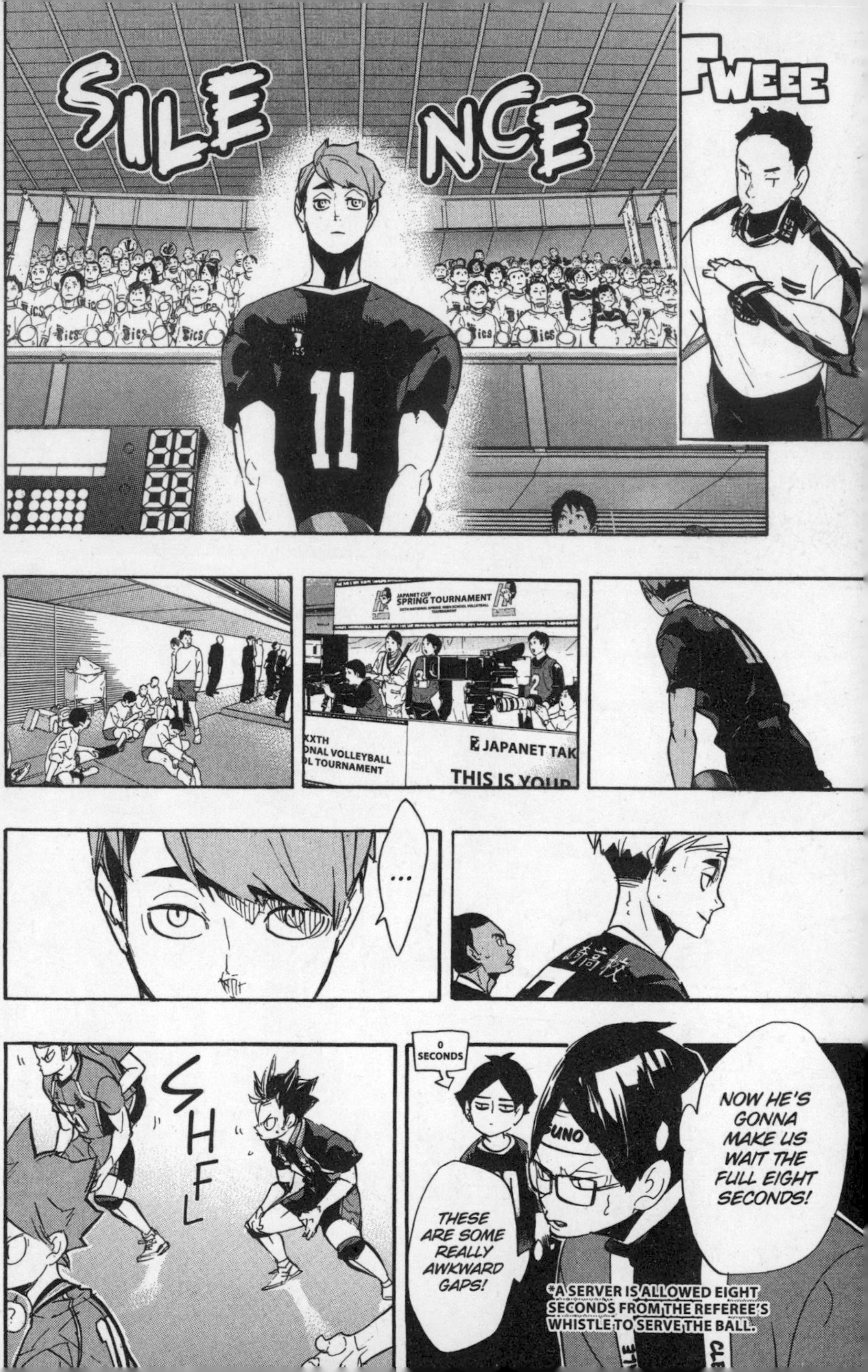
FWEEE
SILENCE
JAPANET CUP
SPRING TOURNAMENT
XXTH
ONAL VOLLEYBALL
OL TOURNAMENT
JAPANET TAK
THIS IS YOUR
...
0 SECONDS
NOW HE'S GONNA MAKE US WAIT THE FULL EIGHT SECONDS!
THESE ARE SOME REALLY AWKWARD GAPS!
*A SERVER IS ALLOWED EIGHT SECONDS FROM THE REFEREE'S WHISTLE TO SERVE THE BALL.
SHFL

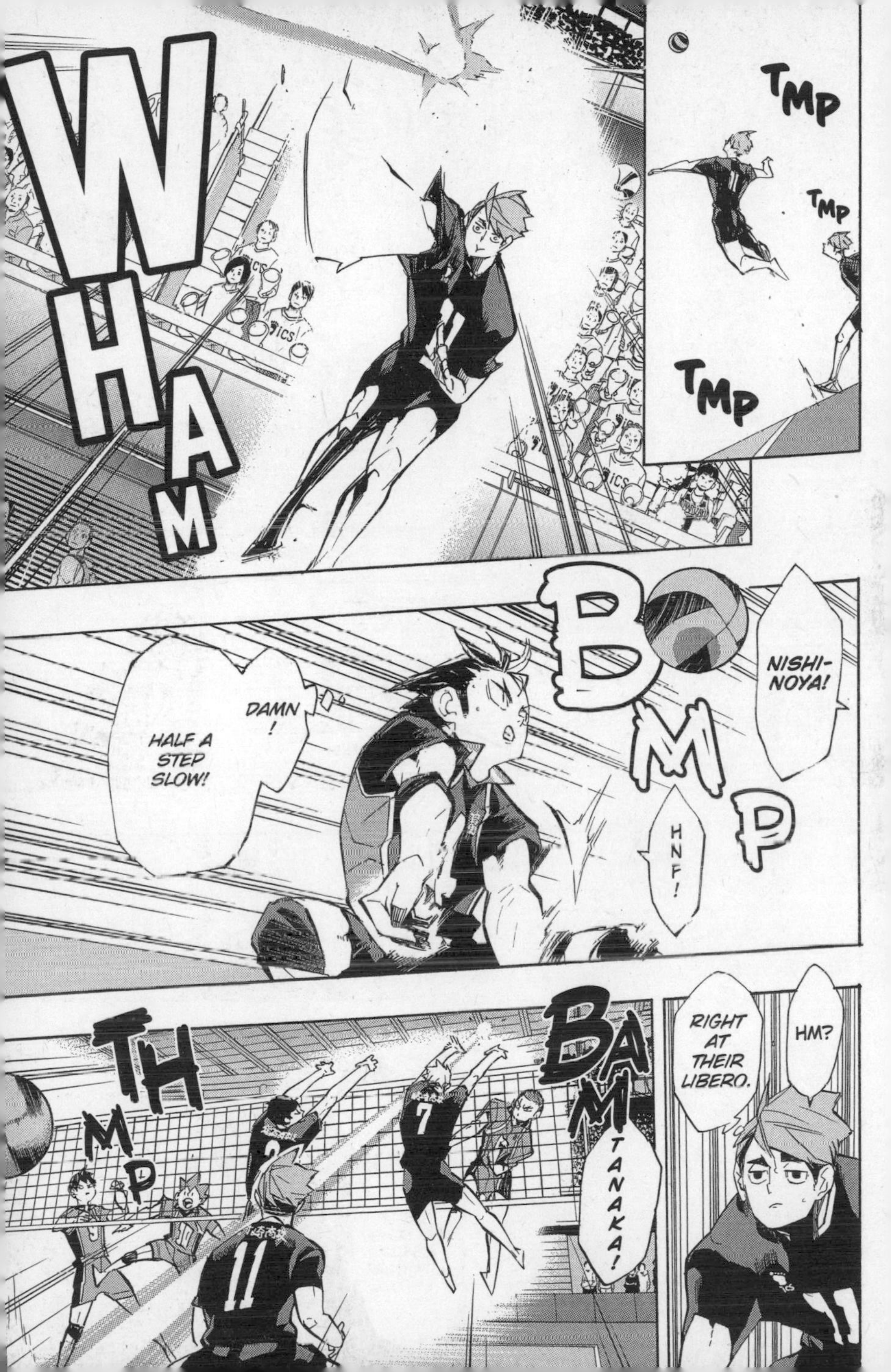
TMP
TMP
TMP
WHAM
NISHI-NOYA!
BOMP
HNF!
DAMN!
HALF A STEP SLOW!
HM?
RIGHT AT THEIR LIBERO.
BAM
TANAKA!
THMP

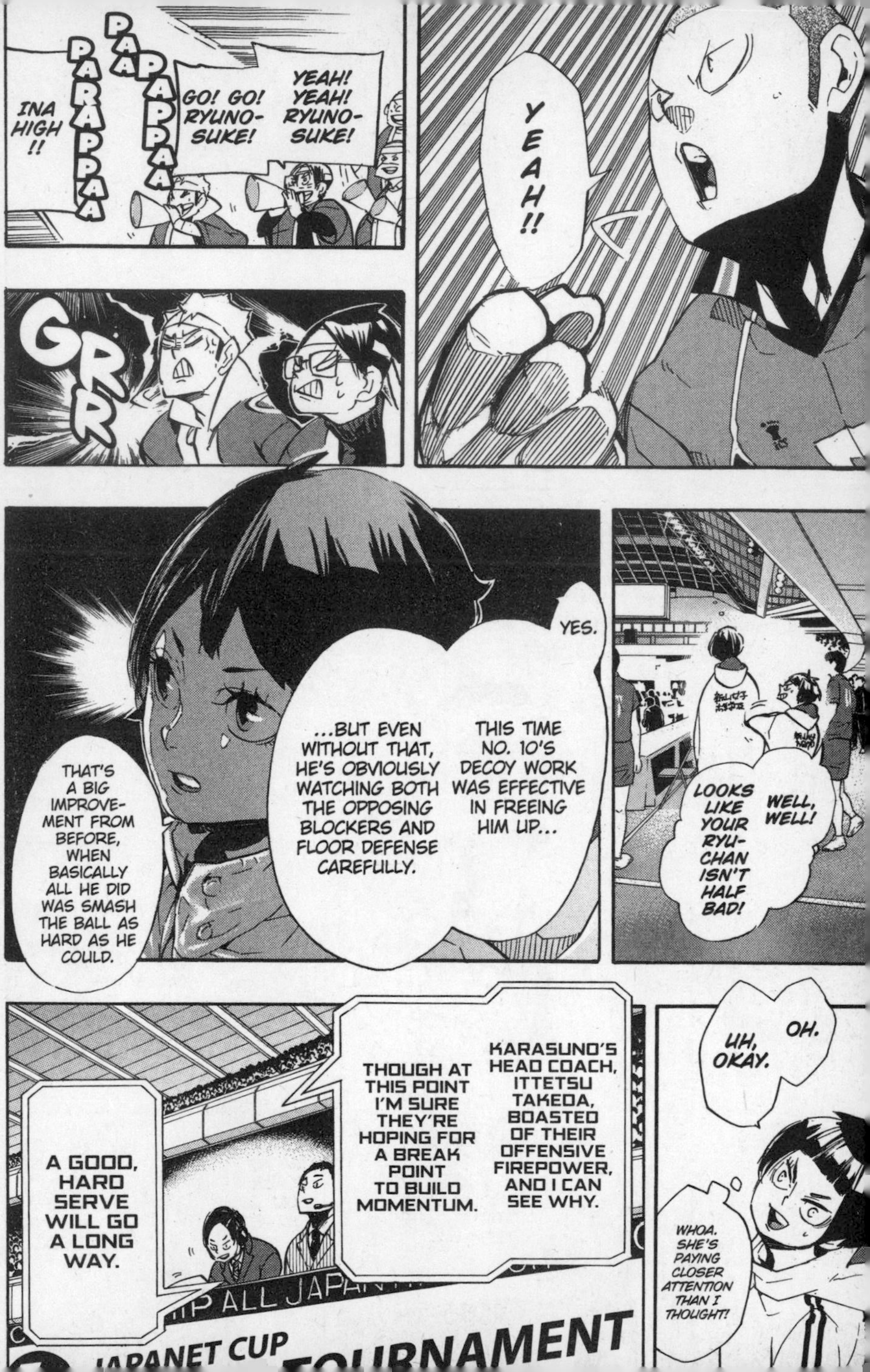

YEAH!!
YEAH! YEAH! RYUNOSUKE!
GO! GO! RYUNOSUKE!
PAAPAPPAA
PARAPPAA
INA HIGH!!
GRR
WELL, WELL!
LOOKS LIKE YOUR RYU-CHAN ISN'T HALF BAD!
YES.
THIS TIME NO. 10'S DECOY WORK WAS EFFECTIVE IN FREEING HIM UP...
...BUT EVEN WITHOUT THAT, HE'S OBVIOUSLY WATCHING BOTH THE OPPOSING BLOCKERS AND FLOOR DEFENSE CAREFULLY.
THAT'S A BIG IMPROVEMENT FROM BEFORE, WHEN BASICALLY ALL HE DID WAS SMASH THE BALL AS HARD AS HE COULD.
OH.
UH, OKAY.
WHOA. SHE'S PAYING CLOSER ATTENTION THAN I THOUGHT!
KARASUNO'S HEAD COACH, ITTETSU TAKEDA, BOASTED OF THEIR OFFENSIVE FIREPOWER, AND I CAN SEE WHY.
THOUGH AT THIS POINT I'M SURE THEY'RE HOPING FOR A BREAK POINT TO BUILD MOMENTUM.
A GOOD, HARD SERVE WILL GO A LONG WAY.
JAPANET CUP
TOURNAMENT

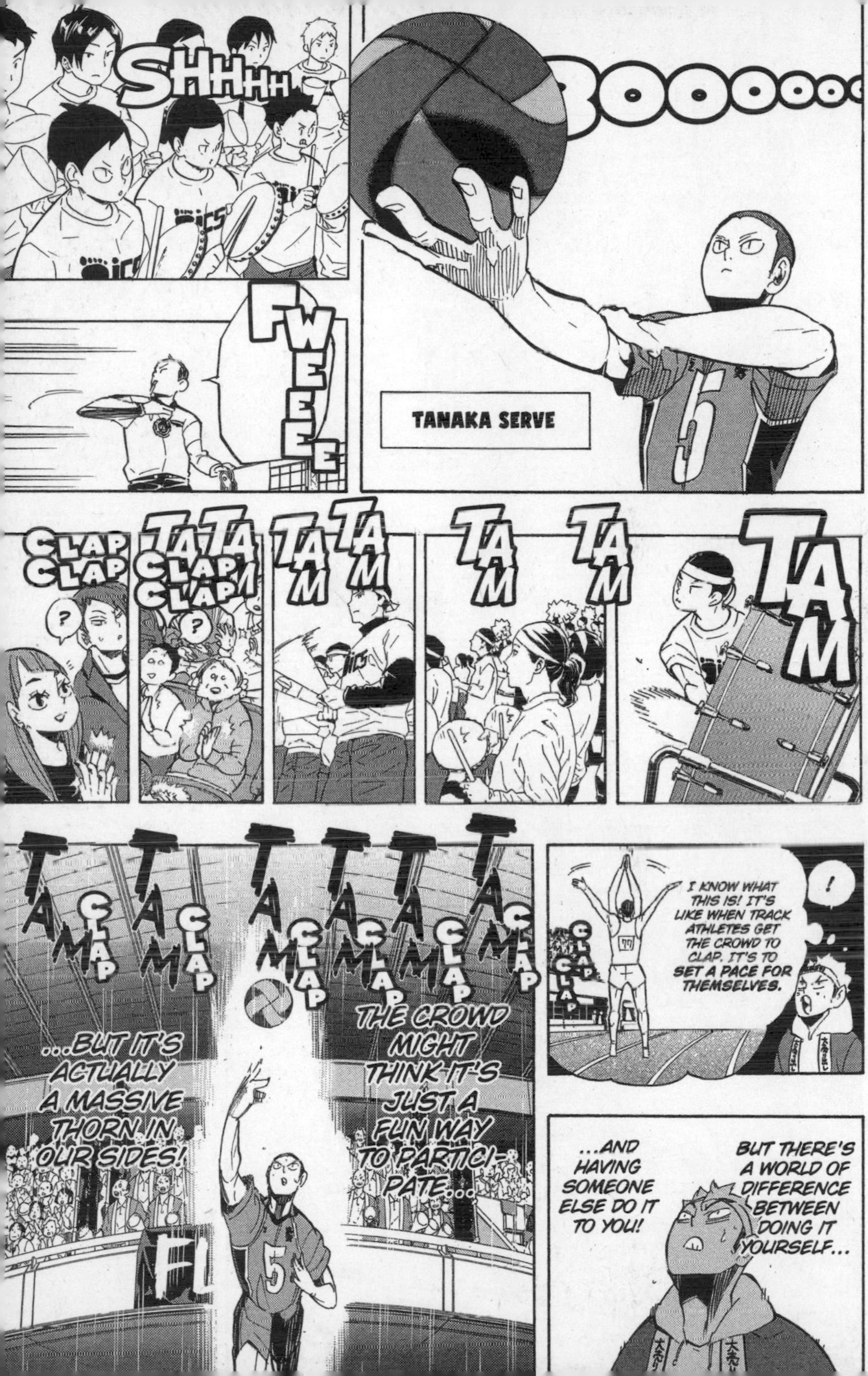

BOOOOO...
TANAKA SERVE
SHHHHH
FWEEEEE
TAM
TA M
TA M
TAM TAM
TATA
CLAP CLAP
CLAP CLAP
!
I KNOW WHAT THIS IS! IT'S LIKE WHEN TRACK ATHLETES GET THE CROWD TO CLAP. IT'S TO SET A PACE FOR THEMSELVES.
CLAP CLAP
BUT THERE'S A WORLD OF DIFFERENCE BETWEEN DOING IT YOURSELF...
...AND HAVING SOMEONE ELSE DO IT TO YOU!
TAM CLAP TAM CLAP TAM CLAP TAM CLAP TAM CLAP TAM CLAP
THE CROWD MIGHT THINK IT'S JUST A FUN WAY TO PARTICI-PATE...
...BUT IT'S ACTUALLY A MASSIVE THORN IN OUR SIDES!
FL

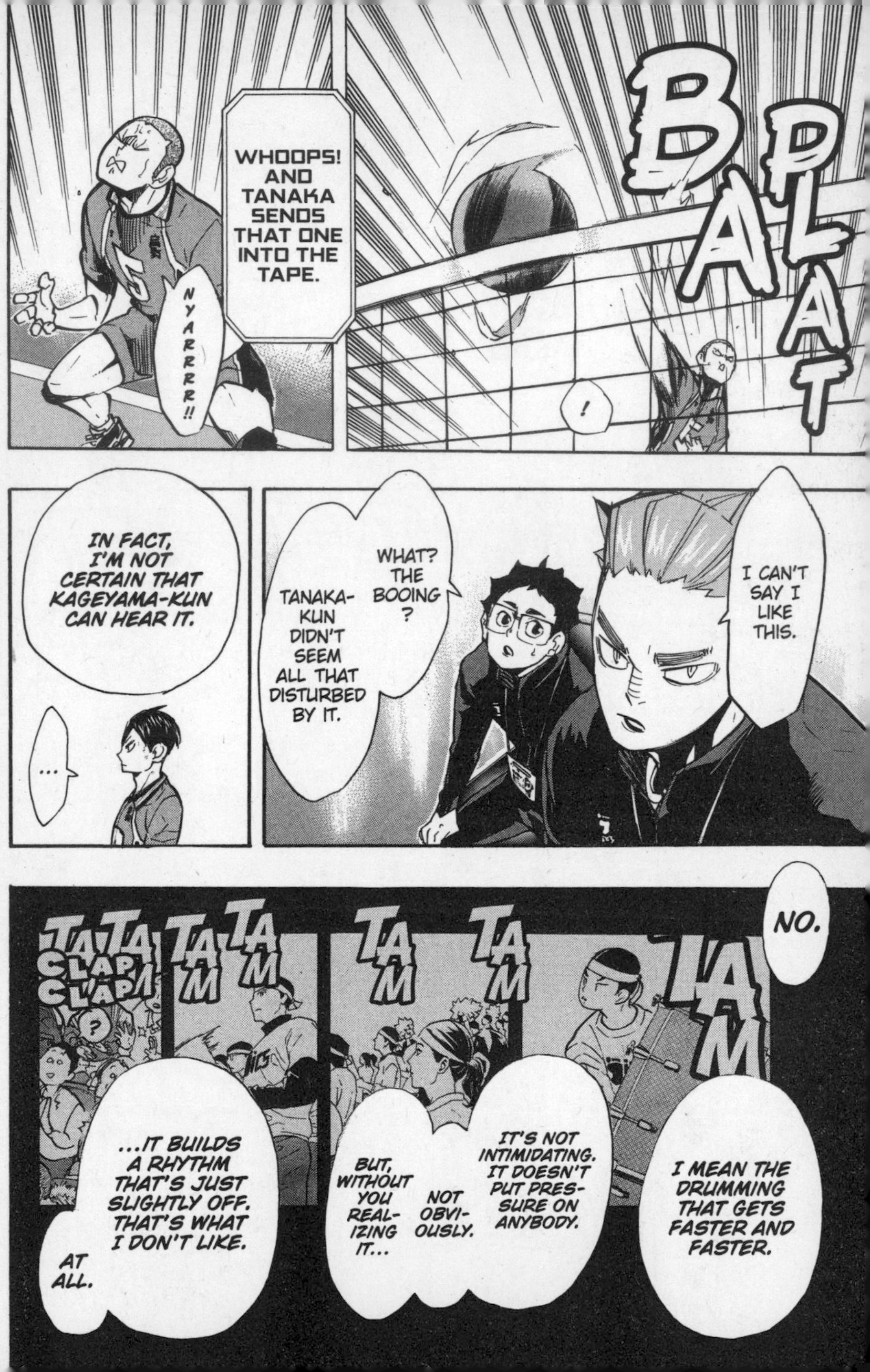
BPLAT
!
WHOOPS! AND TANAKA SENDS THAT ONE INTO THE TAPE.
NYARRRR!!
I CAN'T SAY I LIKE THIS.
WHAT? THE BOOING?
TANAKA-KUN DIDN'T SEEM ALL THAT DISTURBED BY IT.
IN FACT, I'M NOT CERTAIN THAT KAGEYAMA-KUN CAN HEAR IT.
...
NO.
TAM
TAM
TAM
I MEAN THE DRUMMING THAT GETS FASTER AND FASTER.
IT'S NOT INTIMIDATING. IT DOESN'T PUT PRESSURE ON ANYBODY.
NOT OBVIOUSLY.
BUT, WITHOUT YOU REALIZING IT...
TAM TAM
TA TA TA
CLAP CLAP
?
...IT BUILDS A RHYTHM THAT'S JUST SLIGHTLY OFF. THAT'S WHAT I DON'T LIKE.
AT ALL.

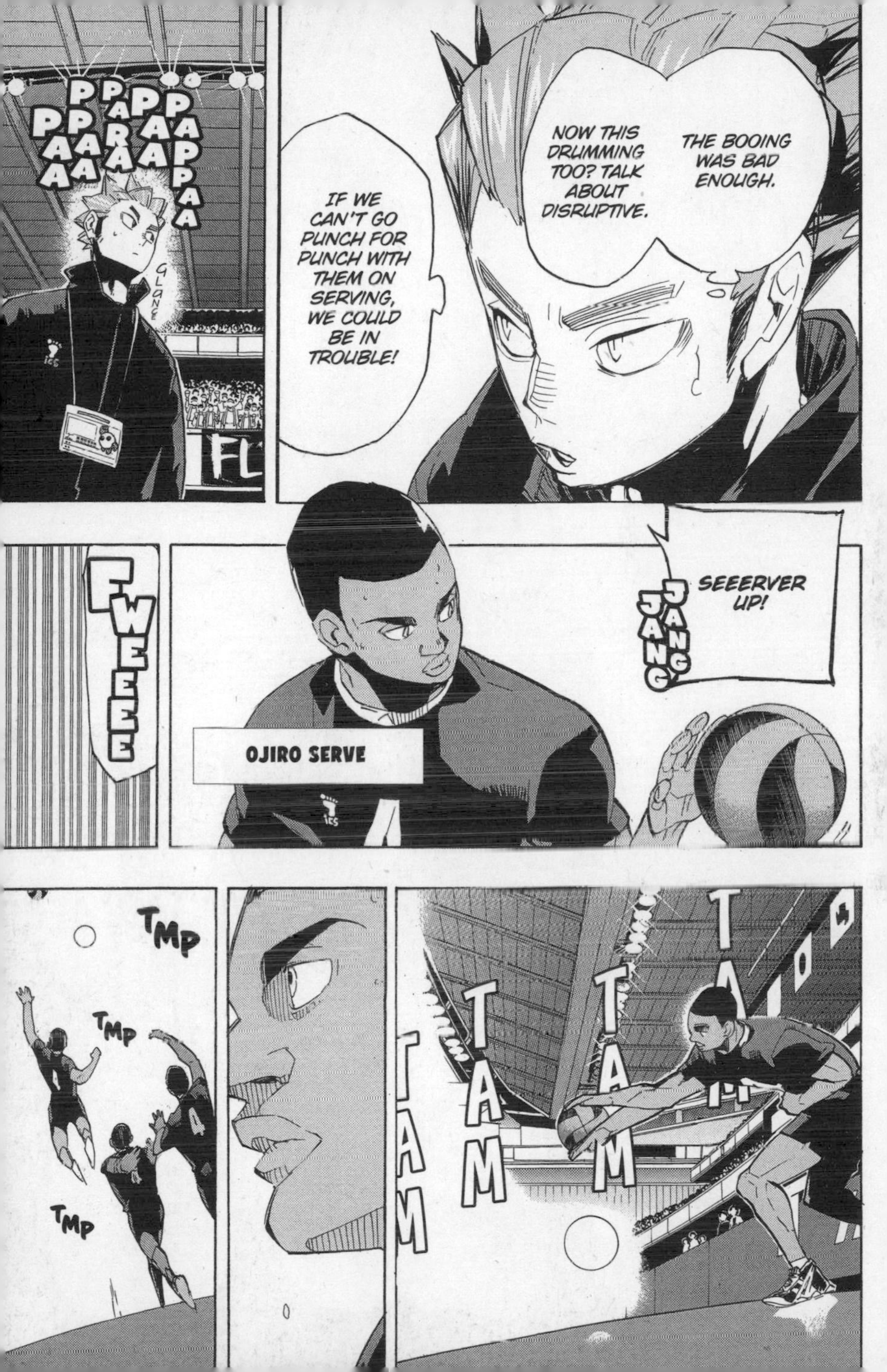
THE BOOING WAS BAD ENOUGH.
NOW THIS DRUMMING TOO? TALK ABOUT DISRUPTIVE.
IF WE CAN'T GO PUNCH FOR PUNCH WITH THEM ON SERVING, WE COULD BE IN TROUBLE!
PAPAPAPAPAPAPAPAPA
GLANCE
SEEERVER UP!
JANG JANG
OJIRO SERVE
FWEEEE
TA
TAM
TAM
TAM
TMP
TMP
TMP

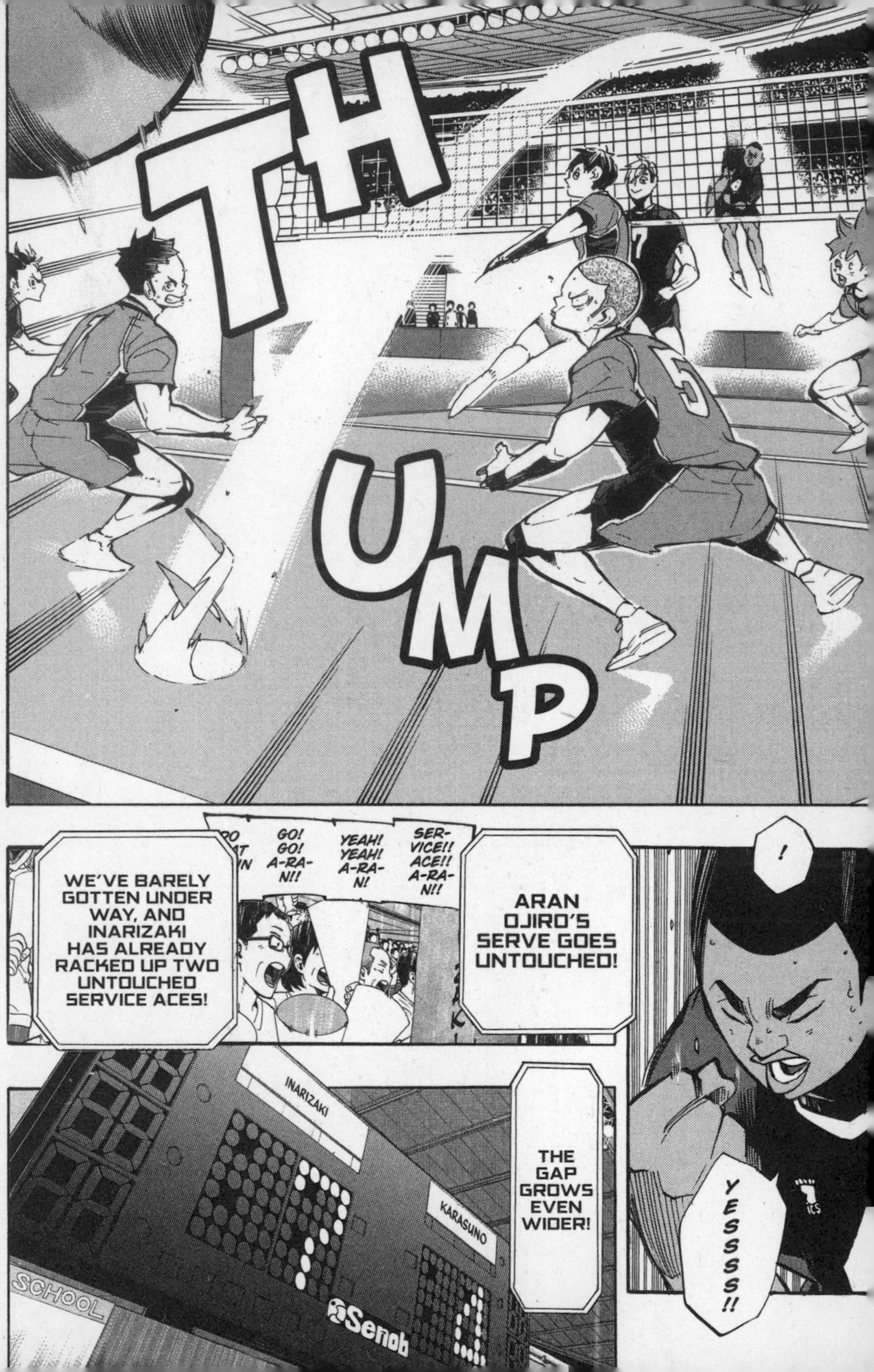
THUMP
!
YESSSS!!
ARAN OJIRO'S SERVE GOES UNTOUCHED!
SER-VICE!! ACE!! A-RA-N!!
YEAH! YEAH! A-RA-N!
GO! GO! A-RA-N!!
WE'VE BARELY GOTTEN UNDER WAY, AND INARIZAKI HAS ALREADY RACKED UP TWO UNTOUCHED SERVICE ACES!
THE GAP GROWS EVEN WIDER!
INARIZAKI
KARASUNO
SCHOOL
Senob

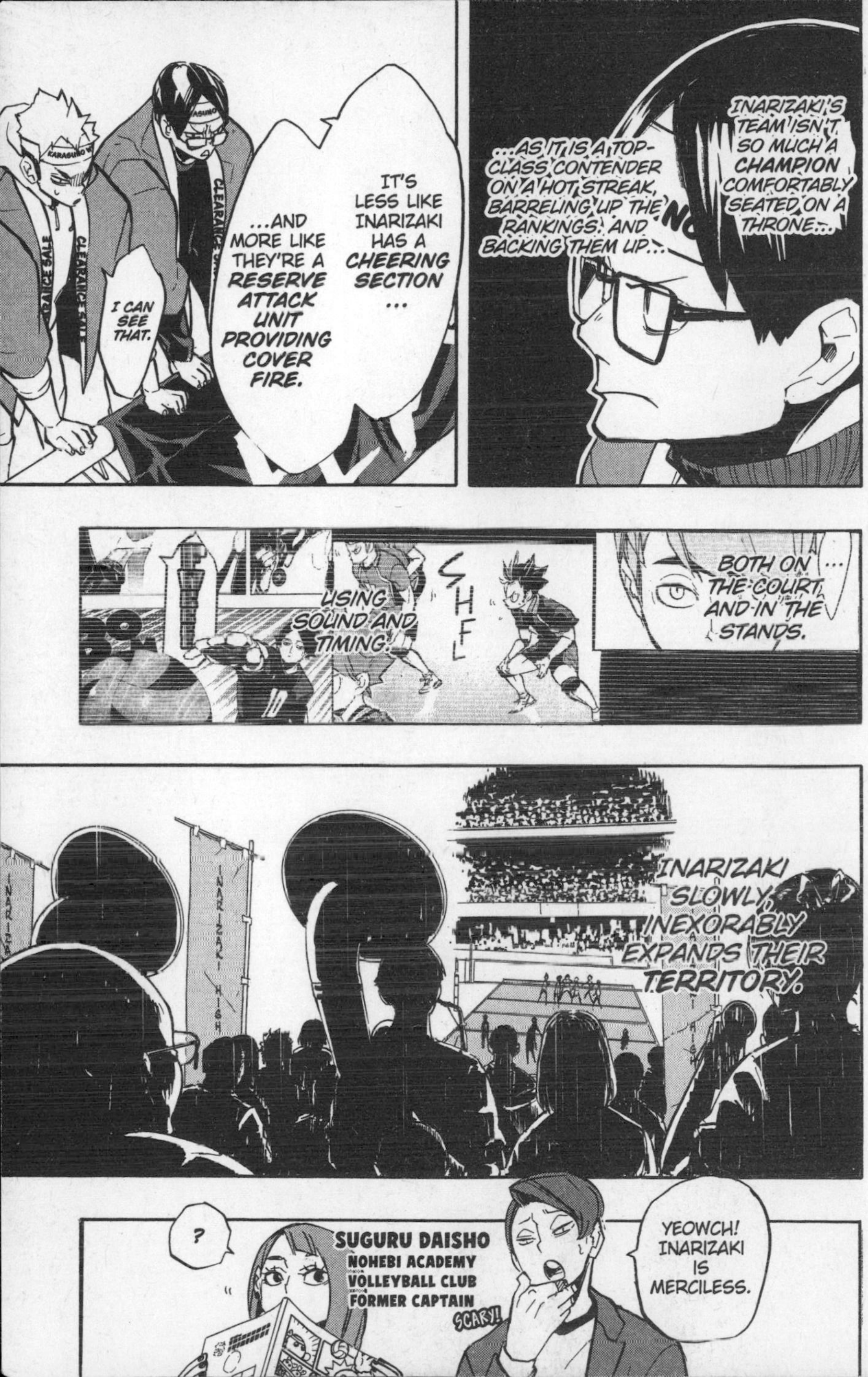
INARIZAKI'S TEAM ISN'T SO MUCH A CHAMPION COMFORTABLY SEATED ON A THRONE...
...AS IT IS A TOP-CLASS CONTENDER ON A HOT STREAK, BARRELING UP THE RANKINGS. AND BACKING THEM UP...
IT'S LESS LIKE INARIZAKI HAS A CHEERING SECTION...
...AND MORE LIKE THEY'RE A RESERVE ATTACK UNIT PROVIDING COVER FIRE.
I CAN SEE THAT.
...
BOTH ON THE COURT AND IN THE STANDS.
SHFL
USING SOUND AND TIMING.
INARIZAKI SLOWLY, INEXORABLY EXPANDS THEIR TERRITORY.
YEOWCH! INARIZAKI IS MERCILESS.
SCARY!
SUGURU DAISHO
NOHEBI ACADEMY VOLLEYBALL CLUB FORMER CAPTAIN
?

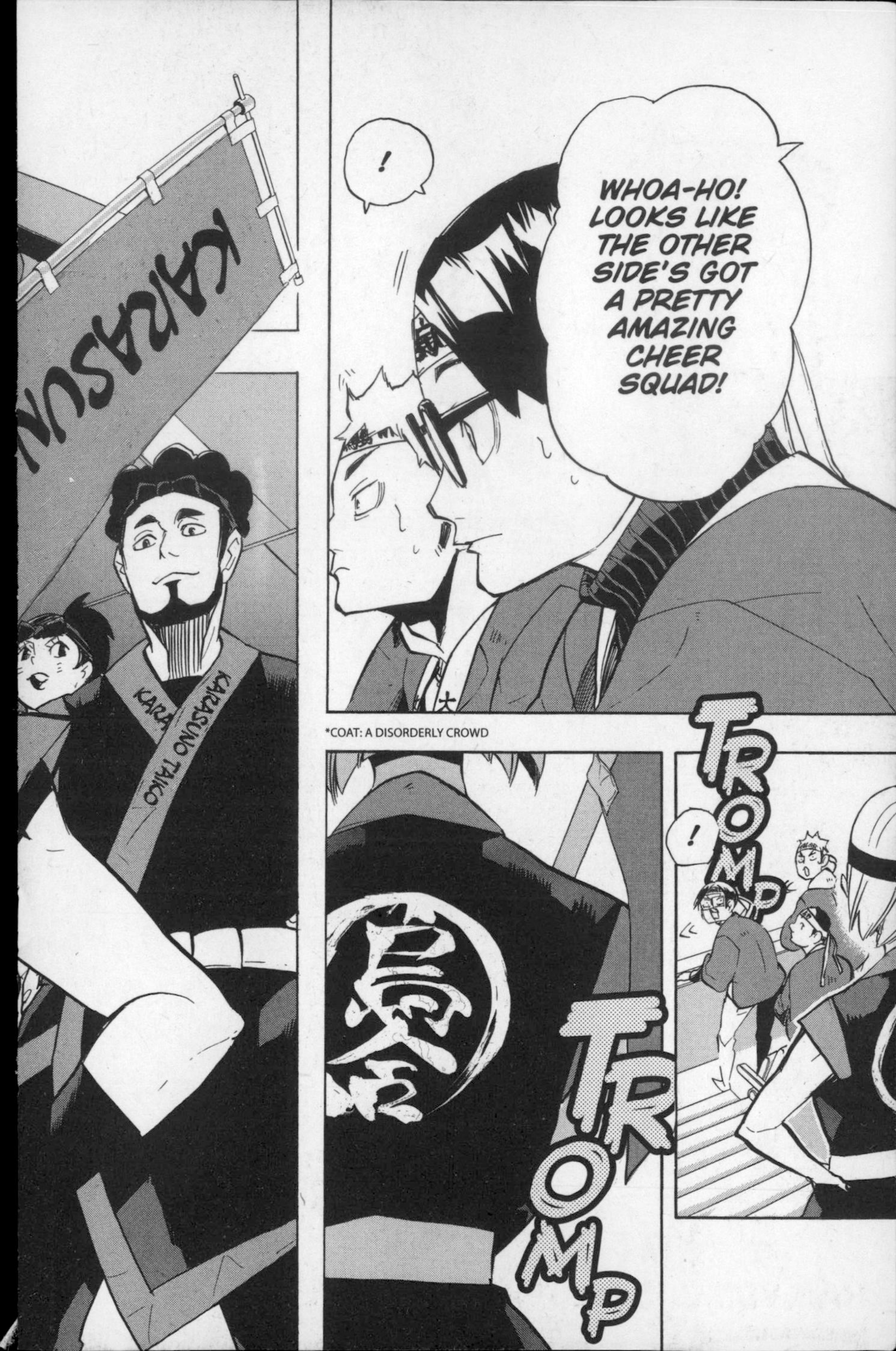
WHOA-HO! LOOKS LIKE THE OTHER SIDE'S GOT A PRETTY AMAZING CHEER SQUAD!
!
*COAT: A DISORDERLY CROWD
TROMP
!
TROMP
KARASUNO
KARASUNO TAIKO
KARA

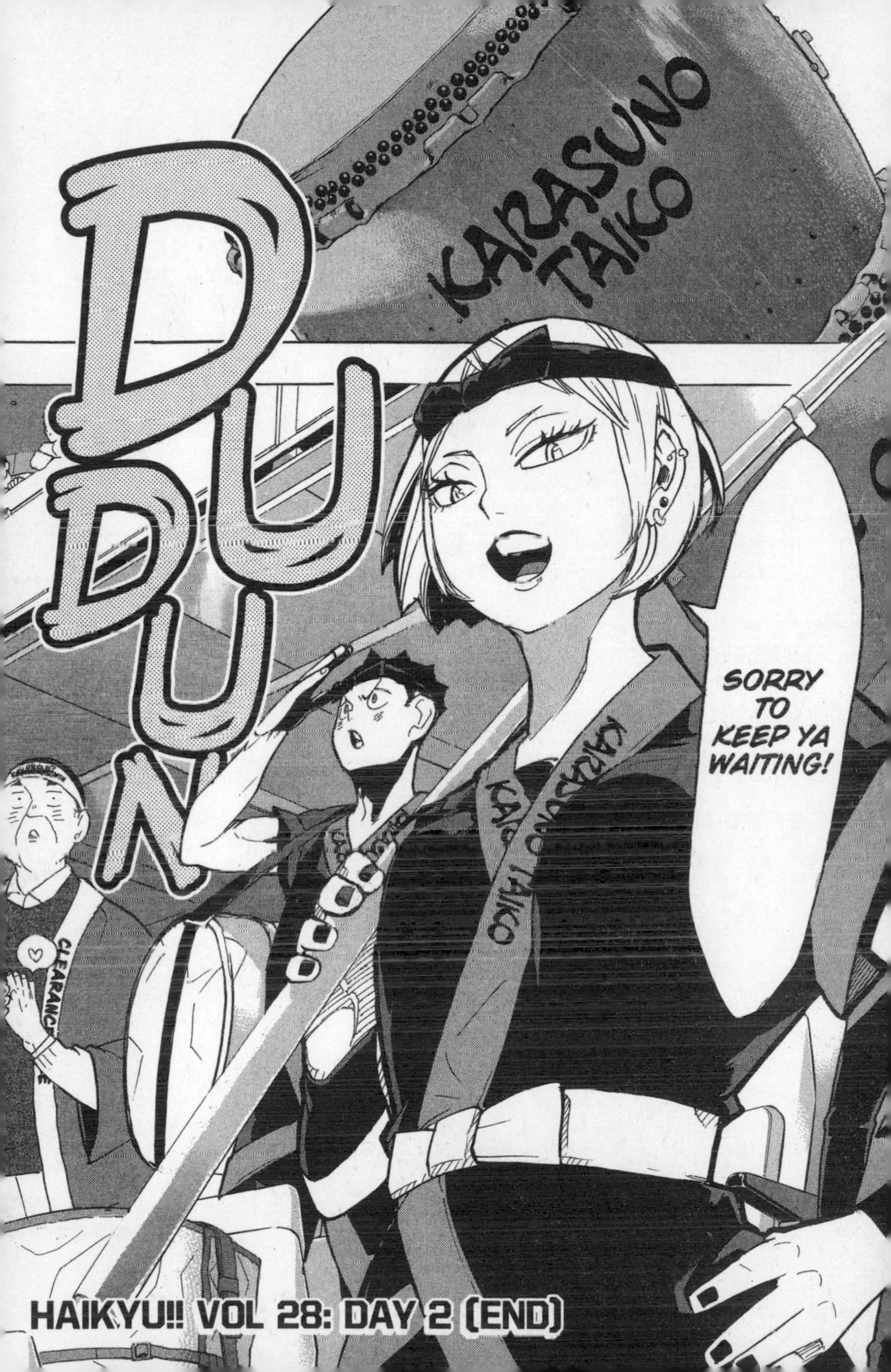
KARASUNO TAIKO
SORRY TO KEEP YA WAITING!
DUDUDUN
KARASUNO TAIKO
CLEARANCE
HAIKYU!! VOL 28: DAY 2 (END)

ATSUSHI NAMIKIRI

BIRTHDAY: SEPTEMBER 3
FAVORITE FOOD: PEACH PARFAIT
CURRENT WORRY: LOSING CONCENTRATION
PARTWAY THROUGH A TASK.

ABILITY PARAMETERS
(5-POINT SCALE)

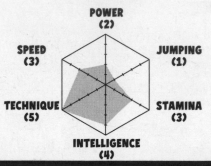

POWER
(2)

JUMPING
(1)

SPEED
(3)

STAMINA
(3)

TECHNIQUE
(5)

INTELLIGENCE
(4)

MIYAKO WATAHASHI

BIRTHDAY: MAY 28
FAVORITE FOOD: SEA URCHIN
CURRENT WORRY: WITHOUT AUTORUN HER FINGERS
START TO HURT.

ABILITY PARAMETERS
(5-POINT SCALE)

SHF SHF SHF

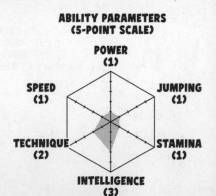

POWER
(1)

SPEED
(1)

JUMPING
(1)

TECHNIQUE
(2)

STAMINA
(1)

INTELLIGENCE
(3)

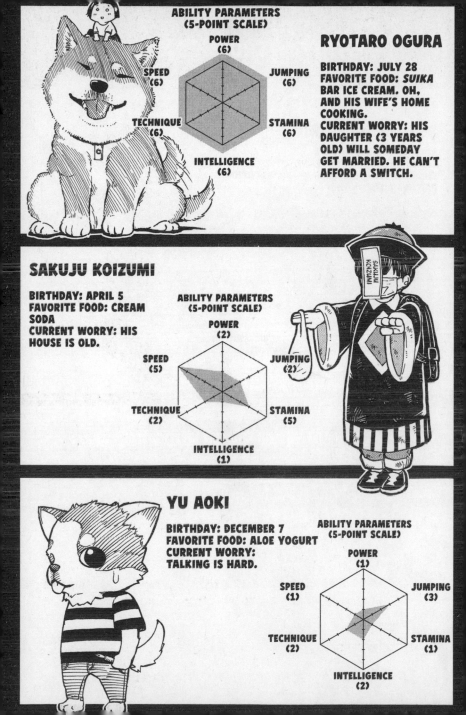

ABILITY PARAMETERS
(5-POINT SCALE)

POWER
(6)

SPEED
(6)

JUMPING
(6)

TECHNIQUE
(6)

STAMINA
(6)

INTELLIGENCE
(6)

RYOTARO OGURA

BIRTHDAY: JULY 28
FAVORITE FOOD: *SUIKA*
BAR ICE CREAM. OH,
AND HIS WIFE'S HOME
COOKING.
CURRENT WORRY: HIS
DAUGHTER (3 YEARS
OLD) WILL SOMEDAY
GET MARRIED. HE CAN'T
AFFORD A SWITCH.

SAKUJU KOIZUMI

BIRTHDAY: APRIL 5
FAVORITE FOOD: CREAM
SODA
CURRENT WORRY: HIS
HOUSE IS OLD.

ABILITY PARAMETERS
(5-POINT SCALE)

POWER
(2)

SPEED
(5)

JUMPING
(2)

TECHNIQUE
(2)

STAMINA
(5)

INTELLIGENCE
(1)

YU AOKI

BIRTHDAY: DECEMBER 7
FAVORITE FOOD: ALOE YOGURT
CURRENT WORRY:
TALKING IS HARD.

ABILITY PARAMETERS
(5-POINT SCALE)

POWER
(1)

SPEED
(1)

JUMPING
(3)

TECHNIQUE
(2)

STAMINA
(1)

INTELLIGENCE
(2)

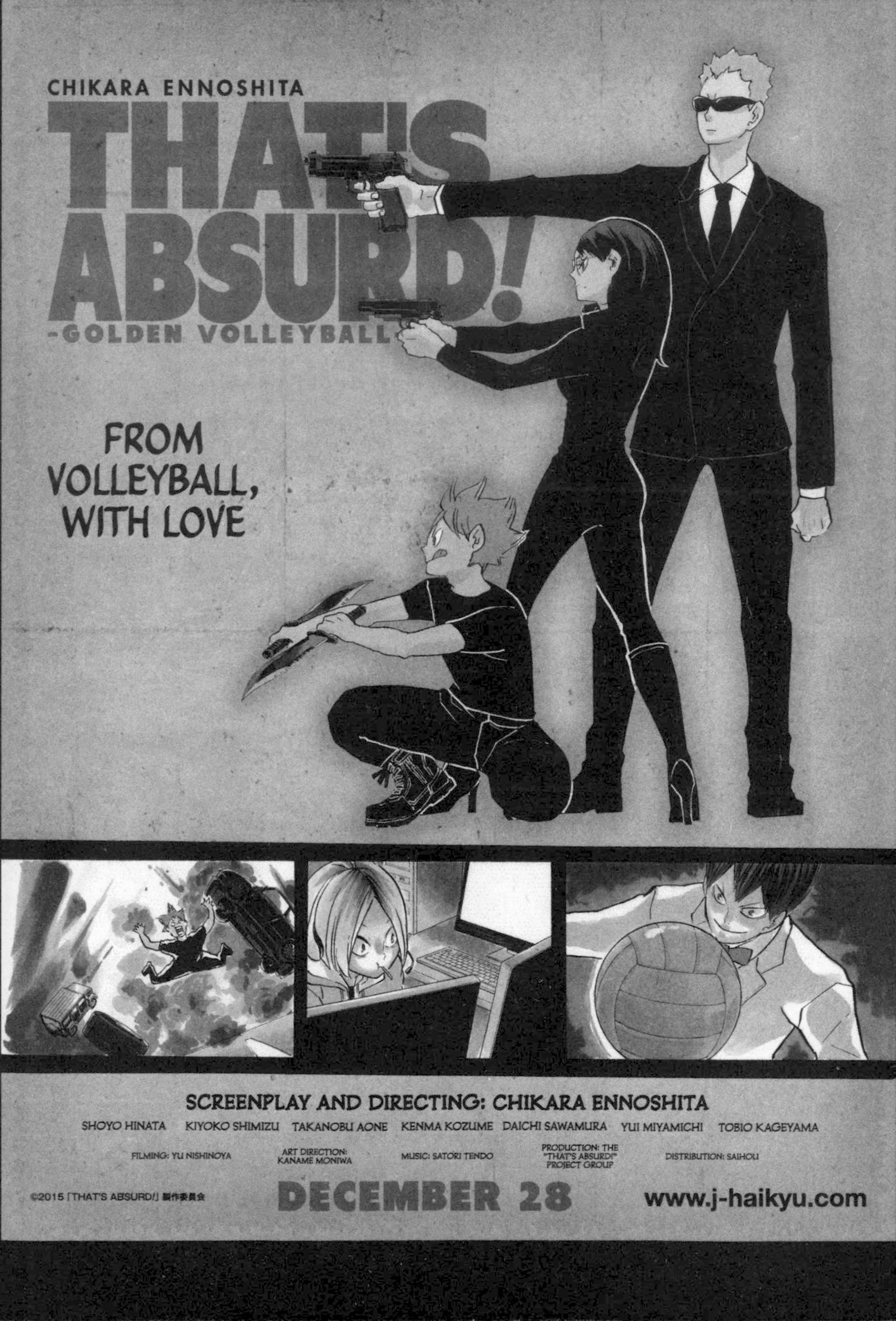

CHIKARA ENNOSHITA
THAT'S ABSURD!
-GOLDEN VOLLEYBALL
FROM VOLLEYBALL, WITH LOVE
SCREENPLAY AND DIRECTING: CHIKARA ENNOSHITA
SHOYO HINATA KIYOKO SHIMIZU TAKANOBU AONE KENMA KOZUME DAICHI SAWAMURA YUI MIYAMICHI TOBIO KAGEYAMA
FILMING: YU NISHINOYA
ART DIRECTION: KANAME MONIWA
MUSIC: SATORI TENDO
PRODUCTION: THE "THAT'S ABSURD!" PROJECT GROUP
DISTRIBUTION: SAIHOU
©2015「THAT'S ABSURD!」製作委員会
DECEMBER 28
www.j-haikyu.com

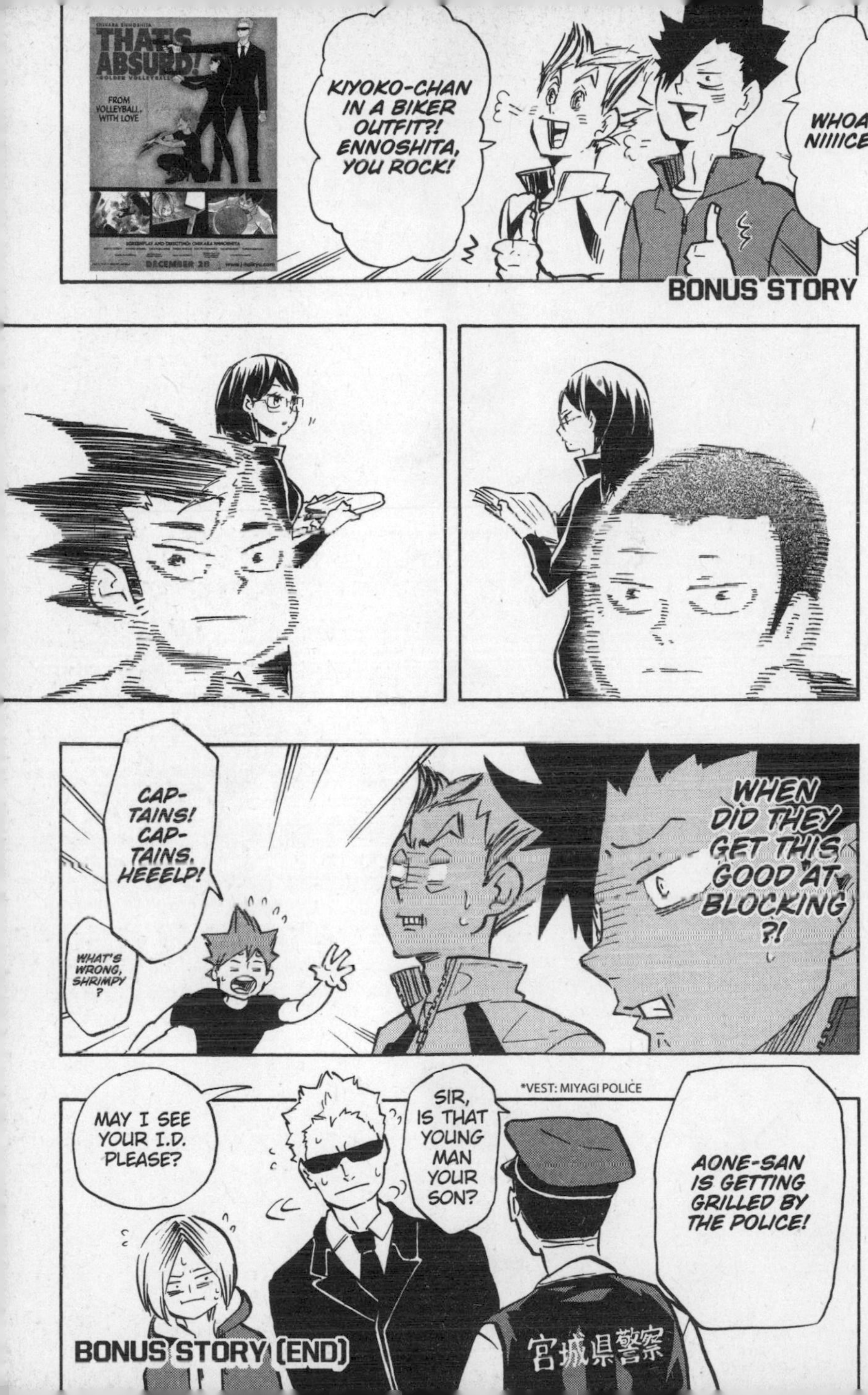
WHOA, NIIIICE!
KIYOKO-CHAN IN A BIKER OUTFIT?! ENNOSHITA, YOU ROCK!
THAT IS ABSURD!
FROM VOLLEYBALL, WITH LOVE
DECEMBER 28
BONUS STORY
WHEN DID THEY GET THIS GOOD AT BLOCKING?!
CAP-TAINS! CAP-TAINS. HEEELP!
WHAT'S WRONG, SHRIMPY?
*VEST: MIYAGI POLICE
AONE-SAN IS GETTING GRILLED BY THE POLICE!
SIR, IS THAT YOUNG MAN YOUR SON?
MAY I SEE YOUR I.D. PLEASE?
宮城県警察
BONUS STORY (END)

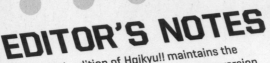

EDITOR'S NOTES

The English edition of Haikyu!! maintains the honorifics used in the original Japanese version. For those of you who are new to these terms, here's a brief explanation to help with your reading experience!

When saying someone's name in Japanese, a suffix is often attached to indicate how familiar the speaker is with the person. Some are more polite and respectful, while others are endearing.

1. **-kun** is often used for young men or boys, usually someone you are familiar with.

2. **-chan** is used for young children and can be used as a term of endearment.

3. **-san** is used for someone you respect or are not close to, or to be polite.

4. **Senpai** is used for someone who is older than you or in a higher position or grade in school.

5. **Kohai** is used for someone who is younger than you or in a lower position or grade in school.

6. **Sensei** means teacher.

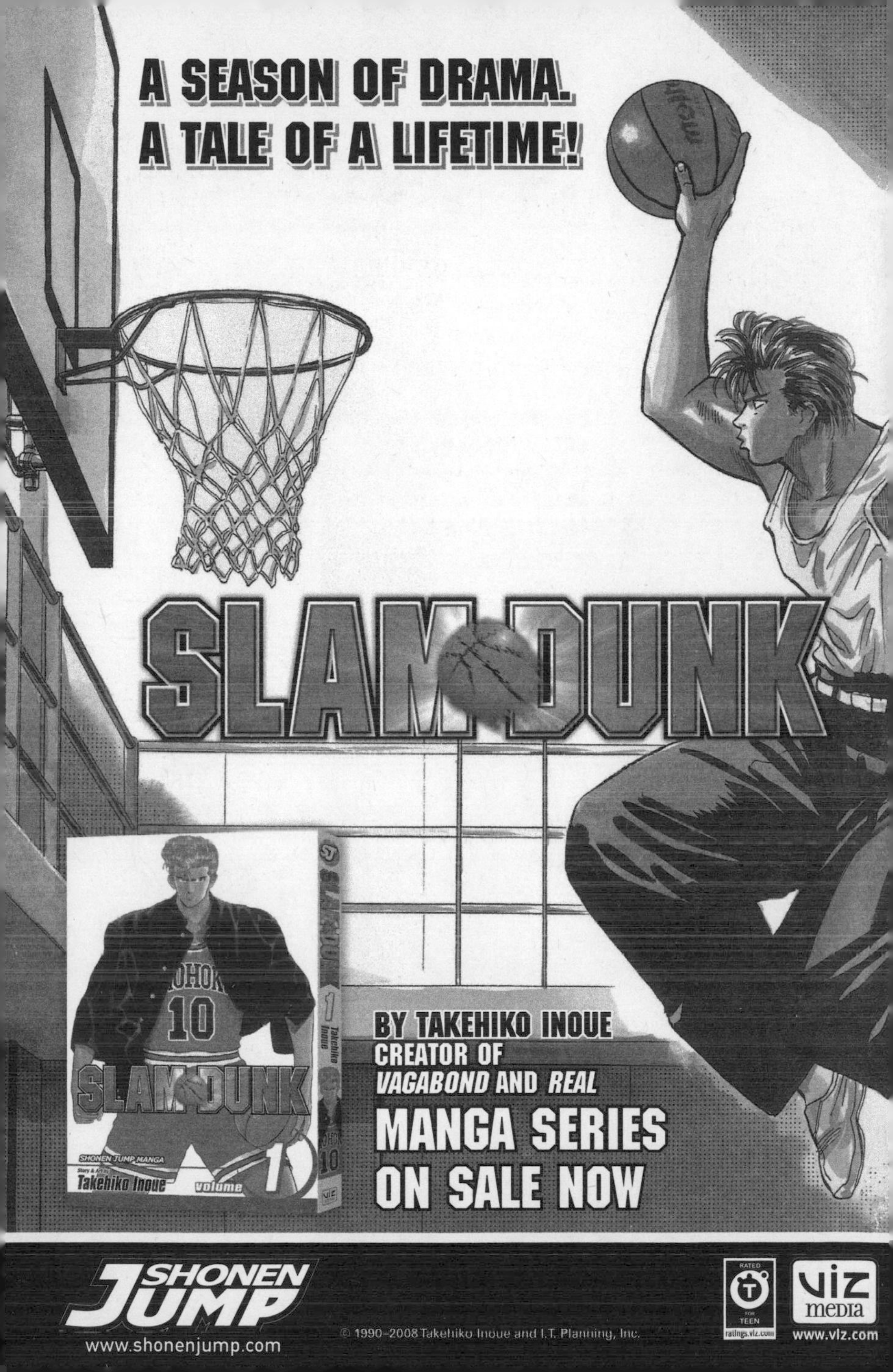

A SEASON OF DRAMA.
A TALE OF A LIFETIME!
SLAM DUNK
BY TAKEHIKO INOUE
CREATOR OF
VAGABOND AND REAL
MANGA SERIES
ON SALE NOW
SHONEN JUMP MANGA
Takehiko Inoue
volume 1
SHONEN JUMP
www.shonenjump.com
© 1990–2008 Takehiko Inoue and I.T. Planning, Inc.
RATED T FOR TEEN
ratings.viz.com
VIZ media
www.viz.com

Kuroko's BASKETBALL

TADATOSHI FUJIMAKI

When incoming first-year student Taiga Kagami joins the Seirin High basketball team, he meets Tetsuya Kuroko, a mysterious boy who's plain beyond words. But Kagami's in for the shock of his life when he learns that the practically invisible Kuroko was once a member of "the Miracle Generation"—the undefeated legendary team—and he wants Kagami's help taking down each of his old teammates!

THE HIT SPORTS MANGA FROM *SHONEN JUMP* IN A 2-IN-1 EDITION!

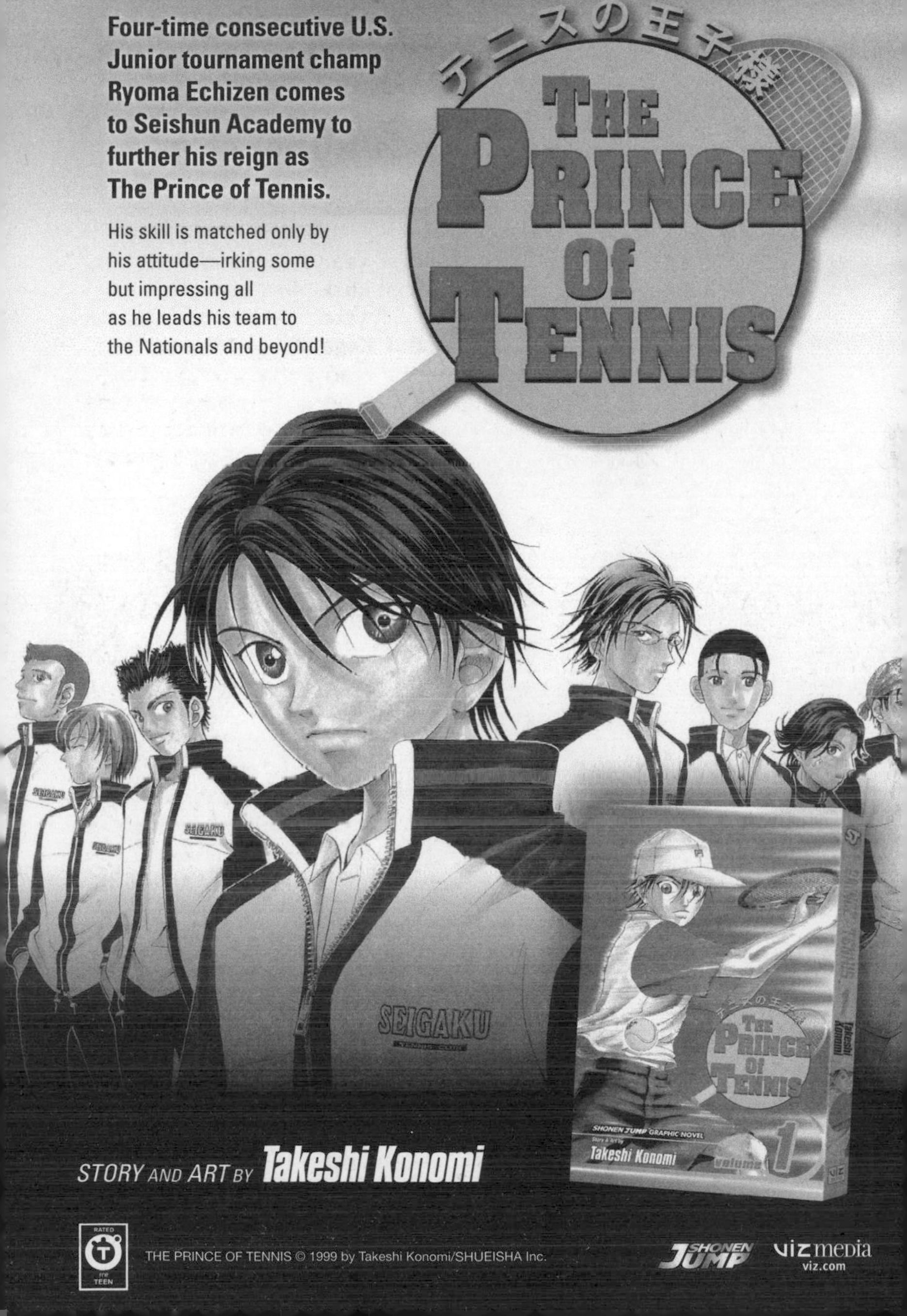

Four-time consecutive U.S. Junior tournament champ Ryoma Echizen comes to Seishun Academy to further his reign as **The Prince of Tennis.**

His skill is matched only by his attitude—irking some but impressing all as he leads his team to the Nationals and beyond!

テニスの王子様

THE PRINCE OF TENNIS

STORY AND ART BY **Takeshi Konomi**

RATED **T** TEEN

SHONEN **JUMP**

viz media
viz.com

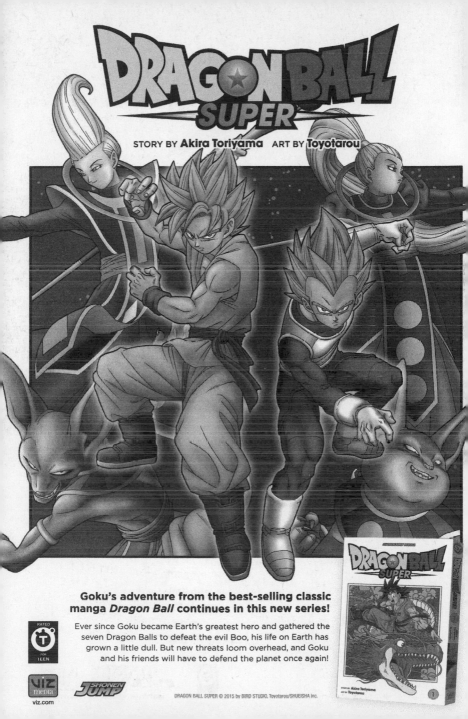

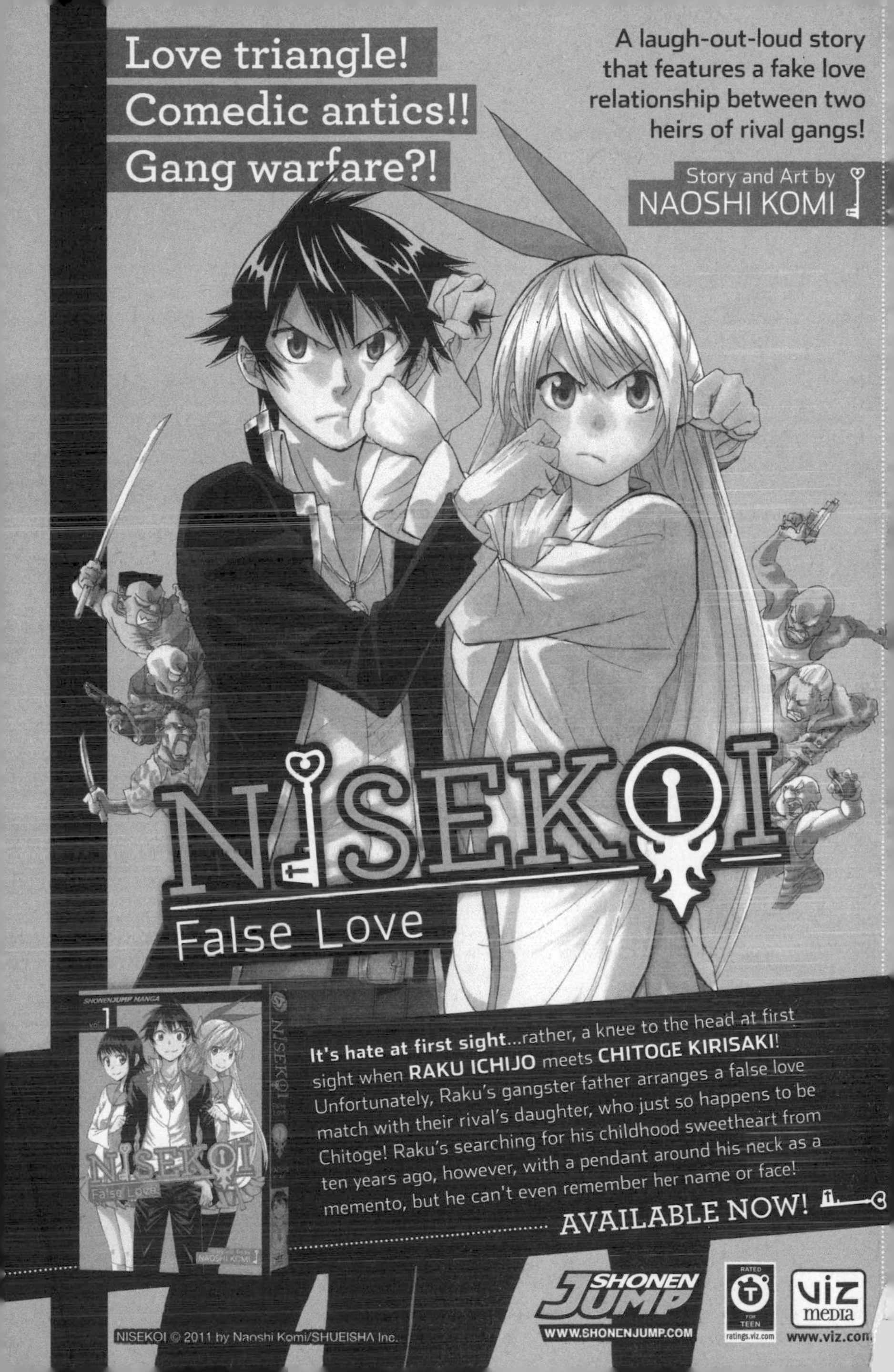
Love triangle!
Comedic antics!!
Gang warfare?!
A laugh-out-loud story that features a fake love relationship between two heirs of rival gangs!
Story and Art by NAOSHI KOMI
NISEKOI
False Love
SHONEN JUMP MANGA
VOL. 1
NISEKOI False Love
NAOSHI KOMI
It's hate at first sight...rather, a knee to the head at first sight when RAKU ICHIJO meets CHITOGE KIRISAKI! Unfortunately, Raku's gangster father arranges a false love match with their rival's daughter, who just so happens to be Chitoge! Raku's searching for his childhood sweetheart from ten years ago, however, with a pendant around his neck as a memento, but he can't even remember her name or face!
AVAILABLE NOW!
SHONEN JUMP
WWW.SHONENJUMP.COM
RATED T FOR TEEN
ratings.viz.com
VIZ media
www.viz.com
NISEKOI © 2011 by Naoshi Komi/SHUEISHA Inc.

You're Reading the
WRONG WAY!

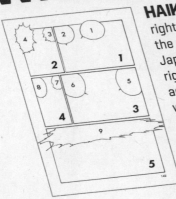

HAIKYU!! reads from right to left, starting in the upper-right corner. Japanese is read from right to left, meaning that action, sound effects and word-balloon order are completely reversed from English order.